Stalinism

Stalinism

Russian and Western views at the turn
of the millennium

Alter Litvin and John Keep

LONDON AND NEW YORK

First published 2005 by Routledge
2 Park Square, Milton Park, Abingdon, Oxon OX14 4RN

Simultaneously published in the USA and Canada
by Routledge
711 Third Ave, New York, NY 10017

Routledge is an imprint of the Taylor & Francis Group

© 2005 Alter Litvin and John Keep

Typeset in Baskerville by Keystroke, Jacaranda Lodge, Wolverhampton

British Library Cataloguing in Publication Data
A catalogue record for this book is available from the British Library

Library of Congress Cataloging in Publication Data
A catalog record for this book has been requested

ISBN 0–415–35108–1 (hbk)
ISBN 0–415–35109–X (pbk)

Contents

Introduction

This volume is designed as a contribution to the ongoing debate in Russia and the West on the Soviet past, and more particularly on the years 1929–53, during which virtually all power was concentrated in the hands of J.V. Stalin and a handful of associates in the upper echelons of the ruling Communist Party, then known as the AUCP(b). The immediate aim is to give students and the interested general public a sense of what has been achieved of late by professional historians in the Russian Federation and in Western countries: to 'take stock' of this literature, to offer encouragement or constructive criticism where it seems to be called for, and to indicate how the gaps in our knowledge might best be filled by future researchers. It is hoped that the bibliographical references will be helpful, even if for practical reasons many of the works cited may at present be hard to obtain. With the rapid development of computer-assisted research tools, this situation is sure to improve in the years to come.

The 1930s, which have been better studied than the post-war era, were years of massive social turbulence, marked by the influx to the towns and construction sites of millions of rural folk displaced by collectivization. Crisis in some sectors of the economy, notably agriculture, was the price paid for rapid growth in others. Giant construction projects symbolized the spirit of the era. The 'administrative command' system of managing the economy led initially to chaos: plan targets were under-fulfilled and statistical data manipulated to conceal the fact. Later, the pace of advance slackened a little; more sophisticated methods of catering to popular needs were developed that paid greater attention to the quality of the goods produced. Nevertheless, the interests of the consumer always took second place to those of the state, eager to promote the development of capital-intensive heavy industry, not least for reasons of national defence.

In the 1930s, the USSR saw itself as an embattled country, a bastion of socialism under siege by ruthless imperialist powers. This image, though exaggerated for propaganda reasons, was not wholly unrealistic since both Japan and, from 1933, Nazi Germany represented serious latent threats to Soviet security. In response, Moscow relaxed its initial hard ideological stance towards limited co-operation with 'bourgeois' democratic states and joined the League of Nations. However, these moves did not signify any departure from Leninist principles of irrevocable class struggle, as interpreted by the current leader.

Josef Stalin's personality impregnates the era and will continue to fascinate historians for generations to come. No fully satisfactory biography of the man has yet been written, although there is no lack of worthwhile attempts to do so. Still less information is readily available about the character and careers of his leading associates, such as Molotov, Kaganovich or Zhdanov, although here too biographers are at work. In general, current historiographical fashion favours the study of structures over that of personalities. The way government was carried on has become much better known. There have also been innovative investigations into the plight of the peasantry during the 1929–31 collectivization drive, the ensuing famine, and many other aspects of social life in town and country. Such matters are now usually studied 'from below'; the 'masses' are no longer simply treated as the object of official policies. The discipline of gender studies boasts several noted specialists on Russian affairs, and the 'cultural turn' has led to work on a wide range of topics from religious beliefs to manners and morals within the working-class household.

This veritable explosion of knowledge stems from the opening up of the former Soviet archives since 1991. This marked the beginning of a new era in scholarship on the Stalin years, both in the Russian Federation and in Western lands. At first, in view of the strict censorship that had prevailed hitherto, every scrap of information was seized on as a revelation. There were, however, remarkably few sensational 'scoops', and within a few years the tone adopted by researchers became more dispassionate and restrained. The documents that have since been published, in such rich profusion as to make a critical overview difficult, have tended to confirm what independent researchers had long suspected; for example, that the hyper-centralized administration creaked badly, or that there was a good deal of grumbling among the mass of Soviet citizens, which coexisted with genuine enthusiasm among zealots and those eager to rise up in the social hierarchy. Efforts made to establish the degree of support for Party policies among different segments of the population, on the basis of correspondence, petitions and official opinion surveys (*svodki*) are still in their infancy, but seem to show that the scale of disaffection was greater than had previously been thought.

Fresh details have also become available about the scale and timing of the successive waves of repressive action taken by the Party leadership, with 'technical' assistance from the security services, against real or supposed enemies: former Oppositionists, people with foreign associations, 'socially dangerous elements' who had come into conflict with the law, and so on. Severe punitive measures were applied against all these groups of offenders, including terms of imprisonment in what is today for simplicity's sake usually referred to as 'the Gulag'. It has become abundantly clear that the Moscow show trials, and their counterparts in the provinces, were merely the tip of the iceberg, which for decades concealed from historians' attention the 'mass operations' conducted, especially from August 1937 onwards, against a whole host of targets. Within little more than a year these state-sponsored massacres led to the loss of some three-quarters of a million lives by execution alone, not counting those who died in prisons or Gulag camps. The precise reasons for this vast blood-letting are not yet entirely clear, but research in this area is proceeding apace. It is even harder to specify the short- and long-term consequences of the Terror, which were clearly momentous and extend far beyond our cut-off date of 5 March 1953.

The years of the Great Patriotic War (1941–5) are not included in this survey, mainly for reasons of space: to deal adequately with the many facets of this titanic conflict would require another volume, and neither of the two authors claims expertise in military history. For similar reasons coverage of foreign policy matters is restricted to two sub-periods, and little has been said here about one of the most important aspects of Soviet domestic history: the nationalities problem, although this is very much a 'growth area' in current historiography worldwide, for reasons that need no explanation. We have here deliberately confined ourselves to political, economic, social and cultural matters, and even so have had to be selective.

This work is divided into two distinct parts. Part I, by Alter Litvin (Kazan'), is concerned with scholarship in Russian. Part II, by John Keep (Bern), deals with writings in three major Western languages. The boundary is sometimes less sharply defined than one might expect. Scholars in the Russian Federation co-operate with colleagues abroad in writing articles or editing conference papers. Some Russian academics have emigrated, especially to the USA or Israel, and express themselves with enviable fluency in English as well as their native tongue. We have kept to a rule of thumb in such cases. As the twenty-first century advances, such international collaboration is becoming the norm and is to be warmly welcomed. May knowledge of the past assist in leading people in all lands towards a peaceful, integrated world, in which the sufferings that marred the age of Stalin will seem of mere antiquarian interest.

In Part I, Alter Litvin sets out to evaluate what professional historians and publicists have written about the Stalin era since the Soviet Union's collapse in 1991 against the background of the contemporary political situation. He argues that their work reflects a basic polarization between adherents of two major schools. On one hand, there are the 'patriots', nostalgic for a past when a mighty Soviet state, resting on foundations built by the Stalinists in the 1930s, became one of the world's two superpowers. They are inclined to ignore or whitewash what Westerners usually call the 'purges' (and Russians the 'mass repressions') and other sins of the regime. Some historians, such as A.S. Seniavsky, consider that harsh measures to discipline the population were historically necessary and justified, since there was a good deal of concealed opposition that threatened national unity in the face of foreign foes. Others, such as Yu. N. Zhukov, claim that the responsibility for the abuses of power lies less with the leadership than with rank-and-file members of the Party apparatus, who forced Stalin's hand.

On the other hand, those historians of a more liberal disposition, and greater contact with their Western confrères, view the Stalin years as a melancholy time of despotic, totalitarian rule when unforgivable crimes were committed and Soviet citizens were deprived of their basic rights. A.N. Sakharov, for instance, condemns the generation of 'new men' whom Stalin elevated to positions of power and influence as half-educated zealots who first deified their leader only to 'tread on him' once he was dead, while preserving the fundamentals of his system.

These debates among the professionals reflect divisions in public opinion generally. For example, a poll taken in November 2001 showed that less than one fifth of the 2,000 or so respondents were interested in Soviet history at all; of these, 45.3 per cent identified the Stalin era with military prowess and Russia's great-power status; 32.9 per cent assessed Stalin's personal achievements positively (a considerable rise since 1990, when the comparable figure had been 6 per cent); 41.3 per cent expressed negative views about the former leader. Among intellectuals, opinion is noticeably more critical. One film producer, for instance, labelled Stalin 'the cruellest ruler of any slave-owning state' and added that 'the unforgettable Iosif Vissarionovich lives on in each of us'.

Alter Litvin considers that this pluralism of historical opinion is up to a point a progressive development, especially when compared to the outward conformity that reigned in Soviet times. He offers a broad-ranging survey of recent academic and popular historical writing on the Stalin theme, paying particular attention to the degree to which authors' arguments are supported by documentary evidence. Over the last decade or so, a vast mass of primary source material has appeared, both official papers and unofficial writings (memoirs, correspondence and so on), all of which offers a solid basis for future research, even if independent scholars have not yet been able to explore every recess of the vast archival edifice.

In Part II, John Keep has restricted coverage to monographs and articles that have appeared in print since 1997, although where appropriate reference is made to earlier publications, especially where there is a sequential aspect to such work. There is no mystical significance to these years being 'the turn of the millennium': they might be seen rather as the third distinct phase in the evolution of historical 'sovietology' (as it was once called) since the end of the USSR, a phase of 'settling down' or routinization that has seen major advances in concrete research and the successful application of new methodologies. This has led to a more consensual view in some fields, such as foreign policy, as well as to vigorous debate on many other issues that are of interest to historians of the twentieth century in general, and not merely to specialists on the USSR.

The aim has been to assess the current state of knowledge while rendering justice to all contending schools of thought, both the more traditionally minded empiricists and the practitioners of various post-modernist tendencies. (Incidentally, the two are *not* mutually exclusive.) A full theoretical accounting with these new methodologies has not been attempted here: rather it is a matter of judging the trees by their fruit. Both the innovators and the traditionalists are found to have made valuable contributions. Where criticism has been ventured, one hopes that no offence has been given. Some well-known scholars may have received less attention than is their due, while others toiling in less familiar environments have been favoured. A particular attempt has been made to cover German-language scholarship, which is sometimes unjustly overlooked in work by American or British writers. The cut-off date is the end of 2002, but where possible the most important works that appeared in 2003 and the first months of 2004 have also been considered.

Research in this field is still in its initial phase and new work is appearing weekly. For any unjustifiable omissions or crass errors, the author begs the reader's indulgence.

Acknowledgements

John Keep (who also translated Part I) thanks warmly Christophe von Werdt, Barbara Lothamer and others at the Schweizerische Osteuropa-Bibliothek, Bern, for tireless and invaluable technical help in preparation of the typescript and for providing an enviable working environment. Thanks are also due to Bernhard H. Bayerlein (Mannheim/Cologne), Michael Ellman (Amsterdam), Heinz-Dietrich Löwe (Heidelberg), Carmen Scheide (Basle), and Lynne Viola (Toronto), each of whom kindly read sections of the MS in advance of publication. None of them of course bears any responsibility for the remaining imperfections.

Finally, both authors are indebted to Ilia V. Gerasimov (Kazan') for uncomplainingly helping to maintain electronic communication between them. Their partnership has been trouble-free and mutually enriching.

Abbreviations

APRF	Archive of the President of the Russian Federation
ASSR	Autonomous Soviet Socialist Republic
AUCP(b)	All-Union Communist Party (bolshevik)
CC	Central Committee (of CPSU)
CCP	Chinese Communist Party
Cheka	*see* Vecheka
CPC	Council of People's Commissars
CPGB	British Communist Party
CPSU	Communist Party of the Soviet Union
ECCI	Executive Committee of the Communist International
FSB	Federal Security Service
FSU	former Soviet Union
FYP	Five-year Plan
GARF	State Archive of the Russian Federation
GDR	German Democratic Republic
GRU	Main Intelligence Administration
GULag	Main Administration of (Labour) Camps (of the NKVD/MVD)
IR	international relations (theory)
IRI	Institute of Russian History (of the Russian Academy of Sciences)
ITK	corrective labour colony(ies)
ITL	corrective labour camp(s)
JAFC	Jewish Anti-fascist Committee
KGB	State Security Committee
KPRF	Communist Party of the Russian Federation
LMG	League of Militant Godless
MGB	Ministry of State Security
MVD	Ministry of Internal Affairs
NATO	North Atlantic Treaty Organization
NEP	New Economic Policy
NKID	People's Commissariat of Foreign Affairs
NKVD	People's Commissariat of Internal Affairs
OGPU	Unified State Political Administration
PCF	French Communist Party

PDRK	People's Democratic Republic of (North) Korea
PLA	People's Liberation Army (China)
PM	post-modernism
PUR	Political Administration of the Red Army
RAN	Russian Academy of Sciences
RGASPI	Russian State Archive of Social and Political History
RGVA	Russian State Military Archive
Rosarkhiv	Russian Archival Administration
RSFSR	Russian Socialist Federated Soviet Republic
SED	Socialist Unity Party (GDR)
SMAG	Soviet Military Administration in Germany
SRs	Socialist-Revolutionaries
TsA FSB RF	Central Archive of the Russian Federal Security Service
Vecheka	All-Russian Extraordinary Commission to Combat Counter-Revolution, Sabotage and Speculation
YCL	Young Communist League (Komsomol)

The following abbreviations are used for journal titles:

AHR	*American Historical Review*, Bloomington, IN
CMR	*Cahiers du monde russe*, Paris
EAS	*Europe-Asia Studies*, Glasgow
Forum OIZ	*Forum für osteuropäische Ideen- und Zeitgeschichte*, Weimar/Vienna
IA	*Istoricheskii arkhiv*, Moscow
IRSH	*International Review of Social History*, Amsterdam
JGOE	*Jahrbücher für Geschichte Osteuropas*, Munich
JHK	*Jahrbuch für historische Kommunismusforschung*, Mannheim
JMH	*Journal of Modern History*, Chicago
Kritika	*Kritika: Explorations in Russian and Eurasian History*, Bloomington, IN
OA	*Otechestvennye arkhivy*, Moscow
OI	*Otechestvennaia istoriia*, Moscow
RR	*Russian Review*, Lawrence, KS
RSS	*Religion, State and Society*, London
SR	*Slavic Review*, Urbana-Champaign, IL
VI	*Voprosy istorii*, Moscow

Part I

Coping with the legacy of Stalinism

Recent Russian writing

1 Sources

Archives

The quest for truth about the Stalin era must begin with a look at the situation in Russian archives. In the 1990s, this improved greatly for scholars who wanted to consult documents from that period. The declassification of hitherto secret papers led to the publication of many works, some of very high quality. But as the years passed, political developments made things more difficult. It used to be much easier to gain access to sensitive material under Boris Yeltsin than it is today.

R.G. Pikhoia, who headed the Russian Federal archive service from 1990 to 1996, has stated that in Soviet times up to 90 per cent of the documents in the archives of the Communist Party (CPSU), and 20 per cent of those in state repositories, were considered secret or were otherwise subject to restrictions. The regulations on release of official documents to the public domain were not adhered to. Among those kept under lock and key were those containing data on the mass repressions under Stalin and the activities of central state organs, including the armed forces and police.

In 1992–3 the Russian state authorities took over the archives of the former CPSU. Of its files, 74 million were declassified; so too were more than 600,000 from the central archives of the ex-KGB (security service) and about 400,000 from Soviet ministries and other state agencies that had ceased to exist.[1] Between 1992 and 1997, a total of over 5 million previously closed files in the state archives were declassified, and no fewer than 285 documentary volumes saw the light.[2] However, especially in the former KGB archives and those of the President of the Russian Federation (APRF) progress has not been so rapid and it is extremely difficult to gain access to material held there.

The documentary volumes on the Stalin era that have appeared since 1991 are as a rule compiled according to subject matter. They are also selective; that is to say, they do not reproduce an entire archival collection (*fond*) in its entirety. In St Petersburg, some scholars did start publishing all the documents relating to the so-called 'Academy case' (1929–31), in which a number of historians were arrested, but their edition remained incomplete. The same thing happened with a project to publish all of the material from the investigations into those accused during Stalin's Great Terror.[3]

Stalin died on 5 March 1953 at the ripe old age of 75, after an active and varied life, first as a revolutionary – he joined the Bolshevik party's Central Committee in 1912 – and from 1922 until his death as *de facto* head of the Soviet state. It is therefore only to be expected that material about him should be scattered around in several archival repositories, in Russia and elsewhere. According to Pikhoia, the Stalin *fond* alone contained about 80,000 to 100,000 files, while there were no fewer than 10.6 million in the ex-KGB archives.[4] In the 1990s scholars doing research on Stalinism focused their attention on the papers that had hitherto been practically inaccessible: documents in Stalin's personal collection (*fond*) and in the former KGB's central archive. In analysing this material, Russian researchers were chiefly concerned with trying to find out how the totalitarian state apparatus was built and functioned.

Part of Stalin's personal collection is held in what is now known as RGASPI (Russian State Archive of Social and Political History); this was formerly the Communist Party's central archive (officially known as the Central Party Archive of the Institute of Marxism–Leninism attached to the Central Committee of the CPSU, or TsPA IML). Another part is in the APRF. So long as Stalin was alive, and for some time thereafter, his *fond* bore the number 3 (no. 1 was reserved for Marx and Engels, and no. 2 for Lenin). Today the number given to the Stalin *fond* in RGASPI is 558. In 1996 it was said to hold 16,174 files, in Russian and Georgian.[5]

This means that the bulk of Stalin's personal papers are in APRF. This archive, set up on 31 December 1991, contains the personal collections of 51 major Soviet leaders and political personalities. In 1998 (on 2 August) President Yeltsin confirmed a document listing which categories of files were henceforth to be kept by the state. Among those listed was Stalin's personal *fond*.[6] About a year later, in October 1999, 1,445 files from this *fond*, of very unequal quality, were transferred from APRF to RGASPI, along with 20 inventories (*opisi*) relating to 100 collections of the Politburo.[7] Further transfers were made over the next three years. In 2003, when I was working in RGASPI on documents in *fond* no. 558, I tried to find out how many files from Stalin's personal archive were held in this archive, how many of them had been put in its secret repository (*spetskhran*), and when they would be declassified – but this was a riddle that I was unable to solve.

Part of Stalin's archive was destroyed: on this point all the specialists concerned agree. General D.A. Volkogonov, who had unlimited access to information about the archives while he served as advisor to the President of the Russian Federation, wrote that many documents had been done away with on Stalin's own orders, while others had disappeared after his death. According to Volkogonov,

> When Beria was arrested [in 1953] Khrushchev ordered the 'arrest' of his personal archive, which contained a number of documents that Stalin had sent to the NKVD. A commission set up for this purpose took the view that the best course would be simply to burn 11 sacks of documents that were apparently unique, without first reading them . . . The members of the highest Party collegium were afraid that among these papers there was some material compromising them.[8]

The Medvedev brothers, Zhores and Roi, incline to the view that material from Stalin's personal archive was destroyed along with many documents from the archives of Beria and Mikoian. (Neither Khrushchev nor M.A. Suslov, the CC secretary, kept personal archives, and the same was true of A.N. Poskrebyshev, Stalin's long-time private secretary.)[9]

In 1994 a catalogue came out called *Stalin's Special File*. It listed nearly 3,000 documents addressed to Stalin between 1944 and 1953 by the NKVD (or MVD, as it later became). Most of these were simply items of information, for instance about earthquakes in various parts of the USSR, drafts of decrees and orders, or just documents needing Stalin's signature.[10] When Khrushchev made his so-called 'secret speech' criticizing Stalin at the XXth Party congress in 1956, and again at the XXIInd congress in 1961, he made use of documents from Stalin's personal archive, but otherwise publication of materials from this *fond* had to await the Soviet Union's collapse. The subsequent appearance of several such publications shows that many documents in the Stalin *fond* were indeed preserved; the fact that scholars have yet to set eyes on some of them does not mean that they are non-existent. From July 1994 onward, the bimonthly periodical *Istochnik* ('Source') published a supplement entitled 'Herald of the Archive of the President of the Russian Federation'. A number of documents from Stalin's personal *fond* appeared for the first time in its pages. One can only regret that early in 2004 *Istochnik* had to cease publication because of financial problems – according to its editor, S.V. Kondrashov (pers. com.).

Scholars working on *fond* no. 558 in RGASPI will find there, among other papers, writings by Stalin from the years 1906 to 1917 that were not included in his published *Collected Works*. Certain articles (from various years) have a note appended to the effect that they were written not by Stalin but by G.Ya. Sokol'nikov (1888–1939), people's commissar of Finance from 1921 to 1926, who was later shot. The collection also contains two film scripts, 'Lenin in 1918' and 'The First Cavalry Division', bearing Stalin's corrections, along with numerous memoranda to Stalin from the police chief G.G. Yagoda. According to one of these notes, on 30 January 1933 Stalin sent a telegram to the authorities in Petrozavodsk (Karelia) telling them how important it was to utilize prison labour in forestry work. There are also several propaganda articles that E.M. Yaroslavsky sent to Stalin for him to pronounce on. One of those he approved, by O. Chaadaeva and P. Pospelov, contained sharp criticism of A.G. Shliapnikov's memoirs on 1917.[11]

The Stalin archive contains some materials which at first glance do not appear relevant: for example, the manuscript diary of I.I. Prezent from 28 June 1928 to 15 September 1930. Prezent was a faithful myrmidon of Stalin and T.D. Lysenko, who played a sinister role in the fate of Soviet genetics and its leading representative, Academician N.I. Vavilov (1887–1943). In his diary, Prezent mentioned Maxim Gorky's hostile attitude towards the poet Demian Bednyi, whom he called 'a fat, uncultured beast'. But probably the real reason why the diary found its way into Stalin's personal archive was an entry of 7 July 1929 about the author's meeting a certain Zorin. The latter told him he knew Stalin, and recalled how, when he had met him in Moscow in 1924, Stalin had invited him into the government box at the Bol'shoi. Once, Stalin saw Zorin talking to L.P. Serebriakov and asked him: 'Why are you friendly with him?' 'He's a good comrade', replied Zorin. 'That's true, but one has to distinguish between friendship and politics.'[12]

Scholars doing research in the accessible part of Stalin's personal *fond* and other material about the purges of the 1930s are faced with a host of problems in dealing with such sources. One of them is to determine how reliable and authentic they are. Academician A.A. Fursenko, who was on a board set up by Rosarkhiv (the chief archival authority), had the chance in the late 1990s to see many documents that were closed to other people. He came to the conclusion that the medical report on Stalin's death had been forged in order to show that Stalin's associates had not had anything to do with it, for the 20-page typewritten report differs from the hand-written ones compiled earlier whenever Stalin had been ill.

> The document is not dated, but the rough draft bears the date July 1953, i.e. four months after Stalin's death. This in itself is enough to make one suspicious. From the text it is clear that the report was compiled on the basis of a medical journal that had been kept between 2 and 5 March. Yet this journal is missing from the file on Stalin's last illness . . . and was evidently destroyed. There are indeed a few loose sheets of paper there entitled 'Draft Records of Medicines Prescribed and Diagram of Duty Rosters During I.V. Stalin's Illness, 2–5 March 1953'. In front is a cut-out piece of cardboard, which served as a cover for the *earlier* file with the same title on the course of Stalin's illness. To judge by the numbers on the pages, which have been crossed out, the document originally had two dozen sheets, but several of those at the beginning are missing – and it is precisely they that would tell us when medical treatment was started. Also lacking are the duty roster and the doctors' conclusions after each changeover of personnel. Finally, on the cut-out lid of the cardboard cover of the 'Draft Records . . . ' file there is a mark 'Volume X', which shows that there were nine previous volumes relating to Stalin's fatal illness. What happened to them is also unclear.

Fursenko takes the view that the 'Draft Records' and the medical journal 'contained data that did not accord with the official conclusions' on the causes of Stalin's death, which explains why they were removed:

> One cannot overlook the fact that the typewritten text of the conclusions was compiled a few days after Beria's arrest on 26 June 1953. When Beria's case was being investigated, it seems likely that someone in the Kremlin leadership wanted to destroy the medical journal so as to get rid of any possible evidence that Stalin had not been properly cared for but had been done to death. At the CC plenum in June 1957 Molotov criticized Khrushchev, who had been appointed chairman of the commission on Stalin's archive, for not having called a meeting of it for four years.[13]

In an article written jointly with V. Yu. Afiani, Fursenko tells us a bit more about how this commission was set up and what became of it. On 4–5 March 1953, the Bureau of the CC Presidium (as the Politburo was then known) entrusted Beria, Malenkov and Khrushchev with the job of bringing Stalin's papers 'into appropriate order'. On 3 September of that year, members of the Presidium asked Malenkov and Khrushchev to report on the materials in the late leader's archive – but they failed to do so. On 28 April 1955, another commission was set up to inspect Stalin's documents, this time with Khrushchev in the chair (the other members were Bulganin, Kaganovich, Malenkov, Molotov, Pospelov and Suslov), and it was to this body that Molotov's remark refers. Probably Khrushchev used these records in his struggle against his adversaries in the leadership.

The two authors disagree with the opinion held by Svetlana Allilueva, Stalin's daughter, and the Medvedev brothers that the documentation on the leader's illness was destroyed on his orders already in 1952, when he had his personal physician, V.N. Vinogradov, arrested. The medical histories of Stalin's illnesses from the 1920s onward have been discovered in the archive of the USSR Health Ministry's Fourth Department. (This was the successor to the so-called 'Kremlin hospital' that catered for members of the Party and governmental élite.) These records are incomplete. Who took the missing ones and why, or whether they have been preserved, it is impossible to say. Fursenko and Afiani show that the integrity of Stalin's personal archive was breached long ago; some documents were transferred elsewhere and others destroyed.[14]

In March 2003, Rosarkhiv staged an exhibition to mark the fiftieth anniversary of Stalin's death. As well as documents, one could view the generalissimo's dressing gown, coat, uniform breeches and boots – inside one of which was an orthopaedic pad, since as is generally known Stalin had one leg shorter than the other. But the *pièce de résistance* was the draft of Khrushchev's 1956 'secret speech', from which he apparently decided at the last moment to omit an anecdote about Stalin shouting at him 'What are you sitting there for? Are you afraid I'll shoot you? Don't be scared, I won't!'[15]

Investigation records

The reliability and authenticity problem crops up when working in the ex-KGB's central archive, too, but here it takes a rather different form, especially when one considers the grim legacy of Stalin's terror, with its millions of victims. Many innocent citizens convicted between 1918 and 1953 were later rehabilitated by the Procuracy, which found they had not committed any criminal offence. This means that the evidence against them in the investigation transcript (*protokol*), which served to convict them, was falsified. Some scholars have accordingly raised the question whether it is right to publish such fraudulent documents. I personally am convinced that it is, since they constitute important evidence as to the arbitrary and illegal nature of the totalitarian regime. But working with such tendentious material requires a fine touch: one has to weigh each sentence, each word of evidence. One cannot take the transcript as a true record of the accused's testimony, because the investigator may have rewritten it. In the local KGB archive in Kazan', I found one transcript that had been completed by the investigator in the accused's absence, yet on the basis of it the man was sentenced (again in his absence) to be shot by a three-man tribunal (*troika*). Later, in 1940, it was the investigator's turn to be investigated. He admitted that he had forged the testimony of alleged 'enemies of the people' in order to meet his allotted quota of arrests and executions. Even where the accused's signature appears at the bottom of each page of the transcript, this does not count as proof that the statements in it are authentic, because they might have been made under duress, after physical or psychological torture.

Generally, historians working on tendentious material go by the maxim that information contradicting the compiler's intentions is more reliable than any which endorses them. But in dealing with Soviet investigation transcripts, it is difficult to keep to this rule because, by and large, they do not contain *any* information contradicting the charges.

If one analyses such documents carefully, it becomes apparent that an accused might well be sentenced to be shot whether or not he or she had confessed to 'criminal' acts. A.V. Svechin, a former tsarist general who later commanded a Red army division and then became a professor in the General Staff Academy, categorically denied all the evidence brought against him, which had been beaten out of his colleagues. At a closed hearing before a circuit session of the USSR Supreme Court's Military Collegium on 29 July 1938, he pleaded not guilty. Yet all the same, he was sentenced to be shot for having allegedly belonged to a mythical organization of 'monarchist ex-officers' that had been concocted by the NKVD.[16]

A number of accused stated that the investigation transcript had been tampered with by the official who questioned them. For example, the historian V.I. Picheta, rector of Belarus State University, was arrested in 1929 in connection with the so-called 'Academy case', another OGPU invention. In a plea for help (12 November 1931) to his professional colleague, Academician M.N. Pokrovsky, written from Viatka province, where he was living in exile, he explained what his investigation had been like:

> After my interrogation was over they handed back my testimony and asked me to substitute certain words by others more incriminating. They compelled me to alter the conclusions of my testimony and told me what style and tone I should adopt when giving evidence. I would have to invent evidence; if I refused to do so, they said, it would be to my disadvantage ... They forced me to confess to belonging to an organization that I had no idea existed. I signed everything written down by the investigator ... It was a forgery ... I couldn't protest, for they would have condemned me for doing so.[17]

The illegal methods used in distorting interrogation records and carrying out judicial investigations are described by Yevgeniia Ginzburg, who later wrote a well-known account of her sufferings entitled *Into the Whirlwind*. On 9 May 1953 she sent a letter from her place of exile in Magadan *oblast'* to K.E. Voroshilov, in his capacity as chairman of the USSR Supreme Soviet, from which this quotation is taken:

The session of the USSR Supreme Court's Military Collegium on 1 August 1937 at which my case was considered lasted six minutes, including questioning and reading the lengthy text of the sentence. My judges were in such a hurry that they did not answer any of my questions or statements. Among the methods used during preliminary investigation were deprivation of sleep for eight days and nights running, filthy curses, threats and so on . . . The absurdity of the charges of 'terror' is obvious merely from a superficial glance at the records of my case, so that there is no need to contest them here. In 1937 I asked the chairman of the court which politician I was accused of murdering. He replied with a strange, complicated syllogism: the Trotskyists had killed Kirov in Leningrad, you didn't struggle against El'vov in Kazan', and so you must be treated as a terrorist.[18]

Investigation transcripts generally consist of a printed form authorizing the arrest of the accused, filled in by hand, followed by the interrogation records. The latter are quite simple in structure and consist of statements by successive investigators, which differ from one another in form. The arrested person would first try to prove his or her innocence by making credible statements about their political loyalty. But after a month or so, he or she would start to give the evidence the investigator wanted to hear, such as having used an official position to engage in 'wrecking activities'. The absurdity of these confessions did not faze the investigators, since they were actively engaged in fabricating an indictment. They went so far as to think up bogus 'subversive' organizations, as we have just seen. M.P. Yakubovich, who was sentenced at the 1931 Menshevik trial to a term of exile, wrote after his release to the USSR Procuracy on 10 May 1967 as follows:

No such body as the 'Union Bureau of Mensheviks' existed in reality. Those convicted in this case did not all know each other and not all of them had been members of the Menshevik party . . . The first 'organizational' session of the 'Union Bureau' took place a few days before the trial began . . . At this 'meeting' the accused became acquainted with one another and agreed what conduct they would adopt in court.[19]

Investigation transcripts do not contain any references to torture, blackmail, threats against relatives of the accused and so on. We know about such matters from memoirs written by survivors of the Terror, from the sparse acknowledgements made by their tormentors when they themselves were put on trial, and from documents on the subsequent rehabilitation of the accused. There is as yet no accepted methodology for working on sources of this kind, but there is much common ground between the various political trials staged during the Soviet era, both as regards their organizers' intentions and the results of the policy of repression.

Scholars consider that it is quite justifiable to apply the rules elaborated for publication of documents on earlier epochs. They use documents from central (federal) and local archives, as well as those of various government agencies. But in nearly every instance, they have found it necessary to draw on material held in RGASPI and the security service archive (TsA FSB RF) as well. This explains why these two repositories have loomed so large in the foregoing account.

Documentary publications

One of the earliest documentary volumes to appear in the 1990s containing material from Stalin's personal archive revealed how the leader had himself corrected the text of his official 'brief biography'. This work was first published in 1939, with a print run of over 4 million copies. Over 13 million copies came out of the second edition (1947). Along with the *Short Course* of Party history (1938), these manuals were obligatory reading in schools and universities, as well as in the vast number of courses organized by the Party's Agitprop department and the Komsomol (Communist Youth League). Stalin's comments, on the draft of the second edition, bolstered the myth that he had been a major Bolshevik leader before 1917, had master-minded 'decisive military operations' during the civil war, and had become Party leader already in 1921 while yet remaining 'a worthy pupil of Lenin'.[20]

A similar purpose was served by Stalin's editorial corrections to the draft of the *Short Course*. Each chapter was given a contemporary political twist; all references were removed to those now categorized as 'enemies of the people' and shot; and the RSDRP was no longer called a Marxist party because Stalin thought Western social democrats had become 'opportunists' and thus the term was no longer fitting for their erstwhile Russian comrades either. By stressing his own role in the struggle against Mensheviks, Trotskyists and other 'enemies of the Party' he sought to legitimize the show trials of ex-oppositionists then in progress.[21]

The documentary volumes published in recent years deal with different topics; they were put together by various people without co-ordination from above, so that in some cases political expediency took precedence over observance of professional standards. This was most evident in the criteria adopted when deciding which documents to choose and whether to publish them in full or not. The volume *Stalin's Politburo in the 1930s* (1995)[22] was certainly an eye-opener for many historians, who later came to regret that a lot of sources relevant to the operation of this body had not been included.

V.P. Danilov is the leading specialist on Soviet agrarian history in the Russian Academy of Sciences' Institute of Russian History, and has published a large number of documentary volumes on this topic. He has often stated what a tremendous advantage it has been for him and his colleagues to be free from the bonds of Marxist–Leninist ideology. This freedom has enabled a fresh approach to be taken to the study of the peasantry, who comprised the bulk of the population in the 1920s but thereafter suffered catastrophe.

In 1992 the institute's learned council decided to publish two series of documentary volumes, *The Soviet Village in the 1920s and 1930s Seen Through the Eyes of the Vecheka, OGPU and NKVD* and *The Tragedy of the Soviet Village: Collectivization and Dekulakization, 1927–1939*. André Bérélowitch, Nicolas Werth, and Theodor Shanin were among the foreign scholars associated with this project. A key source is the reports (*svodki*) on popular attitudes compiled for the benefit of the leadership by secret-police informants. Danilov calls them 'a really unique and highly reliable source about politically significant events that are inadequately treated in other available sources'. When working on collectivization the compilers had to deal with classified material, for from May 1927 onward the Soviet censorship authorities prohibited publication of anything about what was really going on as regards farming and food supply. Thus the publication of these secret orders and reports is a boon to future researchers.[23]

The documents published in these volumes, along with those in the Smolensk archive (now also available in Russian), show what a terrible tragedy Stalin's forced collectivization of agriculture was for peasant farmers, who were subjected to cruel and indiscriminate violence. Volume 3 of *The Tragedy* tells of the harsh fate that awaited the so-called 'kulaks' sent into exile as 'special settlers' (*spetspereselentsy*) (pp. 96–100) and the man-made famine of 1932–3. Published here for the first time (pp. 634–5) is a directive dated 22 January 1933, signed by Stalin and Molotov (with the former's autograph signature), forbidding starving peasants from leaving the afflicted areas in Ukraine and elsewhere. Population experts and historians have put the number of famine victims at 5 million or more. The Stalinist leadership's responsibility for this atrocity is abundantly confirmed in these pages.[24] Although these editions are not yet complete, the documents published so far constitute an indispensable basis for further research.

Next in importance is the 10-volume work *Top Secret*, of which six volumes (in nine books) had appeared by the beginning of 2004.[25] Jointly edited by a team of Russian and foreign specialists, it contains reports to Stalin by the security police on the situation in the country between 1926 and 1934.

It is worth noting that contemporary Russian historians disagree about the reliability of sources drawn from the ex-KGB archive. V.P. Danilov, who has worked on them a lot in recent years, considers that the reports on public opinion *are* reliable because the police were keen to collect as much information as possible, even of a negative kind. But in 1930–1 some leading OGPU officials tried to slow down the pace of dekulakization and ease conditions for the peasants. Stalin raised the matter in the Politburo (25 July 1931) and as a result those who took this moderate line were sacked. Already in March of that year, the OGPU's Information department had been dissolved, and thereafter the reports no longer contained so much concrete data; instead they mainly reflected the official interpretation of events.[26] From Danilov's analysis, it follows that police reports *cannot* be considered entirely reliable beyond March 1931.

The editors of *Top Secret* also view as authentic the OGPU's monthly surveys of political and economic conditions. These surveys were based on *svodki* supplied by local agencies of the Information department along with other reports by secret bodies charged with surveillance of 'counter-revolutionaries'. The text as published here is taken directly from the archival original, without any cuts. The surveys were designed to provide a basis for policy decisions by Stalin and the Politburo. Copies were also sent to local police chiefs for operational guidance. They reveal that there was constant opposition to the Soviet regime in the 1920s and early 1930s: workers demanded better economic conditions, peasants opposed collective farming, and ministers of religion defended their right to carry out their duties.

V.K. Vinogradov, who wrote one of the introductory chapters, notes that already in 1929 monthly reports on political conditions ceased to be compiled, and that in 1930 the information supplied became much vaguer.[27] Thus there is a two-year gap between Vinogradov and Danilov as to when the deterioration of quality occurred. Vinogradov pointed out that the shifts in information policy were logically connected with the change in the Party line, when the security police were given new tasks to fulfil. The lack of reliable information from 1929 onward influenced the regime's attitude towards society. J. Arch Getty (Riverside CA), in his introduction to volume 3, raises the question how far the OGPU's role in 'producing' information told its 'consumers' in the top Party leadership what they wanted to hear. He does not have an answer, but still considers the information surveys a valuable historical source.[28] A. Edgar (Santa Barbara, CA) is even more affirmative about their value, but stresses that the themes they dealt with were those requested by the political bosses: 'Since it was the central Party authorities that stood behind the call for information, in the shape of reports and surveys from the OGPU, and required it to be presented in a certain format, these documents can tell us much about the concerns, anxieties and confusion of those at the top.'[29] It is probable that these surveys also served the security police as a means of showing the Party authorities how important this agency was, so as to get more funds and cadres.

The material in these volumes reveals for the first time, on such a broad scale and with such frankness, the hidden side of Stalin's 'socialist construction': the total surveillance exercised by the police over various strata of the population, and the widespread grass-roots disaffection with official policy – to which the Party responded by unleashing the purges.

How faithfully did the reports by local OGPU agencies, which served as the basis for the surveys, convey actual facts? A thorough examination of this point has yet to be undertaken, but much of what was reported can be confirmed from other publications based on regional police documents.[30]

Some Russian historians take a highly critical view of all documentary sources on the Soviet era. The most radical in this respect is I.V. Pavlova, who argues that:

> These sources are not merely heavily coloured by ideology but actually perverted the sense of the events they reported on in a fundamental way. An ideocratic state order leaves behind records couched in a language full of taboos which reflects the distorted outlook of the addressees.

She maintains that the investigation records held in the former KGB archive were the most falsified of all Stalin-era documents.[31] I think it is wrong to view the matter so subjectively, for even in the falsified data regarding individuals arrested for political offences one does come across authentic documents written by the accused (manuscripts, diaries, letters and so on), and the biographical data in these files, too, are accurate. Moreover, the ex-KGB archive also contains various reports and surveys of the political situation whose accuracy the editors accept.

In 2003, there appeared the first major publication compiled on the basis of documents in Stalin's personal archive, entitled *Stalin and the Vecheka-GPU-OGPU-NKVD*. According to the compilers, B.N. Khaustov and V.P. Naumov, who also contribute an introduction to the volume, its value lies in its revelation of the mechanism whereby the security organs became a tool in maximizing Stalin's personal power. The documents show how he used them to suppress any opposition to his rule and extended their scope to cover every sphere of people's lives. In this way, they were turned into instruments of personal despotism. For instance, the Politburo adopted what were properly judicial decisions, such as 'to exile Trotsky abroad for anti-Soviet activity' (10 January 1929) or 'to shoot Ya. Bliumkin' (5 November 1929); and later Stalin made handwritten corrections to the lists whereby whole groups of offenders were sentenced to death or exile.[32]

Most documentary volumes are based on holdings of the TsA FSB RF. One of them deals with the chiefs of the security apparatus, while others treat these organs' role in the purges, the Gulag economy, and the show trials of the 1930s.[33] The most comprehensive of all the works on the Gulag was compiled from materials of the Interior ministry (MVD) and its Gulag subordinate, held in GARF (State Archive of the Russian Federation). The documents are arranged thematically: penal policy, the Gulag's organization, statistics, make-up of the prisoner population and their disposition (entry, exit, transfer), living and working conditions, and contribution to the economy. Special attention is given here to the latter point, for Gulag convicts were employed to construct roads and canals, the new building of Moscow State University, and nuclear facilities, as well as in mining (coal, gold), drilling oil wells and so on.

Documents in this volume fill out what is known from other published sources; for example, about the construction bureau staffed by prisoner scientists such as the aircraft designers A.N. Tupolev and V.N. Petliakov, as well as the rocket engineer who devised the first *Sputnik*, S.P. Korolev. On 4 July 1939, Beria reported to Stalin that the NKVD had set up seven 'technical bureaux' for aircraft construction, diesel propulsion, shipbuilding, artillery, munitions, poisonous substances and reinforced steel. He suggested that 316 specialists working there should be sentenced to lengthy terms of imprisonment, their sentence being gradually reduced to provide an incentive or as a reward for specially meritorious work.[34]

In 1943, forced labour (*katorga*) was introduced as a penalty. In such camps, the regime was particularly harsh and prisoners had to wear a number on their outer clothing, as they did in Nazi concentration camps. Between 1948 and 1952, 12 'special' camps were set up for ex-Oppositionists sent for a second time to the Gulag – for their initial 'offence'. By 1953 there were twice as many regional ITL[35] administrations as there had been in 1949.

The documents that have recently appeared on the Gulag are couched in less emotional language than survivors' accounts or Solzhenitsyn's *Gulag Archipelago*, but have the merit of authenticity. They represent a fundamental source for scholarly investigation of the system of repression. The dispassionate tone of these documents does not detract from the horrors. On the contrary, the arbitrary and cruel nature of the machinery devised to crush the populace emerges from these pages with fresh force.

There are a great number of such publications, for virtually each republic and district in the Russian Federation has found it necessary to put out 'books of memory' with lists of the victims in its territory, along with other relevant documents.[36]

The documents in Stalin's personal *fond* show that in the early 1920s not all Bolshevik leaders agreed that repression was the only effective way of dealing with discontent. L.B. Kamenev thought that under the NEP there should be fewer shootings on political grounds. Zinoviev dissented, as did Stalin, who wrote 'Kamenev is inflating the question but simplifying it in a way that harms our cause'. Just at that time, in 1923, the leaders were discussing what to do about M.Kh. Sultan-Galiev (1892–1940), the Tatar Communist leader who had worked under Stalin in the Nationalities commissariat. He stood for conferring equality and full rights on autonomous republics within the new Soviet federation, and opposed Stalin's plan to build what was in effect a 'pan-Russian empire'. Zinoviev and Bukharin thought it wrong to arrest Sultan-Galiev, fearing this might provoke a Muslim revolt. But Stalin got his way and later had him shot.[37]

As already noted, in the mid-1950s Khrushchev, engaged in a power struggle to become sole leader, made use of the Stalin archive to discredit his comrades. In June 1957, a CC plenum met to condemn the so-called 'anti-Party group' (Malenkov, Kaganovich, Molotov and others). Among the archival materials made available were the execution lists that Stalin and Molotov had signed in 1937–8. A memorandum prepared for Khrushchev on the basis of these documents stated that between 27 February 1937 and 12 November 1938 Stalin and other Politburo members told the NKVD that they sanctioned the Military Collegium's conviction of 38,679 individuals. On one single day, 12 November 1938, Stalin and Molotov ordered 3,167 persons to be shot.[38]

Recently published documentary collections about the regime's relationship with the artistic and scientific intelligentsia show that not a single group of Soviet citizens escaped the vigilant eye of the state security apparatus. One of these volumes lists chronologically all major decisions taken by the Party and state authorities from 1917 to 1953 designed to crush freedom of speech and people's right to dissent.[39]

As already noted, the numerous volumes of material that have appeared of late on various topics to do with Stalinism, as well as Stalin himself,[40] raise two methodological questions: whether they should be published in full and what criteria to use in selection. Of course, some formerly classified sources have become accessible, but one can only guess how many more are still awaiting perusal and study. There is not much chance at present of any improvement in this regard. One would have thought that A.N. Yakovlev, chairman of the official Commission on Rehabilitation of Victims of Political Repression (and founder of the 'Democracy' fund), would be allowed to see anything he wanted. But when he began to publish the multi-volume series of documents from the archives of the Party CC and the ex-KGB, he encountered great difficulty in getting hold of the papers about the NKVD's shooting of about 20,000 Polish POW at Katyn' and elsewhere in 1940, and also of the records of the negotiations with Germany prior to the 1939 Nazi–Soviet pact. Talking later to S. Filatov, former chief of President Yeltsin's administration, he said sadly 'I don't know what to do about the "Russia: Twentieth Century: Documents" series. The archives have been closed and I'm not being given any material, the President won't see me . . . Somebody is turning Russia into a "guided democracy".'[41] So today, historians are saying that if Yakovlev cannot get them, it is not worth while for them even to try . . .

Selection criteria have changed in the recently published documentary collections: instead of reproducing sources that would expose the iniquities of Stalin's regime, editors have turned to academic analysis of its structure; instead of focusing on negative features of the dictatorship they seek to give a more objective picture. Historians have become better aware that it is their duty to approach the evidence fearlessly but with due scepticism. This more scholarly and critical attitude is apparent *inter alia* from a recent analysis of the Stalin-era edition of the first 13 volumes of the leader's *Works* (1946–51).[42]

The fiftieth anniversary of Stalin's death in March 2003 was marked by the appearance of further relevant documents, some of them historically significant. Among them are the following: stenographic minutes of Stalin's conversation with Winston Churchill on 9 October 1944 about the Soviet–Polish border and other current international issues; a document stressing the need for an accurate English translation of Stalin's last major work, *Economic Problems of Socialism in the USSR*; and the record of talks he had with the SED leaders Pieck, Grotewohl and Ulbricht (4 May 1950, 1 and 7 April 1952) about German reparations and other matters.[43]

Particularly interesting are those that throw light on Stalin's personality and behaviour in certain situations. On 22 October 1936, C. Hatter, Moscow bureau chief of Associated Press, wrote asking Stalin for an interview because foreign newspapers were carrying reports that he was seriously ill 'and even dead'. Four days later, Stalin replied with black humour: 'As far as I can tell from foreign press reports I have long since left this sinful world and betaken myself to the next. Since one cannot but trust reports in the foreign press . . . I ask you to credit them and not to disturb my peace in the beyond.'

Stalin behaved curiously when, on 19 July 1949, he discussed the *Great Soviet Encyclopedia* with S.I. Vavilov, president of the USSR Academy of Sciences. Vavilov asked whether it should include articles on 'our enemies' such as Trotsky. Stalin said it should do so, for 'you'll put Napoleon in, and after all he was a great scoundrel'.

Also published in 2003 were letters written by individuals and institutions directly after Stalin died offering suggestions as to how he should be immortalized: building a pantheon, for instance, or renaming Moscow State University in his honour.[44] Other new documents deal with his role in Party and government after the war[45] and his relations with members of his family. On 13 September 2003,

Izvestiia reported that Stalin's granddaughter, Galina Yakovleva Dzhugashvili, had been given papers from US archives relating to her father's death. A lieutenant in the Red Army, Yakov Iosifovich (1907–43) was taken prisoner by the Germans on 16 July 1941 and sent to Sachsenhausen concentration camp. A file containing the conclusions of a special commission of the Reichssicherheitshauptamt was found in Himmler's personal archive by the Americans in 1945. It contained reports about Dzhugashvili's death by the camp commandant, eye-witness testimony and photographs, as well as minutes of his interrogation.[46] A graphological examination of these materials was undertaken by V. Zhiliaev, who put forward the hypothesis that Yakov Iosifovich was actually killed in action and that the documents about the prisoner had been concocted by German intelligence for propaganda purposes.[47] This does not seem very plausible, for there is too much evidence about how the prisoner met his death. One of the guards, Konrad Harfisch, told the camp commandant that

> Yakov Stalin thrust his right foot into an empty square in the barbed-wire fence and put his left foot on the electric wire. For a moment he stood there motionless, with his right foot thrust forward and his body leaning back. Then he called out 'Harfisch, you're a soldier! Don't funk, shoot me!' So I shot him.[48]

Other material on Stalinism has come out in the specialized periodical *Istoricheskii arkhiv* ('Historical Archive'), which ceased publication in 1963 and was not revived until late 1992: one need only look at the index for the last 10 years.[49] It was this journal that featured the lists of visitors to Stalin's office from 1924 to 1953.[50] In the course of 30 years he received there practically the entire Soviet *nomenklatura*. There were 30,000 visits by about 2,800 different individuals[51] – and Stalin also met people *outside* his office. A close analysis of these lists shows some editorial confusion over people with the same name or the jobs they held. Thus in 1935 (22 May, 31 May, 25 July), Stalin received three visits from a certain Kuibyshev, but this was not the Politburo member Valerian Vladimirovich, as stated, for he had died in suspicious circumstances on 29 January of that year, but his brother, Nikolai Vladimirovich (1893–1938).[52]

Many Russian historians are currently busier publishing documents than doing serious original research. The reasons for this are that they are keen to exploit the 'new' material so long as it is still accessible, and that their readers want to know about the past at first hand. They do not have much confidence in the authors of scholarly monographs, who often adjust what they write to the mood of the moment. In any case, putting out these documentary volumes has been one of the main achievements of Russian historians over the last few years.

Memoirs, diaries and correspondence

Memoirs

The memoirs about the Stalin era that appeared in the 1990s are an odd bunch. The leader's principal associates had either published their reminiscences earlier or else were not anxious to get into print. From the 1960s to the 1980s, we were treated to autobiographical accounts by ministers (such as A.I. Mikoian), army leaders, aircraft designers, planners and other functionaries. The memoirs of Boris Bazhanov first appeared in a Russian periodical in 1989, and in book form three years later.[53] The new Russian editions include materials from his interrogation by French intelligence officials, who were keen to find out how stable the USSR was internally and how Bazhanov got on with Russian emigrés in France.[54]

Khrushchev dictated his memoirs in 1967–71, but they did not appear in Russia until the 1990s. He devoted a good deal of space to his relations with Stalin and acknowledged that at first he had worshipped him for all his cruelty. To justify his indifference to the fate of friends of his who fell victim to the Terror in the 1930s, when he occupied leading posts in the Party, Khrushchev claimed that he could not have helped them because 'the Cheka was above the Party'.[55] In his view, Stalin was both a great leader and a brute, a devoted Marxist and the executioner of his people. He kept to this ambivalent view all through his memoirs, convinced that the 'cult of the individual' was responsible for the people's miseries rather than the merciless repressive system that he and other Party leaders helped Stalin to sustain.

This notion, that Stalin was 'a great statesman but a bad human being and Communist', is found in many other functionaries' memoirs. They were products of his regime and found it hard to dissociate themselves from it after 1956. Like Khrushchev, they tended to blame the 'Chekists' for everything that had gone wrong and to exculpate themselves and the Party. This self-serving attitude was demolished by A.N. Yakovlev, himself a former Party official, when he wrote 'the Party élite and the security service élite were twins who committed their crimes together'. The entire leadership of Party and state were responsible for the repressions, but most guilt attaches to Stalin, who 'organized atrocities and destroyed Lenin's Russia'.[56]

This radical stance calls for a certain correction: Stalin already held important posts while Lenin was still alive, becoming Secretary-General of the Party in April 1922; even then he was known for his irreconcilable, merciless attitude to other people, of which he had given ample proof in his direction of Red Army operations and the Nationalities commissariat, as well as supervisor of the Cheka. In those early years, he did much to shape the Soviet regime and was bolstered in his leading position by an élite of functionaries, of whom some later wrote memoirs.

Accordingly, one can divide Soviet (and post-Soviet) memoirs into two groups: those in which Stalin is portrayed more or less positively, and critical ones written by dissidents and survivors of the purges. This subjective element can be explained largely by the political situation at the time they were written. Especially in the 1990s, memoirists' views were influenced by the Soviet collapse and the Communists' loss of their power monopoly – as well as by attempts to restore the old system. Since there was no longer any censorship and a plurality of opinions flourished, writers' attitudes varied immensely.

For instance, M. Lobanov, who has compiled a collection of memoirs (along with some other material), endeavours to represent Stalin as a 'great statesman'. His book consists of flattering excerpts from contemporary sources: Stalin's speeches against Trotsky, the falsified 'evidence' presented at the Moscow show trial of January 1937 and so on. For Lobanov, Stalin is a wise and omnipotent ruler, merciless towards enemies of the state, and a victorious commander-in-chief during World War II.[57] Much the same can be said of another miscellany compiled by E. Gusliarov. His *Stalin As He Lived* . . . is highly complimentary about his private life and relationships with friend and foe; nothing is included by repression victims, who are not even mentioned.[58] Given the current political situation, it is not surprising that propagandist literature of this kind should come out.

Svetlana Allilueva (1926–99), like the children of other senior officials,[59] seeks to exculpate her father, although she did not like him interfering in her private life: he destroyed her first two marriages, to G. Morozov and A. Kaplin, primarily because both men were Jews. Kira Pavlovna Allilueva is a niece of Stalin's second wife, Nadia. Her father was a Red Army general who died in unexplained circumstances in 1938, and both she and her mother were repressed. But now, many years later, she can tell a reporter that Stalin was a 'charming man' and 'goodness itself'.[60] Such behaviour is hard to explain: presumably some people just prefer to forget the past. Of course, there are other memoirists who write about Stalin and his repressive rule from a very different standpoint, such as Alexander Solzhenitsyn, Yevgeniia Ginzburg, Nadezhda Mandel'shtam, Lev Razgon, or Varlam Shalamov, all of whom spent time in the Gulag.[61]

Among the curious episodes mentioned in memoirs is a story that is still going the rounds among workers in a Moscow car factory. This once had the job of making an armoured limousine for Stalin, who had an original way of testing the glass and armour: the engineers responsible were seated in the vehicle, which was then peppered with rifle and revolver fire. The armour held up and the engineers emerged – still alive but with hair turned grey.[62]

Some memoirs underwent changes when they were re-edited. Marshal G.K. Zhukov's suffered particularly from this. The first edition appeared in 1969, the eleventh in 1992.[63] Many of the cuts restored in the later edition had to do with his appraisal of Stalin, which did not (and still does not) accord with what the authorities would like to see. Zhukov was first received by Stalin on 2 June 1940, on his return from defeating the Japanese at Khalkin-gol in Mongolia. Apparently, the encounter went well, for two days later he was promoted and appointed chief of the army's general staff. After war broke out with Germany Zhukov, as a member of the Stavka (general headquarters), saw Stalin on several occasions. Historians have corrected a number of factual errors in the marshal's memoirs,[64] but this does not affect the passages where he offers varying opinions about Stalin. After the war, Zhukov was demoted and humiliated, yet he remained grateful to the leader for having spared him from arrest in the late 1940s, when several other top-ranking officers suffered this fate.

Reminiscences have been published in recent years by some people who were personally close to Stalin: his bodyguard A.T. Rybin, for instance, or G.N. Kolomentsev, who was in charge of the Kremlin's special kitchen. He claims that Stalin died already in the night of 1/2 March 1953. When he was alive his favourite dishes were baked potatoes and *pel'meni*, washed down with Georgian cognac.[65] Another bodyguard, Yu.S. Solov'ev, recalls details of how Stalin's body was removed from the Mausoleum, where it had lain next to Lenin's mummified corpse, and taken to a grave dug nearby. Solov'ev noticed that the building workers involved

> made a frame of reinforced concrete slabs on the bottom and along the sides of the grave. Instead of soil being put on top of the coffin, liquid concrete was poured on in quantities that would have filled a car. The reburial was organized by Major-general Zakharov, chief of the KGB's Ninth department. Before Stalin's mortal remains were removed from the coffin in the Mausoleum, Zakharov ordered five large and several small gold buttons to be cut off his generalissimo's uniform.[66]

People are still reminiscing about their reactions to the dictator's death. The writer Daniil Granin recalls that he was 'shaken' by it, and the journalist S.V. Kondrashov relates how tense the editors of *Izvestiia* were while they waited for news of the ailing leader's state of health. When his death was announced, they were told by the Party CC not to write anything themselves but to publish only the official documents – and to add that in China people were studying Stalin's *Works*.[67]

Many of Stalin's close associates, notably Molotov and Kaganovich, have since given interviews either to historians, such as G.A. Kumanev and V.T. Loginov, or to journalists like F.I. Chuev, and their accounts are well known.[68] Most of these senior functionaries expressed favourable opinions about their leader. Molotov told Chuev in 1970 that '1937 was necessary'[69] – in other words, he justified the wave of repression he had himself helped to engineer. One of Kumanev's most recent articles is based on conversations he had in 1978 with V.S. Yemel'ianov (1901–88), who managed the government's Committee on Standards during the war, and Marshal I.T. Peresypkin (1904–78), who was in charge of army signals. Both had good things to say about their meetings with Stalin to discuss improvements in Red Army equipment.[70]

In the archives, there are records of Stalin's meetings with all kinds of people; for instance, with a group of Soviet writers early in September 1933. No minutes were taken, but what he said was noted down by several of those present. One was N.N. Nakoriakov (1881–1970), then director of the State Publishing House (*Gosizdat*). He recalled that Stalin had referred to writers as 'engineers of human souls' and suggested they set up a single country-wide union. This notion was backed by Maxim Gorky, who then became president of the Union once it was set up in 1934.[71] Interviews that Stalin gave to the German and French writers Emil

Ludwig and Romain Rolland in 1931 and 1935 respectively were publicized at the time, but now we also know what was left out of the published texts.[72]

To mark the fiftieth anniversary of Stalin's death some Volgograd communists came up with the idea that their city should revert to the name by which it was known between 1925 and 1961, Stalingrad. In this connection, *Istochnik* published, from the leader's personal archive, a letter of January 1925 from Stalin to the local Party boss, B.P. Sheboldaev (1895–1937), asking that he himself should not be mentioned when Sheboldaev changed the city's name from Tsaritsyn, that is, in essence sanctioning it.[73]

In Soviet times, the authorities were none too happy about people publishing their reminiscences, even if they had been in the armed services during the war. The writer Konstantin Simonov asked the Brezhnev leadership in January 1979 about putting out a collection of such memoirs but was told this was inadvisable, since a good many 'corrections and changes of a principled nature' had had to be made in the memoirs of Marshals Zhukov and Konev, as well as others.[74] The same negative approach was taken in regard to other writers of memoirs, too, as the documents show.

Stalin's character was complex: he was extremely strong willed and determined to achieve his goals; and his merciless cruelty, even towards relatives and comrades who had worked with him for years, continues to amaze those who study his personality. Was he paranoid? Professor V.M. Bekhterev (1857–1927), the well-known psychiatrist, who examined him in 1927, thought so.[75] Several memoirists note his marked suspiciousness. Admiral I.S. Isakov (1894–1967) told a journalist that he was once walking with Stalin along a corridor in the Kremlin; Isakov said he was surprised at the bright lighting and the profusion of guards, to which Stalin replied: 'The problem isn't the lights or the number of guards, but that I don't know which of those blackguards will put a bullet in the back of my neck and when.'[76] This suspiciousness was also remarked on by associates such as L.B. Kamenev, who recalled an occasion when the leaders were discussing what they liked to do most in life. Merry after drinking a bottle of wine, Stalin said: 'pick one's victim, prepare everything, wreak merciless vengeance, and then go to bed'.[77]

If Stalin fell ill, this was treated as a state secret (after all, the Leader was supposed to be 'immortal'). Not until the 1990s did one learn from D.A. Volkogonov that he had suffered several strokes which led to loss of consciousness due to spasms in the brain. The first one occurred at the end of 1949. But when his physician Professor V.N. Vinogradov (1882–1964) advised him to slow down, Stalin construed his advice as malicious in intent and eventually had Vinogradov arrested. Of the doctors who attended on Stalin in March 1953, several have left memoirs.

I.A. Valedinsky (1874–1954) kept watch on Stalin's health during his vacations in Sochi between 1926 and 1940. He was well disposed towards the leader, to whom he was indebted for a spacious Moscow apartment and the release of his son, an engineer arrested in 1937. In Valedinsky's view, Stalin's health at this time gave no grounds for concern, although he had pains in his joints and muscles that diminished his ability to move around.[78] Another professor of medicine, N.A. Kipshidze, was personal physician to Stalin's mother, Yekaterina Georgievna

Dzhugashvili, who suffered from diabetes. The first time he met the leader was in 1935, when he arrived on a visit. In his memoirs, he records the scene:

> My conversation with him was in Russian, which his mother did not under-
> stand and so I could tell him frankly all about her state of health. She was then
> 79. After that Stalin switched to Georgian and there was an interesting
> exchange between mother and son. Comrade Stalin told us both that when
> he was young he had frequently been beaten by his mother . . . Turning to
> her, he said he hadn't been a bad son and asked: 'Why did you beat me so
> often?' She replied: 'So that you should turn out as well as you have.'[79]

At the time, he and the others present could laugh about this, but there was also a serious side to the matter. Stalin's mother related an incident when the boy had been badly beaten by his drunken father, who had lifted him up and thrown him violently on to the earthen floor. In later years, too, Stalin had to put up with physical violence when under arrest or in exile. Did these experiences make him appreciate that brute force could affect people's will-power and favour coercive measures?

Professor A.L. Miasnikov (1899–1965) was one of the doctors called to Stalin's bedside on 2 March 1953. He reminisced later:

> Stalin, who was short and fat, was lying in a cramped position, his face
> contorted, the fingers of his right hand stretched out like the thongs of a whip.
> He was breathing heavily, now faintly and now more strongly . . . Thank
> heavens, there was no doubt about the diagnosis: an effusion of blood in the
> left hemisphere of the brain due to high blood pressure and arteriosclerosis.
> A profusion of drugs was prescribed.

On the third day, the doctors came to the unanimous conclusion that the leader's death was inevitable. A post-mortem examination held on 6 March confirmed their diagnosis. Miasnikov suggested that Stalin had been a very sick man for years, and that this might explain his cruelty, suspiciousness, fear of enemies, failing judgement and stubbornness. If he is right, then the Soviet state had long been run by a leader with 'areas of softening' in the brain.[80]

Diaries

Diary entries and letters are usually dated, which adds to their authenticity. In the 1990s, when documents of this kind came to be published in much greater quantity than before, it emerged that under Stalin diaries had been kept by all kinds of professional people, including writers and scholars.[81] Some of these 'ego-documents' have been treated to historiographic analysis, in particular, Jochen Hellbeck's work on Stepan Podlubnyi.[82] At the beginning of the tragic year 1937, the historian N.M. Druzhinin (1886–1986) noted in his diary: 'one must be prepared for anything: ferocious struggles, agonizing suffering, one's own death and that of millions of others'.[83] His professional colleague S.S. Dmitriev (1906–91) described the grim moral atmosphere among Moscow historians in 1949–53, during the 'anti-cosmopolitan' campaign, when study of Stalin's writings on linguistics and economics was obligatory. On 30 June 1956, the Central Committee published a decision on 'overcoming the cult of the individual' that tried to limit the damage done by Khrushchev's 'secret speech'. Dmitriev was sceptical, noting that it contained no criticism of the existing system and was likely to encourage 'those powerful forces that backed and still back the so-called cult of the individual'. In May 1991, he noted pessimistically that 'Russia's twentieth century . . . is ending in poverty, bloodshed and humiliation.'[84]

Quite different in tone and substance is the diary of V.A. Malyshev (1902–57), who from 1939 onward held various senior defence-related appointments. When he first met Stalin he was charmed and stunned: he wrote, with evident sincerity, that 'I am ready to devote all my strength to justify c. Stalin's great confidence in me . . . What tremendous intelligence he possesses . . . After he has spoken even the most complex and incomprehensible questions become simple, clear and readily understandable.' He describes in detail his encounters with Stalin during the war, when Malyshev was in charge of tank production, a matter in which the leader took a close interest. But his diary also reveals that what Stalin expected above all from loyal subordinates was that they should carry out orders from above, not display initiative. On 28 December 1946, he gave Malyshev a 'very serious' warning not to 'take liberties' over locomotive output, 'or else we shall punish [you]'. He went on: 'ours is not a party of individuals with their own views: there are only the views of the Party'. And since he identified his own opinion with that of the Party, leading functionaries developed a survival instinct; they were in effect not much more than lackeys of 'the Boss'.

In his diary, Malyshev kept to matters that concerned him directly and did not touch on contemporary politics – except on 1 December 1952, when he noted that the CC Presidium had discussed 'wrecking' in the public health administration and the situation in the MVD. On that occasion, Stalin had told the ministers that they ought to be 'politicians and intelligence operatives' since 'every Jew is a nationalist, a spy for the US'. Our diarist offered no comment on the leader's remarks.[85]

In the Stalin era, it was dangerous to keep a diary. Many people destroyed theirs, fearing trouble if arrested; others were confiscated by the NKVD but then disappeared. This makes those diaries that have survived even more valuable. They show that the regime was unable to impose uniformity of views by force.

Correspondence

Letters from this time can be divided roughly into several categories: correspondence between the leaders; letters by Soviet citizens to various official bodies; and ordinary communications between friends. Stalin's surviving letters, especially those he sent to his closest relatives, are of the greatest interest. One of the first to publish those to his mother was L.M. Spirin. He obtained them from Shota Chivadze, a colleague of his at the Institute of Marxism–Leninism who had been asked to translate them from Georgian into Russian. There were 11 of them in all, dated between 1922 and 1934. They are very brief, more like notes, and each contained a stereotyped wish for her 'to live for a thousand years'. In 1935, Stalin's mother got only an hour's warning that her son was coming to see her, and the following exchange took place:

> 'Iosif, what are you up to these days?'
> 'I'm secretary of the Central Committee of the AUCP(b) . . . You remember the tsar, Mama?'
> 'Of course I do.'
> 'Well, I'm a sort of tsar.'
> The old lady fell silent for a while and then said with a sigh: 'It would have been better if you'd become a priest.'[86]

Much of Stalin's correspondence that has been published is official in character. In December 1969 his closest associate V.M. Molotov, then 79, gave the Central Party Archive (now RGASPI) 77 letters and memoranda he had received from the leader. They first appeared in print in 1990, but it was five years before the complete set came out in book form.[87] The compilers describe the correspondence as unique evidence of the frank way the Soviet leaders initially formulated what were to become official Party and government decisions. Apart from information about economic conditions, Stalin's letters to Molotov contain much about the political struggle being waged at the top, first against Trotsky and his supporters and then against A.I. Rykov, N.I. Bukharin and other 'rightists'. In 1930–1, Stalin followed closely the OGPU's concoction of the cases brought against members of the so-called 'Industrial party' and the 'Union Bureau of Mensheviks'. Thus, in August 1930, we find him suggesting 'the arrest of Sukhanov, Bazarov and Ramzin', who were among the accused. He also took decisions on the appointment of senior staff in people's commissariats concerned with various branches of the economy. Molotov usually agreed to whatever Stalin proposed; it is a pity we do not have his replies, which were probably destroyed.[88]

The published edition of letters between Stalin and L.M. Kaganovich is fuller, since in this case we *do* have what his correspondent replied. They are drawn from various collections in RGASPI as well as Kaganovich's personal archive. From 1930, he was Stalin's deputy as Party leader, and did his bidding with dog-like loyalty. The correspondence contains much about the 'revolution from above': forced collectivization, peasant resistance and its repression, the supply crisis, and the famine of 1932–3. It is clear from these letters that the leaders were unwilling to acknowledge the real reasons for the famine or to assist the victims. On 18 June 1932, Stalin put the food shortages down to inefficiency in the local supply organs, as a result of which 'several tens of thousands of Ukrainian collective farmers are going around the whole European part of the USSR disorganizing our *kolkhozy* with their complaints and whining'.

A letter of 20 July 1932 to Kaganovich and Molotov reveals that Stalin was personally responsible for the decree of 7 August of that year whereby starving peasants who picked up a few ears of grain from the collective fields were arrested and punished for 'stealing socialist property'. Within the next six months, as we now know, 103,000 people were sentenced under this decree, and 4,880 of them were shot. Kaganovich, who lived on until 1991, remained a convinced supporter of Stalin and his methods of rule, as did Molotov, too.[89] These letters show how far removed the country's leaders were from the people's needs and interests. In effect, they stood for the construction of 'barracks socialism', a powerful bureaucratic and punitive apparatus bolstering their personal power; how ordinary folk actually lived was of little account to them. These letters supplement a volume of correspondence between the leaders during the NEP era (1921–7), published in 1996. It was then that this powerful machine was forged, for already in 1922 people used to speak of 'marching ahead under Stalin'.[90]

Quite different in character are the statements, petitions and denunciations which Soviet citizens sent between 1917 and 1927 to representatives of authority, which up to a point may be seen as an expression of public discourse, a sort of dialogue with the state power.[91] We find here complaints at arbitrary behaviour by local bureaucrats, along with suggestions as to how to combat drunkenness, banditry and official malfeasance. The letters are written in the hope that the central authorities will intervene to improve matters. One wishes the compilers of this volume had provided a commentary to tell us whether these appeals were successful or not.

Petitions submitted in the 1930s and later are quite different from those of the NEP era. The later ones are mostly appeals on behalf of people who had been repressed; they contain no protests against the regime nor even evidence of the accused's innocence, just appeals for mercy. Among the most emotionally worded is that written to Stalin by the famous poet Anna Akhmatova asking him to pardon her son, L.N. Gumilev. A student of history at Leningrad university, he was sentenced on 26 July 1939 to five years in custody. He and two other students were accused of belonging to a non-existent 'terrorist youth organization', concocted by the NKVD, which had allegedly sought to assassinate the city's Party boss, A.A. Zhdanov. In her letter (6 April), Akhmatova besought Stalin to save her only child, a gifted historian innocent of any crime 'against the Motherland and the government'. Alas, the letter did not reach its addressee. Gumilev stayed behind bars until 1944, when he volunteered for service at the front.[92]

Maxim Gorky's letters to Stalin and the police chief G.G. Yagoda abound in expressions of loyalty towards the regime and its powerful chiefs. The contrast with those written by humble petitioners is striking. Gorky returned to Moscow from his self-imposed Italian exile in 1928 and was treated to a grandiose top-level reception. His sixtieth birthday, which fell that year, was marked by stage-managed celebrations, as the writer M.M. Prishvin (1873–1954) noted in his diary:

> [Gorky's] jubilee was arranged . . . by the Soviet government in the same way
> as all other state festivals. Today the government says 'Kiss Gorky!' and

everyone will kiss him. Tomorrow they'll say 'Spit on Gorky!' and they'll all spit . . . Unless there is some shift of policy Gorky will soon be turned into a nullity.

Gorky knew it was all a charade but took part in it willingly. To one woman writer he complained: 'Everywhere they're paying me honours. I'm an honoured baker, an honoured Pioneer. If I were to go and look at an insane asylum today, they'd make me an honoured madman, you'd see.'[93]

Gorky's correspondence with Stalin ran from 1929 to 1936, the year of his death, and consists of about 90 letters, notes and telegrams. The fullest collection of these came out in the journal *Novyi mir*. Until 1934, Gorky used to go back to Italy annually because of his bad lungs, and from there he would send off veritable panegyrics about conditions in the USSR. For instance, on 2 November 1930, he approved of the arrests of intellectuals, writing: 'I am pleased with the work of the GPU, this tireless and valiant guardian of the working class and the Party.' He thought the trial of the non-existent Industrial party in 1930 'brilliant', and expressed his 'deep comradely affection' for Stalin (12 November 1931), calling him 'a good person' and 'a firm Bolshevik' whose courage made him irreplaceable.[94]

Gorky's frequent letters to Yagoda, who was in charge of the security police from 1932 to 1935, at first glance appear businesslike. As a propagandist for the regime, he sometimes tried to use his position to ease the lot of writers who had been arrested or were in disgrace, and would address Yagoda as 'dear comrade and fellow-countryman' (they both hailed from Nizhnii Novgorod). But some of Gorky's letters were not much better than denunciations. Early in June 1930, he wrote from Sorrento telling Yagoda that he had been asked by the poet Boris Pasternak to help him and his family get permission to go abroad in order to meet some emigré relatives. Gorky turned down Pasternak's request on the grounds that another writer who had been let out, A.P. Kamensky, had written an 'anti-Soviet' article in the emigré press and had refused to return to the USSR. 'That's the way it always is', he wrote soothingly, 'decent people have to pay for the misdeeds of rogues, and now it's your turn.' He reported to Yagoda that, although Pasternak was a 'completely honourable person', weakness of will might lead him to defect, and so he should not be granted an exit visa. On 25 November 1932, Gorky congratulated Yagoda on the fifteenth anniversary of the Cheka, whose officers he described as heroes.[95]

The oddest thing about Gorky's correspondence with Stalin and Yagoda is that he was writing from Italy, where he was beyond their grasp, yet found it expedient to declare his devotion to them both. Why? In 1922 he had defended the Socialist-Revolutionaries who had been put on trial, but during the show trials of 1929–31 he inveighed against the accused. What happened in the interim to his understanding of events in the USSR? Literary scholars have yet to explain this satisfactorily. But Gorky's letters do show clearly that, whether he wanted to or not, he became a stooge of a regime dedicated to the extirpation of all dissent.

The letters to Stalin from other Soviet writers such as Mikhail Bulgakov, Alexander Fadeev, Mikhail Sholokhov or Ilya Ehrenburg are now familiar territory. Of the scientists who corresponded with him, Academician P.L. Kapitsa is best known for having interceded on behalf of a fellow academician, the physicist L.D. Landau (1908–68), who went on to win the Nobel prize. Landau was arrested in April 1938 for 'anti-Soviet utterances', but after a year was freed, on Kapitsa's personal responsibility, after the latter told Stalin he was the country's foremost theoretical physicist.[96]

It is still uncertain whether Ehrenburg signed a letter to Stalin in 1953 backing the deportation of Jews from European Russia to the Far East and Kazakhstan in connection with the 'doctors' plot' affair. Close examination shows that he did not agree to sign the first draft of the collective letter, but instead wrote to Stalin offering to edit the text of another letter that was going around. In the event, he signed this second text after it had been redrafted, on Stalin's order, in such a way as to distinguish between Jews in general, who were to be spared, and 'Jewish nationalists', who were to be tried and punished.[97] But not many such letters have been preserved.

In the Stalin era, thousands of letters to the leader were published, all written in stereotyped servile language. One of the few that stand out for a touch of humanity was written by N.K. Krupskaia, Lenin's widow, after Stalin's wife, Nadezhda Allilueva, had committed suicide in 1932: 'these days you are continually in my thoughts and I want to shake your hand. It is hard to lose someone so close'.[98]

To sum up: the current study of archival sources, published documents, memoirs and correspondence from the Stalin era has brought to light a large amount of fresh information. Scholars and the general public continue to take a good deal of interest in the phenomenon of Stalinism. But all these texts have only begun to receive the careful historiographic analysis they merit, and it is in this direction that research now needs to go.

Notes

1 R.G. Pikhoia, *Sovetskii Soiuz: istoriia vlasti, 1945–1991* (Moscow: RAGS, 1998), 6.

2 V.P. Kozlov, *Rossiiskoe arkhivnoe delo: arkhivno-istochnikovedcheskie issledovaniia* (Moscow: ROSSPEN, 1999), 331.

3 *Akademicheskoe delo, 1929–1931 gg.*, fasc. 1: *Delo po obvineniiu akademika S.F. Platonova* (St Petersburg: Izd. Biblioteki Rossiiskoi Akademii nauk, 1993); fasc. 2: *Delo po obvineniiu akademika E.V. Tarle*, pts 1, 2 (St Petersburg: RAN, 1998); *Dva sledstvennykh dela Yevgenii Ginzburg* (Kazan: Taves, 1994). One reason why such publications in full had to be abandoned was that they included relatively insignificant or falsified material. See D.B. Pavlov, *Otechestvennye i zarubezhnye publikatsii dokumentov rossiiskikh partii* (diss., Moscow, 1998), 65.

4 E. Maksimova, 'Ten', otbroshennaia v proshloe: pochemu arkhiv Stalina vse eshche pod zamkom', *Izvestiia*, 2 November 1995, which includes an interview with Pikhoia; V.V. Bakatin, *Izbavlenie ot KGB* (Moscow: Novosti, 1992), 149.

5 *Putevoditel' po fondam i kollektsiiam lichnogo proiskhozhdeniia* (Moscow: Rossiiskii tsentr khraneniia i izucheniia dokumentov noveishei istorii, 1996), 233.

6 'Arkhiv Prezidenta Rossiiskoi Federatsii, 1991–2001 gg.', *Istochnik*, 2001, nos. 5, 7, 9.

7   E. Maksimova, 'Lichnyi fond Stalina stanovitsia obshchedostupnym: no pochemu lish' chastichno?', *Izvestiia*, 30 October 1999.

8   D.A. Volkogonov, *Sem' vozhdei* (Moscow: Novosti, 1995), bk 1, 260–1.

9   Zh. and R. Medvedev, *Neizvestnyi Stalin* (Moscow: Folio, 2002), 114, 116–9.

10 V.A. Kozlov and S.V. Mironenko (eds), *'Osobaia papka' I.V. Stalina: arkhiv noveishei istorii Rossii: iz materialov Sekretariata NKVD-MVD SSSR, 1944–1953 gg.: katalog dokumentov* (Moscow: Blagovest', 1994).

11 RGASPI, f. 558, op. 11, d. 45, 94, 184, 186,187, 201, 202, 1100. There are several precedents for the erroneous attribution of writings to Soviet leaders. The first edition of Lenin's *Works* in the 1920s contained some articles by V.V. Vorovsky; some by Lenin appeared in a collection of Zinoviev's works; and even the fifth edition of Lenin's *Collected Works* (1960s) credited him with 'The Socialist Fatherland Is in Danger!' (1918) – which was in fact written by Trotsky.

12 RGASPI, f. 558, op. 11, d. 189, ll. 15, 86–7. On Zorin's harmful role in Soviet genetics, see M.G. Yaroshevsky (ed.), *Repressirovannaia nauka*, vol. I (Leningrad: Nauka, 1991), 58–60. Serebriakov (1888–1937), a CC member in 1919–21, was liquidated in the 1930s.

13 A.A. Fursenko, 'Konets ery Stalina', *Zvezda*, 1999, no. 12, 184–5. The document 'Istoriia bolezni I.V. Stalina (sostavlena na osnovanii zhurnal'nykh zapisei techeniia bolezni so 2 po 5 marta 1953 g.' is currently held in RGASPI, f. 558, op. 11, d. 1486, ll. 101–20.

14 A.A. Fursenko and V.Yu. Afiani, '1953: mezhdu proshlym i budushchim', in *Katalog vystavki '1953: mezhdu proshlym i budushchim'* (Moscow, 2003, 7–11). See also S.I. Allilueva, *Dvadtsat' pisem k drugu* (Moscow: Zakharov, 2000), 114; Medvedev, *Neizvestnyi Stalin*, 13.

15 *Komsomol'skaia pravda*, 1 March 2003.

16 TsA FSB RF, d. 1657. Svechin was rehabilitated on 8 September 1956.

17 RGASPI, f. 147, op. 2, d. 11, l. 15. After release from detention Picheta (1878–1947) was elected as a full member (Academician) of the USSR Academy of Sciences.

18 *Dva sledstvennykh dela Yevgenii Ginzburg*, 90–1. Ginzburg (1904–77) spent 18 years in camps and exile. She was the mother of the writer V.P. Aksenov. N.N. El'vov (1901–37) was a professor of history at Kazan' University. He was arrested on 10 February 1935 on a charge of 'Trotskyism', shot on 15 September 1937 and rehabilitated posthumously.

19 A.L. Litvin (ed.), *Men'shevistskii protsess 1931 goda: sbornik dokumentov v 2 kn.* (Moscow: ROSSPEN, 1999), bk 2, 457, 462. B. Unfried, 'Foreign Communists and the Mechanisms of Soviet Cadre Formation in the USSR', in B. McLoughlin and K. McDermott (eds), *Stalin's Terror: High Politics and Mass Repression in the Soviet Union* (Basingstoke, UK and New York: Palgrave Macmillan, 2003) 175–93, who has worked on this material, correctly warns that investigation records are misleading, for much the same reasons as I give here.

20 'I.V. Stalin o sebe: redaktsionnaia pravka sobstvennoi biografii', *Izvestiia TsK KPSS*, 1990, no. 9, 113–29; *I.V. Stalin: kratkaia biografiia* (Moscow: Gospolitizdat, 1939); G.F. Aleksandrov *et al.* (comps), *I.V. Stalin: Kratkaia biografiia: 2. izd., ispravlennoe i dopolnennoe* (Moscow: Gospolitizdat, 1947).

21 'I.V. Stalin v rabote nad "Kratkim kursom istorii VKP(b)"', *VI*, 2002, no. 11, 3–29, no. 12, 3–26, 2003, no. 4, 3–25.

22 O.V. Khlevniuk *et al.* (comps), *Stalinskoe politburo v 30-e gody: sbornik dokumentov* (Moscow: AIRO-XX, 1995).

23 V.P. Danilov, 'Problemy otbora i publikatsii rassekrechennykh dokumentov po istorii sovetskogo krest'ianstva', in *Problemy publikatsii dokumentov po istorii Rossii XX v.* (Moscow: ROSSPEN, 2001), 63, 66, 68–9.

24 A. Bérélowitch and V. Danilov (eds), *Sovetskaia derevnia glazami VChK-OGPU-NKVD:*

dokumenty i materialy v 4 tt. (Moscow: ROSSPEN, 1998–). The following volumes have appeared to date: vol. 1 (1918–22), 2 (1923–9), 3 (1930–4), bk 1 (1930–1). V. Danilov *et al.* (eds), *Tragediia sovetskoi derevni: kollektivizatsiia i raskulachivanie: dokumenty i materialy v 5 tt.* (Moscow: ROSSPEN, 1999–). Vol. 1 covers the period May 1927 to November 1929, vol. 2 November 1929 to December 1930, vol. 3 the end of 1930 to 1933. "'Smolenskii arkhiv" kak "zerkalo sovetskoi deistvitel'nosti'", *VI*, 2003, no. 9, 3–27, no. 11, 3–34, no. 12, 3–26. See also *Spetspereselentsy v Zapadnoi Sibiri, 1930–vesna 1931 g.* (Novosibirsk: Nauka, 1992); two sequel volumes (spring 1931 to beginning of 1933, 1933–8) were published in that city by Ekor (1993, 1994).

25   G.N. Sevostianov *et al.* (eds), *'Sovershenno sekretno': Lubianka – Stalinu o polozhenii v strane (1922–1934 gg.)* (Moscow: IRI RAN, 2001–). Vol. 1 covers 1922–3, vol. 2 1924, vol. 3 1925 (in 2 pts), vol. 4 1926 (in 2 pts), vol. 5 1927, vol. 6 1928.

26   V.P. Danilov, 'Neobychnyi epizod vo vzaimootnosheniiakh OGPU i Politburo (1931 g.)', *VI*, 2003, no. 10, 117, 121, 126–8.

27   V.K. Vinogradov, 'Ob osobennostiakh informatsionnykh materialov OGPU kak istochnika po istorii sovetskogo obshchestva', in *"Sovershenno sekretno"*, vol. 1, pt 1, 31–73.

28   A. Getty, 'Tsennyi istoricheskii istochnik', in ibid., vol. 3, pt 1, 32–3.

29   A. Edgar, 'Tsennyi istochnik', in ibid., vol. 5, 18.

30   L. Viola, S. Zhuravlev *et al.* (eds), *Riazanskaia derevnia v 1929–1930 gg.: khronika golovokruzheniia: dokumenty i materialy* (Moscow and Toronto, 1998); *'Al'metevskoe delo': tragicheskie stranitsy iz istorii krest'ianstva al'meteveskogo raiona (konets 20-kh – nachalo 30-kh gg.): sbornik dokumentov i materialov* (Kazan', 1999); *Obshchestvo i vlast': Rossiiskaia provintsiia, 1917–1980-e gg. (po materialam Nizhegorodskikh arkhivov)*, vol. I: *1917 – seredina 30-kh gg.* (Moscow, Nizhnyi Novgorod and Paris, 2002).

31   I.V. Pavlova, 'Ponimanie stalinskoi epokhi i pozitsiia istorika', *VI*, 2002, no. 10, 6, 8.

32   A.N. Yakovlev (ed.), *Lubianka: Stalin i VChK-GPU-OGPU-NKVD: sbornik dokumentov, ianvar' 1922 – dekabr' 1936* (Moscow: Mezhdunar. fond 'Demokratiia', 2003), 180, 213, 669.

33   A.L. Litvin (ed.), *Genrikh Yagoda: narkmom vnutrennykh del SSSR, General'nyi komissar gosbezopasnosti: sbornik dokumentov* (Kazan', 1997); V.P. Naumov (ed.), *Nepravednyi sud: poslednyi stalinskii rasstrel: stenogramma sudebnogo protsessa nad chlenami evreiskogo antifashistskogo komiteta* (Moscow: Nauka, 1994); M.I. Khlusov (comp.), *Ekonomika Gulaga i ee rol' v razvitii strany: 1930-e gody: sbornik dokumentov* (Moscow: IRI RAN, 1998); Litvin (ed.), *Menshevistskii protsess* (see n. 19); A. Artizov *et al.* (comps), *Reabilitatsiia: kak eto bylo: dokumenty Prezidiuma TsK KPSS i drugie materialy* (Moscow: Mezhdunar. fond 'Demokratiia', 2000); A.I. Kokurin and N.V. Petrov (comps), Shostakovsky, V.N. (ed.), *GULAG (Glavnoe upravlenie lagerei), 1918–1960* (Moscow: fond 'Demokratiia', 2002), 7, 9, 13.

34   "'Vinovnost' arestovannykh podtverzhdena . . . '": konstruktorskoe biuro pri OGPU-MGB SSSR', *Istochnik*, 2003, no. 4, 46–50.

35   ITL (*ispravitel'no-trudovye lageria*) were camps that in principle catered for long-term prisoners and usually had more severe regimes than colonies, or ITK (*ispravitel'no-trudovye kolonii*).

36   See, for example, A.V. Semenov *et al.* (eds), *Zabveniiu ne podlezhit: kniga pamiati zhertv politicheskoi repressii Omskoi oblasti*, vol. 1 (Omsk: Omskoe kn. izdat., 2000), whose 416 pages merely list those whose names begin with the letters A and B; the series is in progress.

37   RGASPI, f.558, d. 24, ll. 11, 12, 25. See also I.R. Tagirov (ed.), *Neizvestnyi Sultan-Galiev: rassekrechennye dokumenty i materialy* (Kazan': Tatarskoe knizhnoe izd., 2002).

38   'Resheniia Osobykh troek privodit' v ispolnenie nemedlenno', *Istochnik*, 1999, no. 5, 81–5.

39   A. Artizov *et al.* (comps), *Vlast' i khudozhestvennaia intelligentsiia: dokumenty TsK RKP(b) – VKP(b), VChK-OGPU-NKVD o kul'turnoi politike, 1917–1953 gg.* (Moscow: Mezhdunar.

fond 'Demokratiia', 1999). (This is one of the volumes in A.N. Yakovlev's invaluable series *Rossiia: XX vek: dokumenty.*)

40 Yu.G. Murin (comp.), *Iosif Stalin v ob'iatiiakh sem'i* (Moscow: Biblioteka zhurnala 'Istochnik', 1993).

41 *A.N. Yakovlev: Svoboda – moia religiia: k 80-letiiu so dnia rozhdeniia: sbornik statei* (Moscow: Vagrius, 2003), 276, 313, 316–17, 330–1; Yakovlev, *Sumerki* (Moscow: Materik, 2003), 675–7.

42 M.A. Leushin, *Dokumenty VKP(b)/KPSS kak istochnik po istorii istoricheskoi nauki v SSSR: 1945–1955* (Moscow: RGGU, thesis abstract, 2000). Volumes 14 to 16 of Stalin's *Works* appeared in Russian, ed. R.H. McNeal (Stanford, CA: Hoover Institution, 1967), with an annotated bibliography in English. In Russia, they appeared in 1997, compiled and edited by R.I. Kosolapov.

43 *Istochnik*, 2003, no. 2, 45–56; no. 3, 100–28.

44 Ibid., no. 2, 33–5; no. 4, 40–4, 63–74.

45 O.V. Khlevniuk *et al.* (comps), *Politburo TsK VKP(b) i Sovet ministrov SSSR 1945–1953* (Moscow: ROSSPEN, 2002).

46 *Izvestiia*, 13 September 2003.

47 V. Zhiliaev, '"Plennik": byl li syn Stalina v nemetskikh kontslageriakh?', *Rodina*, 2002, no. 9, 88–95.

48 *Izvestiia*, loc. cit.

49 I.A. Kondakov and A.A. Chernobaev (comps), *'Istoricheskii arkhiv', 1919–2001 gg.: ukazatel' opublikovannykh materialov* (Moscow: ROSSPEN, 2002).

50 *Istoricheskii arkhiv*, no. 6, 1994; 1995, nos. 2–6; 1997, no. 1. For an analysis see Chapter 7, n. 24.

51 Ibid., 1998, no. 4, 3.

52 For further details see A.A. Pechenkin, 'Prezhde vsego – tochnost': posetiteli Kremlevskogo kabineta I.V. Stalina', *OI*, 2003, no. 3, 152–7.

53 Before his defection on 1 January 1928 Bazhanov had been a member of the CC Secretariat (1923–7) and his memoirs first came out abroad: B. Bajanov, *Stalin: der rote Diktator* (Berlin: Paul Aretz, 1931). A French-language edition (1930) was republished in 1980. See now B. Bazhanov, *Vospominaniia byvshego sekretaria Stalina* (St Petersburg: Vsemirnoe slovo, 1992).

54 '"Unichtozhit'" vragov, predvaritel'no ikh obmanuv": Materialy doprosa pomoshchnika General'nogo sekretaria Tsk VKP(b) Borisa Bazhanova frantsuzskimi spetssluzhbami', *Istochnik*, 2001, no. 6, 31–41.

55 N.S. Khrushchev, *Vospominaniia: izbrannye fragmenty* (Moscow: Vagrius, 1997), 23, 24, 60; see also idem, *Vremia: liudi: vlast', v 4 tt.* (Moscow: Moskovskie novosti, 1999).

56 Yakovlev, *Sumerki*, 28, 222.

57 M. Lobanov (comp.), *Stalin: v vospminaniakh sovremennikov i dokumentakh epokhi* (Moscow: Algoritm, 2002).

58 E. Gusliarov, *Stalin v zhizni: sistematizirovannyi svod vospminanii sovremennikov, dokumentov epokhi, versii istorikov* (Moscow: Olma-press, 2003).

59 S.I. Allilueva, *Dvadtsat' pisem drugu* (Moscow: Zakharov, 2000); S. Beria, *Moi otets Lavrentii Beria* (Moscow: Sovremennik, 1995); A.G. Malenkov, *O moem ottse Georgii Malenkove* (Moscow: Technoekos, 1992); G.Ya. Dzhugashvili, *Ded, otets, Ma i drugie* (Moscow: Olimp, 1993).

60 *Izvestiia*, 1 March 2003.

61 For example, Z. Veselaia, *Vospominaniia* (Moscow: Moskovskii rabochii, 1990), 7–35; A.M. Larina-Bukharina, *Nezabyvaemoe* (Moscow: Vagrius, 1989), N.Ya. Mandelshtam, *Vospominaniia* (Moscow, 1989); L. Razgon, *Plen v svoem otechestve* (Moscow: Kurzhnyi sad, 1994); M.M. Korallova (comp.), *Teatr Gulaga: vospominaniia, ocherki* (Moscow: Memorial, 1995); V. Shalamov, *Vospominaniia* (Moscow: Olimp, 2001); A.I. Solzhenitsyn (comp.), *Pozhivshi v GULAGe* (Moscow: Russkii put', 2001).

62 *Komsomol'skaia pravda*, 23 December 2003.
63 G.K. Zhukov, *Vospominaniia i razmyshleniia*, 2 vols, 11th edn, completed from the author's manuscript (Moscow: Novosti, 1992).
64 V.S. Antonov, 'Tri epizoda iz memuarov znamenitogo polkovodtsa (k kharakteristike vospominanii G.K. Zhukova kak istoricheskogo istochnika)', *OI*, 2003, no. 3, 157–63.
65 A.T. Rybin, *Riadom s Stalinym: zapiski teleokhranitelia* (Moscow: Iris-press, 1994); G.N. Kolomentsev, '"Khoziain Kremlia" umer ran'she svoei smerti', *Argumenty i fakty*, no. 49, December 2002.
66 '*1953 god: mezhdu proshlym i budushchim*' (see n. 14), 27.
67 D. Granin, 'Strakh, kotoryi bol'she strakha smerti', *Rossiiskaia gazeta*, 19 March 2003; S. Kondrashov, 'Ia otkazalsia pisat' o vvode voisk v Chekhoslovakiiu i Afganistan . . . ', *Izvestiia*, 28 December 2003.
68 G.A. Kumanev, *Riadom so Stalinym* (Moscow: Bylina, 1999); V.T. Loginov, *V teni Stalina* (Moscow: Sovremennik, 2000); F.I. Chuev, *Soldaty imperii: besedy: vospominiia: dokumenty* (Moscow: Kovcheg, 1998); idem, *Molotov: poluderzhavnyi vlastelin* (Moscow: Olma-press, 1999).
69 Chuev, *Molotov*, 464.
70 *OI*, 2003, no. 3, 49–70.
71 *Istochnik*, 2003, no. 5, 56–62.
72 *IA*, 1998, no. 3, 216–17; *Istochnik*, 1996, no. 1, 140–52.
73 *Istochnik*, 2003, no. 3, 54–5.
74 Ibid., 2000, no. 2, 45–51.
75 *Literaturnaia gazeta*, 28 September 1988.
76 L. Gurunts, 'Iz zapisnykh knizhek', *Zvezda*, 1988, no. 3, 186.
77 L.D. Trotsky, *Stalin* (Moscow: Politizdat, 1990), 250.
78 I.A. Valedinsky, 'Vospominaniia o vstrechakh s t. Stalinym I.V.', *Istochnik*, 1998, no. 2, 68–70.
79 N.A. Kipshidze, *Vstrechi s vozhdem: vospominaniia vracha* (Tbilisi, 1953).
80 A.L. Miasnikov, 'Konchina', *Literaturnaia gazeta*, 1 March 1989.
81 K.I. Chukovsky, *Dnevnik, 1930–1969* (Moscow, 1994); V.I. Vernadsky, 'Dnevnik 1938 g.', *Druzhba narodov*, 1992, no. 2, 219–69, no. 3, 241–69; idem, *Dnevniki: 1926–1934* (Moscow: Nauka, 2001); M.M. Prishvin, 'Dnevnik 1937 g.', *Oktiabr'*, 1994, no. 11, 144–71; 'Dnevnik N.M. Druzhinina', *VI*, 1995, nos. 9–12, 1996, nos. 1–4, 7, 9–10; Yu.V. Got'e, *Moi zametki* (Moscow: Terra, 1997); English edition: T.T. Emmons (trans., ed.), *Time of Troubles: The Diary of Yuriy Vladimirovich Got'e* . . . (Princeton, NJ: Princeton University Press, 1988); 'Iz dnevnikov Sergeia Sergeevicha Dmitrieva', *OI*, 1999, nos. 3–6, 2000, nos. 1–6, 2001, no. 10, On the latter, see J. Keep, 'Sergei Sergeevich Dmitriev and His Diary', *Kritika* 4 (2003), 709–34.
82 See Chapters 8, n. 49; in Russian, idem, 'Lichnost' i sistema v kontekste stalinizma: popytka pereotsenki issledovatel'skikh podkhodov', in M.K. Gorshkov *et al.* (eds), *Krainosti istorii i krainosti istorikov: sbornik statei* (Moscow: RNISiNP, 1997). On M.A. Bulgakov's diary see V.I. Losev, 'Lichnye arkhivnye fondy russkikh pisatelei XX v. kak istoricheskii istochnik: problemy publikatsii', in *Problemy publikatsii dokumentov po istorii Rossii XX v.* (Moscow: ROSSPEN, 2001), 349–55. On S.A. Piontkovsky's diary for 1928–9, see A. Litvin, 'Dnevnik istorika: predislovie k publikatsii', *Ab imperio*, 2002, no. 3, 419–32.
83 Druzhinin, 'Dnevnik', *VI*, 1997, no. 6, 88.
84 'Iz dnevnikov . . . Dmitrieva', *OI*, no. 2, 144; 2001, no. 1, 163.
85 V.A. Malyshev, 'Dnevnik narkoma', *Istochnik*, 1997, no. 5, 108, 130, 135, 140.
86 L.M. Spirin, '"Zhivite desiat' tysiach let": pis'ma Stalina k materi', *Nezavisimaia gazeta*, 13 August 1992. S. Radzinsky, *Stalin* (Moscow: Vagrius, 1997), 28, says he was able to see these letters in APRF.

87 I.N. Kitaev *et al.* (contrib.), 'Pis'ma Stalina Molotovu', *Kommunist*, 1990, no. 11, 94–106; L. Kosheleva *et al.* (comps), *Pis'ma I.V. Stalina V.M. Molotovu, 1925–1936 gg.* (Moscow: Rossiia molodaia, 1995), 6, 198. See also L.T. Lih *et al.* (eds), *Stalin's Letters to Molotov, 1925–1936* (New Haven, CT: Yale University Press, 1995).

88 On this see Medvedev, *Neizvestnyi Stalin*, 104.

89 O.V. Khlevniuk *et al.* (comps), *Stalin i Kaganovich: perepiska, 1931–1936 gg.* (Moscow: ROSSPEN, 2001), 14–15, 19–20, 179, 235–6; cf. also L. Kaganovich, *Pamiatnye zapiski . . . i sovetskogo-gosudarstvennogo rabotnika* (Moscow: Vagrius, 1996).

90 A.V. Kvashonkin *et al.* (comps), *Bol'shevistskoe rukovodstvo: perepiska, 1921–1927: sbornik dokumentov* (Moscow: ROSSPEN, 1996), 5–6, 263; the sequel volume is *Sovetskoe rukovodstvo: perepiska, 1928–1941 gg.* (Moscow: ROSSPEN, 1999).

91 A.Ya. Livshin *et al.* (comps), *Pis'ma vo vlast', 1917–1927* (Moscow: ROSSPEN, 1998); N.S. Chernushev (comp.), *« Dorogoi nash tovarishch Stalin! » . . . i drugie tovarishchi: obrashchenia rodstvennikov i repressirovannykh komandirov Krasnoi armii k rukovoditeliam strany* (Moscow: Zvenia, 2001).

92 '"Iosif Vissarionovich! Spasite sovetskogo istorika . . . ": o neizvestnom pis'me Anny Akhmatovoy Stalinu', *OI*, 2001, no. 3, 149–57.

93 Cited from A.I.Vaksberg, *Gibel' burevestnika: M. Gor'ky: poslednie 20 let* (Moscow: Terra, 1999). The last remark is reported by the writer and literary scholar K.I. Chukovsky (1882–1969) in his diary.

94 '"Zhmu vashu ruku, dorogoi tovarishch": perepiska Maksima Gor'kogo i Iosifa Stalina', *Novyi mir*, 1997, no. 9, 174, 181, 189; see also *Istochnik*, 1999, no. 5, 116.

95 L.A. Spiridonova (contrib.), 'Perepiska M. Gor'kogo s G.G. Yagodoi', in *Neizvestnyi Gor'kii* (Moscow: Nasledie, 1994), 168, 172, 187, 196. A.P. Kamensky (1876–1941) returned to the USSR in 1937, was arrested and died in custody. His article, 'Demian Bednyi i bednyi Nekrasov (stranichka sovetskogo literaturovedeniia)', was published on 4 June 1930 in *Rul'*.

96 On this see P.E. Riabinina (contrib.), 'Landau, Bohr, Kapitsa: pis'ma 1936–1941 gg.', in *Vospimaniia o L.D. Landau* (Moscow, 1988), 334–48; P.L. Kapitsa, *Pis'ma o nauke, 1930–1980* (Moscow: Moskovskii rabochii, 1989); 'Spravka KGB SSSR ob akademike L.D. Landau', *IA*, 1993, no. 3, 151–61.

97 For the text of Ehrenburg's letter see *Istochnik*, 1997, no. 1, 144–5; cf. B. Sarnov, 'Kak eto bylo', *Lekhaim* (Moscow), 2003, no. 7, 38–9; no. 8, 28–34.

98 *Pravda*, 16 November 1932.

2 Stalin's biography

The young Dzhugashvili

No twentieth-century dictator wielded as much power as Stalin did. Countless books have been written about him, and his character continues to attract attention from historians, psychologists, philosophers, sociologists, writers and artists. During his lifetime, six Soviet towns proudly bore his name.[1] There was even a project to rename Moscow 'Stalinodar' (Stalin's gift), but the leader quashed the idea.[2] Hundreds of streets, avenues, factories and institutions were called after him. Even today, although towns are no longer named for him, books still come out acclaiming the leader (and even his son Vasilii): novels are written about him; and in November 2003 a statue was erected in his honour in the centre of Ishim, a town in Tiumen' district, to mark the fiftieth anniversary of his death.[3] But none of these recent authors uses the fresh sources that have become available, and none of them so much as mentions the Gulag archipelago. Instead, they reproduce material from the memoirs of his marshals and other such sources published before 1991. They are propagating myths about a past that somehow refuses to die.

We still do not have a proper scholarly biography of Stalin. This is why many legends continue to circulate along with verifiable facts, leaving readers confused: what should they credit? Whom should they believe? Stalin himself contributed to the mythologizing process by making false statements about his life and thinking up erroneous 'facts' to confuse biographers.

In 1990, L.M. Spirin published the correct date of his birth: not 21 December 1879, as had hitherto been said, but 6 December 1878. Stalin 'rejuvenated himself' in 1921, when he filled in a questionnaire. Why he did so it is hard to say, but it is clear that falsifying one's birth date was something that could be attempted only by a man confident that no one would be able to challenge what he said.[4] Stalin's father was Vissarion Ivanovich Dzhugashvili, a cobbler who later worked in a shoe factory in Tiflis/Tbilisi. His mother, Yekaterina Georgievna, was a seamstress and the daughter of a serf; her maiden name was Geladze. The family was poor. At the age of five, Iosif came down with smallpox, which nearly killed him. The illness left him with pockmarks on his nose, chin and cheeks. As a child he was often beaten by his father, who was given to drink, and as we have seen his mother, too, used to beat him. Once, he fell and injured his left elbow joint. Gangrene set in, and the quack doctor called in said the wound would heal provided the boy's father made him a pair of shoes. The deal was struck, but Iosif's elbow joint stiffened and dried out, leaving him with a withered arm.

In 1888, the 10-year-old boy was accepted into the preparatory class of a four-year Orthodox Church school. He was bright and forward for his age, but reserved; a good pupil, he took an interest in 'subversive' Georgian literature. On leaving school, he received a laudatory certificate and was recommended for admission to a seminary in Tiflis. Here too he was one of the better students. He wrote poetry in Georgian, which was published in the paper *Iveriia* (1895–6) and again in 1937 in Russian translation. But he did not finish the course at the seminary, for on 29 May 1899 he was expelled. The reason given by the authorities was that he 'had failed to turn up for examinations without a reasonable excuse' and had not paid the fees due. But later, his official Soviet biography gave a different explanation: 'excluded from the seminary for spreading Marxist propaganda'. This was untrue. Stalin himself told a gendarmerie officer interrogating him some time later that he had left because he was fed up with his beggarly existence there – a version that was surely closer to the truth.

Two academics and one writer published books in the 1990s dealing in detail with Stalin's life and activities prior to October 1917: A.V. Ostrovsky, B.S. Ilizarov and E.S. Radzinsky.[5] The last-named work is a partly fictionalized biography that contains a good deal of apocryphal material.

Some of the legends that circulate about Stalin can be substantiated but others remain mere suppositions. Stalin was good at obfuscating the record and liked to present himself as an infallible leader who maintained close ties with ordinary folk. These stories were spread to show him as human, charitable and just. It was often said that he kept up with his fellow pupils from the church school at Gori and the Tiflis seminary. On one occasion, speaking to N.A. Kipshidze, he reminisced about telling the other boys in the seminary that he had doubts about the immortality of the soul; one of them disagreed with him but after a day of reflection came back and said he agreed after all, because in Hell there would not be enough firewood to keep the eternal flames going.[6]

In 1944, so the story goes, Stalin once noticed a large sum of money in the safe kept by his personal secretary, A.N. Poskrebyshev, who told him on enquiry that this was his salary as a deputy to the Supreme Soviet; thereupon he ordered most of the money sent to his former fellow seminarians from Tiflis days.[7] This act of generosity immediately became common knowledge, as did the letter he wrote on 8 June 1938 to V.V. Martyshin, a history teacher at the Moscow special school where his son Vasilii was enrolled. Martyshin had complained that the boy was inattentive and behaving badly. But when he gave Vasilii a grade of two for not knowing a lesson, he was sacked at once by his 'vigilant and frightened' superiors. In his letter Stalin thanked Martyshin for being true to his professional principles and asked him not to show any indulgence towards his son in future. But to judge by a second letter, which Martyshin wrote to Stalin in July 1938, he was *not* reinstated.[8]

In 1898, the young Dzhugashvili joined an illegal Social-Democratic organization in Tiflis. Much later, in 1926, Stalin recalled the major landmarks in his early life when he sent greetings to workers in the main railway workshops there: 'from the status of schoolboy (Tiflis) I graduated to that of apprentice (Baku) and then to that of a craftsman of our revolution (Leningrad) – that, comrades, was the course of my revolutionary training.'[9] This account left out at least two relevant episodes which Russian historians in the 1990s have discussed at length: his participation in 'exes', or expropriations (attacks on banks and the like to raise funds for the Bolshevik party), and his alleged ties to the Okhrana, the tsarist political police, matters that are discussed at length by Professor Ostrovsky.

From the early 1900s, Dzhugashvili was a professional revolutionary living illegally. He was fond of pseudonyms and frequently changed his name. He had signed his first verses 'Soselo'; thereafter he became I. Besashvili, Koba (1906), Koba Ivanovich (1907), K. Stefin (1909), K. Salin (1912), and finally K. Stalin (1913). Among his nicknames were David and Soso (1901), Chopur (1903) and Ivanovich (1906). His surnames included Nizheradze (1908), Totomiants (1909), Melikiants (1910), Chizhikov (1911) and Vasil'ev (1912).[10]

G. Uratadze, a Georgian Social Democrat who shared Stalin's cell in prison at Kutais in 1903 for six months, reminisced later:

> To look at he was ordinary and the pockmarks on his face did not make him appear particularly clean. I should add that all the pictures of him I have seen since he became dictator do not at all resemble the Koba whom I first saw in prison or the Stalin whom I knew for many years thereafter. In prison he had a beard and his long hair was brushed back. He had an insinuating gait, and took small steps. He never opened his mouth wide to laugh but just smiled ... He was absolutely imperturbable.[11]

Historians are in no doubt that Stalin approved of 'exes' and took part in them. On 13 June 1907, robbers seized 250,000 roubles in a raid on the post office in the centre of Tiflis. The *coup* was organized by S.A. Ter-Petrosian ('Kamo', 1882–1922) with Dzhugashvili's assent. Such expropriations had been banned by resolutions passed at the RSDRP's IVth and Vth congresses, and so the matter was investigated by the bureau of the party's Transcaucasian organization. All the participants, Dzhugashvili included, were to be expelled from the party. But Lenin backed him and Kamo, so that the expulsion order did not become effective.[12]

As regards the question of his links to the Okhrana, the evidence is murky. Scholars in Russia and the West have been debating the matter for years. A solution to the riddle depends on the authenticity of three documents. The first dates to March 1910, when the Okhrana department in Baku received information about local Social Democrats' activities from a secret agent who was code-named 'Fikus'. The police had several operatives in the RSDRP's Baku organization, and the frequency of arrests aroused suspicion among the activists. Dzhugashvili, who was arrested in Baku on 23 March 1910, was thought to be 'Fikus'. But now a careful investigation by Z.I. Peregudova has shown that the real 'Fikus' was N.S. Yerikov, whose legal name was D.B. Bakradze. A worker and a party member since 1897, he joined the Baku committee in 1910 and co-operated with the Okhrana from 1909 to 1917.

Close source analysis has also cast doubt on the authenticity of the report submitted by the head of the Moscow department of the Okhrana, A.P. Martynov, to the Police department on 11 November 1912 about Stalin's association with R.V. Malinovsky, who was indeed an agent of the Moscow Okhrana from 1910 onward. Malinovsky (1877–1918) joined the Bolsheviks in 1912 and the next year found himself chairman of their fraction in the IVth State Duma. But it was not until April 1917 that he was exposed as a police agent, and so any contact Stalin had with him before that date, while he was still in the Bolshevik leaders' good graces, cannot be considered deliberate collaboration with the Okhrana.

Finally, there is the 'Yeremin letter', which dates such collaboration by Stalin already to 1906/1908. This letter was put into circulation by V.N. Rossianov, a White colonel who had charge of the so-called 'Siberian Okhrana documents' prior to his flight to China. Dated 12 July 1913, it is signed by Colonel A.M. Yeremin, head of the Special section of the Police department, and addressed to A.F. Zhelezniakov, head of the Okhrana in Yeniseisk. Both 'external' and 'internal' analyses of this document show it to be a forgery. The letter exists in a single copy; there is no copy in Police department records and it is not listed in its register of outgoing mail. It bears the number 2,889, but in 1913 the Special department was under instructions to use numbers starting with 93,001. It therefore follows that the department did not issue it. Furthermore, a comparison of the handwriting with Yeremin's on other documents shows that the former is forged – most probably by none other than Rossianov, 'discoverer' of the letter. Peregudova stresses that her inquiry is concerned, not with Stalin's character, but solely with the authenticity of the documents concerned: 'Any archivist would be the first to say that Stalin was an Okhrana agent if reliable documentary evidence to this effect were found; but all the documents currently at historians' disposal do not permit such a conclusion to be drawn.'[13] I am not quite so convinced that all archivists are as honest as Peregudova suggests – in Soviet times some of them would remove papers from files or keep scholars out of the archives – but I do agree with her that new evidence on Stalin may well come out first in the form of rumours. In any case, so far there are no documents other than those just discussed that mention Stalin as an Okhrana agent.

Private life

Post-Soviet historians have concentrated on Stalin's private life in an effort to understand what made him tick, rather than his role in public life. Ostrovsky has much to say about his amorous entanglements, which are of some interest. In 1906 he married Yekaterina Svanidze (1885–1907), who died the following year of peritoneal typhus after bearing him a son, Yakov. The fate of his wife's kin was tragic, for they were all repressed in the Soviet era. In 1910 the Baku police reported that Dzhugashvili was living with Stefaniia Petrovskaia, a noblewoman from Kherson' province, whom he considered his wife. He even asked the city governor to let him marry her. Permission was granted, but Stalin then left to go into exile, and nothing more is heard of Petrovskaia. In February 1911, when he was in exile at Sol'vychegodsk, the local police registered his civil marriage to a fellow-exile, Serafima Khoroshenina. In June of that year, he was allowed to move to Vologda, where police watchdogs soon discovered that he had a liaison with Pelageia Anufrieva, but their relationship was brief since he fled shortly thereafter. In 1914 Stalin was sent to northern Siberia, to the village of Kureika near Turukhansk. Here he lived with Lidiia Pereprygina, who had a son by him named Alexander (1917–67). The child's name was registered as Dzhugashvili but he later took that of his stepfather, Davydov.[14]

In 1918 Stalin, by now a leading member of the Party and government, married Nadezhda Allilueva (1901–32). They had a son, Vasilii, born in 1921, and in 1926 a daughter, Svetlana. The marriage cannot be called a happy one, for the pair quarrelled a lot, and it ended in tragedy: on 9 November 1932 Nadezhda committed suicide. Twenty-two years his junior in age, she shot herself with a pistol given her by her brother. Svetlana records that Stalin did not go to his wife's funeral. Reproached for causing her death, he confided his thoughts to a post-mortem letter, which has not survived.[15]

As we have seen, in 1943 Stalin's son from his first marriage, Yakov Dzhugashvili, was killed in captivity by the Germans. Svetlana, who died in 1999, failed to find happiness in her several marriages. She left the USSR in 1967 and thereafter wrote three volumes of memoirs – *Twenty Letters to A Friend* (London, 1967), *Only One Year* (New York, 1969) and *The Faraway Music* (Delhi, 1984) – in which she criticized the Soviet regime and her father's methods of rule. In the second of these books she wrote:

> He gave his name to this bloodbath of absolute dictatorship. He knew what he was doing. He was neither insane nor misled. With cold calculation he had cemented his own power, afraid of losing it more than of anything else in the world. And so his first concentrated drive had been the liquidation of his enemies and rivals.[16]

Svetlana's brother Vasilii (1921–62) was a source of scandal. He joined the air force, became a captain at the age of 20 and reached lieutenant-general's rank when only 24. His unprecedented, fairy-tale-like career came to a sudden end six weeks after his father died. He was expelled from the armed forces without the right to wear uniform, which was equivalent to dishonourable discharge. Arrested on 28 April 1953, he was sentenced to eight years in custody for 'abusing his service position, appropriating a large amount of state funds, forgery for personal gain, and acquisition of material goods' – to cite from the indictment. (Soviet tradition required that the charges should also include criticism of Khrushchev and the CPSU, which was tantamount to anti-Soviet propaganda and agitation.)

It is tempting to conclude that Vasilii Stalin was a victim of his father's system, but nothing could be further from the truth. At that time, no prisoner in the land of the Soviets enjoyed such privileges as the former leader's son. He was freed from prison at least twice without any decision being taken by the Procuracy. The first occasion was in the winter of 1954–5, when he was put in the prison hospital in readiness for transfer to the government sanatorium 'Barvikha' and then to a *dacha* – this at least is was what Khrushchev told Svetlana Allilueva. The hospital was only nominally a prison outfit, and so Vasilii again fell into bad company, drank to excess, made scenes, and assumed a threatening demeanour. As a result, he was put back in prison. But in 1960 he was released: this time Khrushchev received him and treated him well. He was given back his general's rank along with a Moscow apartment and even a Party card. But it was not long before Vasilii once more started drinking and behaving rowdily, and so back he went to jail. In the spring of 1961, he was let out for medical reasons. The diagnosis was cirrhosis of the liver, a stomach ulcer and complete physical exhaustion. He was exiled for a five-year term to Kazan'.

The judicial proceedings against Vasilii Stalin were held in secret, and so the view gained currency that the authorities were victimizing someone who might otherwise serve as a rallying point for opponents of the regime or even organize a *coup*. But there were no grounds for such beliefs. Vasilii was least of all a politician: for him power just meant cavorting with actresses, patronizing football players, gambling at the races and getting drunk. He was no more than a playboy who owed everything to being the son of the once mighty tyrant. If Trotsky was correct to call Stalin 'a splendid mediocrity',[17] then Vasilii was a mediocre mediocrity. His personal qualities made him quite unfit for any role in politics.

He stayed in Kazan' from 29 April 1961 until his death on 19 March 1962. Eleven volumes of documents have survived to testify to the fact. They are replete with reports by local KGB agents, who did not let him out of their sight for a moment, even putting a listening device into his room. I came across these tomes when working on the Tatarstan republic's commission for the rehabilitation of former political prisoners. The papers record his drunken affairs and physical degradation. He died of alcoholic abuse and was buried on 21 March 1962 at the Arsk cemetery in Kazan'. There was no funeral service and no military honours were rendered to the ex-general and generalissimo's son. The expenses of his burial – 405 roubles and 5 kopecks – were borne by the local KGB.

Vasilii Stalin's last wife, M.I. Shevargina, tried for the rest of her life to get him rehabilitated. But it was not until 30 September 1999 that the Military Collegium of the Russian Supreme Court looked into the case. It quashed the political charges in the indictment but left in those of 'exceeding the powers of his service position [and] negligence with serious consequences'. His term of imprisonment was reduced to four years, which meant that he was posthumously amnestied.[18] On 20 November 2002 his body was exhumed, at the request of Shevargina's children, and reburied next to his wife's grave in Troekurovsky cemetery in Moscow.

The attention paid here to Vasilii Stalin is connected with the efforts made in recent years to reanimate his father's system. Many elderly people feel nostalgic for an era when, whatever else may have happened, at least they were young.[19]

The leader had 10 grandchildren. Although the Alliluev family was repressed, some of its members are still alive. Stalin's grandchildren try to defend his record and write only good things about their parents and distant relatives. This is under-standable in human terms, but these undocumented emotional outpourings cannot be taken as reliable historical sources.

After Nadezhda's death, Stalin did not remarry, although when she died he was still only 54 and in good health. Instead he made do with girlfriends, whom he treated properly; he would ask them to drop in for a glass of good Georgian wine. So far as is known, none of them refused. Among the ladies close to him were three Moscow actresses (Vera Davydova, Marina Semenova and Alla Tarasova) and Kaganovich's niece, Roza.[20] He had nothing to do with his illegitimate children. Stalin exuded a certain masculine charm – as did Rasputin, for that matter.

At the end of his book on the pre-revolutionary Stalin, Professor Ostrovsky points out that, once in power, he ordered documents about himself to be removed from local archives and brought to Moscow, where they were kept under lock and key. No doubt he had good grounds for doing so: not just a desire to keep his past secret and to destroy compromising material, but also to be able to present the story of his life in an attractive light. By 1917 Stalin, a veteran Bolshevik, knew all there was to know about conspiracy and underground organizations. Ostrovsky is quite right to say that his career to date had been crowned with success, and to challenge Trotsky's claim that he owed his rise to power to chance factors, and later to intrigues and mastery of the Party apparatus.[21]

Stalin in power

B.S. Ilizarov focuses attention on Stalin's life and relationships after he became Party leader. By analysing his marginal jottings in books and other personal documents, he seeks to give a psychological portrait of the man. Stalin, he writes, took over Nietzsche's belief in a Superman.[22] His oratorical style was didactic, like that of a preacher. He considered his statements beyond criticism, especially from the late 1920s onward, when he called himself 'Lenin's great disciple'. He was a good draughtsman and left many ink and pencil sketches of his associates, soon to become his enemies. These men were just as cruel as he was, but he was smarter than they were in struggling to win sole power. He put up with Bukharin's effusions so long as the latter was useful to him in worsting Trotsky, Zinoviev and Kamenev, but by 1928 it was Bukharin's turn. It was then that the latter called Stalin 'Jenghis Khan with a telephone'; Stalin's crude term for him was 'a cross between a fox and a pig'. Years later, when K.V. Pauker (1895–1937), his chief bodyguard, mockingly described Zinoviev's execution, with details of how the once mighty Party functionary had fallen to his knees before his executioners pleading for mercy, the leader and his new favourites laughed merrily. One of Stalin's surviving sketches (1930) shows N.P. Briukhanov (1878–1938), a people's commissar of Finance, hanging by the genitals.

Stalin was always afraid of assassination and regarded his physicians and the security chiefs as his most dangerous foes. In 1938 he organized a judicial inves-tigation into the so-called 'case of the killer doctors', which led to the death of three professors of medicine: I.N. Kazakov, L.G. Levin and D.D. Pletnev. This was the moment when he also liquidated two successive heads of the NKVD, G.G. Yagoda and N.I. Yezhov. In 1953 he was preparing a new round of butchery. It began with the 'anti-cosmopolitan' campaign and the 'doctors' plot affair', which stimulated anti-Semitic feelings among the populace to serve as cover for the planned extermination of innocent Jewish people. Only Stalin's timely death saved many potential victims from his 'guillotine'.[23]

His cruelty knew no bounds. D.A. Volkogonov relates how in September 1941 Zhdanov and Zhukov told Stalin that German forces attacking Soviet positions outside Leningrad were using women, children and elderly civilians as a human shield. They called out 'don't shoot! We're your own people!' The Soviet soldiers were in a quandary as to what they should do. Stalin replied:

> I'm told that some Leningrad Bolsheviks are against using firearms on delegates of this kind. I think that if there are such people among the Bolsheviks, they should be shot first. My advice is not to be sentimental but to strike the enemy and his willing or unwilling helpers in the teeth . . . Strike the Germans and their delegates with full force and mow them down.[24]

Yet at the same time, Stalin did have a coarse sense of humour. Milovan Djilas (1911–95), the Yugoslav politician, recalls him enjoying the following story that Djilas told him:

> A Turk and a Montenegrin are chatting during a momentary armistice. The Turk asks why the Montenegrins are always fighting. 'To get booty', says the Montenegrin, 'we are a poor people, always on the lookout where there's something to be had for nothing. But what do you fight for?' 'For honour and glory', says the Turk. The Montenegrin fires back: 'well, you see, each of us fights for what he hasn't got.'[25]

Thus Stalin's character had many contrasting sides. It is not really surprising that some people should see him as an evildoer, others as a genius.

Historians have tried to refine their verdict on his character by studying what books he had in his library, going by the old adage 'tell me what you read and I'll tell you what sort of person you are.' In 1961 a group of library workers from the Institute of Marxism–Leninism was summoned to the Kremlin to sort out the over 20,000 books stored in Stalin's apartment and *dacha*. They found 11,000 volumes of belles-lettres, which were handed over to the Lenin (now Russian State) Library. His collection also contained copies of the works of Trotsky, Bukharin, Zinoviev, Kamenev and others that had been removed from the open shelves of public libraries.

Unfortunately, some of the books he collected went astray, but several hundreds of them bearing his annotations have been studied.[26] Let us note in passing that while he was alive the mere possession of works by his enemies could lead to one's arrest. If confiscated, as a rule they were either burned or kept in special repositories (*spetskhrany*), a sort of literary Gulag. One might say that in the 1930s Stalin was the freest reader in the country, since he could possess whichever books took his fancy and express his opinion about them frankly.

From the 1950s to the 1980s, my friend and teacher L.M. Spirin (1917–93) was a research scholar ('scientific worker') in the Institute of Marxism–Leninism. He told me how the books from Stalin's *dacha* at Kuntsevo were brought there via the Kremlin and put in the basement. They were treated badly: some were pilfered and the director of the Institute's library even suggested burning them. Many were stamped 'Library of I.V. Stalin' and bore his characteristic marginalia. In 1992, when the Party archives were reorganized, 391 of these volumes, including those with the marginal notes, landed up in RGASPI; the rest presumably fell into private hands. Spirin calculated that of the former 46 were published before 1917, 300 between 1918 and 1940, and 35 between 1941 and 1952; 10 bore no publication date. Apart from the belles-lettres, Stalin's library had a strong political emphasis. Most works were by Communist writers: 70 by Zinoviev, for instance, and about 60 by Trotsky. Stalin's marginal remarks were categorical: he was not a man given to doubt. Spirin's study led to the conclusion that Stalin, while no genius, was certainly one of the twentieth century's most ferocious characters – a view it is hard to dissent from.[27]

In the 1930s, a translation of Hitler's *Mein Kampf* circulated on a restricted basis among members of the ruling élite. One of those who read it was M.I. Kalinin, chairman of the CEC, who noted on the first page 'verbose, windy . . . for small shopkeepers' – in other words, he echoed the view taken at the time in Soviet propaganda. Stalin underlined the passage in which Hitler said he was eyeing territory in the east for German expansion.[28] He realized that this meant he was planning war against the USSR.

During the Gorbachev years and later, much Russian historical work on the Stalin era was devoted to unmasking the 'cult of the individual'. The leader was accused of liquidating vast numbers of people and of departing from the ideas of Marx and Lenin. Historians, philosophers and economists wrote masses of articles in the press about the need to get away from Stalin's methods of rule.[29] But what was lacking in this 'unmasking' literature was a critical attitude towards the regime as such and the CPSU's role in establishing its monopoly of power. Such works are, however, being produced today, as is only natural, for there are people still alive who experienced personally what it meant to be branded by the Stalinist regime an 'enemy of the people', or victims' relatives who endured all kinds of deprivation on their account. A.V. Antonov-Ovseenko, son of a famous Bolshevik revolutionary in 1917, sees Stalinism as a mendacious 'theatre of the absurd' staged and directed by the dictator.[30]

Works are also coming out that deal with the criminal deeds of Stalin's associates: A.Ya. Vyshinsky, his Procurator-General, and others officials in the judiciary, as well as NKVD chiefs like G.G. Yagoda and N.I. Yezhov.[31] These authors make it clear that the leader himself took a close interest in the work of the punitive organs, which in effect he directed (see Chapter 4).

Stalin's impact was so far-reaching that writers on virtually any subject in Soviet history between 1922 and 1953 cannot avoid mentioning him, and so making a contribution to his biography. Some of his defenders complain that the first people to criticize him were functionaries who had previously carried out his orders. For instance, they hold Khrushchev responsible for 'murdering' Stalin and Beria, whom they see as 'true communists' and builders of the state. It is impossible to argue with such people since they do not base their arguments on historical evidence but just unleash a torrent of emotional abuse against those who apply scholarly criteria and seek to arrive at an accurate view of the past.

After World War II, many of Hitler's cronies were sentenced by the Nuremberg tribunal for carrying out criminal orders. In the Russian case, matters are different. Unlike Berlin, Moscow was not liberated by foreign armies, and only to a limited degree did members of the Soviet *nomenklatura* express contrition for their crimes. After 1956, these men retained their power, or at the most made *pro forma* concessions which fostered hopes of genuine democratic change. Of course, Khrushchev had nothing to do with Stalin's death, and the execution of Beria was carried out (by General P.F. Batitsky) in accordance with a judicial decision, namely a death sentence passed by the country's Supreme Court.[32]

Earlier studies of the Soviet *nomenklatura* by emigrés such as A. Avtorkhanov and M. Voslensky[33] have been followed up in Russia over the last decade, for example, in various reference works and articles on Stalin's associates.[34] His personal secretariat had a staff of at least ninety persons. He wrote the scenario for all the Party congresses held during his tenure of sole power. Thus, the typewritten text of his report to the XVIIIth congress (1939) bears notes in his hand, in black ink, marking the places where there were to be 'applause', 'stormy prolonged applause', 'general laughter', cries of 'hurrah for comrade Stalin' and so forth.[35]

Stalin made great efforts to ensure that the mighty Soviet state should have a strong, well-equipped army backed by an ideologically homogenized population. To this end, he attended meetings of the general staff and interfered constantly in education and, indeed, every aspect of culture. In his letter of 1931 to the editors of *Proletarskaia revoliutsiia*, he told historians to ignore sources that were 'incorrect' and three years later ensured that schoolchildren should use only textbooks with the right dose of 'patriotic' content. Recent Russian studies show that he was directly involved in the repression of the Red Army leadership during the Terror, when he destroyed the bulk of the country's military élite (see Chapter 4). He was the prime author of the doctrine of 'socialist realism' in literature and the arts, and anyone who transgressed against it was crushed. E. Gromov writes that during the 1930s 'letters by even minor writers and artists were constantly landing on Stalin's table'. After the war, with the nuclear stand-off, he took greater interest in letters from scientists active in the defence industries.[36]

Stalin understood that symbols matter a lot in public life. On his initiative, various rituals were introduced to bolster the leader cult, such as Stalin prizes and scholarships. He personally edited the new Soviet anthem which replaced the *Internationale* in 1943. The first draft was composed by two poets, S.V. Mikhalkov and G.A. El-Registan, to music by A.V. Alexandrov, conductor of the Red Army ensemble. Instead of the words 'Noble union of free peoples', Stalin inserted 'Unbreakable union of free republics'; and he amended the last quatrain to read:

'And the great Lenin lit up our way/ brought us up,/ Stalin inspired us to keep faith with the people,/ to work and achieve great deeds.'[37] Incidentally, Mikhalkov corrected the text of the anthem twice. The first time was in 1977, when Stalin's name was removed; the second time was in 2000, when he supplied new words to the old music. This made some people nostalgic but displeased others, including me: we feel that the revival of Communist symbols (the music of the old anthem and the Red flag in the army) will not help to create a civil society in the new Russia, and is an offence to those who suffered under the old regime. When this matter was being discussed in the press, the satirical writer Vladimir Voinovich jocularly put forward his own version, which had the refrain: 'Glory to our freedom-loving fatherland,/ Glory to the servile Russians, too,/ Who repeatedly alter their symbols/ As if they had nothing better to do.'[38]

Stalin was, as we have seen, the only man in the USSR allowed to have a personal library of forbidden books; he was also the only man permitted to criticize publicly the so-called 'classics of Marxism–Leninism', citations from which were regarded as the ultimate truth.[39] In 1934 Stalin opposed the inclusion in the Party's chief theoretical journal, *Bol'shevik*, of Friedrich Engels's article 'The Foreign Policy of Russian Tsarism'; his remarks, which became widely known at the time, were later published (1941). As scholars have recently pointed out, these comments helped to construct a new mythologized view of history based on 'Soviet patriotism' and stressing the unity of all the peoples of the USSR; it led to a radical revision of what had formerly been said about the war of 1812 or World War I, for instance – and left absolutely no place for Engels's view of tsarist foreign policy as thoroughly reactionary.[40]

In order to bolster a positive image abroad of the Soviet leadership, Stalin arranged to meet well-known contemporary writers, such as H.G. Wells, Leon Feuchtwanger, Romain Rolland, George Bernard Shaw and Henri Barbusse. Their exchanges with him, and their impressions, have recently been analysed in detail by Russian historians. It has become clear that these writers' accounts actually did a lot to expose the myth of the Soviet Union as 'progressive'. They were critical of the all-powerful Soviet bureaucracy, headed by a charismatic ruler, and the harsh punitive policy in force.[41]

At the end of the war, Stalin reached the zenith of his glory. R.G. Pikhoia has calculated that in 1946–53 the ruling élite was only about 3,000 strong.[42] Scholarly interest in the late Stalinist epoch has been growing in recent years, even if much attention continues to be paid to the earlier years.[43] Historians have explored the repressive measures taken against military leaders, including Marshal Zhukov in 1946–7, the 'Leningrad affair' of 1949, the 'Mingrelian nationalist group' (1951), and last but not least state-sponsored anti-Semitism.[44] In 1948, Stalin gave orders for the murder of S.M. Mikhoels, the famous actor and chairman of the Jewish Anti-fascist committee of the USSR. The 'anti-cosmopolitan' campaign that got under way at this time peaked in the 'doctors' plot' affair of 1952–3.[45]

Simultaneously, an ideological offensive was launched. Anna Akhmatova and Mikhail Zoshchenko were publicly defamed and their works withdrawn from circulation. The cultural blight affected films and operas, classical music (Dmitrii Shostakovich's work), biology and genetics, physics, philosophy, linguistics and economics.[46] Stalin sought to present himself as the ultimate arbiter in scientific controversies, which in his view were basically ideological in nature. His ultimate purpose was to reassert the dictatorial controls that had been somewhat relaxed during the war and to destroy any illusions among the intelligentsia that there would now be some sort of liberalization. The 'iron curtain' policy adopted from 1946 onward served to buttress the Party's interference in all spheres of domestic life. For example, scientific and scholarly contacts with specialists abroad were curbed, which led to a prevalence of pseudo-scientific thinking in several branches of knowledge.

Although post-war Soviet society was paralysed by fear, many people resisted inwardly. For example, Shostakovich, besides composing music for the cinema, created the musical cycle 'From Jewish Folk Poetry'. I myself remember how, when I was studying in the historical–philological faculty of Kazan' State University in the autumn of 1950, regular lectures were suspended in favour of a course on 'Stalin's teaching on linguistics', which was obligatory in all universities. The same thing happened when his work *The Economic Problems of Socialism* came out in 1952. We students 'voted with our feet', but a few of us stayed behind so that our absence should not be construed as a political offence. In the late Stalin era, ambivalent behaviour of this kind was typical: people fulfilled their norms and outwardly obeyed orders, while writing something 'for the drawer' or acting in the way they thought right whenever they had a chance.

After suffering his first minor heart attack in October 1945, Stalin reduced his work load and stopped smoking; soon he began to put on weight and suffered from high blood pressure. He started to devote more thought to the succession problem. The XIXth Party congress in October 1952 was the last one he managed. The battle behind the scenes during his last years has now been reconstructed by historians with access to his personal archive and to the papers left by some of his associates (Malenkov, Molotov, Voroshilov) and the memoirs of Mikoian, Shepilov and Khrushchev in particular.[47]

One of the most interesting points to emerge is that he continued to resort to repressive measures to maintain his personal power and get rid of those whose loyalty he was not sure of, so that there was some degree of turnover among the leading cadres. What he wanted was not active decision-makers but subservient executants of his will. As already mentioned, these functionaries responded to his suspicious attitude by developing a survival instinct. After 1945 the influence of the 'old guard' declined. Molotov and Mikoian both lost their ministerial jobs in 1949, while others came in for criticism at the XIXth congress. Stalin's death saved many of this generation from ending up as 'enemies of the people' and prepared the way for the next round of struggle among his heirs.

Recent writers have also thrown light on Stalin's attitude towards his cult in the mass media. In November 1945 Molotov allowed Moscow newspapers to publish Winston Churchill's enthusiastic appreciation of Stalin's wartime leadership. Stalin was very annoyed at this, because from a strict Leninist viewpoint any acclaim by a 'class enemy', even if he was a temporary ally, was inexcusable. In a telegram to Molotov, he made this point: 'Soviet leaders do not need the plaudits of foreign ones. So far as I am concerned they merely shock me.'[48]

A struggle developed for Stalin's favour between Leningraders under Zhdanov and Muscovites under Malenkov. Zhdanov's death on 31 August 1948 shifted the balance of forces up to a point, for many Party officials in the old capital were removed as a consequence of the 'Leningrad affair', so that the conflict was now fought out between members of the leader's old entourage. It is now thought that he probably marked out M.A. Suslov (1902–82) as his successor.[49] He had worked in the CC apparatus since 1941, was one of its secretaries, and in 1949–50 *Pravda* editor. From 1946 to his death, he was the Party's chief ideologist and a Stalinist to his fingertips. Talking to the writer Vasilii Grossman in the early 1960s, Suslov said: 'We exposed the errors that accompanied Stalin's cult of the individual, but we shall never condemn Stalin for fighting the enemies of the Party and the state. We condemn him [only] for striking at his own kind.'[50]

Suslov was among those who 'struck at his own kind', for in the 1930s he played an active role in the mass repressions, as he did later in liquidating the Jewish Anti-fascist committee, deporting people from the Baltic republics, and persecuting intellectuals. Moreover, it was Suslov who organized Khrushchev's deposition in 1964 and afterwards delivered the report to the CC condemning him for *his* cult. He was for long referred to as the 'Red cardinal'. But he could never have become leader of the Party and the country, for he shunned publicity, preferring to operate behind the scenes.

As for the leader cult, this had begun already in Lenin's day, and here, too, Stalin merely proved himself a loyal disciple. It reached its peak towards the end of his life, and so it was logical that any measures of liberalization, any softening of the punitive system, would have to start with de-Stalinization. This was a peculiar process: in July 1953, at the CC plenum called to endorse the ousting of Beria, there was talk only of the 'morbid forms and scale' of the cult and Stalin's name was not even mentioned – as if Beria could have done anything without the boss's sanction. Not until 1956 did Khrushchev summon up enough courage to tell a Party congress about Stalin's crimes. As historians today stress, he instrumentalized the condemnation of Stalin in his struggle against his former comrades in the leadership, who disapproved of his behaviour as First Secretary.[51]

In Russia, with its autocratic traditions, the transfer of power from one ruler to another has always threatened social stability. It took Stalin some 15 years to gain recognition as leader; in Khrushchev's case, the term was only five years. During that time, Malenkov, Molotov and many other members of Stalin's 'old guard', who opposed his reforms, fell from grace.

By the end of his life, Stalin had won a plenitude of honours and awards. He held the rank of generalissimo and was a Hero of the Soviet Union; his medal as a Hero of Socialist Labour dated from 1939; later, he secured a prestigious Lenin order (1949) as well as one named for Suvorov (1st class, 1943), a Victory medal (1944) and so on. (Even so, with only nine medals he lagged some way behind Brezhnev.) He had a flat in the Kremlin and two private *dachas* near Moscow –

Zubalovo with 12 rooms, Kuntsevo with 10; he could also vacation with his chums and foreign guests at any of 16 state *dachas* in the Crimea and Transcaucasia.

In recent years, Russian historians have devoted more attention to Stalin the man than to the life of the society over which he ruled. This is a reaction to the secrecy that surrounded leaders' personal lives in Soviet times, when official biographies lacked any trace of a human touch. R.G. Pikhoia has written of the 'struggle of the crown princes' in the ailing Stalin's last years. A.V. Ostrovsky has brought greater precision to our knowledge of many facts about Stalin's early life, such as the allegation that he collaborated with the Okhrana. Alongside these critical scholarly studies we have the apologetic literature, for instance, about his military role in World War II.[52] The prevailing view is that the Soviet regime's first decade was a 'good' time, whereas others (myself included) reckon that it was precisely then, under Lenin and during NEP, that the foundations of Stalinist totalitarianism were laid; Lenin's successor merely took it to an absurd pitch of 'perfection'.

The biographical approach will probably remain popular in Russia, for some themes never die: as the great historian V.O. Kliuchevsky once wrote, 'why do people like to read about the past? For the same reason that, when a fugitive stumbles and gets up again, he likes to look back at the spot where he fell'.[53]

Notes

1 They were as follows: Yuzovka/Stalino (1924), Tsaritsyn/Stalingrad (1925), Dushanbe/Stalinabad (1929), Kuznetsk/Stalinsk (1932), Tskhinvali/Staliniri (1934) and Bobriki/Stalinogorsk (1934).

2 *Argumenty i fakty*, 17 April 1989, no. 13; *Izvestiia TsK KPSS*, 1990, no. 12, 126–7.

3 G.L. Liparteliani, *Stalin velikii* (St Petersburg: Roza, 2001); A.V. Sukhomlinov, *Vasilii, syn vozhdia* (Moscow: 'Sovershenno sekretno', 2001); V.V. Karpov, *Generalissimus*, 2 bks (Kaliningrad: Yantarnyi skos, 2002); *Rossiiskaia gazeta*, 13 November 2003.

4 L.M. Spirin, 'Kogda rodilsia Stalin: popravka k ofitsial'noi biografii', *Izvestiia*, 25 June 1990.

5 E. Radzinsky, *Stalin* (Moscow: Vagrius, 1997); B.S. Ilizarov, *Tainaia zhizn' Stalina: po materialam ego biblioteki i arkhiva: k istoriosofii stalinizma* (Moscow: Veche, 2002); idem, 'Dusha Koby podlinnogo', *VI*, 2002, no. 7, 84–97; A.V. Ostrovsky, *Kto stoial za spinoi Stalina?* (St Petersburg: Neva, 2003). The last named is a professor in St Petersburg and an associate of the Institute of Russian History in RAN.

6 N.A. Kipshidze, *Vstrechi s vozhdem: vospominaniia vracha* (Tbilisi, 1953), 59.

7 D.A. Volkogonov, *Triumf i tragediia: politicheskii portret I.V. Stalina* (Moscow: Novosti, 1989), 40–1.

8 Sukhomlinov, *Vasilii, syn vozhdia*, 51–8.

9 I.V. Stalin, *Sochineniia* (Moscow: Gospolitizdat, 1948); vol. 8, 175.

10 RGASPI, f. 71, op.10, d. 173, ll. 2–6.

11 G. Uratadze, *Vospominaniia gruzinskogo sotsial-demokrata* (Stanford, CA: Hoover Institution, 1968), 66.

12 Ostrovsky, *Kto stoial . . .* , 212–16, 246.

13 Z.I. Peregudova, *Politicheskii sysk Rossii, 1880–1917* (Moscow: ROSSPEN, 2000), 243–67, 272; V.P. Kozlov, *Obmanutaia, no torzhestvuiushchaia Klio: podlogi pis'mennykh istochnikov po rossiiskoi istorii v XX v.* (Moscow: ROSSPEN, 2001), 106–23. The miscellany compiled by Yu.G. Fel'shtinsky, *Byl li Stalin agentom Okhranki?: sbornik statei,*

materialov i dokumentov (Moscow: Terra, 1999) contains various viewpoints. See also R.C. Tucker, *Stalin as Revolutionary, 1879–1929: A Study in History and Personality* (New York: Norton, 1973), 111–14. On Malinovsky the classic Western work is R.C. Elwood, *Roman Malinovsky: A Life Without a Cause* (Newtonville, MA: ORP, 1977).

14   Ostrovsky, *Kto stoial...?*, 253, 325–34, 355–7, 406–8; V.A. Torchinov and A.M. Leontiuk, *Vokrug Stalina: istoriko-biograficheskii spravochnik* (St Petersburg: Filologicheskii fakul'tet Sankt-Peterburgskogo gos. universiteta, 2000), 173, 420–3; V. Filippov, 'Vologodskii roman Stalina', *Izvestiia*, 17 October 1996.

15   *Argumenty i fakty*, 25 February 1989. The rumour that Allilueva was shot is still circulating; see *Komsomol'skaia pravda*, 14 April 1998.

16   S. Allilueva, *Only One Year*, trans. P. Chavchavadze (New York and Evanston, IL: Harper & Row, 1969), 181–2.

17   Trotsky, *Stalin*, vol. 2, 252.

18   *Izvestiia*, 1 October 1999.

19   For more details see A. Litvin, 'Delo "Fligera": Kazanskaia ssylka Vasiliia Stalina', *Rodina*, 2003, no. 2, 41–3.

20   V.G. Tkachenko (K. and T. Enko), *Chastnaia zhizn' vozhdei: Lenin, Stalin, Trotskii* (Moscow: Tsentrpoligraf, 2000), 145–62, 215–34; N.A. Zenkovich, *Tainy ukhodiashchego veka – 3* (Moscow: Olma-Press, 1999), 31.

21   Ostrovsky, *Kto stoial...?*, 462, 600, 614–15.

22   On this point see now B.G. Rosenthal, *New Myth, New World: From Nietzsche to Stalinism* (University Park, PA: Pennsylvania State University Press, 2004).

23   Ilizarov, *Tainaia zhizn'*, 66, 78, 86, 92–3, 117, 123, 129.

24   D.A. Volkogonov, *Triumf i tragediia* (Moscow: APN, 1989), bk 2, pt 1, 194–5.

25   Cited from E. Gusliarov, *Stalin v zhizni...* (Moscow: Olma-Press, 2003), 705.

26   L.M. Spirin, 'Glazami knig: lichnaia biblioteka Stalina', *Nezavisimaia gazeta*, 25 May 1993; Medvedev, *Neizvestnyi Stalin*, 119–24.

27   Spirin, 'Glazami' and personal information.

28   Ilizarov, *Tainaia zhizn' vozhdia*, 137; Volkogonov, *Triumf i tragediia*, bk 2, pt 1, 24.

29   *Vozhd', khoziain, diktator: sbornik gazetnykh i zhurnal'nykh publikatsii 1987–1989 gg.* (Moscow: Patriot, 1990).

30   A.V. Antonov-Ovseenko, *Teatr Iosifa Stalina* (Moscow: ACT, 2000).

31   For example, A.I. Vaksberg, *Tsaritsa dokazatel'stv: Vyshinsky i ego zhertvy* (Moscow, 1992); English edn: *The Prosecutor and the Prey: Vyshinsky and the 1930s Moscow Show Trials*, trans. J. Butler (London: Weidenfeld & Nicolson, 1990); M.M. Ilinsky, *Narkom Yagoda* (Moscow: Veche, 2002); A.I. Poliansky, *Yezhov: istoriia 'zheleznogo' narkoma* (Moscow: Veche, 2003); V.F. Nekrasov (ed., comp.), *Beriia: konets kar'iery* (Moscow: Politizdat, 1991); V.P. Naumov *et al.* (comps), *Lavrentii Beriia, 1953: stenogramma iul'skogo plenuma TsK i drugie dokumenty* (Moscow: Mezhdunar. fond 'Demokratiia', 1999); V.V. Sokolov, *Narkomy strakha: Yagoda, Yezhov, Beriia, Abakumov* (Moscow: ACT-Press, 2001); V.I. Berezhkov, *Piterskie prokuratory: rukovoditeli VChK-MGB, 1918–1954* (St Petersburg: Blits, 1998).

32   Yu.I. Mukhin, *Ubiistvo Stalina i Beriia* (Moscow: Forum, 2002), 7, 256.

33   A. Avtorkhanov, *Proiskhozhdenie partokratii*, 2 vols (Frankfurt: Possev, 1973); M.S. Voslensky, *Nomenklatura: gospodstvuiushchii klass Sovetskogo Soiuza* (Moscow: Sovetskaia Rossiia, 1991); French edn: *La Nomenklatura: les privilégiés en URSS*, trans. C. Nugue (Paris: P. Belfont, 1980).

34   For example, K.A. Zalessky, *Imperiia Stalina: biograficheskii entsiklopedicheskii slovar'* (Moscow: Veche, 2000); Torchinov and Leontiuk (comps), *Vokrug Stalina* (see n. 14); N.V. Romanovsky, 'Liudi Stalina: etiud k kollektivnomu portretu', *OI*, 2000, no. 4, 65–76.

35   RGASPI, f. 558, op. 1, d. 3221.

36   A.A. Pechenkin, '1937 god: Stalin i Voennyi sovet', *OI*, 2003, no. 1, 52: V.A.

Shentalinsky, *Raby svobody: v literaturnykh arkhivakh KGB* (Moscow: Parus, 1995); English edn: *The KGB's Literary Archive*, tr. J. Crowfoot (London: Harvill, 1995); E. Gromov, *Stalin: vlast' i iskusstvo* (Moscow: Respublika, 1998), 190; B.S. Ilizarov, 'Stalin i roman L'va Tolstogo "Voskresenie"', *OI*, 2003, no. 1, 22–35.

37 For more details, see Volkogonov, *Triumf i tragediia*, bk 1, pt 2, 113–14.

38 Yu.N. Afanas'ev, *Opasnaia Rossiia: traditsii samovlastiia segodnia* (Moscow: RGGU, 2001), 154–7; V. Voinovich, 'Moi gimn', *Izvestiia*, 7 December 2000.

39 I recall attending a meeting in the Institute of Marxism–Leninism in the mid-1970s, when the lecturer told a critic who turned his back on him 'by turning away from me you are turning your back on Marxism–Leninism'. The fellow duly turned round to face him.

40 B.D. Kozenko, 'Otechestvennaia istoriografiia I-oi mirovoi voiny', *NNI*, 2001, no. 3, 10; I.A. Shein, 'Stalin i Otechestvennaia voina 1812 g.: opyt izucheniia sovetskoi istoriografii 1930-kh –1950-kh gg.', *OI*, 2001, no. 6, 97–108: 'I.V. Stalin – "O stat'e Engel'sa 'Vneshniaia politika russkogo tsarizma'" i ideologicheskaia podgotovka k mirovoi voine', *VI*, 2002, no. 7, 3–40. For Western literature see Chapter 5, 000–00.

41 G.B. Kulikova, 'SSSR 1920–1930-kh gg. glazami zapadnykh intellektualov', *OI*, 2001, no. 1, 22; idem, 'Pod kontrolem gosudarstva: prebyvanie v SSSR inostrannykh pisatelei v 1920–1930-kh gg.', *OI*, 2003, no. 4, 43–59; B.S. Lel'chuk, 'Beseda I.V. Stalina s angliiskim pisatelem G. Uellsom (dokumenty, interpretatsiia, razmyshlen-niia)', in A.A. Fursenko (ed.), *Istoricheskaia nauka na rubezhe vekov* (Moscow: Nauka, 2001), 326–52.

42 R.G. Pikhoia, *Sovetskii Soiuz: istoriia vlasti, 1945–1991* (Moscow: RAGS, 1998), 10.

43 Yu.V. Yemelianov, *Stalin: put' k vlasti* (Moscow: Veche, 2002).

44 At this time a number of people who had been released from the Gulag on completion of their sentences were re-arrested, tried and convicted on the former charges.

45 Pikhoia, *Sovetskii Soiuz*, 41–96; M. Geizer, *Solomon Mikhoels* (Moscow: Prometei, 1990); G.V. Kostyrchenko, *Tainaia politika Stalina: vlast' i antisemitizm* (Moscow: Mezhdunar. otnosheniia, 2001); Ya.L. Rapoport, *Na rubezhe dvukh epokh: delo vrachei 1953 g.* (St Petersburg: Pushkinskii fond, 2003); Zh.A. Medvedev, 'Stalin i "delo vrachei": novye materialy', *VI*, 2003, no. 1, 78–102. An earlier work by Kostyrchenko was translated as *Out of the Red Shadows: Anti-Semitism in Stalin's Russia* (Amherst, NY: Prometheus, 1995); see also J. Rapoport, *The Doctors' Plot of 1953* (Cambridge, MA: Harvard University Press, 1991).

46 M.G. Yaroshevsky (ed.), *Repressirovannia nauka* (Leningrad: Nauka, 1991); S.E. Shnol', *Geroi i zlodei rossiiskoi nauki* (Moscow: Kron-press, 1997); Yu.I. Krivonosov, 'Politicheskie igry Stalina pod vidom filosofskoi diskussii', in M. Heinemann and E.I.Kolchinsky (eds), *Za 'zheleznym zanavesom': mify i realii sovetskoi nauki* (St Petersburg: Dm. Bulanin, 2002).

47 Pikhoia, *Sovetskii Soiuz*, 41–96; Romanovsky, 'Liudi Stalina'; A.A. Danilov, 'Vysshie organy vlasti SSSR v pervye poslevoennye gody', in Fursenko (ed.), *Istoricheskaia nauka*, 302–25; A.V. Pyzhikov, 'Poslednie mesiatsy diktatora (1952–1953 gg.)', *OI*, 2002, no. 2, 152–8.

48 Fursenko (ed.), *Istoricheskaia nauka*, 303.

49 Medvedev, *Neizvestnyi Stalin*, 72–6.

50 *Rodina*, 1989, no. 6, 73.

51 Yu. Bokarev, 'Mea culpa! Chto skryvalos' za kritikoi "kul'ta lichnosti"', *Rossiia. XXI* (Moscow, 1995), no. 5–6, 158–80; A.V. Pyzhikov, *Khrushchevskaia 'ottepel'* (Moscow: Olma-Press, 2002); idem, 'Problema kul'ta lichnosti v gody khrushchevskoi ottepeli', *VI*, 2003, no. 4, 47–57.

52 B.G. Solov'ev and V.V. Sukhodeev, *Polkovodets Stalin* (Moscow: Eksmo-Press, 2001).

53 V.O. Kliuchevsky, *Pis'ma, dnevniki: aforizmy i mysli ob istorii* (Moscow: Nauka, 1968), 25.

3 Assessing Stalin's role as leader

Recent appraisals

In November and December 2002 the historian Yu.N. Zhukov was interviewed by a journalist named A.D. Sabov. His replies to the questions put to him were published in successive issues of the popular newspaper *Komsomol'skaia pravda* under the general title 'Stalin as Bugbear',[1] and were clearly designed to build up a positive image of Stalin's place in Soviet history. Citing the US historian J. Arch Getty, Zhukov argued that prior to 1937 the leader had sponsored some three years of liberal reforms, and only their failure had led to the repressions, 'which it is wrong to call Stalinist'. He goes on to claim that Stalin's acquisition of sole power 'saved the country and the world', for otherwise Trotsky, Kamenev and Zinoviev, as zealots for world revolution, would have dragged the USSR into war much earlier than was eventually the case. Zhukov even goes so far as to claim that all the show trials of oppositionists in the 1920s and early 1930s were staged not by Stalin but by Bukharin; if Stalin initiated mass repressions thereafter, from the mid-1930s, he did so at the behest of Soviet citizens eager to purge society from 'enemies of the people'. Given the popular mood at the time, the Procurator-General A.Ya. Vyshinsky emerges as someone holding 'liberal views'. Zhukov takes the confessions of the former oppositionists and military leaders seriously, and reckons that there was indeed a plot against Stalin, who was forced to strike a preventive blow against the conspirators. In his view, it was local Party functionaries rather than Stalin who initiated the Great Terror, the number of whose victims he for some reason puts as low as from 300,000 to 400,000. Allegedly, it was Stalin who put a stop to the terror by getting rid of Yezhov; he imagined that prisoners in Gulag camps were undergoing re-education.

Many readers of *Komsomol'skaia pravda* considered Zhukov's arguments provocative, but he found some grateful admirers, too. On 21 December 2002, a reporter on the paper's staff, O. Kuchkina, offered an analysis of his remarks, which she wrote off as fallacious and baseless. The interview would not be worth our attention had it not appeared in a state-run youth paper with a print run in the millions, whereas serious scholarly works are printed in editions of 300 to 500 copies and are priced out of the reach of ordinary people. Some readers drew a parallel between Yurii Zhukov and Nina Andreeva, whose article in *Sovetskaia Rossiia* on

13 March 1988 was widely taken to be a manifesto by opponents of Gorbachev's *perestroika*; she too defended Stalin, whose name, she averred, was 'linked with an epoch of incomparable achievements by the Soviet people', yet was 'subjected to frantic attacks by his critics'.[2]

A year later, on 18 December 2003, *Komsomol'skaia pravda* returned to the topic of Stalin with an article by the writer Vladimir Karpov in connection with the 125th anniversary of the leader's birth. For Karpov, Stalin is a heroic figure who had turned Russia into a great power, and all the charges levelled against him are contrived. Karpov's article was accompanied by one in a very different spirit by the journalist L. Mlechin, who wrote that the Soviet people had been morally crippled by Stalin's criminal deeds. Such ambivalence towards Stalin's rule is much in evidence today, for there are still many people in Russia unwilling or unable to shed Stalinist ways of thinking.

At least in the scholarly community one finds few who share the opinions of Zhukov or like-minded popular writers. To my mind one of the most estimable historians writing on Stalin's 'socialist state' is I.V. Pavlova of Novosibirsk. She takes a healthily critical approach to official sources from the period, appreciating that many documents have been destroyed or else are inaccessible. She points out that these sources are fundamentally distorted by ideological preconceptions and that we need to adopt ethical criteria in evaluating them. Pavlova indicts a number of her Russian and Western colleagues for taking too apologetic a line towards the dictatorship or exaggeratedly praising the economic modernization and the 'cultural revolution' that Stalin pushed through in the 1930s.

Pavlova agrees with Martin Malia that Stalin's rule was totalitarian, and attacks Western revisionist social historians for writing studies of daily life (considered in Chapter 9) that pay insufficient heed to the political context. This error, she suggests, stems from treating official sources too uncritically. One of her targets is A.K. Sokolov, a researcher at the RAN's Institute of Russian History, who (like some Western revisionists) argued that under Stalin the state was actually quite weak and that it was too inefficient in running the economy to be considered totalitarian; moreover, the Party line changed frequently and the provincial administration was 'chaotic and disorganized'.

Pavlova insists that in Stalin's USSR there was a broad gulf between appearances and reality: the 1936 constitution and other official documents spoke of 'soviet democracy', but the government's guiding principles were actually conspiracy against the people, a blackout on information from abroad, and deliberately mendacious propaganda. She points out that in 1937 the electoral campaign for the Supreme Soviet was held while the Terror was in progress[3] and that this sham 'parliament' had no real power anyway. Pavlova pulls no punches in condemning historians who try to weigh up the positive and negative characteristics of Stalinism. Far from the USSR being modernized in the 1930s, it was actually regressing, since such elements of modernity as had developed prior to the 1917 revolution were being destroyed. Stalinism's only achievement was to build a powerful military–industrial complex: this was 'the only area in which our totalitarianism was able to compete on equal terms with the Western liberal democracies'. Stalinist-style modernization marginalized the populace, turning it into a *lumpenproletariat*; one-third of Soviet citizens went through the concentration camp experience.[4] In short: Pavlova's work exemplifies the tendency among the best historians in today's Russia to seek common ground with the more objective of their Western *confrères* and to look with a critical eye on the Soviet documentary legacy.

The famous culturologist S.S. Averintsev also sees Stalinist rule as totalitarian. He explains the current nostalgia for it by the fact that the fall of the Soviet regime led to a compromise between the old *nomenklatura* and its democratic opponents: 'we had to pay for this bloodless outcome by leaving the old leaders by and large still in place'. Communism was not brought down by defeat in war or popular insurgency, but was dismantled by the Party élite itself.[5] The resurgence of neo-Stalinism in the late 1990s, he contends, can also be attributed to the economic crisis, to corruption and mafia-like activities at the top, and to a reaction against what is perceived as Western military and cultural supremacy.[6]

The Party

The mainspring of the Stalinist regime was the Communist Party, which Stalin once referred to as 'an order of sword-bearers'. During the 1920s there was a ban on forming factions within the Party, but debate continued all the same. From the mid-1930s, however, all such debate ceased and the Party became an obedient instrument in the leader's hands. His personal despotism was reinforced by the Great Terror, which liquidated much of the old Party élite, including those leaders who favoured solving problems by discussion.

We do not yet have a scholarly history of the CPSU by a post-Soviet historian, although recent work has yielded several fragments of information that show how this body was transformed into the chief organ of government. A crucial moment in this process came with the Stalinists' victory at the XIVth congress in 1925, which put an end to intra-party democracy. Members of the Leningrad organization objected that articles written by their leaders (including N.K. Krupskaia) had not been passed for publication, to which Stalin replied: 'we are not liberals. For us the Party's interests are higher than formal democratism'. Henceforth the bosses always claimed to be 'defending the Party's interests'. This congress also legalized denunciation by Party members of one another for heretical conduct and saw the birth of the Party *nomenklatura*. Yu.S. Novopashin, who has written an article on this topic, comes to the discouraging conclusion that the line then adopted was perpetuated at the next two congresses (XVIth, 1930 and XVIIth, 1934). These gatherings, he writes,

> were no longer arenas where like-minded souls exchanged views, where a collective effort was made to decide matters with respect for minority and majority opinion. Instead they became something akin to conclaves of Hitlerite storm-troopers ready to carry out the Führer's orders, even if they knew they were criminal.[7]

Novopashin's article is indicative of the current situation among Russian historians: the more works appear written in an apologetic mode, the more radical are the ripostes by their anti-Stalinist adversaries.

A great deal of work on the Party and its leaders in the 1930s has been done by V.Z. Rogovin and O.V. Khlevniuk.[8] The former managed to complete a projected seven-volume series of studies on the theme 'Was there an alternative to Stalinism?' in which he conceptualizes the whole tragedy suffered by our country between 1922 and 1941. He draws attention to many interesting unknown (or barely known) facts about the ruling Party's inner life, and arrives at a highly negative view of the Stalinists. Only the 'genuine Bolsheviks', represented by Trotsky and the Left Opposition, he argues, offered a real alternative. Rogovin sees the consolidation of the Stalin regime as a 'counter-revolutionary *coup*' and the Great Terror as 'the only weapon Stalin had to fight Bolshevism'.[9] What he has to say about the intra-Party struggles for power and privilege, especially about the role played by the Left Opposition, is of considerable interest; however, his basic argument is unconvincing. The only real alternative to Stalinist totalitarianism was not Trotskyism but democracy, which has long remained a dream for enlightened Russians. Trotsky certainly deserves our respect for being the only man in Lenin's cohort not to kneel in homage before Stalin, whom he lambasted as a traitor to the revolution. But both these leaders were Lenin's pupils and both helped to build a totalitarian state. During the 1918–20 civil war Trotsky shot anti-Bolsheviks without mercy, decimated mutinous Red Army units, and authorized the construction of concentration camps; his record shows that he had no real alternative to Stalin. The Bolsheviks' drive to construct socialism by coercion and administrative controls is now widely recognized as intrinsically flawed. Nor did any of the other leaders (Trotsky, Bukharin, Zinoviev, Kamenev and Rykov) have a real answer to the question how Lenin's design could be implemented in practice. Certainly, any challenge to Stalinism deserves study, but it does not necessarily follow that the people would have been better off if the anti-Stalinists had won the struggle for power.

O.V. Khlevniuk's work is less ideological and more factually based than Rogovin's. In exploring the role of the Politburo and its individual members in taking major decisions, he pays due attention to the state of the sources. He points out that because for various reasons not all the documents we would need are available, we cannot say that the Politburo was divided between 'moderates' and 'radicals' in the 1930s; or that Stalin wavered between these two groups before finally siding with the advocates of terror. He convincingly substantiates his view that not a single decision of major importance was taken in those years without Stalin's knowledge or approval, and that his orders were decisive in launching both the terror and the earlier 'reforms'.

Khlevniuk states that there is no documentary evidence that S.M. Kirov belonged to a 'moderate faction' in the Party.[10] What is more, research into the circumstances of his assassination (1 December 1934) have not turned up any information to suggest that he had a political programme, or that he deviated in any way from the radical Stalinist line. Here the work of A.I. Kozlov and N.A.

Yefimov, who have examined Kirov's early career, is relevant. In March 1917 he came out in support of the Provisional government, but joined the Bolsheviks after they took power. In 1919 he was directly involved in shooting down striking workers in Astrakhan'; later he sided with Stalin against the supporters of Trotsky and Zinoviev, replacing the latter as Leningrad Party chief (1926) and becoming Stalin's loyal henchman. In the late 1920s and early 1930s, he did all he could to promote the violent collectivization drive in the north-western region of the USSR. He also helped to organize the veritable pogrom of the Academy of Sciences in 1929, when the NKVD fabricated the 'Academy case'. It is well known, too, that Kirov had a fondness for young ballerinas and arranged orgies in his palace, which had once belonged to Maria Kseshinskaia, the famous dancer. Some writers (A. Kirilina, Yu. Zhukov) think that L. Nikolaev, Kirov's assassin, acted out of jealousy, because the Leningrad leader was having an affair with his wife, M. Draule, who worked as a waitress in the Smol'nyi canteen. Others, such as Ya.G. Rokitiansky, hold that Kirov was killed on Stalin's orders to provide a pretext for unleashing the Great Terror.[11]

Khlevniuk and Pavlova agree that the reason why Stalin eased the pressure in 1932–4 (prior to Kirov's assassination) was not that he wanted to introduce a 'neo-NEP' but because forced-drive industrialization, and the accompanying collectivization campaign, had plunged the country into a socio-economic crisis. Famine was raging. This was why he had to moderate the tempo of planned economic expansion in the second FYP, free Zinoviev, Kamenev and other former leaders from detention, and reorganize the security police by turning the OGPU into the NKVD. All these measures were just temporary concessions, essential to ensure his own survival, and nothing more. As Stalin was fond of saying, 'You can't afford to yawn and doze when you're in power.'[12]

Economic modernization

His apologists usually argue that he promoted Russia's modernization, that is, the massive shift from a traditional rural society to an urban industrialized one. In fact, the modernization process had got under way much earlier, already in tsarist days. The methods of advance favoured under Soviet rule are evaluated differently by Russian historians today. The variety of views they hold can best be appreciated by looking at a volume of essays published as a *Festschrift* for Yu.A. Poliakov on his eightieth birthday. One of the contributors, the liberal historian V.P. Danilov, takes the view that industrialization, the provision of rudimentary social services, and progress in science and culture 'were not achieved thanks to Stalinism but despite the obstacles it created and the huge losses that resulted. His "revolution from above" was accompanied by a veritable war against the peasantry and a famine that cost millions of lives'. What was officially called 'dekulakization', he argues, had the object, not just of crushing mass resistance to collectivization, but of creating a pool of cheap forced labour with which to develop the remoter northern and eastern regions of the country. Danilov shows in detail how Stalin's 'great break', the drive to fulfil unrealistically high targets during the first FYP, led to enormous loss of life and also of material resources. For him, the methods employed to modernize the USSR were simply criminal.[13]

A very different point of view is presented by A.S. Seniavsky, who also has an article in this *Festschrift*. He takes the line that the mass of Russian peasants, with their communal system of land tenure and traditional ways, stood to benefit from collective farming. The villagers who objected to it were 'only kulaks' (in support of this view, he at least refrains from citing Stalin's *Short Course*, where this argument was put forward). Seniavsky thinks that a modern industry could not have been built except on the basis of public ownership and that the socialist state therefore fulfilled a 'civilizing' mission. Logically enough, there is no place in his scheme for democratic change, private property, or economic competition – all of which he associates with the 'catastrophe' that allegedly befell Russia in the 1990s, when she followed a Western path instead of remaining true to her historic 'peculiarities'.[14]

These two examples suggest that contemporary Russian historians of Stalinism are divided between partisans of a liberal approach and those who stand for a conservative restoration. The liberals lay emphasis on the coercive methods employed and the human losses incurred. They also point out that much of the new technology introduced in the 1930s was imported from the West, and that development was unbalanced, since investment was concentrated in heavy industry, especially the defence sector and branches producing new categories of goods (motor vehicles, especially tractors), the construction of hydroelectric plants and so on.

After 1945, when the Soviet economy had to be reconstructed after wartime damage and destruction, recourse was had to the forced labour of 'special settlers' (*spetspereselentsy*) and ex-enemy POW in the Gulag, which was inefficient. V.P. Popov makes the point that the use of coercive methods in lieu of incentives during the post-war years was one reason why thereafter the Soviet economy continued to lag behind the advanced Western countries both technologically and as regards labour productivity. This is why Stalin's brand of modernization eventually collapsed.[15]

For his part, O.V. Khlevniuk stresses the point that the Stalin regime kept to the same system of economic management after the war that had been set up in the 1930s; the repression of the planner N.A. Voznesensky and the Leningrad Party leaders was in the tradition of the Great Terror, when the managerial élite had suffered badly. Another economic historian, V.S. Lel'chuk, adds that Russia's industrialization is still far from complete: 'now we have to catch up on post-industrial "information society", which will be extremely difficult precisely because the command economy lasted so long and left us in such dire straits'.[16]

The more liberal-minded historians are particularly critical of forced collectivization. Most of their work on this topic has dealt with the repressive aspects, the fate of those exiled as alleged 'kulaks', and the mass movement of protest against violence by the authorities. Draconian laws were passed to safeguard the inviolability of collective 'socialist' property, as a result of which thousands of rural dwellers were sentenced to death or long terms of imprisonment in the Gulag. In 1930 OGPU security troops brutally put down thousands of local revolts and outbreaks (the figures vary from 7,382 to 13,754). Heavy mortality among the peasants sent into exile, as a rule as 'special settlers', threatened to undermine the state's plans to develop the regions to which they were despatched. Some 2.5 million people fell into this category, of whom about one third died from hunger, cold and disease: that is to say, 800,000 individuals, predominantly elderly people or children. These settlements were not dismantled until 1954, after Stalin's death.[17]

Of late, Russian historians have also thrown light on the critical condition of the country's industry, finance and supply systems in the early 1930s. In 1930 and 1931, state grain procurements were fixed at an intolerably high level, a large proportion of the crop was exported and harvests were generally poor. All this, coupled with the policy of forcing peasants to join under-equipped collective farms and expropriating the most hard-working farmers (categorized as 'kulaks') and shoving them off into exile, led to the famine of 1932–4. How many victims of 'dekulakization' and famine were there? Historians have come up with different figures. In the late 1980s, V.P. Danilov, in an exchange with Robert Conquest (who had previously written of 14.5 million casualties) suggested that the famine victims alone numbered 3 million. Conquest replied that his data showed a total of 11 million peasant deaths between 1930 and 1937, comprising about 7 million famine victims plus 4 million who died when exiled to Kazakhstan. From later research, it seems that the true figure is around 4 to 5 million, although higher estimates are encountered.[18]

Recent studies by specialists in agrarian history have highlighted such particular issues as the harm done by collectivization to nomadic reindeer herders in the Arctic regions; the problems encountered in Kaliningrad *oblast'* (the former East Prussia) in the late 1940s, when efforts were made to set up *kolkhozy* there with immigrants from other parts of the USSR; and the internal passport system introduced in 1932. As regards the latter, it emerges that not until 1976–81 did peasants actually get documents allowing them to leave their place of residence and live elsewhere.[19]

Historians of the conservative persuasion argue that it is wrong to focus on shortcomings or the Gulag because the process of modernization was on such a grandiose scale: it turned Russia into a mighty state with an advanced industrial base. Seniavsky, whom we have just met, argues that the collapse of Soviet civilization resulted in 'a catastrophe because, under the pretext of carrying out essential modernizing measures, an attempt was made to westernize the country. Liberal reforms actually led to *de*-modernization . . . and threw us back by several decades'.[20] Other conservatives contend that Stalinist industrialization made the USSR a superpower and was in tune with the general thrust of world history.[21]

The disagreements between contemporary Russian historians over these issues are partly due to the lack of reliable statistics, but basically to their taking an emotional approach to what is becoming for Russians an 'accursed question', namely: do people exist for the benefit of the state or does the state exist for the benefit of the people? While the conservatives are nostalgic for totalitarian rule and the command economy, liberals hold that administrative coercion and repressive methods are incompatible with economic dynamism and popular well-being.

The heavy costs of Stalinist 'planning' and forced economic growth touched off a theoretical discussion about what realistic alternatives there were *c.* 1927–8 within the confines of NEP, but this debate did not lead far, since most historians preferred to concentrate on what had actually occurred.

R.W. Davies and O.V. Khlevniuk, in an article written jointly, point out that the Kremlin leaders adhered to a simple logical scheme: by concentrating all the country's resources in state hands and purchasing up-to-date technology abroad, the USSR would be able to catch up rapidly on the more advanced West. This inevitably meant bureaucratic centralization and the widespread use of coercion, which imposed heavy costs and strain on the population – with consequences that determined the future shape of Soviet society.[22]

Much attention has been paid over the last fifteen years to a problem that it would have been unthinkable to write about in the Soviet era: the contribution of Gulag prisoners to economic growth. Galina Ivanova has shown that in 1929–31 a network of forced-labour camps was set up whose inmates were employed in forestry, farming, building, coal mining and oil extraction. Officially, these installations were termed 'corrective-labour camps' (ITL). The first major project was to construct the White Sea–Baltic (Belomor) canal. Here prisoners toiled for only two to three months before dropping dead from exhaustion.[23] Later Gulag labour was used in the construction of several new towns north of the Arctic circle, as well as industrial plants, railway lines and dams. Prisoners were often exposed to dangerous amounts of pollution, for instance when mining for mercury or uranium to make nuclear weapons. A number of eminent scientists and engineers who were sentenced to terms of imprisonment or exile worked in special construction bureaux and laboratories known as *sharashki*.[24] In 1949 Gulag prisoners produced 100 per cent of the Soviet Union's platinum and over 90 per cent of its gold; for other minerals the percentages were: tin over 70, copper 40, and nickel 33, while for timber it was 13 per cent. In that year, the MVD accounted for over 10 per cent of the country's gross industrial output. Ivanova makes it abundantly clear how irrational and inefficient forced labour was. Zhores Medvedev writes that the Gulag, which played a major role in carrying out the regime's plans to build the A-bomb and the H-bomb, constituted 'a unique giant reserve of highly mobile, qualified slave labour'.[25]

The results of Stalin-style modernization, an essential feature of the totalitarian order, are evident in Russia's economic and political life even today, sometimes in ways one would not expect. In 1999 I happened to tour an exhibition of Dutch masters in a New York gallery. The guide mentioned that certain works by Rembrandt had once formed part of the Hermitage collection in St Petersburg but had been sold off by the Soviet authorities in the 1930s. The 'Fordson' tractors that were bought in exchange have long since rotted away, but the Rembrandts continue to appreciate in value and are in fact priceless. This, too, is one lamentable result of Stalin's 'great leap forward'. In the name of a utopian goal, millions of citizens suffered imprisonment or worse, while works of art were exchanged for rapidly ageing technological artefacts. While the state grew more powerful, the people were reduced to beggary.

Notes

1 *Komsomol'skaia pravda*, 5, 6, 12–14, 16, 19, 20 November 2002. Zhukov is a leading researcher at the Institute of Russian History in RAN. This idea that the purges were justified by the existence of a military plot, organized by Tukhachevsky, was already put forward by V. Suvorov, *Ochishchenie: zachem Stalin obezglavil svoiu armiiu?* (Moscow: AST, 1998).

2 *Komsomol'skaia pravda*, 3 December 2002.

3 On the link see Chapter 11, p. 176.

4 I.V. Pavlova, *Stalinizm: stanovlenie mekhanizma vlasti* (Novosibirsk, 1993); idem, *Mekhanizm vlast' i stroitel'stvo sotsializma* (Novsibirsk: SO RAN, 2001), 15, 17–18; idem, 'Vlasti' i obshchestvo v SSSR v 1930-e gg.', *VI*, 2001, no. 10, 46, 53, 54; idem, 'Ponimanie stalinskoi epokhi i pozitsiia istorika', *VI*, 2001, no. 10, 5, 6, 16; idem, '1937: vybory kak mistifikatsiia, terror kak real'nost'', *VI*, 2003, no. 10, 20, 21, 36. Malia's view was presented to Russian readers in *OI*, 1999, no. 3, 139. Cf. also A.K. Sokolov, *Kurs sovetskoi istorii, 1917–1940: uchebnoe posobie dlia VUZov* (Moscow, 1999), 9, 239, 271.

5 S. Averintsev, 'Preodolenie totalitarizma kak problema: popytka orientatsii', *Novyi mir*, 2001, no. 9, 146; idem, 'Totalitarizm: lozhnyi otvet na real'nye voprosy', *Rodina*, 2002, no. 10, 122–4.

6 For more on this see R.G. Suny, 'Sotsializm, postsotsializm i normativnaia modernost': razmyshleniia ob istorii SSSR', *Ab imperio* (Kazan'), 2002, no. 2, 25.

7 Yu.S. Novopashin, 'XIV s'ezd RKP(b): sovremennyi vzgliad', *VI*, 2003, no. 7, 43, 45–7, 52.

8 V.Z. Rogovin, *Stalinskii neonep* (Moscow: Moskovskaia tipografiia, 1994); idem, *1937* (Moscow: Novosti, 1996); idem, *Partiia rasstreliannykh* (Moscow: V. Rogovin, 1997); idem, *Konets oznachaet nachalo* (Moscow: Shcherbinskaia Tip., 2002); O.V. Khlevniuk, *1937–i: Stalin, NKVD i sovetskoe obshchestvo* (Moscow: Respublika, 1992); idem, *Stalin i Ordzhonikidze: konflikty v Politburo v 30-e gg.* (Moscow: Molodaia Rossiia, 1993); idem, *Politburo: mekhanizmy politicheskoi vlasti v 1930-e gg.* (Moscow: ROSSPEN, 1996).

9 Rogovin, *Konets oznachaet nachalo*, 362, 363.

10 Khlevniuk, *Politburo*, 8, 257, 259, 260–1.

10 M. Rosliakov, *Ubiistvo Kirova: politicheskie i ugolovnye prestupleniia v 30-kh gg.: svidetel'stvo ochevidtsa* (Leningrad, 1991); A. Kirilina, *Neizvestnyi Kirov* (St Petersburg: Neva, 2001); Yu.N. Zhukov, 'Sledstvie i sudebnye protsessy po delu ob ubiistve Kirova', *VI*, 2000, no. 2, 33–51; N.A. Yefimov, 'Kakim byl podlinnyi S.M. Kirov', *VI*, 2002, no. 5, 139–44; A.I. Kozlov, *Stalin: bor'ba za vlast'* (Rostov-on-Don, 1991), 159–62; Ya.G. Rokitiansky, in *OI*, 2003, no. 4, 209–12 (review of Kirilina).

12 Khlevniuk, *Politburo*, 140; Pavlova, *Mekhanizm vlasti*, 207, 281, 304.

13 V.P. Danilov, 'K probleme al'ternativ 20-kh gg.', in G.N. Sevost'ianov *et al.* (eds), *Etot protivorechivyi XX vek* (Moscow: ROSSPEN, 2001), 219, 226.

14 A.S. Seniavskii, 'Sotsial'naia dinamika Rossii v XX v. v kontekste modernizatsii', in ibid., 284, 286.

15 V.P. Popov, 'Stalin i sovetskaia ekonomika v poslevoennye gody', *OI*, 2001, no. 3, 74, 77, 86–7.

16 O.V. Khlevniuk, 'Sovetskaia politika na rubezhe 1940–1950-kh gg. i "delo Gosplana"', *OI*, 2000, no. 3, 74, 77, 86–7; V.S. Lel'chuk, 'Vystuplenie na zasedanii "kruglogo stola": "50 let bez Stalina: nasledie stalinizma i ego vlianie na istoriiu I-oi pol. XX v."', *OI*, 2004, 1, 202–3. Cf. also Pavlova, *Mekhanizm vlasti*, 220–2; V.L. Piankevich, *Vosstanovlenie ekonomiki SSSR (seredina 1941–seredina 1950-kh gg.): istoriografiia* (St Petersburg: Nestor, 2001).

17 I.E. Zelenin, 'Byl li "kolkhoznyi neonep"?', *OI*, 1994, no. 2, 111; idem, '"Revoliutsiia sverkhu": zavershenie i tragicheskie posledstviia', *VI*, 1994, no. 10, 34–5; V.N. Zemskov, 'Sud'ba kulatskoi ssylki', *OI*, 1994, no. 1, 120–1, 138–9; V.F. Zima, 'Genrikh Yagoda i neob'iavlennaia voina s sovetskoi derevnei', *OI*, 2003, no. 4, 178, 179, 182.

See also O.M. Verzhbitskaia, *Rossiiskoe krest'ianstvo ot Stalina k Khrushchevu: seredina 40-kh–nachalo 60-kh* (Moscow, 1992); N.A. Ivnitsky, *Repressivnaia politika sovetskoi vlasti v derevne, 1928–1933* (Moscow: IRI RAN, 2000).

18 V.P. Danilov, 'Diskussiia v zapadnoi presse o golode 1932–1933 gg. i "demograficheskoi katastrofe" 30–40-kh gg. v SSSR', *VI*, 1988, no. 3, 130; idem, 'O tonal'nosti nauchnykh diskussii: otvet istoriku Robertu Konkvestu', *Moskovskie novosti*, 14 May 1989; R. Conquest, 'Svidetel'stva neochevidtsa', ibid., 26 March 1989; Yu.N. Afanas'ev *et al.* (eds), *Sovetskoe obshchestvo: vozniknovenie, razvitie, istoricheskii final* (Moscow: RGGU, 1997), vol. I, 130.

19 L.V. Alekseeva, 'Nachalo kollektivizatsii na severe Zapadnoi Sibiri', *VI*, 2004, no. 2, 146–7; Yu.V. Kostiashov, 'Na kolkoznom sobranii: shtrikhi k istorii zaseleniia Kaliningradskoi oblasti v 1946 g.', *VI*, 2003, no. 9, 132–8; V. Popov, 'Pasportnaia sistema sovetskogo krepostnichestva', *Novyi mir*, 1996, no. 6, 185–203.

20 A.S. Seniavsky, 'Tsivilizatsionnyi podkhod v izuchenii rossiiskoi istorii XX v.: nekotorye teoretiko-metodologicheskie aspekty', in A.N. Bokhanov *et al.* (eds), *Rossiia i mirovaia tsivilizatsiia* (Moscow: IRI RAN, 2000), 567, 600, 604, 609.

21 V.V. Alekseev and E.V. Alekseeva, 'Raspad SSSR v kontekste teorii modernizatsii i imperskoi evoliutsii', *OI*, 2003, no. 5, 8, 11.

22 R.U. Devis [Davies] and O.V. Khlevniuk, '"Razvernutoe nastuplenie sotsializma po vsemu frontu"', in Afanas'ev (ed.), *Sovetskoe obshchestvo*, vol. I, 167, 169–70.

23 A mass grave containing the bodies of over 500 political prisoners employed on this project was discovered recently; see *Izvestiia*, 20 September 2003.

24 In addition to A.N. Tupolev, S.P. Korolev and V.M. Petliakov, whom we have already mentioned, they included V.P. Glushko, V.M. Miasishchev, A.L. Mints, B.S. Stechkin and N.A. Timofeev-Resovsky.

25 G.M. Ivanova, *GULAG v sisteme totalitarnogo gosudarstva* (Moscow: Mosk. obshchestvennyi nauchnyi fond, 1997), 85–6, 90–1, 131, 136; Eng. trans: *Labor Camp Socialism: the Gulag in the Soviet Totalitarian System*, trans. D.J. Raleigh (Armonk, NY: Sharpe 2000); *Sovetskoe obshchestvo* (see n. 18), vol. 2, 233; S.G. Ebedzhans and M.Ya. Vazhnov, 'Proizvodstvennyi fenomen GULAGa', *VI*, 1994, no. 6, 188; N.A. Morozov and M.B. Rogachev, 'GULAG v Komi ASSR (20–50-e gg.)', *OI*, 1995, no. 2, 182–7; Zh. Medvedev, 'Stalin i atomnyi GULAG', in Zh. and R. Medvedev, *Neizvestnyi Stalin* (Moscow: Folio, 2002), 234.

4   Terror

Victims

Stalin's 'repression' (to use the common term) is the subject of a vast number of works by Russian and Western scholars, and these have in turn been critically examined by specialists in historiography.[1] These authors correctly point out that to understand this tragedy, which afflicted virtually everyone in the USSR, one has to begin by looking at the institutional machinery set up to carry out such massive crimes. The perpetrators necessarily loom large in recent Russian studies; notably, the Gulag administration and the NKVD (later MGB), of which it formed a part. (The security organs' nomenclature, as is well known, changed several times during the Soviet era.)

No reliable figure has yet been established for the total number of victims of political repression. One of the best informed researchers in this domain is A.N. Yakovlev, chairman of the official Rehabilitation commission. He states that between 1921 and 1953, according to incomplete data, 5,951,364 persons were arrested for political offences, of whom 4,060,306 were sentenced to various penalties either by regular courts or by extra-judicial tribunals (*troiki*, *dvoiki*, 'special conferences' and so on). Between 1936 and 1961, over 3.5 million individuals were repressed on national (ethnic) grounds. Within the RSFSR alone, 11 nations were deported in their entirety, while 48 suffered this penalty in part. Yakovlev estimates that during the Soviet era the total number of people who lost their lives for political reasons (that is, executed plus deaths in camps or prisons) was somewhere between 20 and 25 million (in the USSR alone). This figure includes the victims of successive famines: over 5.5 million during or just after the 1918–21 civil war plus over 5 million in the 1930s. The Soviet penal system, he notes, inflicted suffering on such a vast scale that it is hard to grasp. In the RSFSR alone, the total number of individuals convicted between 1923 and 1953 was in excess of 41 million. (This figure includes those sentenced for common crimes as well as, for example, workers who were put behind bars for being late or collective farmers who failed to earn enough 'labour days' in the 'socialist sector'.)

Yakovlev uses the term genocide for these excess deaths and indicts the CPSU élite as primarily responsible: the top leaders like Stalin and Molotov and senior police or judicial functionaries (N.I. Yezhov, L.P. Beria, A.Ya. Vyshinsky, V.V.

Ul'rikh).[2] Exactly why Stalin destroyed millions of innocent lives cannot be explained satisfactorily. As well as simple hatred of actual or potential enemies, and sheer love of power, 'an incomprehensible, mystical and devilishly sadistic element is involved'.[3] Yakovlev sees the Party officials and their counterpart in the security organs as two poles in the system, which is debatable. It must be said that the latter were also Party members who did what they were told, and even took the initiative themselves in finding ways to carry out criminal orders passed down from above – what students of German Nazism have called the phenomenon of 'working towards the Führer'. O.V. Khlevniuk has shown that during the Great Terror Yezhov's actions were directed and controlled by Stalin. The *Vozhd'* personally drafted the principal orders for the 'mass operations', supervised NKVD investigations of arrested suspects, and wrote the scenarios for the show trials. From the record of visitors to his office, we know that Yezhov called on at least 270 occasions and spent over 840 hours with the leader. And all the NKVD orders for the 'mass operations' and the major trials were endorsed by members of the Politburo.[4]

But why did Stalin in person sign execution lists and authorize torture? For that matter, why did Hitler eliminate some of his closest associates along with millions of innocent people? Answers to these simple questions must be sought in the nature of the totalitarian state. Long ago Hannah Arendt argued that communism and fascism were ideological twins: both movements mythologized their leaders, the state, the ruling party and so on; both believed in their enemies' collective guilt (for one it was the imperialists and for the other the Jews who were responsible for all ills). In the Soviet case, as V.P. Buldakov points out, this sacralization of power began already with the October revolution, when the Bolsheviks developed a thought pattern that justified whatever Authority said or did. As he puts it, 'it is no coincidence that even today a leader with thousands of victims on his conscience is not considered just a criminal but as a historical personage'.[5]

Added to this is the circumstance that in official documents and publications put out at the time great pains were taken to conceal the real nature of the punitive measures being undertaken. Instead the media were full of slogans about the need to combat 'counter-revolutionaries', 'enemies of the people' and so forth. In Soviet Russia, the regime lost no time in unleashing state terror against its opponents: already in February 1918 the Vecheka was authorized to set up *troiki* empowered to administer the death penalty without any judicial formalities. So it is wrong to distinguish between Stalin's 'Great' Terror and a relatively 'petty' one under Lenin – especially if one bears in mind that during the civil war at least 1.5 million peaceful citizens fell victim to violence by the Reds or the Whites.

I.V. Pavlova points out that whereas the earlier 'Red terror' could be explained in part by revolutionary enthusiasm and the existence of genuine adversaries, this was not the case under Stalin, when the country was at peace. The 'Great Terror' was rather a deliberate undertaking, part of Stalin's project of 'socialist construction', and the culmination of earlier waves of repression against peasants, workers and intellectuals.[6] In the opinion of V.Z. Rogovin, forced collectivization in 1928–33 was a civil war launched to conquer the rural population, while the 1937–8 terror was 'a preventive civil war against the Leninist Bolsheviks'.[7] I do not quite agree with the last phrase, since it does not properly describe the groups that were actually targeted.

The title of his book is misleading, too. 'The party of the executed' is a term originally and more accurately used of the French Communist Party (PCF), which suffered so heavily in the Resistance after 1940. Among the victims of Stalin's repressions the portion who were Bolsheviks is variously put at 116,885 and 1.2 million.[8] The casualty figures at the top level are familiar and expressive: in the CC, which had 139 full and candidate members at the XVIIth congress in 1934, 98 were dead by the time of the XVIIIth congress five years later. Of the 1,966 delegates to the former gathering, 1,108 were repressed. In Ukraine, where Khrushchev became first secretary in January 1938, only three of the 86 members of the republican Party CC survived the purges. Among former members of the all-Union Party Politburo who were shot one may mention S.V. Kosior, Ya.E. Rudzutak, and A.I. Rykov. Punitive action was taken against their families as well: among the wives jailed or exiled were those of Molotov, Kalinin, and even Stalin's loyal private secretary, A.N. Poskrebyshev.[9] Even so it is incorrect to speak of the AUCP(b) as 'the Party of the executed', as Rogovin does, chiefly because its leaders, far from resisting Stalin's tyranny, helped to build and stoke the infernal machine. Such provincial bosses (*obkomsecs*) as P.P. Postyshev and R.I. Eikhe had previously purged local Party organizations and mercilessly scourged the population; they were shot by fellow members of *their own* political party, in whose very name they had acted. The same is true of the military: Marshal V.K. Bliukher voted for the liquidation of Marshal M.N. Tukhachevsky, only to be liquidated himself shortly afterwards.

This state of affairs naturally made everyone afraid, even of close friends who might denounce them at any moment. K.B. Radek (1885–1939), known for his wit, was once sitting together with Gorky and Yezhov; raising his glass, he proposed a toast 'to our bitter reality'. The philosophical writer G.S. Pomerants, who was arrested after the war and survived the camps, wrote later that the inmates had not seen any difference of substance between Stalin and Kirov, and therefore said 'it doesn't matter which of those two serpents eats the other'. But he did pay tribute to one of his fellow inmates, O.G. Shatunovskaia, whom in 1960 Khrushchev put on the 'Shvernik commission' to investigate Kirov's assassination and to rehabilitate Stalin's victims. According to her data, during the six and a half years between 1935 and July 1941 no less than 19,840,000 people were arrested, of whom 7 million were shot. She had access to the 64 volumes of investigation records into the Kirov affair and was convinced that he was murdered by Stalin with the aid of I.V. Zaporozhets (1895–1937), a senior NKVD official whom the dictator despatched to Leningrad for that purpose.[10] Neither her version of what occurred nor her figures for the number of victims has been confirmed by later research – but they have not been conclusively disproved, either. In recent years, lists of those repressed have been published in many cities and regions, and these should be helpful in establishing the truth about the numbers of casualties.[11] One thing is already clear from the volumes that have been published: over 60 per cent of the victims were non-Party peasants.

Pavlova argues that Stalin's repressions cannot be explained by reference to any supposed 'general laws of world-historical development' but that they were deliberately devised in order to get rid of actual or potential opposition to the ruling clique. The latter claimed the credit for every success scored in 'building socialism' and attributed every shortcoming or reverse to intrigues by class enemies – in other words, disinformation was practised on a massive scale. The writer M.M. Prishvin noted in his diary (1 November 1937): 'most of all I hate *Pravda* as the embodiment of the worst lying the world has ever known.' By such mendacious means the regime succeeded in associating the mass of the population actively with the repression. At public meetings people would vote solidly in favour of the extirpation of supposed enemies. The CC plenums held in February/March and June 1937 signalled further turns of the screw. According to NKVD records that have become accessible since 1991, the number of people arrested in 1937–8 was 1,344,923, of whom 681,692 were shot.[12]

The Gulag

E.Yu. Solov'ev, in his study of the Gulag, distinguishes three phases in its history. The first, the 'Belomor canal era', was preparatory: it was then that the basis was laid for a system of 'state slavery'. In the second phase, 1936–41, the camps became sites of extensive forced labour (*superkatorga* is his term), and most prisoners were expected to remain there for life. Solov'ev contests the notion that one of the chief reasons for the camp system's extension was the need for cheap labour to promote economic development.

> The Bolshevik state needed a Zone in which people could be driven to their death daily without fear of the consequences. The millions detained there – a population the size of Switzerland's – enabled the regime to keep 140 million other Soviet people in a state of servitude or semi-servitude, so that they could be mobilized in the struggle for modernization.

The third phase in the Gulag's history began towards the end of the war, when 'it turned into a gigantic workhouse'. The profits from slave labour formed an integral part of the planned economy; in this respect Beria's rule differed from Yezhov's.[13]

Solov'ev's view of the Gulag as a system for exploiting prisoners' forced labour does not contradict Pavlova's view that its purpose was to terrorize the rest of the population, for these functions were compatible. The Gulag's main object was to ensure the regime's survival by demonstrating its limitless potential for cruelty. In the later 1940s several 'secret' cities, closed to outsiders, were set up for nuclear weapons and missile production; they were inhabited by some of the country's most qualified workers and engineers, who if not actually under arrest were prohibited from leaving the area assigned to them.

Recent years have seen publication of a number of memoirs by ex-prisoners, but in particular also reference works about the Gulag and documents that show how it functioned, both at the central and the local level.[14] As a result, we now have a much clearer idea of the geography of the 'Archipelago' (to use Alexander Solzhenitsyn's graphic term), the development of the legislative edifice that governed its workings, and the economic tasks that prisoners in various camp complexes were obliged to fulfil. Thus in 1950 the number of inmates of camps (ITL) and colonies (ITK) reached its peak: approximately 2,800,000. There were separate camps for ex-enemy prisoners of war, whose numbers declined, through death and release, from over 2 million in 1946 to 19,000 in 1953. At the end of the latter year, the prisoners in 48 of the 68 camp complexes were employed either in forestry work or in building military installations (including nuclear ones). It was not until 1960 that Stalin's Gulag was finally dismantled.[15]

Rural terror

Other recent studies have examined the impact of Stalinist repression on particular groups of the population: peasant farmers, the army, the Party, the creative intelligentsia and so on. V.P. Danilov writes that 'the exaction of "tribute" from the peasantry was the heart of agrarian policy throughout the Stalin era', and buttresses this view by pointing to the vast number of farmers arrested during collectivization (95,208 in the first year, 1929, alone). He sees the countryside as the principal target of the dictatorship, which aimed to turn peasants into 'human material' with which to build the future socialist society in conformity with the leader's grand design.[16]

Terror in the countryside reached its climax in 1937–8, according to I.E. Zelenin. The repressions unleashed by the directives of July/August 1937 led to the arrest of 248,300 people, of whom 108,100 (43 per cent) were ex-'kulaks'. Most of these – 83,600 – fell into Category I and so were shot. Zelenin agrees with the American specialists Sheila Fitzpatrick and Roberta Manning that ordinary people did not believe the central authorities' efforts to persuade them that the repressions were primarily the work of local leaders.[17]

The film *The Chairman* (1963–4: director A.A. Saltykov, screenplay by Yu.M. Nagibin) gives a realistic portrayal of the totally impoverished state of rural Russia after World War II and the inhabitants' poor morale. One of the characters in the film, a collective farmer, describes his plight as follows: 'I'm afraid of our own people and I'm afraid of outsiders, too. I'm scared of all officials and of their orders. And worst of all, I can't manage to feed my family . . . The people are tired. They've lost faith in everything.'

In the USSR, films on historical topics had a fairy-tale quality. Stalin paid a lot of attention to the cinema as a propaganda instrument and once said 'a good film is worth several divisions'. Historians of the Soviet cinema have described how the medium changed as revolutionary internationalism gave way to national Bolshevism.[18] But *The Chairman* was exceptional and gave a very different picture of village life from that portrayed, for instance, in I. Pyr'ev's fantasy *Kuban Cossacks* (1950).

The intelligentsia

Along with peasants, intellectuals were another favourite target of Soviet penal policy. They figured prominently among those falsely charged with belonging to various non-existent parties and the like at the show trials. The security organs created a vast network of informers to control creative artists and scholars, and these men often filed misleading reports about what they said or did. Such reports were sometimes forwarded by the NKVD up to Stalin for a decision. For example, in 1938 he received those compiled on several poets (Dem'ian Bednyi, Mikhail Golodnyi, Mikhail Svetlov and Iosif Utkin), which have since been published by A.N. Yakovlev.[19]

I also have published a few such documents, which give one a good idea of the way cases were cooked up against prominent people, such as the well-known opera singer S.Ya. Lemeshev in 1942. Suffering from tuberculosis in one lung, he was advised by doctors to go to Yelabuga on the river Kama, where he could relax and breathe the fresh air of the pine forests. No sooner had he arrived than the local Chekists received a wire from their superiors ordering them 'to arrange agent surveillance of Lemeshev'. The order was carried out to the letter: guards were mounted round the clock at the house where he and his wife were staying; the other tenants, and people they used to play cards with, were enrolled as secret informers (*seksoty*), who on pain of arrest had to report whatever the artist said to the local NKVD. The Chekists sought to build up a file of compromising material (*kompromat*) on Lemeshev and worked out elaborate plans how to get hold of it: for example, told that the couple were suspected of spying for the Nazis, they plotted the 'discovery' of a radio transmitter in the woods where they went for a stroll. Luckily for the Lemeshevs, they left Yelabuga before the zealous security men could put together yet another case.[20]

Much more information has become available of late about the repressive measures taken against members of particular professions such as historians, biologists, physicists, writers and artists. Whole books have been written about the tragic fate of the great theatrical director Vsevolod Meierhold, the poet Osip Mandel'shtam, the novelist Isaak Babel', and the journalist Mikhail Kol'tsov, to name but a few, as well as on a number of famous scientists.[21] A.N. Yakovlev has described, on the basis of archival materials, 'incredible facts about how world-famous individuals were tortured in special cells at the Lubianka and in Lefortovo jail' (Moscow). He also gives data on the mass execution of clergy during the Great Terror: in 1937 alone, 136,900 priests were arrested, of whom 85,300 were shot. Military men were likewise systematically victimized.

The military

From 1929 onwards, the Chekists claimed almost annually to have 'unearthed counter-revolutionary organizations' in the Red Army. Most of the alleged members were officers who had once served in the tsarist armed forces. That they had professed loyalty to the Soviets after the revolution did not save them from repression. The CC plenum of February/March 1937, and Stalin's programmatic speech of 5 March, had tragic consequences for the Red Army leadership. Seen as potential opponents of the regime, Marshal M.N. Tukhachevsky and several other senior officers were arrested and shot. And that was just the beginning: within a few weeks several tens of thousands of officers were seized, among them 16 commanders of military districts, 5 naval fleet commanders and 76 divisional commanders; of the 108-man Military Council only 10 were left by November 1938. On the eve of the German invasion, the Soviet Union's armed forces had been beheaded and rendered unfit to fight.[22]

Military historians in particular continue to debate these drastic measures and the harm they did. O.F. Suvenirov presents a veritable martyrology of the victims, whose rank ranged from marshal to private, and their families. It is clear that Stalin's main purpose was to subject the Red army to his own personal control. Whether there was indeed a 'Tukhachevsky plot' is still under discussion, but most scholars think there was not. The figure of approximately 40,000 repression victims is often cited, but the exact toll has yet to be satisfactorily established; some of those sent to prison or the Gulag survived and were later reincorporated into the army's ranks.[23]

The military purge is logically connected with the punitive measures taken against Red Army soldiers taken prisoner during the Soviet–German war who escaped only to fall into the hands of SMERSH, the military counter-intelligence outfit. Soviet sources list 4,590,000 POW, whereas the German figure is higher: 5,270,000. Additionally, over 5 million civilians were deported to the Reich. Some 2 million POW and over 1,230,000 civilian deportees met their death in enemy hands. After the war more than 1.8 million former POW and at least 3.5 million civilians were repatriated, but over 450,000 (including about 160,000 ex-POW) refused to return to the USSR. Yakovlev gives frightening figures on the wartime activities of military tribunals, which sentenced to various penalties nearly 1 million (994,000) Soviet military personnel, of whom over 157,000 were shot – the equivalent of 15 divisions. One can imagine what a considerable contribution to victory such divisions might have made had they existed and been committed to action. Most of these men were soldiers who had escaped from positions surrounded by the enemy or else from POW camps.

In 1955 civilians who had collaborated with the German occupiers, for instance by serving in police formations, were amnestied. But the ex-POW had to wait another 40 years, until January 1995, before their turn came to be granted civil rights.[24] At various junctures official sources have offered different figures for Soviet casualties in World War II. The latest estimate puts them at 38,794,000, of which military losses account for 17,774,000. There were 471,000 arrests for 'counter-revolutionary offences' (out of a total of approximately 2.5 million people sentenced). About 225,000, or over 9 per cent, of those convicted were executed.[25]

The national minorities

One aspect of Stalin's nationality policy that continues to attract attention among Russian historians is the forcible deportation of entire ethnic groups. Already in the 1930s, several peoples living close to the border (Poles, Koreans, Karelian Finns), as well as Germans and Kurds, were deemed 'politically unreliable' and moved to regions in the interior. Another foretaste of things to come was the incarceration of political emigrés, especially from Germany, Austria and Poland, who sought safety in the USSR.[26] As soon as the Soviet–German war broke out, the Volga German ASSR was liquidated and the population herded off to Siberia and Kazakhstan. Later the same fate was meted out to Kalmyks, Crimean Tatars, Chechens, Balkhars and others whose reliability was suspect, even though they had committed no offence.

The deportation of these 'punished peoples' (R. Conquest) has now been extensively studied and many relevant documents published.[27] Even after they were rehabilitated, they could not automatically return to their original area of residence. The Volga German ASSR was never re-established, with the result that many Germans emigrated to the Federal Republic; nor could the Meskhetian Turks return to Georgia, and today they are still languishing in the Krasnodar region of the Kuban'. The massacre of over 22,000 Polish officers and other citizens by the NKVD at Katyn' remained a closely guarded state secret until the late 1980s, when the truth belatedly came out.[28] Yakovlev recalls that in December 1991 Gorbachev passed on to Yeltsin a packet containing all the relevant documents, and thinks the former was wrong not to make the affair public while he was in power.[29]

Soviet propaganda extolled the equal rights allegedly enjoyed by all the peoples of the USSR, and was highly critical of national chauvinism and anti-Semitism. But the reality was very different. State-sanctioned anti-Semitism, a factor already in the 1930s, reached its apotheosis after the war with the anti-cosmopolitanism campaign and then the so-called 'doctors' plot'.[30] Jews were suspected of entertaining pro-Zionist sympathies, but they were not the only group to face charges of what was officially termed 'bourgeois nationalism'.[31]

Some Russian scholars take the view that in the long term Stalin's nationality policy was a fiasco, since ultimately all three Communist-run federal states (the USSR, Czechoslovakia and Yugoslavia) broke up.[32] Once the pertinent documents became available, a start could be made on exposing the falsifications spread by Stalinist apologists such as V.V. Karpov, who based his reasoning in part on the confessions extracted from alleged 'bourgeois nationalists'. He ran into criticism from V.P. Danilov, who pointed out that he gave no source references for his assertions, which were based solely on his imagination. In particular, Danilov demonstrated the fallaciousness of Karpov's claim that 90 per cent of repressed 'enemies of the people' were Jews, a claim that simply reflected the author's anti-Semitic prejudice. Danilov went on to provide a breakdown of the ethnic composition of the 1,420,711 individuals arrested between 1 January 1936 and 1 July 1938, at the height of the Great Terror (see Table 4.1).

Table 4.1 National composition of arrested persons,[*] 1 January 1936–1 July 1938

Nationality	Number	Percentage
Russians	657,799	46.3
Ukrainians	189,410	13.3
Poles	105,485	7.4
Germans	75,331	5.3
Belarusians	58,702	4.1
Jews	30,542	2.1
Others	303,442	21.5
Total	**1,420,711**	**100.0**

Source: V.P. Danilov, 'Stalinizm i sovetskoe obshchestvo', *VI*, 2004, no. 2, 173–5. V.V. Karpov's views are in his *Generalissimus* (Kaliningrad: Yantarnyi skos, 2002).

Note: [*] Principal categories only

The first post-Soviet scholars to analyse repression statistics were V.N. Zemskov and V.P. Popov, whose findings are still often cited. Zemskov classified those arrested according to three principal groups: people charged with 'traditional' offences like anti-Soviet agitation; peasants and SRs; and 'nationals' (that is, ethnic minorities). He was criticized for this by A.F. Stepanov, who argued that it would be better to take the type of offence for which they were sentenced, so that the second group ought to be called 'kulaks'. Zemskov effectively countered his critic by saying that, while this would certainly be the correct procedure in a *Rechtsstaat*, in the Soviet case one had to distinguish between those sentenced by regular courts and the victims of extra-judicial tribunals. Zemskov's point has been substantiated by research done recently in Kazan'.

The fate of individual victims and their families is another topic that has been increasingly studied of late. As a rule, biographers trace their subject's career from the revolution onwards and show how their initial enthusiasm for the Soviet order gave way to disenchantment. In this respect, one is reminded of Arthur Koestler, author of *Darkness at Noon*, who on returning from a visit to the USSR quoted the Old Testament passage in which Jacob discovers that his uncle Laban has substituted the ugly Leah for her beautiful sister Rachel, whom he loved, and exclaims: 'what is this thou hast done unto me? . . . Wherefore then hast thou beguiled me?' (Gen. 29:25).[33]

From the documents we also learn of people's reactions when they were suddenly arrested. Their anguish is often palpable, and some protested as best they could against this bacchanalia of terror. Take, for example, the denunciations by informers contained in records of the Tatarstan *troika* for late 1937. On 23 August 1937 this gremium examined 30 cases; 28 of the accused were shot and 2 sentenced to 10 years behind bars. Two peasant women, R. Aleeva and T. Bochkareva, were shot for making the following 'counter-revolutionary statements': 'Soviet power robs the peasants, takes their last grain and leaves them to starve' and 'I must honestly say I cannot accept the situation I have been placed in by Soviet power.'[34] It would be interesting to have a close analysis of these cases and the light they shed on the victims' psychology at this crucial moment in their lives.

Perpetrators

In recent years, a number of historians have examined the penal and judicial system under Stalin. Thus L.P. Rasskazov, in a study of the relevant legislation, highlights the role of the 'special conferences' set up within the NKVD by a decree of 10 July 1934, which were permitted to sentence political offenders extra-judicially. A later edict of 7 April 1935, as is well known, allowed children aged 12 or over to be prosecuted, and another in 1937 raised the maximum term of imprisonment from 10 years to 25.[35] Meanwhile the security organs were themselves being readied for the Terror by personnel and structural changes.

At the summit of the secret police hierarchy, as V.R. Menzhinsky's control was attenuated by illness, a struggle broke out between Yagoda's partisans, a 'north Caucasus group' around Ye.G. Yevdokimov (1891–1940) and M.P. Frinovsky (1898–1940), 'Ukrainians' under V.A. Balitsky (1892–1937), and Leningraders led by L.M. Zakovsky (1894–1938).[36] Yagoda won out, but after his dismissal (26 September 1936) his successor Yezhov was able to purge his supporters from the apparatus. Once he in turn fell from power (28 November 1938: he was not arrested until 10 June 1939), his men were liquidated by Beria. There was thus a considerable turnover of the NKVD's 'leading cadres'.

Data have now been published on the size and composition of the security police. As the number of officials at the centre increased, from 96 in 1934 to 182 at the beginning of 1941, so their average age declined. In 1937 more than half were 40 or over, but in 1939–40 most were in their early thirties. The purge also affected the NKVD's ethnic make-up: Poles, Latvians and Germans were expelled and the number of Jews declined from 37 in 1934 to 10 in early 1941. In 1938 a high proportion of the NKVD leadership had received no more than a primary education (42.6 per cent) or else were ex-inmates of children's homes (12.7 per cent). Most of those who perpetrated the Great Terror (77 per cent in 1937, 71 per cent in 1938) had joined the organization between 1917 and 1925, while it was still under Dzerzhinsky. This shows that it is wrong to draw a contrast between 'honest Chekists' of that generation and supposedly corrupted officials under Yezhov and Beria. The high liability to arrest in the 1930s made the police functionaries nervous, encouraged the practice of denunciation, and undermined patronage links. M.P. Shreider, an NKVD official convicted in 1938, later recalled that 'we old Chekists, who were fairly well informed, continued to worship Stalin and so reckoned that everything going on must be in order'. He stressed the point that at the time NKVD officials were subordinate solely to Stalin and Yezhov (later to Beria), each of whom 'by a stroke of the pen could destroy any individual in the country'. Out of the 322 men who headed NKVD administrations at republic, *oblast'* and *krai* level between July 1934 and September 1938, 241 (nearly 75 per cent) were arrested, most of them in 1938–9 after Beria had taken over.[37]

Historians of the security organs have also touched on the sort of life these officials led.[38] It is hard for us to imagine the mental state of someone who could put his signature to a list of individuals to be executed, or who actually shot an innocent person in the back of the neck with his Nagant revolver. Common to all such perpetrators was a total indifference to the value of human life; cruel and drunk with power, they gloried in their ability to turn people into 'camp dust' (*lagernaia pyl'*), as the phrase went. The 'officials for special assignments' were as a rule ill-educated thugs, and Party members to boot. For their gory deeds they were rewarded with distinctions and medals, such as 'Honoured Chekist'. Some of these characters could claim to have despatched as many as 10,000 human beings to the next world. But not all NKVD men were of this type: the organization also gave employment to skilled chemists, for instance, who worked in its poison laboratory. At the top were functionaries who reached general's rank: Yagoda actually became the equivalent of a marshal (his title was General Commissar of State Security). But their survival rate was low: S.A. Goglidze was shot in 1953, Yu.D. Sumbatov-Topuridze, arrested after Stalin's death, died in a mental home in 1960; G.S. Liushkov, who fled to Manchuria in June 1938, was killed by the Soviets in Dairen in 1945.

Before the 1990s, Western students of the security set-up had to rely mainly on press reports and the memoirs of former agents who defected, such as A. Orlov or V. Krivitsky. The documentary evidence available over the last decade or so has enlarged our knowledge considerably. Among other things, it has clearly shown that Stalin and his clique played a cardinal role in the repressions and that local Party committees exercised control over the NKVD during the Terror.[39] Students of the Soviet judicial system have also benefited from access to archival material, which has shown that the regular courts coexisted alongside, and were to some extent compromised by, the extra-judicial terror apparatus.[40]

Scholars have also noted the element of continuity in the history of the security organs. For instance, I.A. Serov (1905–90), who became KGB chairman under Khrushchev (1954–8), joined the NKVD in 1939 and worked in the central apparatus as deputy commissar for security; he was one of those who organized the 1940 Katyn' massacre as well as the deportation of Chechens and Ingush in 1944 and of Baltic peoples after the war. Many others who earned their spurs under Beria, unless they happened to be particularly close to their chief, continued their careers without hindrance in the post-Stalin era.

The Terror and Russia's collective memory

In Russia today, historians and journalists frequently ask whether the terror was historically necessary and what consequences it had. On the first point, most writers are critical of Stalin's measures, but there are also a few apologists who try to justify them: Stalin allegedly 'had to' destroy internal enemies in order to forge national unity against the external foe. But this argument is scarcely convincing: if there really had been a 'fifth column' in the USSR in the 1930s, the Great Terror failed to eliminate it, for during the war no fewer than 1.2 million

Soviet citizens collaborated with the invader one way or another, for example, by joining General A.A. Vlasov's 'Russian Liberation Army' or by serving in auxiliary police units.

But *was* there a 'fifth column'? Most military historians do not think so. Nor do they accept the argument that the purge served to eliminate older officers whose professional experience dated from the civil war and who were no longer technically up to date. This is a red herring. It is true that Marshals S.M. Budennyi and K.E. Voroshilov showed little talent for fighting in modern conditions, but officers of ability who rose to the top during the war, like Marshals G.K. Zhukov and K.K. Rokossovsky, had also served in the earlier conflict. From the late 1920s onwards, Stalin cashiered and arrested practically all the ex-tsarist officers, yet his closest military adviser, B.M. Shaposhnikov (1882–1945), had graduated from the General Staff Academy in 1910 and risen to colonel's rank before the revolution; he was the only Soviet marshal with whom the dictator was on first-name terms.[41]

Defenders of Stalin tend to be elderly men nostalgic for the 'glorious past', but some of them are youngsters who simply cannot imagine the horrors of the Gulag and suchlike. G.Kh. Popov, for example, is at heart a democrat, but he thinks that the Great Terror was organized in order to consolidate 'state socialism', and since this was historically progressive then the Great Terror must have been justified, too.[42] Such reasoning is unacceptable: state socialism turned out to be rotten at the core and eventually collapsed. This means there can be no excuse for the Terror either: it is in fact unpardonable from every point of view. In the Soviet era, its only defenders were the people responsible for it; the rest just went along with them out of fear.

Stalin's Gulag and the fascist concentration camps created a kind of 'terror-istic background' in the minds of ordinary folk, who got on with their lives as best they could, showing little initiative and convincing themselves that freedom meant fulfilling orders from above. There is as yet no serious scholarly work comparing the Soviet and Nazi experience, although the topic is a popular one. On 13 February 2003 *Izvestiia* asked its readers whether they thought the victims of each system should have the same status. Most respondents thought they should, but this poll did not lead to any concrete result – nor is it likely to.

In Russia, 30 October is set aside every year as a memorial day for victims of political repression. In many towns, the descendants of Gulag inmates make their way to a commemorative plaque, usually situated opposite former NKVD headquarters. In Kazan' I, too, go along, since my father was branded an 'enemy of the people' and severely punished. These gatherings in my experience are dismal affairs: the only people who turn up are elderly, miserable and in tatters. Usually, some minor official appears and tells us that everyone in authority would like to help us but unfortunately there isn't any money . . . and that's all. The commem-orative plaques are never turned into proper memorials and so aren't treated with respect. Our leaders are pretty indifferent and would prefer us to forget this unpleasant page of history. They are much keener on getting school textbooks rewritten so as to reflect their own view of what the collective historical memory should be about.

Students of Stalin's repressions generally pay a good deal of attention to the punitive organs responsible for carrying them out. Up to a point, this is understandable: it is certainly important to know how the state machinery functioned, and attractive to work with sensitive documents that were kept secret for so long. But there is also an uglier angle to such institutional studies, in so far as they are promoted by members of the security establishment itself. In the late 1990s a number of books were published glamorizing individual Chekists as patriots who had performed their professional duties successfully. This self-congratulatory tendency has accelerated since 2000, when V.V. Putin was elected President. His first four years in office were marked by a massive influx into senior administrative posts of people who had served in the 'power ministries' (that is, the military and police). Sociologists have calculated that their share has risen from 5 per cent in the late Soviet era to over 50 per cent today. They comprise about 70 per cent of the sizeable staffs of the central government's newly appointed regional chiefs, and their role is likely to increase further in the near future.[43] Today's security officials are anxious to cultivate a positive image of themselves and, if challenged about the NKVD's role in Stalin's repressions, say they did not have anything to do with illegal activities.

In this climate, it is only to be expected that books recently published about the Cheka and its successors take an apologetic line. They say little or nothing about the 'organs'' role in terrorizing the population, and instead make much of the losses they incurred through Stalin's purges, when allegedly 1,361 officials were discharged and 884 arrested[44] – figures that are a bit dubious. To encourage favourable historical studies of the 'organs', a series of evening meetings was held at the Lubianka, which historians of varying persuasions were invited to attend.[45]

Meanwhile, critically minded historians have not been idle. Two handbooks have appeared which provide biographical data on the leading officials and explore the institution's complex administrative history.[46] N.V. Petrov and K.V. Skorkin cast doubt on the inflated number of 'repressed Chekists' (approximately 20,000) that circulated widely at one time, which suggested that there had been massive resistance to Stalin's repressive policies within the NKVD by 'the men of Dzerzhinsky's generation'. These two scholars point out that on 1 March 1937 the organs had a total staff of about 25,000, so that it is impossible for so many of them to have been arrested. The actual number of arrests between 1933 and 1939 is 22,618; but this figure includes regular police (*militsiia*), fire brigades, border troops, Gulag guards and so on. Moreover, most of these men were charged with criminal offences or abuse of their official position (corruption). Under Yezhov, from 1 October 1936 to 15 August 1938, 2,273 NKVD men were arrested, of whom 1,862 were charged with counter-revolutionary offences. When Beria took over, 7,372 men were sacked (22.9 per cent of listed operative cadres). Of Yezhov's men 937, the most odious investigators and torturers, were arrested. Between 1953 and 1959, after Stalin was no more and Beria had fallen from power, 20 out of 182 senior officials who had been in service in early 1941 were brought to trial. They were charged with being stooges of Beria, V.S. Abakumov or M.I. Bagirov. In the

1950s there was no question of punishing the NKVD men implicated in Stalin's repressions – and that remains the case today.

What is more, in the late 1990s efforts were actually made to rehabilitate such monsters as Yezhov, Beria and Abakumov.[47] The last-named, head of the MGB (State Security ministry) from 1946 to 1951, was tried in Leningrad on 19 December 1954 and shot immediately thereafter. In 1994 the case was re-opened and the Military Collegium of the Russian Supreme Court partially rehabilitated him. He was acquitted of the charge of treason and so no longer officially classed as a state criminal. In December 1997 the Presidium of the Supreme Court reduced his sentence from death to 25 years' deprivation of liberty.

On 4–5 June 1998 *Izvestiia* reported that Yezhov's case had been reviewed. After a one-day closed hearing, he had been shot on 4 February 1940, in a cellar on Nikol'skaia street in Moscow. The Military Collegium now decided, after hearing a statement by the Procuracy, that Yezhov's crimes were so immense that he should not be rehabilitated, but the charges of espionage and conspiracy to kill Stalin were dropped.

Finally, on 30 May 2000 *Izvestiia* carried a notice that the Military Collegium had partially rehabilitated three of Beria's close associates: Pavel Meshik and Vladimir Dekanozov, who were Internal Affairs ministers in Ukraine and Georgia respectively, and Lev Vlodzimirsky, head of the investigation department for specially important cases. They too were acquitted of the charges of espionage and terrorism. Instead their offence was described as 'abuse of power and of official position with serious consequences'. Beria, who had been put to death on 23 December 1953 (in an underground bunker of Moscow military district, by General P.F. Batitsky), was *not* rehabilitated.

During Gorbachev's *perestroika* in the late 1980s, the media often touched on the problem of responsibility for Stalinism. *Repentance* (1987), a film by Tengiz Abuladze (1924–94), was shown to mass audiences. After the attempted *coup* of August 1991, President Yeltsin of Russia issued decrees banning the CPSU and dissolving its organizations. The Constitutional Court sat in judgement on the former ruling party. But its proceedings soon turned into a farce. The CPSU was not convicted and prohibited, as the Nazi party had been in post-1945 Germany; none of its leaders had to stand trial; and former Communist functionaries easily managed to recreate their party under a new name, the KPRF. Its leaders continue to participate in national politics and in presidential elections its candidate usually comes second.

Rehabilitation: legal aspects

Contemporary Russian law does not specify who should be considered a criminal guilty of crimes against the people – which is why there have been efforts to rehabilitate the NKVD chiefs, as we have just mentioned. Indeed, at first glance there would appear to be good legal grounds for such appeals. On 4 February 1988 the USSR Supreme Court, meeting in plenary session, decided to rehabilitate N.I. Bukharin, A.I. Rykov and all the others convicted in the last great show trial, held almost 50 years earlier – except for G.G. Yagoda. Why? At that trial Yagoda, along with his fellow accused, was charged with having organized Kirov's assassination, killed Gorky, Menzhinsky and Kuibyshev, and attempted to murder Yezhov. Reviewing this case, the Procuracy had no trouble in proving that the accused had been tortured and their evidence tampered with, and noted that in 1939–40 the NKVD investigators responsible (Yezhov, Frinovsky, Ushakov and others) had themselves been convicted of crude dereliction of duty. The Supreme Court ruled that none of the accused had been in contact with foreign intelligence services or had conspired to commit terrorist acts. So naturally the questions arise: why did not the court rehabilitate Yagoda? Why did it not go on to rehabilitate the later NKVD chiefs? After all, they too had neither engaged in espionage nor plotted to kill Stalin. This is why some jurists and historians (such as O.V. Khlevniuk) have suggested that the charges levelled against Beria, for instance, should be amended. For did he not push through several liberal measures after Stalin's death?[48]

I am convinced, however, that there are no legal grounds at all for rehabilitating the Soviet-era secret police chiefs, just as there are none for revising the judgements at Nuremberg. In neither case should a statute of limitations apply. All these men were responsible for horrendous criminal acts (authorizing extra-judicial procedure, legalizing torture and so forth) covered by Article 58 of the penal code and by the principle of so-called 'socialist legality'. Although Beria purged Yezhov's men from the NKVD for infringing this principle, he himself invoked it when he subsequently killed or imprisoned millions of innocent citizens.

The RSFSR law of 18 October 1991 on 'the rehabilitation of victims of political repression' does not clarify the legal situation. The relevant article states simply that individuals 'who have committed offences against justice' are not to be rehabilitated.[49] But *which* justice? The crimes committed under Stalin were carried out in accordance with 'socialist legality', and so it is *this* principle that needs to be repudiated; in other words, the court needs to issue a formal declaration to the effect that the USSR was no *Rechtsstaat*. During the Terror, police and judicial officials carried out their duties in accordance with the will of Stalin and the Party CC. Each of these officials bears a specific degree of responsibility for his actions. The rehabilitation procedure instituted in the 1950s, and taken up again in the 1980s, did not go far enough and left a legal vacuum. Only once the Soviet regime itself has been indicted as criminal can one go on to judge those who committed crimes in its name; only then can a court decide which of them might qualify for rehabilitation.

According to *Izvestiia* of 18 January 2003, by the year's end the chief Military Procurator intended to complete his review of the cases of all victims of political repression in the 1930s and 1940s. During 2002, it was stated, his office had reviewed the cases of over 47,000 'enemies of the people', of whom 17,706 had been rehabilitated; but in 41,057 cases this had been refused – mainly because the accused had collaborated with the occupation authorities during the war. The evidence against Beria, in 39 folders, is still secret. But a number of other notorious killers, such as M.D. Berman (1898–1939), who for many years administered the

Gulag camps, and S.F. Redens (1892–1940), who headed the NKVD department for Moscow *oblast'* in 1934–8, have been posthumously rehabilitated. This has led to protests by former political prisoners, who have said that they have no wish for their rehabilitation claims to be handled in the same way as those of leading NKVD officials.[50]

The undeserved rehabilitation of these men has given a fillip to irresponsible white-washing of the Stalin era and of the NKVD's role in it. One writer even goes so far as to call the Gulag 'a devilish product of Russo-Jewish bolshevism'.[51] As we have seen, popular journals have published interviews with people who met Stalin and praised him extravagantly. But the lessons of the Terror should never be forgotten, nor should the guilt of those who perpetrated it. We have certainly come a long way in understanding the phenomenon, but what we really need is a multi-volume scholarly history of the Gulag as well as of the security organs as a whole.

Notes

1 A.L. Litvin, 'Rossiiskaia istoriografiia Bol'shogo terrora', in L.V. Stoliarova *et al.* (comps), S.O. Shmidt (ed.), *U istochnika: sbornik statei v chest'... S.M. Kashtanova* (Moscow: MPU Signal, 1997), pt 2, 546–75; A.S. Kan, 'Postsovetskie issledovaniia o politicheskikh repressiiakh v Rossii i SSSR', *OI*, 2003, no. 1, 120–33; S. Wheatcroft, 'The Scale and Nature of German and Soviet Repression and Mass Killings, 1930–1945', *EAS* 48 (1996), 1319–53; idem, 'Victims of Stalinism and the Soviet Secret Police...', *EAS* 51 (1999), 315–45 and 52 (2000), 1143–59; M. Ellman, 'Soviet Repression Statistics: Some Comments', *EAS* 54 (2002), 1151–72; J. Keep, 'Stalinism in Post-Soviet Historical Writing', in K. McDermott and J. Morison (eds), *Politics and Society under the Bolsheviks: Selected Papers from the Vth World Congress of Central and East European Studies, Warsaw, 1995* (Basingstoke and New York: Macmillan, 1999), 102–39; idem, 'Recent Writing on Stalin's Gulag: An Overview', *Crime, History, Societies* 1 (Paris, 1997), 2, 91–112.

2 A.N. Yakovlev, *Sumerki* (Moscow: Materik, 2003), 26, 217–22. V.V. Ul'rikh (1888–1951) was chairman of the Military Collegium of the USSR Supreme Court during the purges.

3 Ibid., 26, 222.

4 O.V. Khlevniuk, *Politburo: mekhanizmy politicheskoi vlasti v 1930-e gg.* (Moscow: ROSSPEN, 1996) 207–8. On the 'mass operations' see Chapter 11, p. 177.

5 V.P. Buldakov, *Krasnaia smuta: priroda i posledstviia revoliutsionnogo nasiliia* (Moscow: ROSSPEN, 1997), 244.

6 I.V. Pavlova, *Mekhanizm vlasti i stroitel'stvo stalinskogo sotsializma* (Novosibirsk: SO RAN, 2001), 269, 308.

7 V.Z. Rogovin, *1937* (Moscow: Novosti, 1996), 17–18.

8 Idem, *Partiia rasstreliannykh* (Moscow: Novosti, 1997), 487–8.

9 Pavlova, *Mekhanizm*, 251–2.

10 S.G. Pomerants, 'Gosudarstvennaia taina pensionerki', *Novyi mir*, 2002, no. 5, 142–3.

11 See, for example, A. Artizov *et al.* (comps), *Reabilitatsiia: kak eto bylo: dokumenty Prezidiuma TsK KPSS i drugie materialy* (Moscow: Demokratiia, 2000), vol. 1, *mart 1953 – fevral' 1956*; *Martirolog Bashkortostana* (Ufa, 1999), 2 vols; *'Belaia kniga' Samarskoi oblasti* (Samara: Samarskii dom pechati, 1997–2003), 19 vols; A.V. Semenov *et al.* (eds), *Zabveniiu ne podlezhit: kniga pamiati zhertv politicheskikh repressii Omskoi oblasti* (Omsk: Omskoe knizhnoe izd., 2000–2), 4 vols; Yu.A. Shestov *et al.* (eds), *Ne predavat' zabveniiu: kniga pamiati zhertv politicheskikh repressii* (Pskov, 1998), 5 vols to 1998. In 2002 in the republic of Tatarstan,

4,104 individuals were rehabilitated and 1,335 persons were recognized as victims of political repression.

12   Pavlova, *Mekhanizm*, 267, 287, 290, 301, 310, 317–24, 330.

13   E.Yu. Solov'ev, 'Pereosmyslenie Taliona: karatel'naia spravedlivost' i iuridicheskii gumanizm', *Novyi mir*, 2004, no. 1, 132–4.

14   U. Riutta and I. Togi, *Osuzhdennyi po 58-i stat'e: istoriia cheloveka, proshedshego ural'skie lageria* (St Petersburg: Bibliia dlia vsekh, 2001); A. Biriukov, *Kolymskoe triedinstvo, ch. 1: Poslednyi Riurikovich* [i.e., Prince D.P. Sviatopolk-Mirsky] (Magadan: Maobti, 2000); M.B. Smirnov *et al.* (eds), *Sistema ispravitel'no-trudovykh lagerei v SSSR, 1923–1960: spravochnik* (Moscow: Zven'ia, 1998); A.I. Kokurin and N.V. Petrov (comps), *GULAG (Glavnoe upravlenie lagerei), 1918–1960: dokumenty* (Moscow: Demokratiia, 2002); Yu.A. Brodsky, *Solovki: dvadtsat' let Osobogo Naznacheniia* (Moscow, 2002); S.A. Papkov, *Stalinskii terror v Sibiri, 1928–1941* (Novosibirsk, 1997); N.M. Yakovlev, 'Zhertvy stalinskikh repressii v Iakutii', *VI*, 2003, no. 12, 122–8.

15   Smirnov *et al.*, *Sistema*, 51, 54, 59, 62; cf. also L. Sitko, 'Dubrovlag pri Khrushcheve', *Novyi mir*, 1997, no. 10, 142–66; *Istoriia politicheskikh repressii i soprotivleniia nesvobode v SSSR: kniga dlia uchitelia* (Moscow: Mosgorarkhiv, 2002).

16   V.P. Danilov, 'Stalinizm i sovetskoe obshchestvo', *VI*, 2004, no. 2, 171–3.

17   I.E. Zelenin, 'Kul'minatsiia "Bol'shogo terrora" v derevne: zigzagi agrarnoi politiki, 1937–1938 gg.', *OI*, 2004, no. 1, 176–7. Fitzpatrick's article of 1993, 'How the Mice Buried the Cat', was published in *Sud'by rossiiskogo krest'ianstva* (Moscow: RGGU, 1996); R. Manning, *Bel'skii raion, 1937 god*, trans. from English by E.V. Kodina (Smolensk: SGPU,1998).

18   T.M. Dimoni, '"Predsedatel'": sud'by poslevoennoi derevni v kinokartine I-oi poloviny 1960-kh gg.' and V.E. Bagdasarian, 'Obraz vraga v istoricheskikh fil'makh 1930-kh – 1940–kh gg.', *OI*, 2003, no. 6, 31, 33, 44, 93.

19   Yakovlev, *Sumerki*, 165–73.

20   A.L. Litvin, *Bez prava na mysl': istoriki v epokhu Bol'shogo terrora: ocherki sudeb* (Kazan': Tatknigoizdat, 1994); idem, 'Sudebnyi protsess nad nesushchestvuiushchei partiei', in idem (ed.), *Men'shevistskii protsess 1931 g.: sbornik dokumentov v 2-kh kn.* (Moscow: ROSSPEN, 1999), vol. I, 3–36; idem, 'Dos'e na artista', *Rodina*, 1993, no. 4, 74–7.

21   V. Fradkin, *Delo Kol'tsova* (Moscow: Vagrius, 2002): M.G. Yaroshevsky (ed.), *Repressirovannaia nauka* (Leningrad: Nauka, 1991); V.A. Kumanev (ed.), *Tragicheskie sud'by: repressirovannye uchenye AN SSSR* (Moscow: Nauka, 1991); V.N. Soifer, *Vlast' i nauka: razgrom kommunistami genetiki v SSSR* (Moscow: CheRo, 2002); M. Heinemann and E.I. Kolchinsky, *Za 'zheleznym zanavesom': mify i realii sovetskoi nauki* (St Petersburg: Dm. Bulanin, 2002): S.E. Shnol', *Geroi i zlodei rossiiskoi nauki* (Moscow: Kron-press, 1997). An English translation (by L. and R. Gruliow) of an earlier work by Soifer was *Lysenko and the Tragedy of Soviet Science* (New Brunswick, NJ: Rutgers University Press, 1994).

22   Yakovlev, *Sumerki*, 174, 185, 187–96.

23   O.F. Suvenirov, *Tragediia RKKA, 1937–1938* (Moscow: Terra, 1998); M.I. Mel'tiukhov, 'Repressii v Krasnoi armii: itogi noveishikh issledovanii', *OI*, 1997, no. 5, 109–21; Ye.G. Plimak and V.S. Antonov, 'Taina "zagovora Tukhachevskogo"', *OI*, 1998, no. 4, 123–8; V. Suvorov, *Ochishchenie: zachem Stalin obezglavil svoiu armiiu?* (Moscow: AST, 1998); 'Tak byl li "zagovor Tukhachevskogo"?', *OI*, 1999, no. 1, 176–86; M.A. Tumshis and A.A. Papchinsky, 'Pravda i lozh' A. Orlova', *OI*, 1999, no. 6, 179–82; I.I. Gol'dfain, 'Dvusmyslennye chisla', *VI*, 2002, no. 6, 170–3.

24   Yakovlev, *Sumerki*, 197–201; see also 'Nezakonchennoe srazhenie marshala Zhukova: o reabilitatsii sovetskikh voennoplennykh, 1954–1956 gg.', *IA*, 1995, no. 2, 108–25; A.G. Bezverkhiy *et al.* (eds), *SMERSH: istoricheskie ocherki i arkhivnye dokumenty* (Moscow: Glavarkhiv g. Moskvy, 2003).

25   A.I. Muranov and V.E. Zvegintsev, *Dos'e na marshala* (Moscow: Andreevskii flag, 1999), 134; V.G. Pervyshin, 'Liudskie poteri v Velikoi Otechestvennoi voine', *VI*, 2000, no. 7,

121–2; A.S. Kan, 'Postsovetskie issledovaniia o politicheskikh repressiiakh v Rossii i SSSR', *OI*, 2003, no. 1, 129.

26 M.M. Panteleev, 'Repressii v Kominterne (1937–1938 gg.)', *OI*, 1996, no. 6, 161–8; W.J. Chase, *Enemies Within the Gates? The Comintern and the Stalinist Repression, 1934–1939*, Russian documents trans. V.A. Staklo (New Haven, CT and London: Yale University Press, 2002).

27 For example, O.L. Milova (comp.), *Deportatsii narodov SSSR (1930–1950-e gg.)*, 2 pts (Moscow: Institut etnologii i antropologii RAN 1992–5); *Repressirovannye narody Rossii: chechentsy i ingushi: dokumenty, akty, kommentarii* (Moscow, 1994); A.I. Osmanov *et al.* (eds), *Repressii 30-kh gg. v Dagestane: dokumenty i materialy* (Makhachkala: Jupiter, 1997); A.E. Gur'ianov (comp.), *Repressii protiv poliakov i pol'skikh grazhdan* (Moscow: Zven'ia, 1997); *Repressii protiv rossiiskikh nemtsev* (Moscow, 1998).

28 R.G. Pikhoia *et al.* (eds), *Katyn': plenniki neob'iavlennoi voiny: dokumenty i materialy* (Moscow: Demokratiia, 1997); I.S. Yazhborovskaia *et al.*, *Katynskii sindrom v sovetsko–pol'skikh i rossiisko–pol'skikh otnosheniiakh* (Moscow: ROSSPEN, 2001); V.D. Oskotsky, 'Katyn'–imia naritsatel'noe', *VI*, 2003, no. 6, 94–107.

29 Yakovlev, *Sumerki*, 419.

30 G.V. Kostyrchenko, *Tainaia politika Stalina: vlast' i antisemitizm* (Moscow: Mezhdunarodnye otnosheniia, 2001); I.A. Al'tman, *Zhertvy nenavisti: Kholokost v SSSR, 1941–1945 gg.* (Moscow: fond Kovcheg, 2002).

31 H. Kuromiya, 'Stalinski "velikii perelom" i protsess nad "Soiuzom osvobozhdeniia Ukrainy"', *OI*, 1994, no. 1, 190–7; B.F. Sultanbekov, *Stalin i 'tatarskii sled'*, Kazan': Tatknigoizdat, 1995); E.Yu. Zubkova, 'Fenomen "mestnogo natsionalizma": "estonskoe delo" 1949–1952 gg. v kontekste sovetizatsii Baltiki", *OI*, 2001, no.3, 89–102; E.Yu. Borisenok, 'Ukreplenie stalinskoi diktatury i povorot v natsional'noi politike na Ukraine, 1930-e gg.', *OI*, 2003, no. 1, 152–70.

32 O.G. Bukhovets,'Klio na poroge XXI veka: iskushenie natsionalizmom . . . ', *VI*, 2002, no. 3, 148.

33 A. Zuskina-Perel'man, *Puteshestvie Veniamina: razmyshleniia o zhizni i sud'be evreiskogo aktera Veniamina Zuskina* (Moscow: Mosty kul'tury and Jerusalem: Gesharim, 2002); N. and M. Ulanovskaia, *Istoriia odnoi sem'i: memuary* (St Petersburg: Inapress, 2003); A. Koestler, 'Avtobiografiia (fragmenty knigi)', *Inostrannaia literatura*, 2002, nos. 7, 8.

34 Arkhiv KGB Tatarii (now Upravleniia FSB RF po Respublike Tatarstan), f. 109, op. 2, t. 108, ll. 1, 34.

35 L.P. Rasskazov, *Karatel'nye organy v protsesse formirovaniia i funktsionirovaniia administrativno-komandnoi sistemy v sovetskom gosudarstve, 1917–1941 gg.* (Ufa, 1994), 231–305, 306–20.

36 A. Papchinsky, 'Repressii v organakh NKVD v seredine 30-kh gg.', in *Politicheskii sysk v Rossii: istoriia i sovremennost': sbornik* (St Petersburg: Sankt-peterburgskii gosudarstvennyi universitet, 1997), 284–94.

37 N.V. Petrov and K.V. Skorkin, *Kto rukovodil NKVD: 1934–1941: spravochnik* (Moscow: Zven'ia, 1999).

38 E. Lukin, *Na palachakh krovi net: tipy i nravy Leningradskogo NKVD* (St Petersburg: Bibliopolis, 1996); A.G. Tepliakov, 'Personal i povsednevnost' Novosibirskogo UNKVD v 1936–1946', *Minuvshee: istoricheskii al'manakh* (Moscow and St Petersburg, 1997), vol. 21, 240–93; V.A. Bobrenev, *'Doktor smert' ili varsonofevskie prizraki* (Moscow: Olimp, 1997); B. Sopel'nik, 'Professiia ubivat': palachi stalinskoi epokhi', *Rodina*, 2003, no. 9, 66–9.

39 V.N. Khaustov, *Deiatel'nost' organov gosudarstvennoi bezopasnosti NKVD SSSR v predvoennye gody, 1934–1941 gg.* Thesis abstract (Moscow, 1998).

40 A.I. Muranov and V.E. Zviagintsev, *Sud nad sud'iami: osobaia papka Ul'rikha* (Kazan', 1993); M. Delagrammatik, 'Voennye tribunaly za rabotoi', *Novyi mir*, 1997, no. 6, 130–58; "'Neobkhodimo imet' avtoritetnoe ukazanie TsK . . . '": o sudoproizvodstve glazami narkomov', *Istochnik*, 1999, no. 5, 120–7; I.V. Govorov, 'Sovetskoe

gosudarstvo i prestupnyi mir, 1920-e gg.—1940-e gg.', *VI*, 2003, no. 11, 143–52; P.H. Solomon Jr., *Soviet Criminal Justice under Stalin* (Cambridge: Cambridge University Press, 1996; Russian trans: Moscow: ROSSPEN, 1998).

41 Shaposhnikov served as chief of the general staff from 1937 to 1940 and again during the first 10 months of the Soviet–German war. A story circulates among his admirers in the army as to how Stalin once rang him up in his office at 7 p.m. and asked why he was still at work. When he replied that he still had a lot to do, Stalin told him: 'You're chief of the general staff. You shouldn't spend more than four hours a day in your office. The rest of the time you should stay at home, lie down on your sofa, and think about the next war.'

42 G.Kh. Popov, 'Tridtsat' sed'moi god, ili materializatsiia prizraka', *Moskovskii komsomolets*, 2 August 2002.

43 *Izvestiia*, 16 March 2004.

44 V.A. Sobolev *et al.* (eds), *Lubianka 2: iz istorii otechestvennoi kontrrazvedki* (Moscow: Mosgorakhiv, 1999), 203. See also A. Dienko (comp.), *Razvedka i kontrrazvedka v litsakh: entsiklopedicheskii slovar' rossiiskikh spetssluzhb* (Moscow: Russkii mir, 2002); L.M. Mlechin, *Predsedateli KGB: rassekrechennye sud'by* (Moscow: Tsentrpoligraf, 1999); P.A. Sudoplatov, *Spetsoperatsii: Lubianka i Kreml', 1930–1950-kh gg.* (Moscow: Olma-press, 1997); A.P. Sudoplatov, *Tainaia zhizn' generala Sudoplatova: pravda i vymysly o moem ottse*, 2 bks (Moscow: Olma-press, 1998); A.A. Papchinsky and S.V. Tumshis, *Shchit, rakolotyi mechom: NKVD protiv VChK* (Moscow: Sovremennik, 2001); V.I. Berezhkov and S.V. Pekhtereva, *Zhenshchiny–chekisty* (Moscow: Olma-press, 2003).

45 They were known as 'Historical Evenings at the Lubianka'. See *Rossiiskie spetssluzhby: istoriia i sovremennost': materialy istoricheskikh chtenii na Lubianke 1997–2000 gg.* (Moscow, 2003).

46 Petrov and Skorkin, *Kto rukovodil NKVD*, 501–2; A.I. Kokurin and N.V. Petrov (comps), *Lubianka: organy VChK-OGPU-NKVD-NKGB-MGB-MVD-KGB, 1917–1991: spravochnik* (Moscow: Materik, 2003).

47 On these men, see B.V. Sokolov, *Narkomy strakha: Yagoda, Yezov, Beriia, Abakumov* (Moscow: AST-press-kniga, 2001); K.A. Stoliarov, *Palachi i zhertvy* (Moscow: Olma-press, 1997); M.M. Poliansky, *Narkom Yagoda* (Moscow: Veche, 2002); A.I. Poliansky, *Yezhov: istoriia stalinskogo 'zheleznogo' narkoma* (Moscow: Veche, 2003); A. Knight, *Beria: Stalin's First Lieutenant* (Princeton, NJ.: Princeton University Press, 1993); M. Jansen and N. Petrov, *Stalin's Loyal Executioner: People's Commissar Nikolai Ezhov, 1895–1940* (Stanford, CA: Hoover Institution Press, 2002) and Chapter 11, n. 44–50.

48 O.V. Khlevniuk, 'L.P. Beriia: predely istoricheskoi "reabilitatsii"', in G.A. Bordiugov (ed.), *Istoricheskie issledovaniia v Rossii: tendentsii poslednikh let* (Moscow: AIRO-XX, 1996); cf. Knight, *Beria*, 9.

49 E.A. Zaitsev (comp.), *Sbornik zakonodatel'nykh i normativnykh aktov o repressiiakh i reabiltitatsii zhertv politicheskikh repressii* (Moscow: Respublika, 1993), 196.

50 D. Litovkin, 'V reabilitatsii otkazano', *Izvestiia*, 18 January 2003 (the 47,000 figure should presumably be 57,000?); S. Grigoriants, 'Ne mogu byt'' v odnom riadu s ubiitsei', *Izvestiia*, 13 July 1993.

51 R. Balandin and S. Mironov, *'Klubok' vokrug Stalina: zagovory i bor'ba za vlast' v 1930-e gg.* (Moscow: Veche, 2002), 379; cf. N.G. Sysoev, *Zhandarmy i chekisty: ot Benkendorfa do Yagody* (Moscow: Veche, 2002); V.S. Zhukovsky, *Lubianskaia imperiia NKVD, 1937–1939* (Moscow: Veche, 2001).

5 Foreign policy

The Nazi–Soviet pact

Post-Soviet research on Stalin's foreign policy has focused on two main problems: the Nazi–Soviet agreements of August–September 1939 and the origins of the Cold War. During the 1990s, certain documents came into the public domain that had previously been thought lost or non-existent: notably, the secret protocols to the non-aggression pact of 23 August 1939 and the text of the friendship treaty concluded one month later, on 28 September. Molotov, who was people's commissar for Foreign Affairs at the time, denied that any such documents existed. On 29 April 1983, he was interviewed by the journalist F. Chuev, and the dialogue went like this:

> CHUEV: 'In the West they keep on writing that some secret agreement was concluded along with the pact in 1939.'
> MOLOTOV: 'There wasn't one.'
> 'There wasn't one?'
> 'No, it's absurd.'
> 'But surely now one can talk about it.'
> 'Of course, there are no secrets about the matter. In my view rumours are being put about to soften us up, as they say. No, no, in any case I think everything that happened was entirely above board and there couldn't have been any such agreement. After all, I was very close to things, indeed I was in charge, and I can state firmly that this is certainly a fiction.'[1]

Another witness, A.N. Yakovlev, records that 'Boris Yeltsin once rang me up and said that the "secret protocols" everyone had been looking for were in the Presidential archive and that Gorbachev knew about this . . . I was dumbfounded by the discovery.' His reaction is not surprising, for in 1989 Yakovlev himself had been in charge of the foreign policy commission of the Party CC, which had declared that the pact conformed to international legal norms and condemned the 'secret protocols' for dividing up European territory in such arbitrary fashion. Gorbachev and Yakovlev assured delegates to the 1989 Congress of People's Deputies that the originals of the protocols did not exist.[2]

But even after the original documents had been found and published, some Russian historians still argued that the Soviet leadership had been justified in signing the secret protocols. Some of them repeated the old Soviet argument that, even though the pact had been imposed by Germany on the USSR, it was a perfectly natural agreement for which there had been good diplomatic grounds, and it had been economically advantageous, too.[3] L.N. Nezhinsky went on to justify Hitler's and Stalin's 're-arrangement' of territory: he argued that after 1917 Russia had lost much territory (Finland, the Baltic provinces, eastern Poland and Bessarabia) and now had a chance to get it back, and even to extend the Soviet borders. He wrote that 'the successes of Stalin's diplomacy' had resulted in 'territorial accretions' and eliminated a 'historic injustice'.[4]

A rather similar line is taken by M.I. Mel'tiukhov: the Soviet–German treaty resolved the diplomatic tug of war between Britain and Germany to draw the USSR into a settlement of European problems. Moscow had managed to stay out of the war and won freedom of action in eastern Europe.[5] At first glance, there may seem to be something to be said in favour of this interpretation. Certainly, Soviet–German relations were mutually beneficial between September 1939 and May 1940: Germany was able to escape the Allied blockade by importing foodstuffs and raw materials from the USSR, while the Soviets got back territory that had once formed part of the Russian empire. But as G.A. Kumanev points out,

> The non-aggression pact of 23 August 1939 itself was in complete conformity with diplomatic norms . . . [but] the secret protocols to the pact are an entirely different matter, as are the secret clauses of the follow-up agreement on friendship and frontiers signed on 28 September 1939. The conclusion of these agreements with Hitlerite Germany can in no way be explained or justified satisfactorily.[6]

It is perfectly clear that, by invading and occupying independent states, the Soviet Union associated itself with Nazi Germany in aggression. It cannot escape its guilt for carrying out a repressive policy in the territories it occupied: from 17 September 1939 to 22 June 1941 over 400,000 people were arrested and deported from the eastern Polish lands which the USSR had annexed, equivalent to 3 per cent of the population: moreover, as is well known, there was collusion between the NKVD and the Gestapo. (The same things happened in the Baltic states later.) As S.Z. Sluch writes, the Red Army's entry into Poland on 17 September 1939 was no different from Hitler's so-called 'police action' two weeks earlier. He goes on to say that the Nazi and Soviet leaders shared common political and military aims in partitioning Poland. The Soviets deployed a large armed force of over 466,000 men with about 4,000 tanks, 2,000 aircraft and 5,500 artillery pieces, and these troops joined with Wehrmacht units in finishing off the Polish army, which was bravely resisting the invader.

The relevant provisions of the treaty of friendship that was concluded on 28 September 1939 established legal equality between the two aggressors. Sluch notes that in the last four months of that year the two powers maintained contact at an unprecedented level of intensity. The German ambassador in Moscow, Count von der Schulenburg, met leading officials on 59 occasions: Stalin and Molotov together four times, and Molotov alone 44 times. The German military command sent various requests to its Soviet counterpart; for example, to station a weather ship in the Atlantic off the British Isles for two months, 'to make it easier to organize flights from the west' against the UK. During the 'phoney war' period, the USSR was actively supporting German military activities against Britain and France.

Sluch gives a detailed analysis of a speech that Stalin is said to have made at a secret session of the Politburo on 19 August 1939, when he allegedly spoke of the leadership's hope of exploiting the forthcoming war between Germany and the Western allies to revolutionize the European continent. On the basis of this speech, several Russian and Western historians have claimed that 19 August 1939 should be regarded as the real date of the USSR's entry into World War II. However, Sluch's analysis shows that there was no such speech: the texts of it are forgeries. Even so, we have other evidence (such as Dimitrov's record of remarks by Stalin in the same sense); it cannot be denied that the USSR's foreign policy in 1939–41 was expansionist, and drew the country indirectly into the war long before the German invasion on 22 June 1941 – though this does not controvert the established view that it was the Nazis who were responsible for the outbreak of the Soviet–German war of 1941–5.[7]

This standpoint, which many Russian historians endorse, is best expressed by M.I. Semiriaga:

> The assertion that the USSR and Germany were equally responsible for unleashing World War II because they both had totalitarian regimes is not plausible. The chief responsibility for this international crime lies with the Nazi leaders. The Soviet leaders bear a share of the responsibility in that, by signing the non-aggression pact, they created certain conditions which contributed to the outbreak of war . . . [between the Western powers and] Hitler.[8]

This discussion of who was to blame for the war was set in motion, with explosive force, by the publication of works by 'V. Suvorov', the pen name of V.B. Rezun, an intelligence (GRU) agent of the Soviet general staff who defected to Britain. It was he who put into circulation the theory that Stalin was preparing to launch a 'preventive strike' against Germany, to be delivered on 6 July 1941.[9] This earned him vociferous criticism, not least from partisans of the traditional Soviet interpretation of events, and obliged historians to examine closely the evidence on which his claim rested.[10]

This research confirmed what had previously been known about Soviet–German military co-operation during the Weimar republic,[11] but no documentary evidence was found to buttress the 1941 'preventive strike' theory. On the contrary, the materials published of late show rather that the Stalinist leadership was unable to avert a German attack or to prepare the country to face one. Stalin and Molotov were guilty of a gigantic strategic miscalculation that would lead to a national catastrophe and cost several tens of millions of lives, even though victory was achieved in the end.

Historians in Russia today no longer subscribe to the Soviet myth that the invasion was a 'surprise attack' on the USSR. They know that Hitler's decision to invade was taken on 22 July 1940 and that his generals had got 'Operation Barbarossa' ready by the end of that year. Naturally, the Soviet leadership learned many details of these war preparations, not least through its intelligence agents abroad.[12] But for a variety of reasons, chief among which was Stalin's confident belief that Hitler would not attack the USSR until he had dealt with Britain, the necessary measures to strengthen border defences were not taken.

Moreover, after Stalin's rather aggressive speech to military academy graduates on 5 May 1941, Defence commissar S.K. Timoshenko (1895–1970) and chief of general staff G.K. Zhukov (1896–1974) worked out a plan for putting the army on to a war footing and striking a preventive blow against the German forces in Poland – only to find that Stalin was mightily angry with them. When the two generals referred to his speech of 5 May, he told them cynically (according to Zhukov's account): 'I just said this to encourage those present to think of victory instead of saying the German army is invincible.' By turning down the military leaders' plans for a preventive strike, Stalin tied their hands. M.I. Mel'tiukhov casts doubt on Zhukov's story about Stalin preparing a preventive strike in 1941 and argues that he actually did so as early as 1940, and that Zhukov deliberately confused the date when in 1965 he discussed the matter with the historian V.N. Anfilov. After studying the documents on Soviet military planning in 1940 and 1941, Mel'tiukhov comes to the conclusion that the traditional view of Soviet policy as defensive and peace-loving is wrong. He avers that offensive operations *were* being prepared against Germany and her allies, for the formal alliance between the two powers no longer suited their respective national interests and both of them were preparing for war; the Soviet side was ready to strike in mid-July 1941. But all this does *not* mean that the German invasion was a preventive strike, as Hitler claimed at the time – merely that Stalin had an opportunity to avert it by attacking first, which he missed.[13]

Thus Stalin, in effect, pursued a policy of appeasement towards Germany in 1939–40, which failed. The documents show that when the invasion began the Soviet leaders lost their heads. At 5.30 a.m. on 22 June 1941, von der Schulenburg, the German ambassador, arrived at the Kremlin to hand Molotov a note stating that the two countries were now at war. Molotov's reaction was surprising: he said that the German government had not complained of any grievances to the Soviets, and had simply attacked without any reason or pretext; and then he posed the rhetorical question 'Why did Germany sign the non-aggression pact that it has so light-heartedly broken?' But Schulenburg answered that he had nothing to add to his earlier statement.

The surprise for the Soviet leaders was not the German invasion itself but the scale of the defeats which the invaders inflicted on the Red Army and the speed with which their forces advanced towards Moscow.[14] Suffice it to say that by the end of the year our best-trained cadre units had been wiped out and some 3.9

million men had been taken prisoner; the enemy seized territory inhabited by about 40 per cent of the total population.[15] As regards casualty figures, the scale was immensely greater than in the immediately preceding conflicts. The September 1939 operation in Poland cost the Red Army only 737 killed and 1,862 wounded. The Winter War with Finland (30 November 1939 – 12 March 1940) was more costly: 71,214 killed, 16,292 died of wounds, 39,369 missing, 163,773 wounded and 12,064 frostbitten, whereas the Finns lost 23,000 killed and about 60,000 wounded.[16] But irreplaceable losses during the 1941–5 Soviet–German war numbered many *millions*. No wonder that the '1941 syndrome' left a lasting mark on Soviet foreign policy.

So discussions are still going on about whether the USSR could (or should) have struck a preventive blow against Germany in 1941, or how to interpret Stalin's alleged speech of 19 August 1939. The problem is twofold: first, Stalin always tried to leave as little documentary trace as possible of his thinking, and concealed the truth behind 'battalions of lies'; second, some of our historians are unable to overcome traditional interpretations inherited from the Soviet past. After all, it is common knowledge that in the summer of 1939 the breakdown of the tripartite negotiations was not just the fault of the British and French but was partly due also to the position taken by the USSR, and that at that time the Red Army had nearly twice as many tanks and planes as Germany and her allies.[17] To make progress in investigating Stalin's actions we would need more reliable documents than are currently available. For example, we cannot decide whether Stalin really addressed the Politburo on 19 August without the original text of his (alleged) speech, for the text we have has passed through other people's hands; to get at the truth one would really need a thorough-going comparative analysis of different sources. Historians have not been allowed to see all the documents that they would need to arrive at a conclusive judgement.

Cold War origins

The victory of the Allied powers in World War II did not stop them preparing to fight each other on an even grander scale, though the existence of nuclear weapons moderated their belligerent fervour to a considerable extent. When did the Cold War start, and what were its results? On these questions, too, debates are in progress among Russian historians. In Soviet times some of them focused on the basic antagonism between Soviet Russia and the capitalist countries that had been a factor in international politics since October 1917, whereas others reckoned that the East–West confrontation really got under way in 1946. The latter based their reasoning on Stalin's speech of 9 February 1946, in which he said the USSR was ready for competition with the West, and Churchill's speech at Fulton, Missouri on 5 March of that year, when he called on the Anglo-Saxon powers to take the lead in resisting Communist expansion.[18]

A series of academic conferences was held in Moscow (1992–8) and at Yale University (1999) on the evolution of the 'two camps' theory. Those who attended agreed that Stalin had played a decisive role in deepening the Soviet–American geopolitical confrontation. At the 1992 conference, which took a retrospective look at Soviet foreign policy in general, one speaker mentioned that shortly after the end of the war Marshal S.M. Budennyi had said it was a pity that Stalin had not ordered Soviet troops to move on further westward after they had taken Berlin and Prague. This tough-minded old cavalryman wanted 'to chop [our enemies] down from the head to where their legs start'. Unexpectedly, Stalin had replied: 'And how are we going to feed them all?'[19] In other words, he was not averse to setting up a pan-European Soviet order provided the population's nutritional needs could be taken care of.

There is another piece of supporting evidence for this interpretation: on 18 November 1947, Stalin met the PCF leader M. Thorez, who was then head of the French Council of Ministers, and told him, in Molotov's presence, that 'if Churchill had delayed the second front for another year the Red Army would have reached France', and after a pause said 'we even thought of getting to Paris'. Thorez in turn let Stalin know that the French Communists had concealed arms dumps and radio transmitters for contacting Moscow. To this Stalin responded by promising further arms supplies: 'we are all Communists and that's what counts'.[20]

Many Russian historians today see a link between the USSR's postwar expansionist drive and the country's collapse in 1991. Initially, they had access to the papers of some leading policy-makers (such as V.M. Molotov, A.Ya. Vyshinsky and S.A. Lozovsky), as well as to some of those in the Stalin *fond*, but since the October 1993 crisis, the familiar practice of closing off archives to researchers has gathered pace. The sources at their disposal are plentiful but fragmentary, and it is not clear what the secret repositories may contain. The dozen or so monographs and documentary volumes published in recent years show that, like all tyrants, Stalin was eager to confront his foreign adversaries but from time to time sounded a pragmatic note which tempered his messianic zeal.

Unlike their forerunners, post-Soviet historians place the blame for the outbreak of the Cold War on both sides, but to varying degrees. Most of them consider that Moscow did not have a clear-cut line on foreign-policy issues when the war ended, whereas the USA, with its colossal power, was determined to expel the Soviets from the strong points they had won and opposed the notion of an agreement to divide up the world into spheres of influence. As V.O. Pechatnov puts it, 'the USSR was too strong to capitulate and too weak to win. The Cold War imprisoned Stalin in a vicious circle'.

In 1947, when the USSR refused to participate in the Marshall Plan or let its satellites do so, the tension between the two blocs increased markedly: this view is commonly held today. The Cominform was set up in response to what Moscow viewed as an American effort to remove eastern Europe from its zone of influence. Others see the founding of the Cominform rather in long-term perspective, as a means of ensuring total ideological, political and economic control over its eastern European member parties. They have looked closely at Soviet links with the individual countries concerned, the way dictatorial regimes were installed, and the Soviets' role in the repression of non-Communist elements.

Other topics studied are Sino-Soviet relations and the outbreak of hostilities in Korea. In his last years, some think, the ageing Stalin may have been preparing for World War III, and to a considerable degree it was his personal ideas that shaped the country's foreign policy.[21]

East–West tension also had an influence on Soviet domestic policy, since it could be used to justify stricter ideological controls and further economic belt-tightening. E.Yu. Zubkova and V.S. Lel'chuk are among those who, by examining the *mentalité* of ordinary Soviet people after the war, have shown how the regime strove to manipulate public opinion by invoking the image of the United States as a new enemy in place of the Nazis. Yu.I. Krivonosov and O.Yu. Yedin have analysed the harm which the staged ideological discussions did to philosophy as well as to various fields of scientific research, notably biology. G.D. Alexeeva and A.M. Filitov have looked at the part which historians played in facilitating (or, rarely, hindering) the drive for conformity of thought in the face of the external enemy. Alexeeva argues on standard lines that

> It was not the Cold War but the whole course of global development that engendered the struggle of ideas between Western and Soviet historians. The Cold War merely concentrated, focused and sharpened the adversarial relationship. The struggle of two social systems was reflected in the parallel existence of sovietologists in the west and critics of 'bourgeois falsifiers of history' in the east.

Filitov adds that the Cold War came to an end because of 'the unstoppable flood of information about Western realities unleashed by the "spirit of Helsinki" which washed away all trace of the "iron curtain" before the political leaders realized the fact.'[22]

Scholars today are in agreement that East–West tension has much to do with the impoverished state of the post-war Soviet economy. On top of this came the catastrophic famine of 1946–7 that struck Ukraine, Moldavia and other regions. In 1947 alone malnutrition and related diseases took the lives of 1,462,400 persons; in 1946 the comparable figure had also exceeded 1 million (1,059,600). Yet, Stalin persisted in sending grain to Romania and Czechoslovakia, where the population was suffering from severe drought. The Stalinists' economic policy, writes V.P. Popov, was designed to ensure the *nomenklatura*'s dominance over the population and to extend its influence abroad. The 1947 currency reform and the abolition of rationing of foodstuffs and consumer goods were tantamount to acts of pillage. The programme to develop nuclear energy and weapons likewise represented a heavy burden on the inefficient Soviet economy, widening the breach between the military–industrial complex and the civilian sector. As discussed in Chapter 3, Stalin's efforts to achieve economic miracles by non-economic means were bound to fail.[23]

L.N. Nezhinsky adheres to the classical view that the Cold War was a confrontation between two antagonistic systems, one socialist and the other capitalist, fought out on the political, ideological and military plane. Rather different is

A.N. Yakovlev's conception that it was a violent confrontation between two states, which the existence of nuclear weapons rendered idiotic. It was prosecuted by men who were 'suffering from an obsession with ideology at a time when resistance to the adversary could have fatal consequences'.[24] From time to time spokesmen for each side would threaten the adversary with a nuclear riposte. All Soviet leaders from Khrushchev onward uttered such threats – as did Russia's first president, Boris Yeltsin, who in response to foreign criticisms of Russian actions in Chechnia declared that Russia had 'an arsenal full of nuclear weapons' and would not be scared by international sanctions.[25] Today Russia's foreign-policy spokesmen consider that a multi-polar world best suits the country's interests. But the continuing economic crisis, the return to what is in effect single-party rule, and the lack of a civic society in Russia are not calculated to raise her international prestige, so that a return to Cold War high-handedness is on the cards. In my view only when Russians become fully fledged Europeans, able to travel anywhere without visa restrictions and with a convertible currency in their pockets, will one be able to say that the Cold War is definitely over.

Notes

1   F.I. Chuev, *Molotov: poluderzhavnyi vlastelin* (Moscow: Olma-press, 1999), 25–6.
2   *Izvestiia*, 28 December 1989; D.G. Nadzhafov, 'Sovetsko–germanskii pakt 1939 g.: pereosmyslenie podkhodov k ego otsenke', *VI*, 1999, no. 1, 160–1; A.N. Yakovlev, *Sumerki* (Moscow: Materik, 2003), 419.
3   V.Ya. Sipols, *Tainy diplomaticheskie: kanun Velikoi Otechestvennoi, 1939–1941* (Moscow: IRI RAN, 1997), 100; L.A. Bezymensky, 'Sovetsko–germanskie dogovory 1939 g.: novye dokumenty i starye problemy', *NNI*, 1998, no. 3, 13.
4   L.N. Nezhinsky, 'Puti i pereput'ia vneshnei politiki Rossii v XX stoletii', *OI*, 1999, no. 6, 6: idem, 'Vneshniaia politika i natsional'no–gosudarstvennye interesy Rossii v XX stoletii', in A.N. Bokhanov *et al.* (eds), *Rossiia i mirovaia tsivilizatsiia: k 70-letiiu . . . A.N. Sakharova* (Moscow: IRI RAN, 2000), 382.
5   M.I. Mel'tiukhov, '"Kriki ob oborone – eto vual"', in Yu.N. Afanas'ev *et al.* (eds), *Sovetskoe obshchestvo: vozniknovenie, razvitie, istoricheskii final* (Moscow: RGGU, 1997), vol. I, 292; idem, *Upushchennyi shans Stalina: Sovetskii Soiuz i bor'ba za Yevropu 1930–1941 gg.: dokumenty, fakty, suzhdeniia* (Moscow: Veche, 2002), 69.
6   G.A. Kumanev, 'Tainyi vybor: sovetsko–germanskii pakt o nenapadenii', in G.N. Sevost'ianov *et al.* (eds), *Etot protivorechivyi XX vek* (Moscow: ROSSPEN, 2001), 157.
7   S.Z. Sluch, 'Sovetsko–germanskie otnosheniia v sentiabre–dekabre 1939 g. i vopros o vstuplenii SSSR vo vtoruiu mirovuiu voinu', *OI*, 2000, no. 5, 47, 51, 52; no. 6, 17, 18, 23; idem, 'Rech' Stalina, kotoroi ne bylo', *OI*, 2004, no. 1, 113, 130.
8   M.I. Semiriaga, *Tainy stalinskoi diplomatii, 1939–1941* (Moscow: Vysshaia shkola, 1992), 59.
9   V. Suvorov, *Ledokol: kto nachal vtoruiu mirovuiu voinu?* (Moscow: Novoe vremia, 1992; idem, *Den'–M: kogda nachalas' vtoraia mirovaia voina? Prodolzhenie knigi 'Ledokola'* (Moscow: Vse dlia Vas, 1994); idem, *Posledniaia respublika: pochemu Sovetskii Soiuz proigral vtoruiu mirovuiu voinu* (Moscow: AST, 1995); idem, *Zachem Gitler napal na Sovetskii Soiuz?* (Moscow: AST, 2000).
10 M.I. Mel'tiukhov, 'Sovetskaia istoriografiia i polemika vokrug knigi V. Suvorova "Ledokol"', in Yu.N. Afanas'ev *et al.* (eds), *Sovetskaia istoriografiia* (Moscow: RGGU, 1996), 488–521; G. Gorodetsky, *Mif 'Ledokola': nakanune voiny* (Moscow: Progress-

Akademiia, 1995); idem, *Rokovoi samoobman: Stalin i napadenie Germanii na Sovetskii Soiuz* (Moscow: ROSSPEN, 1999).

11 Luftwaffe pilots trained at Lipetsk and armoured units in Kazan', while experiments with the latest chemical weapons were carried out at the 'Tomka' proving ground in the Volga region. All of this helped to maintain good relations between the two states. See now Yu.L. D'iakov and T.S. Bushueva, *Fashistskii mech kovalsia v SSSR: Krasnaia armiia i reikhsver: tainoe sotrudnichestvo, 1922–1933: neizvestnye dokumenty* (Moscow: Sovetskaia Rossiia, 1992); V.A. Zubachevsky, 'Politika sovetskoi Rossii v tsentral'noi Yevrope v nachale 1920–kh gg. (po novym dokumentam)', *OI*, 2003, no. 2, 95, 98–9.

12 A.P.Belozerov *et al.* (eds), *Sekrety Gitlera na stole u Stalina: razvedka i kontrrazvedka o podgotovke germanskoi agressii protiv SSSR, mart–iun' 1941 g.: dokumenty iz Tsentral'nogo arkhiva FSB Rossii* (Moscow: Mosgorarkhiv, 1995); S.V. Stepashin and A.P. Bykov (ed.), *Organy gosudarstvennoi bezopasnosti SSSR v Velikoi Otechestvennoi voine: sbornik dokmentov*, vol. I, 2 bks, *Nakanune*; vol. 2, 2 bks, *1941 god: dokumenty* (Moscow: A/0 Kniga i biznes, 1995, 1998).

13 Mel'tiukhov, *Upushchennyi shans*, 305, 334, 399–400, 402–3. 406, 412.

14 V.K. Volkov, 'Prizrak i real'nost' "Barbarossy" v politike Stalina (vesna–leto 1941 g.)', *VI*, 2003, no. 6, 38, 46, 49, 54–5; '"Sovremennaia armiia–armiia nastupatel'naia": vystupleniia I.V. Stalina na prieme v Kremle pered vypusknikami voennykh akademii, mai 1941 g.', *IA*, 1995, no. 2, 22–39.

15 V.D. Danilov, 'Stalinskaia strategiia nachala voiny i real'nost', *OI*, 1995, no. 3, 40.

16 N.Yu. Kuleshova, 'Krasnaia armiia v kontse 1930-kh gg.: problema boesposobnosti s tochki zreniia istorii povsednevnosti', *OI*, 2003, no. 4, 79–80.

17 I.V. Pavlova, *Mekhanizm vlasti i stroitel'stvo stalinskogo sotsializma* (Novosibirsk: SO RAN, 2001), 355, 356, 365, 425.

18 Churchill's speech was first published in Russian in *Nezavisimaia gazeta* of 28 May 1992.

19 *Izvestiia*, 12 February 1992.

20 Ibid., 5 November 1995.

21 V.M. Zubok and V.O. Pechatnov, 'Otechestvennaia istoriografiia "kholodnoi voiny": nekotorye itogi desiatiletiia', *OI*, 2003, no. 4, 143, 145, 147, 148; cf. also A.O. Chubar'ian (ed.), *Stalin i 'kholodnaia voina': sbornik dokumentov* (Moscow: IRI RAN, 1998); I.V. Gaiduk *et al.* (eds), *Stalinskoe desiatiletie kholodnoi voiny: fakty i gipotezy* (Moscow: Nauka, 1999); G.M. Kornienko, *'Kholodnaia voina': svidetel'stvo ee uchastnika* (Moscow: Olma-press, 2001).

22 E.Ya. Zubkova, *Poslevoennoe sovetskoe obshchestvo: politika i povsedvnevnost'*, *1945–1953* (Moscow: ROSSPEN, 2000) (English translation of an earlier edition: *Russia after the War: Hopes, Illusions and Disappointments, 1945–1957*, trans. and ed. H. Ragsdale (Armonk, NY: M.E. Sharpe, 1998).

23 V.F. Zima, *Golod v SSSR 1946–1947 gg.: proiskhozhdenie i posledstviia* (Moscow: IRI RAN, 1996, 2nd edn. Lewiston, NY, 1999), 163; V.P. Popov, 'Stalin i sovetskaia ekonomika v poslevoennye gody', *OI*, 2001, no. 3, 62, 64, 68–9, 74.

24 Nezhinsky, 'Vneshniaia politika' (*see* n. 4), 246–7.

25 *Izvestiia*, 10 December 1999.

Part II

Wrestling with revisionism

Recent Western writing on Stalinism

6   Old controversies, new approaches

Revisionism and post-modernism

Historical literature on the Stalin era (1929–53) is rich and growing rapidly: in a few years, it may rank in size with that on Hitler's Third Reich. At first glance, this may seem remarkable, for the period in question is more than half a century behind us. But there are two good reasons for this continuing interest. The first is that since 1991 Russian archives, along with those held elsewhere in the former Soviet Union, have in principle been open to foreign researchers. Moreover, thousands of hitherto secret documents have appeared in print. It is true that in practice archive access is often restricted, on one pretext or another, and some files have been tampered with for political reasons. Nevertheless, the opportunities that exist have revolutionized the field of Soviet studies in the West. Today, historians, many of whom are relatively new to the profession, are confidently investigating a broad range of topics on a scale that could scarcely have been dreamed of by their forerunners who toiled in Soviet archives and libraries during the 60 years or so when the ruling Communist Party (CPSU) tightly controlled the flow of information.

Access to primary sources, while yielding a lot of fresh detail, has not fundamentally altered our view of Soviet reality under Stalin. The changes that have occurred are due rather to the widespread adoption of fashionable new methodological approaches. These have opened up a great many questions that lay beyond the purview of the pioneers who founded the discipline known colloquially as 'sovietology' (a term that was initially used with a touch of irony, later forgotten).

This first generation, the 'fathers',[1] concerned itself primarily with matters political: with the ruling Party and its official ideology, the way decisions were taken, popular support mobilized, and the country governed. An important sub-field was 'kremlinology', the arcane study of power relationships at the top. The emphasis was personalist and institutional, but not exclusively so, for at the same time much critical attention was paid to the achievements and shortcomings of the 'planned' economy, not least in the agricultural sector; meanwhile other scholars were studying Soviet Russian literature, not just in its political context but for its own sake, and to a lesser extent the visual arts. As in other fields of historical research, investigators tried to establish chains of cause and effect and to range the factors that had influenced the course of events in some order of priority.

Relatively rare in this initial phase (roughly, 1945–65) was first-hand knowledge of, and interest in, the experiences and aspirations of ordinary people. But here too there were exceptions, such as the remarkable Harvard project on the Soviet social system, based on interviews with emigrés from what until the mid-1950s was an all but hermetically closed world.[2] In the United States, which set the tone for most European countries as well (although German scholars developed their own traditions), the lacunae were strikingly apparent to the generation of 'sons and daughters' that came to the fore in the late 1960s. These were social historians in the main, who often took a critical attitude towards their predecessors, seeing their work as too heavily influenced by 'Cold War' considerations. They had, it was held, over-stressed the violent, coercive aspects of Communist rule. In particular, the relevance to the Soviet political and social order of the term totalitarian was now called in question. The so-called 'revisionists' in this 'new cohort' (Sheila Fitzpatrick) on the whole took a more positive attitude towards the contemporary USSR that had something to do with the international situation at the time. The Vietnam war and the student upsurge that peaked in 1968 made Soviet-style socialism appear, not as a dangerous threat to Western values as heretofore, but rather as an alternative way of coping with problems besetting the entire industrial world. For those concerned with the origins and development of the system this meant endeavouring to write 'history from below'. Attention was redirected to underlying social processes, such as the massive population shifts and dislocations that had accompanied the initial drive to industrialize during the First Five-Year Plan (FYP), along with the emergence of a new élite of officials and managers, the later *nomenklatura*. The main beneficiary of this shift of interest, however, was not the Stalin period but the age of Lenin: the 1917 October revolution was now seen by some western scholars as an authentically popular artefact and no longer as something imposed on people from above by a conspiratorial party. Even the Great Terror of 1937–8 came to be viewed 'as to some extent understandable in its motives, the result of a collective process rather than Stalin's caprice'.[3] It had owed a good deal to input from below by subordinates, as a well as to anxieties that had permeated broad strata of the populace. They credited official claims that the Soviet state order was at risk from artfully concealed internal enemies, so that extreme vigilance was called for. This psychological malaise, it was argued, went far to clarify Soviet citizens' otherwise inexplicable readiness to denounce one another and to confess to implausible crimes when under investigation.

The achievements of the revisionist school were impartially appraised in a series of essays published in the US journal *Russian Review* in 1986.[4] The date was significant, in that Mikhail Gorbachev was just getting into his stride as new CPSU general secretary. His policies of *perestroika* and *glasnost'* would shake the Soviet system to its foundations and within a few years bring about its demise. In the later 1980s, while old dogmas were being cast to the winds in Eastern Europe, Western sovietology found itself in something of a crisis. Its claims to scientific respectability had never been fully accepted elsewhere in the academic establishment, and now its practitioners had to face some awkward questions. In particular, why had they so signally failed to anticipate the epochal changes currently under way? The charge was directed mainly against social scientists, but historians could not entirely escape suspicion of having been complacent about the human cost of Stalin's dictatorship – a matter that was now being enthusiastically debated by civic-minded journalists in the USSR.

Sackcloth and ashes are not part of academic garb, and so few scholars in the field stood up to admit their errors in public. Instead, what happened was that the social historians became subsumed into a broader current unleashed by the so-called 'cultural turn'. A new generation – the 'grandsons' – took the helm. Since the early 1970s, a major shift of landmarks had been taking place in western intellectual life which owed a lot to the seminal influence of Michel Foucault as well as to linguistic philosophers and anthropologists, and history was one of the disciplines that was most profoundly affected. The catch-all term 'post-modernism', which (abbreviated to PM) we propose to use for these new tendencies, risks doing them less than justice, but is perhaps an excusable shorthand designation since we are concerned here solely with their practical implications for students of Stalinism, and not with the broader implications, which extend across the whole range of human thought.

The appellation PM is misleading in two principal respects: first, because such writers do not necessarily see themselves as heralds of a new age chronologically distinct from, or superior to, the modern era;[5] and second, because they do not propose a coherent doctrine which can be encompassed by a single term, but rather put forward a range of disparate but interlinked propositions. Not all of these are set out clearly in generally accessible language, for one of the most intriguing features of PM is its development of a special vocabulary, in which terms may be used in different senses by various authors or not be defined at all. Nevertheless, it can be asserted with some confidence that protagonists of most viewpoints within the PM 'family' adhere to an idealistic world view that denies our ability to perceive reality beyond our own sensations; and that the historically minded among them share a profound scepticism towards grand historiosophic schemes ('metanar-ratives'), according to which mankind is moving forward inexorably towards some ulterior goal, whether this be a communist utopia, a capitalist free-market paradise, or for that matter the Second Coming of Christian theology.

There is no place in PM thinking for universal fixed principles or eternal truths, since all is in flux: to cite a once shocking formula, 'the medium is the message', for we can only know about things or ideas indirectly, from communications about them that register in our minds. Religious and moral values are necessarily at a discount if one starts from the premiss that individuals ('subjects'), or groups of them ('collectivities'), fashion their mutual relationships, and find their place in the surrounding milieu, by making sense of their experiences and prioritizing their preferences, and that therefore each has an equally valid conception of what is true. There is a basic philosophical problem here that we can only touch on. Chris Lorenz (Netherlands) speaks justly of 'the PMs' allergy to the problem of truth'.[6] The more radical theorists question the ability of scholars or scientists, and certainly of traditionally minded empiricist historians, to reach valid conclusions on the basis of an objective examination of evidence, for their employment of it cannot but be slanted by their own subjective assumptions, coloured as these must be by those of the group (class, nation, society) to which they belong; for similar reasons, it makes little sense to inquire into alleged links between cause and effect, since these are not knowable. Lorenz pleads with PMs to accept what he calls 'internal realism': they should recognize that reality *does* after all exist independently of our knowledge of it and that scientific statements refer to this reality; and that professional historians, properly applying well-tried methodologies, are themselves the best judges of the merits of whatever 'truth claims' their colleagues may put forward, since such writers do not try to do more than advance partial, relevant (not absolute) truths.

Lorenz is not alone in seeking common ground between PM historians and the traditionalists. His approach seems preferable to the intransigent one taken by, for example, Beverley Southgate, who writes off the latter as 'Pomophobes' and condemns them for adhering to modernist dogmas long ago discredited, first by the Romantics and Nietzsche, then by Foucault and others in our own day. The 'doubt and unease' experienced by the post-modernist, he avers, are preferable to the supposed certainties of the empiricist, since these rest on fallacious premisses. 'History is now left stranded like some antediluvian beast on the beach of post-modernity, awaiting only nostalgic farewells and final submersion.'[7] We should jettison rationalism, along with the search for logical consistency, and instead make imaginative leaps, following the inspirations of our dreams, and use these insights to build a bright future in this 'decisively post-Christian era', when man has at last acquired the freedom to make choices that will bestow meaning on our chaotic world.

Few writers in the sovietological field have yet gone so far. However original their interpretations may be, judged by conventional standards, they still try to base them on the same sort of evidence as is used by everyone else. Accordingly, there is plenty of room for coexistence and good-natured dialogue between adherents of different schools of thought. The field is not closed off in the way it was in the USSR by Marxist–Leninist thinking; there is a 'discursive space' in which we can all profit from one another's ideas.

Let us now attempt to penetrate the web of PM ideas, picking out those relevant to our topic. Those who have taken the 'linguistic turn', the semioticists, look on the historical record as a 'text' that needs to be 'deconstructed', freed from the fallacious notions that beset those responsible for creating it, so revealing its true meaning. This is deemed particularly necessary where we are dealing with a 'discourse' shaped by some superior agency, whose author(s) wanted to produce a certain effect upon those to whom their messages were addressed. Such authors had a hidden agenda that it is our duty to expose, investigate, criticize. In this way, notions that originated in literary criticism are now freely applied to other areas of human thought and activity. They have inspired fruitful investigations into the way the Stalinist Party-state represented itself symbolically and how the aesthetic code of 'socialist realism' was applied far beyond the realm of the arts – for example, in ceremonial parades or officially sanctioned festivities. These rituals played a major part in people's lives at the time, affecting the way they interacted with each other and with the society as a whole.

Closely related to this is the study of everyday life (*Alltagsgeschichte*). PM-oriented scholars seek to penetrate behind the propaganda screen, which represented Soviet citizens as zealously devoted to upholding the existing order (or, in some cases, as reprehensible backsliders, even covert enemies), and to fill in the gaps which information control left in the public record. How did people in various walks of life *really* live and think? What satisfactions did they enjoy, and how far did they try to improve their lot, by their own actions or by appealing to the authorities? When they complained, or petitioned for redress of grievances, which needs and aspirations were uppermost in their minds?

Naturally, these differed over time, and also between various groups. The social makeup of the population was a major concern of those in the leadership, and the élite generally, who took seriously the aim of building a classless order and who were willing to endorse discriminatory measures and massive physical violence against any elements that did not fit into this vision: members of the former 'ruling classes', for example. But how far did such attitudes spread downwards to rank-and-file members of the Party or Komsomol (Young Communist League), soldiers, or ordinary 'toilers'?

Other groups might be the target of repressive action on grounds of ethnic allegiance, despite the regime's internationalist credo. National minorities suffered disproportionately in the Terror, as has since become all too clear (see Chapter 11), and it is not surprising that many such subjects regarded Soviet rule as something alien to their own culture, imposed on them by external force. Since 1991, several writers have explored the curious paradox whereby Moscow, by carving up the Union's territories administratively more or less on ethnic lines, while refusing to cater to the legitimate aspirations to autonomy of so many non-Russian peoples, allowed national consciousness to persist or even stimulated it where it had not previously existed. Even within the Russian heartland (RSFSR) there were significant differences between people's behaviour in provinces with various socio-economic profiles, and these need to be taken into account, too.

In the West, the 'cultural turn' (or 'anthropological turn', as it might better be termed) fostered study of a whole range of marginalized elements: criminals, beggars, prisoners, the insane and so on, here following, perhaps unconsciously, Foucault's dictum that one can best recognize the contours of any historical entity by inspecting its outer limits: 'it is the extreme that encapsulates the truth'.[8] Their colleagues in the Soviet field long lacked a source base adequate for such investigations, but now a start has been made. Building on works by Alan Ball about two such groups in the 1920s, 'NEPmen' and orphans (*besprizorniki*),[9] historians have examined the fate of those deprived of civic rights (*lishentsy*) and kulaks – peasants with a modicum of property who, barely tolerated under NEP, were deported or shot out of hand during the agricultural collectivization drive after 1929. In the towns, self-employed craftsmen and shopkeepers, along with priests and mendicants, fell into a category of 'marginals' that was severely punished during the Terror.

The social group that most obviously deserves to put in the 'underdog' category is: women – even though they comprised half the population and had been an object of official solicitude from 1917 onward. By Stalin's time, women were seen chiefly as an economic resource. They formed a key segment of the industrial labour force, hard-working and underpaid; harsher still was the lot of the *kolkhoznitsa* (female collective-farm worker). Most recent studies of gender problems in Soviet Russia have been devoted to the progressive, experimental early years, which offer more rewards to the investigator, but attention is increasingly focusing on the period before and after World War II – a struggle in which Soviet womenfolk played a greater part as combatants than was the case in any other belligerent country. Family problems and the domestic environment come into the picture, too. However, PM-oriented cultural historians are less concerned with what women actually *did*, in peace or war, than with trying to establish what Malte Rolf calls their 'gender-specific construction of the self'.

This brings us to the vexed question of identity. Today's historians no longer think it adequate to speak of an individual having a distinct personality or character, whose traits can be itemized by using terms familiar to Plutarch: noble, tolerant, sullen, selfish or whatever; even the insights into the human mind vouchsafed by modern clinical psychiatry do not seem to be highly regarded. The distinction commonly made between someone's private 'inner world' and the mask presented in public is also questioned. Instead, our PM-inspired colleagues prefer to speak, again following Foucault, of 'subject(hood)' and 'the techniques of the self'. By the latter are meant 'the ways whereby an individual ascertains who he/she is and the concepts employed in doing so' (Rolf). These writers take very seriously the Stalinist regime's endeavours to create a 'new Soviet man' imbued with all the politically correct collectivist virtues: resilient, industrious, patriotic and so on. They are also interested in the procedures employed to bring this about and to select leading cadres: Party schools, where the curriculum followed strictly Marxist–Leninist principles, then the still relatively bloodless Party purges ('exchanges of documents'), when members had to attend inquisitorial meetings of their cell at which they might be grilled by their comrades and have to confess any faults; finally, the physical liquidation of alleged heretics during the Terror. It was in this context that some young people eager to get ahead endeavoured to refashion their 'selves' until they fitted the accepted pattern of thought and behaviour.

There is certainly much to learn from examining these matters, but we should bear in mind that conformist pressures affected a relatively small segment of ambitious would-be nomenklaturists and that the mass of common people were concerned only indirectly, if at all. Identity is in any case a highly fluid characteristic, hard to pin down: not only do people's ideas of themselves change rapidly over time, especially in periods of stress, but they may be capable of simultaneously holding contradictory ones and displaying different facets of their 'self' to different interlocutors. Moreover, people may combine allegiance to some superordinate entity (the nation, for instance) with allegiance to a smaller one (region, sect, profession, cultural group and so on) and at any given moment one of these latter may be more prominent. The same considerations apply, with even greater force, to the study of *mentalités*, defined as 'the pattern of unconscious attitudes and interpretations that individuals need in order to cope with the world in which they live'.[10] 'Mentality' is understood as a collective phenomenon, whereas subjectivity is individual; therefore in the former case the potential for misinterpretation is far greater.

Do ordinary folk, in the Soviet Union or anywhere else, really 'construct' their own identity, as is so widely assumed today, or is this shaped unconsciously? It would be good to have more enlightenment on this point, preferably by a qualified psychologist, before unthinkingly following such pioneers as Igal Halfin and Jochen Hellbeck in 'rethinking the Stalinist subject' or 'fashioning the Stalinist soul'.[11] These ground-breaking studies are based in large part on what are now sometimes called 'ego-documents'; that is to say, diaries and correspondence written by those relatively rare individuals intrepid enough to put potentially compromising thoughts to paper so long as Stalin was in charge. Some of these writings have since come to light in the archives (alas, in certain cases in the unfortunate writer's NKVD dossier), and several of them have been published; in optimal circumstances they can be complemented by oral interviews, if the subject lived on to the present day. Most of these survivors had successful careers and learned to 'speak Bolshevik' (S. Kotkin). The sources are, however, as yet too few in number, and too unrepresentative, to sustain the far-reaching edifices that have been erected on such foundations. Speculation can be productive only up to a certain point; in probing the 'self' the investigator needs to be very careful not to stray beyond the limits of the evidence and see what he or she wants to see.

On the crucial issue of what Soviet citizens in the 1930s (and still more in 1945–53) actually thought about the regime under which they lived, much is still unclear, for all the progress that has been made of late. Diary entries can be read in different ways, and it is not always helpful to compare what is said in them with the information contained in *svodki*: reports about the state of public opinion drawn up by secret-police operatives or others for the edification of those at the top. Even more troublesome are transcripts of evidence and signed statements of confession made under investigation. These were liable to falsification by interrogators and cannot be taken at face value. Svetlana Boym (USA) argues trenchantly that Western scholars find it hard to appreciate the very unusual nature of the Stalinist world, so different from their own, and to penetrate the metaphorical language often used by Soviet diarists; instead of generalizing from a slender source base, they should rather seek to show how a particular event was reflected in several such documents.[12]

In more positive vein, one might point out that these studies do at least deal with real individuals, whose hitherto unknown life-stories they have added to our stock of knowledge. Here the cultural historians are in a way completing a circle by rehabilitating the biographical approach adopted by historians for centuries from classical times onward – admittedly, with the important difference that today's 'subjects' usually stem from the depths of society, and the methods of analysis have become more sophisticated.

In so far as one can generalize at all, it is probably true to say that recent Western archive-based studies have revealed a greater degree of opposition to the regime than was recognized by contemporary observers or the first historians to look at the period. We are confronted with what Nicolas Werth calls a 'palette', or broad range, of antagonistic reactions. These might be said to begin with simple disinterest in officially sponsored activities, along with stubborn adherence to traditional patterns of thought and conduct (religious observance, for instance). These practices lead on to actual dissidence: discussing taboo topics *sub rosa*, spreading rumours, telling jokes. If such behaviour is adhered to persistently, it turns into deviance or insubordination. This in turn may be expressed either spontaneously, as by the peasant women who led local insurgencies against the collectivizers in 1930–1, or else in more organized fashion. In the latter case we can indeed speak of resistance, such as occurred in the Baltic lands or the western Ukraine after 1944, or later in some Gulag camp complexes.[13]

PM-oriented historians are not closely concerned with the institutional set-up under Stalin, gladly leaving such relatively well-trodden ground to their empiricist colleagues. It is they who are more likely to explore the implications of single-party rule or personal dictatorship, and to contrast this form of government with more democratic alternatives; they also have more interest in investigating the extravagant abuses of power that took place under Stalin and the ways that such constraints on the leader(s)' freedom of action as initially existed in the USSR were by-passed after 1928–9.

The PM tendency to play down the special characteristics of Stalinist rule seems to be an indirect legacy of Foucault, who had nothing to say, after all, about Soviet Russia and, in so far as he was concerned with state power, thought rather in terms of eighteenth-century French absolutism. Indeed, his work on royal *lettres de cachet* under Louis XV may have influenced recent studies of letters to the press and petitions in Stalin's realm. Foucault preferred the term 'state effect' to 'state'; he spoke loosely of 'domination' by elements of the élite who might or might not be state officials; and in any case he taught that power 'comes from below' and was (or is) widely diffused in society; power relationships were generated at the lowest level, in families and in workplaces, and the whole structure of political–economic domination rested on this basis. Explaining this, Michael Maset comments: 'in Foucault's perspective a view of social space in the form of above and below, basis and superstructure, is deemed inadequate or even counter-productive; his analysis of power is more suggestive of a network [of relationships] filling social space.'[14]

This notion has been taken over by sovietologists of the second and especially the third generation, who are eager to discern evidence of 'input from below' into the political process – even when writing about the Great Terror, which as we now know for certain was initiated by Stalin and a small group of intimates. It is often argued today that officials in the provinces ('periphery' is the preferred term) did more than just passively implement instructions from above; instead they actively helped to shape policy, although they might well do so from careerist or bureau-cratic motives that had little in common with the priorities of 'Moscow'. In other words, power relationships under Stalin were less hierarchical than interactive, fluid and even chaotic. There is certainly a good deal of evidence to support such a view (see Chapter 7), but the argument is not really convincing unless 'the state is brought back in' (Fitzpatrick), that is, full account is also taken of what 'the centre' said and did. Empiricist historians have solid grounds for pursuing a conventional approach that gives due weight to the interplay of personalities, ideas, factions and institutions at all levels, and continues to tease out causal linkages. Indeed, the best results will probably be obtained where the old and new methodologies are employed complementarily.

The totalitarian controversy

Into this context let us now try to fit the hoary totalitarian–revisionist controversy, on which so much ink has been spilled. Probably the most authoritative study of the matter is by the eminent political scientist Juan Linz, whose primary field of interest is Franco's Spain rather than Stalinist Russia.[15] The genesis of the term in the pre-war literature on Mussolini's Italy and its sequels has been thoroughly explored, most recently by Abbott Gleason.[16] At that time, writers generally spoke of 'Caesarism' or 'political religion', and maybe if these terms had been kept to later debates about the USSR would have been less polemical. The term 'totalitarianism' came into general use in the 1940s and 1950s. In the English-speaking world, it owed much to influential works by Hannah Arendt (1951) and Carl J. Friedrich/Zbigniew Brzezinski (1956). The latter listed five principal characteristics of such systems and stressed alleged common ground between the Soviet and Nazi experiences. The view gained currency that a totalitarian regime could not reform itself but was fated to endure unless eliminated by defeat in war (as had happened in 1945) – an untested hypothesis, later disproved by fact. Widespread use of the term in Cold War political rhetoric devalued it and, in the eyes of later revisionist scholars, discredited it entirely. Already in 1956 it was questionable, since Stalin was no more and under Khrushchev the Soviet regime was clearly evolving, if only slowly. Yet even today, more than a decade after the USSR's disappearance, continued usage of the term is still being repeatedly denounced. Why then has it proved so durable and is there anything positive to be said on its behalf? Why are its defenders more often found in eastern Europe than in the West?

After careful consideration of the debate, the Russian historian Nikita Lomagin contends that 'the theory of totalitarianism, deprived of its ideological subtext, is still objectively helpful in understanding better the essence of the political regime that was established in the USSR',[17] a judgement in which the present writer concurs. So far as the Stalin era goes (and Linz rightly pleads for the term 'post-totalitarian' with regard to the years that followed), its use can be defended so long as we are clear in our minds about its limitations. In the first place, totalitarianism cannot claim to be a fully fledged explanatory theory, or even a model: at best it is a suggestive concept, which needs to be tested against historical reality. Second, we need to distinguish between its application to three different sets of phenomena:

1   the ruling Party's 'totalizing aspirations' (Michael David-Fox);[18] that is to say, the utopian dream of recasting entirely not just the economic and social order

but the mental habits of all citizens, to create the 'New Soviet Man' – the Orwellian nightmare, so to speak;

2   the mechanisms of rule, as fashioned by Lenin and further developed by Stalin: pseudo-constitutional forms, a single Party-state, secret decision-making, centralized bureaucratic administration; a powerful security police and successive waves of indiscriminate terror; positive (proactive) censorship; isolation of the country from external influences – to mention just some important features;

3   extensive controls over society: the 'command economy'; mass mobilization of the populace in successive campaigns to attain goals set from above; ramified, pervasive *agitprop*; partisan politicization of culture, science and education; prohibition of autonomous civic activity; efforts to eliminate religious and national distinctions.

If we attempt to break down Stalinism in this way (and admittedly the distinctions are not always clear-cut), we can go on to ask how far the term totalitarian is relevant to the three sets. One answer might be: (1) yes; (2) yes, but with reservations; (3) only to a limited extent.

As to (1), the correspondence between the Soviet leaders that has been published recently confirms the view that they thought ideologically, that is, with ulterior long-range goals in mind, even to the point of obsession, while combining this with short-term pragmatism. Moreover, this style of thinking permeated the apparatus down even to the lowest level of rank-and-file activists; although there was a good deal of backsliding, in the main these men and women *did* see themselves as 'building socialism' – or strengthening the system, which comes to much the same thing – so long as Stalin lived; after 1953, however, these ideological concerns became increasingly irrelevant to members of the *nomenklatura*.

As to (2), in framing day-to-day policy the regime had to make compromises with reality: the bureaucracy was inefficient and divided into contending groups, notably patron–client networks; junior functionaries misinterpreted the centre's commands, sometimes with intent – and were tolerated for a time. But by and large the system of rule *worked* as intended: the military remained loyal, the censors maintained tight control, and the 'iron curtain' was very much a reality (except, of course, during World War II).

As to (3), in trying to determine people's conduct the regime encountered far greater difficulty. There were unplanned population shifts, despite the introduction of internal passports; peasant resistance forced concessions over private plots; workers changed jobs frequently, disregarded appeals to boost productivity, and disliked Stakhanovites or other 'strivers'; ordinary people, and not just the educated, often disbelieved propaganda, preferring to credit rumours instead; writers and scholars produced manuscripts 'for the drawer'; there were 'catacomb' churches underground and religious beliefs were not extinguished; national sentiment remained alive among many minority groups – again the list could be extended.

In sum: Soviet society was not 'atomized', as early spokesmen for the totalitarian interpretation held, since horizontal linkages persisted. But it was indeed severely constrained. The Stalin regime tried very hard to impose total control, especially after 1945, and achieved a remarkable degree of success in doing so. It exercised greater power over the citizenry than any other twentieth-century European dictatorship did, even if there were inevitably many gaps in the control network. These loopholes would grow larger during the decades that followed until the system, although apparently still solid, was hollowed out and forfeited credibility; in the 1980s, when fundamental reform was attempted, it collapsed. That it lasted so long after 1953 is testimony to Stalin's success. During his tenure of power, active resistance was rare, but there was a good deal of opposition (dissidence, deviance) beneath the mask of conformity and indifference to the Great Idea was widespread.

Juan Linz concludes that recent studies of everyday life in Nazi Germany, while making important contributions to knowledge, 'do not call into question the distinctive characteristic of a totalitarian regime . . . nor the shaping of society, behaviour patterns, and values by the system. They only question a simplistic view of totalitarianism that extrapolates from an ideal type of society totally penetrated and shaped by those in power'.[18] This holds good for revisionist work on the Stalin era, too. Some such writers speak of 'negotiation' having occurred between the state and its subjects. Unless the word is used in a specific technical sense it is misleading, for whatever bargaining took place was informal and (from the regime's vantage point) involuntary. Certainly, subordinate functionaries exercised much autonomous power – but at any time they might be called to order, scapegoated for offences that were really the responsibility of the centre, and summarily disposed of. In a system where fear and suspicion were so rampant, input into decision-making from below, though not totally absent, was extremely limited. In the USSR under Stalin, little of consequence occurred (in peacetime, at any rate) that did not have the dictator's explicit or tacit assent. He may indeed have been a fearful man, as Arch Getty insists, but he could intervene at whim in virtually any area without being checked, even if his will might not be carried out exactly as he wished. In the last resort, Stalin was most definitely 'in charge', and millions of victims bear testimony to the fact.

Whether this situation makes the Soviet Union between 1929 and 1953 totalitarian is, in the final instance, a matter of definition, of the label we choose to apply. That it was a tyranny is surely beyond doubt. And since the study of tyranny is as old as the Greeks, empiricist historians have something to contribute to the discussion along with social scientists or others of the post-modernist persuasion. All approaches are valid and there is something to learn from each.

Notes

1 The generational approach is developed by Michael David-Fox in his edited volume of essays *Amerikanskaia rusistika: vekhi istoriografii poslednikh let: sovetskii period* (Samara: Samarskii universitet, 2001); cf. the review by B.N. Mironov in *Kritika* 4 (2003), 201–25.
2 R.A. Bauer *et al.*, *How the Soviet System Works: Cultural, Psychological and Social Themes* (Cambridge, MA: Harvard University Press, 1956).
3 V. Andrle, 'Demons and Devil's Advocates: Problems in Historical Writing on the

Stalin Era', in N. Lampert and G.T. Rittersporn (eds), *Stalinism: Its Nature and Aftermath: Essays in Honour of Moshe Lewin* (Basingstoke, UK: Macmillan, 1992), 32.

4 S. Fitzpatrick *et al.*, 'New Perspectives on Stalinism', *RR* 45 (1986).

5 M. Maset, *Diskurs, Macht und Geschichte: Foucaults Analysetechniken und die historische Forschung* (Frankfurt and New York: Campus, 2002), 22.

6 C. Lorenz, 'Historical Knowledge and Historical Reality: A Plea for "Internal Realism"', in B. Fay, P. Pomper and R.T. Vann (eds), *History and Theory: Contemporary Readings* (Oxford: Blackwell, 1998), 349.

7 B.C. Southgate, *Postmodernism in History: Fear or Freedom?* (London and New York: Routledge, 2003), 107.

8 U. Brieler, '"Erfahrungstiere" und "Industriesoldaten": Marx und Foucault über das historische Denken, das Subjekt und die Geschichte der Gegenwart', in J. Martschukat (ed.), *Geschichte schreiben mit Foucault* (Frankfurt and New York: Campus, 2002), 56.

9 A.M. Ball, *Russia's Last Capitalists: The Nepmen, 1921–1929* (Berkeley, CA: University of California Press, 1987); idem, *And Now My Soul Is Hardened: Abandoned Children in Soviet Russia* (Berkeley, CA and London: University of California Press, 1994).

10 T. Geiger, as cited by T. Undulag in *IRSH* 47 (2002), 35.

11 I. Halfin and J. Hellbeck, 'Rethinking the Stalinist Subject: Stephen Kotkin's "Magnetic Mountain" and the State of Soviet Historical Studies', *JGOE* 44 (1996), 456–63, and other works by these authors listed in Ch. 8, n. 44, 48.

12 S. Boym, 'Kak sdelana "sovetskaia sub'ektivnost'"', *Ab imperio* (Kazan') (2002), 3, 285–96.

13 For more on this typology, see a forthcoming study by N. Werth.

14 Maset, *Diskurs*, 82; J. Plamper, 'Foucaults Gulag', *Kritika* 3 (2002), 255–80.

15 J.J. Linz, *Totalitarian and Authoritarian Regimes* (Boulder, CO: Lynne Rienner, 2000).

16 A. Gleason, *Totalitarianism: The Inner History of the Cold War* (New York and Oxford: Oxford University Press, 1995), 13–30.

17 N.A. Lomagin, *Neizvestnaia blokada* (St. Petersburg: Neva, 2002), vol. I, p. 33.

18 M. David-Fox, *Revolution of the Mind: Higher Learning Among the Bolsheviks, 1917–1929* (Ithaca, NY and London: Cornell University Press, 1997), 7.

19 Linz, *Totalitarian Regimes*, 28.

7 'A peculiar new state'

Politics and government

Stalin and the leader cult

One might have expected Western scholars studying a dictatorial system to concentrate attention on the dictator. That is, however, not the case. This neglect is primarily due to current historiographic fashion, which de-emphasizes the role of personality in human affairs, but it is also partly because the documentary sources recently made available[1] show that Iosif Vissarionovich was very much the man he was always thought to be: capricious, wily, ruthless, blessed with a remarkable memory but suspicious to the point of paranoia, even of his closest counsellors.

We have had to wait until 2003 for a fuller picture. Simon Sebag Montefiore's grandiose study of Stalin's 'court'[2] is based on exhaustive reading in the archives and published sources, as well as interviews with surviving descendants of the mighty (such as A.I. Rykov's daughter Natalia). It aims to portray the dictator in the context of his immediate circle, and so includes a great deal of material on members of his family and those of members of the Politburo, along with secret-police functionaries, generals, writers and so on. Montefiore exploits well unpublished testimony from the diary of Maria Svanidze (wife of Stalin's brother-in-law) and notes compiled by his civil-war crony, S.M. Budennyi. We are offered an enormous amount of data on life in the Kremlin (and Kuntsevo, Stalin's *dacha*), the ever-changing pattern of personal relationships at the top, and the arbitrary way decisions were often taken – especially as regards the fate of any official who incurred the tyrant's displeasure and was 'repressed' (the common euphemism, that is, usually shot with or without trial). Here Montefiore largely follows the approach taken by Robert Conquest, in his *Great Terror* (1968 [1990]), but amplifies his findings in many particulars. Much of this will be familiar ground to specialists, but there is also a good deal of fresh information, all treated in a calm, deadpan tone with flashes of irony and wit.

Montefiore refrains from moralizing in *Stalin* but makes it abundantly clear that Stalin's world was riven by squalid intrigues and scandals. Yet the leader's character had its gentler side, too: he could be charming, liked practical jokes, and treated children kindly (so long as their parents did not fall into the category of 'enemies'). After the death in 1932 of his second wife, Nadezhda Allilueva, Stalin's temperament changed for the worse; 'always alone, even among his convivial entourage' (p. 153), he found little satisfaction in subsequent amorous liaisons or masculine friendships. A prey to fits of paranoia, and convinced of his own greatness, he would strike out unpredictably at actual or potential opponents, fully aware that such random violence caused unjust suffering and death, but reasoning that sacrifices on this massive scale were the price that had to be paid to reach the regime's goals and make its leader feel more secure. Moreover, this inhuman outlook was shared by all those who exercised power at senior level, so that one should not make the mistake of holding Stalin alone responsible for the excesses: all these men were 'frightened fanatics', whose 'evangelical enthusiasm' for bloodshed 'sometimes totters on the edge of tragi-comedy' (pp. 182–3).

For all its brilliance Montefiore's *Stalin* does not present a comprehensive portrait of the man or his reign, for it sets out to be no more than a 'chronicle' without pretension to close analysis of policy. Much of the fascinating detail is of limited historical significance. As the focus continually shifts, the reader is jolted from one incident to another without much explanation of the causes and consequences of each move. For example, did it matter that so many of the top leaders were linked by family ties? On crucial episodes such as S.M. Kirov's assassination or the motives for the Hitler–Stalin pact, Montefiore does offer alternative interpretations, but by and large he is content to let the record speak for itself. Likewise, sources are rarely evaluated for reliability and references to them are bunched together awkwardly at the back of the book. To be sure, these blemishes will only bother other writers keen to check on the accuracy of the facts reported, whereas the general reader will enjoy being swept along by this absorbing narrative of villainy and tragic error. It has no equal as an account of the goings-on at the centre of power, but may annoy those who prefer a more 'bottom-up' (society-oriented) approach.

Quite a different tack is taken by Erik van Ree (Amsterdam), who provides an iconoclastic study of 'Stalin as thinker'.[3] Was he not essentially an opportunist who used ideas as weapons to gain and retain sole power? Were not any political notions he had purely derivative and, towards the end of his life, absurdly remote from reality? Van Ree faces up at the outset (pp. 1–17) to these and other obvious objections, urging us not to apply our own conceptual framework to an alien milieu; rather we should try to penetrate Stalin's 'mental universe' by investigating the ideological constructs within which his thoughts were constrained. Even if he was often deliberately mendacious, he was also a 'true believer' in Marxist–Leninist doctrine as *he* interpreted it; therefore, when analysed thematically, we find that his notions on class struggle, world revolution, or the need for total unity and a strong state under socialism have a perverse inner logic. Practically all the elements in his 'strange compound of Marxism and nationalism' have precedents in the thought of the creed's founding fathers or other Western Marxist leaders. Thus there is more to his teaching than mere deception or manipulation. If one looks at the marginal notes that Stalin scribbled on books in his personal library, it emerges that these were confined to the 'classics', which he took seriously, whereas he left unmarked historical or literary works that occupied only a small corner of his mind.

It is therefore wrong to see him acting consciously as a latter-day Ivan Groznyi or Peter the Great (images that feature in Montefiore's work, as they do in the standard biography by Robert Tucker).[4]

Erik van Ree's thesis in *The Political Thought of Joseph Stalin*, sustained as it is by a thorough examination of Stalin's private jottings and casual conversational remarks as well as his published statements, is open to the objection that these texts do not fully encompass their author's psyche, which had a subconscious dimension less adequately, if at all, reflected in doctrine. His argument is more convincing in regard to long-range strategic issues, notably in the foreign-policy field, than to, say, the Terror, which can scarcely be characterized as 'a climactic form of class struggle' (p. 117) but rather as a perversion of it. 'We have several documents', van Ree goes on, 'to suggest that Stalin was under the impression that the confessions beaten out of his victims were genuine' (p. 120). Maybe so, but it strains credulity too far to see such practices as killing opponents by getting the NKVD to stage a fake car crash as anything other than thuggery, far removed from any political principle, Marxist or otherwise. Even so, van Ree's propositions are cogently argued and deserve careful reading by any future biographer of the dictator.

He or she will also need to consider the original approach of the American historian Alfred J. Rieber.[5] Taking his weapons from the PM armoury, he seeks to establish a complex profile of Stalin's 'multiple identity' as a 'man from the borderlands'; the way he 'constructed' and presented himself helps to explain his appeal to rank-and-file Party stalwarts and thus his rise to power, for he was better able than other contenders to bridge the gap between the core territory and the periphery of the neo-imperial Soviet state. By the mid-1920s, where this sketch stops, Stalin is seen to be skilfully balancing three projections of his self: a commitment to the proletariat as dominant class, to an ethno-cultural region (Transcaucasia) as territorial unit, and to Great Russia as the USSR's political centre. Rieber's approach to his subject is sophisticated and he draws on an impressive range of material, but judgement on its validity must await publication of his forthcoming book, provisionally entitled *Cold War as Civil War: Russia and Its Borderlands*, which will treat later periods as well. Crucial to any evaluation will be the concepts of 'identity' and 'self-representation', on which professional psychologists ought to have much to say.[6] This terminology may have advantages over the traditional historians' limited tools, for can we really speak of 'beliefs' or 'principles' in regard to someone so notoriously unprincipled?

Heinz-Dietrich Löwe (Heidelberg), like Rieber an authority on pre-revolutionary Russia, has recently brought out a two-volume biography of Stalin[7] designed for the general reader – which explains the lack of footnotes; instead there is a thematic bibliography (pp. 401–19) that refers one to the newly available Russian sources. Löwe is in no doubt about Stalin's decisive role in policy-making from the First FYP onward. He declares roundly that 'the Soviet leadership clearly bears the moral guilt [for the 1932–3 famine] . . . since the death of millions could have been at least limited, and probably even prevented, if it had only wished to. But Stalin did not want to do so' (p. 229) – a remark that may raise eyebrows in revisionist circles. Stalin was 'the great radicalizer' who constantly sought to force the pace, yet time and again would suddenly switch course and make concessions when he realized that unremitting extremism would endanger his regime (p. 235). 'He was clever enough to present himself as the initiator of acts of moderation' while plotting the next offensive move against fainthearts in the leadership. In applying terrorist measures Stalin was 'the great doser' who carefully calibrated the amount of violence to be administered, while donning the mask of 'good Tsar'. The minutes of the February–March 1937 Central Committee plenum, published in 1992–5, 'leave no doubt that it was Stalin who set the course or who, as was said then, uncovered major conspiracies and directed the Chekists' work in the proper direction' (p. 257). It was he and his 'paladins' who authorized compilation of lists of those to be repressed (p. 265), 'and therefore the purges did not, as sometimes claimed [by certain revisionists], get out of control; rather they were driven forward in the localities with maximum energy and brutality by the centre, by Stalin's closest intimates' (p. 237).

Most traditional historians would endorse this 'intentionalist' view, although Löwe may be taking it a little too far when he asserts that 'at all times Stalin determined the scale of the repressions' (p. 280), for nuances matter here. It seems rather that local functionaries were granted a certain leeway to interpret what the centre wanted and sensed that excesses would normally be tolerated by their superiors – at least until the line suddenly changed. But the main point is that subordinate officials could not have committed their crimes unless these had been authorized in advance from the top (see Chapter 11, p. 177).

Löwe does not spoil his argument by overdoing the horrors, and includes enough general history to provide context. The leader's diplomatic successes and setbacks during and after the war are duly noted, and his reign ends in a *Götterdämmerung* – the parallel with Hitler's Reich is hinted at – marked by famine, intellectual stultification (except, perhaps, in atomic physics)[8] and further waves of repression, if on a less extensive scale than in 1937–8. The 'anti-cosmopolitan' campaign clearly had Stalin's blessing, although 'he carefully avoided being directly identified with it'. Seeking an explanation for the regime's resort to anti-Semitic measures that so crassly contradicted its 'internationalist' ideology, Löwe suggests that they were primarily a mass mobilization device, 'the best possible means of isolating the Soviet Union from the West', with its threatening ideals of liberalism and democracy (pp. 379, 389–91).[9]

Not much is said here about the leader cult that Stalin fostered with such assiduity from his 'fiftieth' birthday onward.[10] Sarah Davies, in an article on this topic, dates its firm establishment to 1933–4; intensified after Kirov's assassination, it reached its apogee in 1936–7; the momentum petered out two years later, when propagandists placed more emphasis on Molotov, only to revive once the war began. How did people react to it? The upwardly mobile, she argues, responded positively to the suggestion that the charismatic leader was their defender and benefactor, whereas to ordinary folk it was the paternalistic aspect that appealed more, if at all. By and large, people took from the official mythology whatever conformed to their own way of thinking.[11]

Davies's analysis is convincing up to the point where she puts forward a claim that, in the course of a 'constant process of "negotiation" between "official" and "popular" aspirations, [the regime] adjusted its messages in response to pressure from below'. This seems implausible. Certainly, the officials who administered the leader cult had to take some account of the market for their notions, much as commercial advertisers do in an open society, but does this really constitute a 'response'? Unless evidence of such interaction is discovered in Agitprop papers, it seems safer to say that the extent and character of cult literature was determined by the regime's perception of its interests. Jeffrey Brooks (see below) remarks that 'Stalin allowed for innovations from below in the cult's performance'[12] but does not go so far as Davies. No such proposition about popular input into the cult is advanced in an article on the topic by Benno Ennker, author of a major work on its Leninist antecedent.[13] He is surely correct in regarding it rather as an instrumental device to construct, for a society that had lost its sense of absolute values, a point of orientation equally binding on everyone.[14] On the chronology of the cult, he agrees more or less with Davies, noting (p. 177) that after 1934 it acquired a more emotional quality, as evidenced in the use of the term 'beloved Leader'.

Public culture, political institutions

This point is also made by Jeffrey Brooks in his major study of public culture under Stalin.[15] Abundantly illustrated, this rests on a detailed sampling of *Pravda* and some other central press organs; the chief themes and issues are treated in an 'interpretative context' (p. xix), statistical evidence being adduced as appropriate. Naturally, the cult features prominently; according to Brooks, it peaked in December 1939 (*pace* Davies), on the leader's sixtieth (official) birthday, when his near-deification performed the role of a 'creation myth' and lent it 'almost magical power. Stalin's cult and its embellishments in representations of Soviet life had the classic attributes of a primitive ritualistic drama: recurrent themes, stereotypical characters, and symbolic settings. The political theatre of high Stalinism drew in all the active elements of Soviet society, engaging them at once in participation and complicity' (p. 66).

In explaining 'this extended performance' that involved so many actors, Brooks moves beyond the familiar sociological interpretation (its evocation of religiosity and patriarchalism) to a 'culturalist' one: certainly the aim was to legitimize the regime, 'to smooth a very rough system of authority', but it did so by 'adopt[ing] elaborate rituals of theatre to tell a story about the Soviet experience . . . to bring about a national consensus based on his personal and near mythic authority'. Many people probably played along with this 'grand show' because they 'craved some kind of legitimate order', whereas others joined in for opportunistic reasons. They then 'internalize[d] the logic and forms of familiar rituals' and even introduced some innovations in them 'to sustain the expected sequence of behaviour' (pp. 66–9). The most potent source of the cult's appeal lay in the promise of 'a cherished future' of material abundance and national grandeur.

If Brooks's main message relates to the theatrical ('performative') nature of Soviet public culture, a secondary theme is that the press, as the 'hegemon of information' (p. xiv), stimulated popular dependence on the ruler and his state through what is called here 'the economy of the gift' (pp. 83–105). Journalists heaped praise on high achievers held up to the public as models such as Stakhanovites, scientists, or aviators, while they in turn paid tribute to the authorities, and to the Leader personally, for making their exploits possible. Since most citizens could not hope to reciprocate adequately all the benefits allegedly showered upon them, they felt humiliated and fell into a permanent state of moral indebtedness. By repeating such slogans as 'Thank you, comrade Stalin, for a happy childhood' they helped to reinforce the existing hierarchy and to conceal 'an elaborate system of rewards that was not really justified' (p. 84). Brooks recognizes that this adulation was often insincere or ambiguous, but holds that its chief effect was to create 'a circle of obligation, effort, entitlement and reward' that embraced the entire active population (p. 89). He continues the story through the war and post-war years, noting that 'Stalin's final triumph was the enactment of his own funeral', but that once he was dead his charisma evaporated and the country's new leaders tried to base their legitimacy on rational rather than mythic foundations, but in doing so undermined 'Soviet society's essential otherness' (pp. 233, 239).

Perceptive as this study is (though some readers may feel he overdoes the explanatory value of his insights), it does not provide a picture of the propaganda apparatus as an institution, and one hopes that in future some scholar will leap to fill the gap, even if the records of the CC's Agitprop department may not seem very attractive material to work with. What *can* be done in this area has been shown by Michael David-Fox, whose *Revolution of the Mind*[16] deals with an equally unpromising topic: political education in the 1920s, that is, the training in the social sciences given at the Institute of Red Professors, the Sverdlov Communist University, the Socialist (later Communist) Academy, and in a whole gamut of Party schools across the land, all of it highly coloured by the Bolsheviks' peculiar interpretation of Marxism and designed to transform the thinking of an entire people. The 'Party style in intellectual life', with its intolerance, specialized jargon, rituals and rhetoric, shaped the outlook of the 'new class' in a fundamental manner and had a 'devastating effect' on the way science and learning were perceived in Stalin's USSR (and later, too). This was most obvious in the encouragement of an obsessive concern with unmasking hidden enemies ('deviationists'), a practice that began as 'an intellectual game [but] soon would become high political drama' (p. 131). David-Fox presents a 'culturalist' interpretation of Stalinism's roots that is more searching than the familiar one, focussed on factional struggle at the summit of the Party. Since Stalin was 'in many ways a product of his milieu', the drive to eliminate 'impurities' in the Party élite needs to be seen as characteristic of an entire political culture, one that underwent a fundamental shift *circa* 1929. There existed an 'intricate web of interconnections . . . between culture, politics, and intellectual style', explored here with remarkable sophistication and originality (pp. 189–91).

The political history of the 'Great Turn' (1929–30) has been enriched by Catherine Merridale (Bristol), author of an earlier monograph on the capital city around this time, who examines 'the dynamics of political change' there in the light of archival sources.[17] Stalin, she argues, showed 'consummate skill and timing' in securing the dismissal in October 1928 of N.A. Uglanov, the first Party secretary in the capital (p. 74). He was unpopular with the rank-and-file, many of whom supported his ouster from personal conviction – without necessarily approving of Stalin-style wholesale collectivization. They were sceptical about the merits of the rival factions fighting each other at the top, a struggle in which they were unable to participate. Although there was 'a consensus for change . . . there was no massive and unthinking Stalinist clique in Moscow' at that time (pp. 77–8); instead, Party officials in the capital were anxious about the direction in which the country was going and the consequences this would have on their own position. Even after the screw had been tightened in 1929–30 'opposition to Stalin's personal rule and policies continued at all levels of the Party' and 'a sullen silence about official values characterized significant sections of the non-Party population'. In sum: 'support for individual aspects of Stalinist policy was contingent and conditional' (p. 84). These findings are useful in that they illuminate more clearly the context in which M.A. Riutin put forward his 'platform', in which, as is well known, he voiced radical criticism of the General Secretary's policies and may even have forced him to make temporary concessions.

For the years that followed, it is harder to construct detailed studies of Party organizations at republic, city or *oblast'* level, but they will surely follow as more attention comes to be focused on the provinces than on the two metropolitan cities.[18] In the former studies, a great deal of attention is rightly paid to the way officials in outlying areas (the 'periphery') interpreted the instructions they received from the 'centre', sometimes neglecting or ignoring them, or else perverting their intent in order to advance their own personal or sectional interests. This approach has to some extent discredited the view once widely held that these men were unthinking automata, pliant tools in the hands of their masters. Where scholars used to see only top-down hierarchical relationships, they now prefer to speak of interaction between different levels of the power structure. Even if Moscow got its way in the end, so the argument goes, it did so only by applying more coercive means than originally intended, and at much heavier cost. The emphasis is now on the waste and inefficiency besetting any over-centralized bureaucratic system, especially one trying to do too much too quickly.

This approach was pioneered in the 1990s by American revisionist scholars such as Stephen Kotkin, who offered an in-depth analysis of Magnitogorsk, the new city in the Urals that epitomized the Stalin regime's aspirations to industrial might and urban modernity.[19] In briefer compass, but taking a longer time period, Hiroaki Kuromiya (Bloomington) has tackled similarly the key coal-mining region of the Donbas in eastern Ukraine.[20] In two chapters on the Stalin years, he offers a convincing (and largely critical) analysis of political and social realities: the presence during the First FYP era of fugitives with bogus identities (p. 161), the uncovering by zealots of Riutin sympathizers (p. 177), the effect of Stakhanovism on the way work was organized in the mines (p. 215), and the impact of the Great Terror: he notes that of the 377 Poles arrested, 80 per cent were shot (p. 232).

'Throughout all the turbulence', Kuromiya contends, perhaps a little too enthusi-astically, 'the Donbas retained its reputation as the free steppe . . . a potential base for anti-Moscow counter-revolution' (p. 186). In later chapters he turns his attention to the war years, when the region was temporarily under enemy occupation, and the hardships that followed liberation.

The Donbas was viewed with jealous eyes by Party officials in the Urals, or so James Harris reports in a study[21] whose title reflects an ambitious plan for regional development elaborated by provincial officials in 1928–9. They ener-getically battled Gosplan to be allocated high growth rates and so lavish resources from the centre, and in the event got more investment than could readily be absorbed. Funds were grossly squandered, plans repeatedly changed, and targets under-fulfilled. Meanwhile the region became a major dumping ground for deported kulaks (or those so labelled). In effect decision-makers at the centre and in the periphery vied with each other in pushing through irrational measures that cost local residents (not to mention deportees) dearly. 'High-tempo indus-trialization did not disturb the regions; indeed they did everything in their power to encourage the centre to spend and build as much as possible. If Moscow had become infected with "gigantomania", it had caught the disease from the regions' (p. 131).

As evidence mounted of inefficiency and chaos, local officials found themselves charged with malfeasance. Their reaction was to pretend to submit to Moscow's dictates, to submit misleading reports, and to shift the blame on to scapegoats. By 1936, these practices had inflamed local tensions to such a point that the bureau-crats in Sverdlovsk (Yekaterinburg) could no longer control them. Moscow scented conspiracy. 'The call by the Central Committee to round up former oppositionists was the match to the powder keg' and so the Terror got under way in this region (p. 189). Harris does not emulate Kuromiya in giving details of who victimized whom. Instead his account is weighted towards problems of planning and administration. Its principal merit is to offer a view of the origins of the purges from a regional perspective.

Turning back to the scene at the centre, the historian Evan Mawdsley and the political scientist Stephen White (both Glasgow), offer an unprecedentedly thorough analysis of the Central Committee of the CPSU,[22] the tip of the *nomenklatura* that effectively ran the country. This is not a work for easy reading but rather for reference, even though biographical information is provided on the key players which helps to add flesh and blood to what would otherwise be just a statistical or politological exercise. Chapter 2 (pp. 34–90) deals with the period from Lenin's death to the Great Terror, chapter 3 (pp. 91–135) with 'Stalin's New Elite', the men who succeeded its victims. These comprised no fewer than two-thirds of the men who had served on the Party's central executive since 1923. Turnover, which was normal (15–16 per cent) in 1927 and 1930, rose to 34 per cent in 1934 and a horrific 83 per cent in 1939, by when 'the Central Committee [had] devour[ed] itself' (pp. 34, 64, 420). Mawdsley and White offer a plausible explanation for the bloodshed: 'what mattered to [Stalin] was the preservation of his own personal power and the consolidation of what he perceived as the interests of the Revolution', supposedly threatened by hidden foes (p. 83). Yet 'there is little specific evidence of élite opposition', for these senior functionaries were concerned only to preserve a measure of stability in government. But it was precisely this prospect of a tenured, self-conscious bureaucracy that the *Vozhd'* sought to destroy – logically, from his standpoint, and in the end successfully (p. 89), but at incalculable cost.

One must wonder about the degree of success achieved if, as the authors go on to argue, the new élite was 'much more secure than the old' (p. 93), in that the mortality rate among the 1939 and 1941 cohorts was a mere 7 per cent (p. 95). Little change occurred in the 'representation' on the CC of various potential interest groups (managers, military, etc.), but they were more plebeian in origin, less well educated, and addicted to authoritarian methods of governance – the Stalinist type with which one is familiar, in short. One favourably disposed reviewer regrets that the authors did not do more to explore this ossification of the Party élite, a result of the purge and indirectly a cause of the Soviet collapse.[23] Mawdsley and White's treatment of these men (there were precious few women) is exhaustive but unduly austere. One is left wondering whether the authors do not place too much emphasis on age as a determinant of conduct and would have welcomed more context (what did they do with their power and why?); however, this would have required more than a single volume. They have provided just what was promised, a personnel profile of a key institution.

The two authors' approach is with some justice termed 'highly formal and static' by S.G. Wheatcroft (Melbourne), who draws a sharp contrast between the Central Committee (as 'the formal élite') with the *real* 'decision-making élite', the Politburo or those of its members who were particularly close to the leader at certain junctures. Wheatcroft offers an analysis of the 2,800 persons received in Stalin's office – on average about 10 times each – from 1930 onward.[24] Since Stalin also consulted people privately *outside* his office, and we do not know what was said at these meetings, the statistical calculations presented here are perhaps less revealing than Wheatcroft claims, but they do at least show basic trends: for example, in 1938 the state security chiefs made up 14.4 per cent of Stalin's callers, but only 2.0 per cent in 1948 (p. 100). The author sees 'considerable group participation' in decision-making and challenges the once generally accepted image of Stalin as a 'lone dictator' (p. 102).

According to the editor of this volume, E.A. Rees (Florence), the key moment in the establishment of his personal despotism came in 1937;[25] before then he was up to a point dependent on his closest subordinates, who controlled key agencies. These men could influence his thinking but did not 'fence him in' and fell into line once he had settled an issue, so that his pre-eminence was not in doubt. Granting that this was so, it may be a little misleading to speak here of 'oligarchy', but Rees explores the nuances of personal relationships at the summit between 1929 and 1953 more carefully than previous writers, and his distinction between a despot (one who kills his subordinates: p. 206) and a mere dictator certainly merits further discussion.

The operations of the Council of People's Commissars (*Sovnarkom*), the chief government body, were thoroughly scrutinized in 1996 by another British scholar,

Derek Watson (Birmingham).[26] This is institutional history par excellence, which ends with the rather astonishing claim that Sovnarkom 'failed to become a cabinet . . . but did become a remarkably sophisticated body, the procedures of which compare favourably with governments and cabinets in contemporary Western countries'. This seems to put office procedure before substance and to ignore the removal of so much of the government's regular business into the hands of the dictator and his intimates. Even Arch Getty thinks Watson is rather too sanguine about Sovnarkom's efficiency, since there is ample evidence of overlappping, redundancy and sheer chaos.[27] Although V.M. Molotov is featured in the book's title, little is actually said here about him as an individual, but since the man was so notoriously tight-lipped this can scarcely be held against the author.

Since Watson wrote Yoram Gorlizki (Manchester) has taken the story on into the post-war era.[28] As he sees it, the senior government body was afflicted by 'perpetual tension' between modern bureaucratic ways of doing business and despotic practices that allowed Stalin to intervene at will, since he enjoyed 'enormous discretion' (p. 701). The term 'totalitarianism' does less than justice to this complex hybrid situation, but alas, the author's alternative, 'neo-patrimonialism', is unlikely to come so readily to people's lips. He provides fresh data about the Council's eight sectoral bureaux, designed to co-ordinate supervision over various branches of the economy; there was even a ninth one, of deputy premiers, to supervise the others. Hardly surprising, therefore, that efficiency suffered, or that in the last months of his life Stalin apparently became dissatisfied with the system. Whatever draconian measures he may have had in mind, we do not know, and it was left to his successors to go on tinkering with the top-heavy system of administration they inherited (p. 736).

Behind the institutional framework lay a tissue of inter-personal relations, not least those between patrons and clients. A great deal of work remains to be done in this area,[29] to which Sheila Fitzpatrick offers a sparkling *entrée* in a miscellany of 1998.[30] Stalin was by no means the only patron: oppositionists like Bukharin also built up such networks, as did police chiefs (Yagoda, Yezhov) and writers (Lunacharsky, Gorky), but Molotov was one of the most sought after. Clients usually established relations with them through intermediaries ('brokers') and adopted a particular literary style when writing to them (pp. 44–5). The protection they extended might enable an innocent man to survive the Terror, as well as providing material or career benefits of lesser magnitude. The patrons derived some prestige from granting such favours but if they were too generous might well fall from grace – one reason for the drastic action taken against Stalin's old patron Abel Yenukidze (p. 52). Informal links of this kind were the grease that lubricated the system – and contributed to the dependency syndrome described by Brooks; they bolstered the regime's image of 'fatherly concern' for its humble subjects.

This topic is also taken up on a more abstract theoretical plane by the Australian political scientist Graeme Gill.[31] In 1990 he published a weighty tome in which Stalin was allotted a relatively subordinate role in the institutional set-up.[32] He since appears to have modified his views, for he now states that 'the primacy of the personalist principle [was] a crucial feature of the Soviet mechanism of power', which 'shaped administrative processes at respective levels of the structure and moulded relations between those different levels'. But this principle was 'matched' (that is, counteracted?) by 'opposing . . . pressures for the strengthening and routinization of organizational norms'; the tension between the two 'was a major factor structuring the way in which the mechanism of power functioned' (pp. 8, 10–11).

The collection of articles in which these observations occur also contains an important contribution by the editor, Niels Rosenfeldt, on 'The Importance of the Secret Apparatus of the Soviet Communist Party during the Stalin Era' (pp. 40–70) in which he concludes that fresh archival evidence confirms his earlier view 'that the secret Party apparatus played a crucial role in the communication and security system; that it was an important means of information and personnel control; and that it also performed significant analytical tasks for the supreme leadership' (p. 61).[33] All these specialized institutional studies usefully complement works written from a more 'personalist' perspective such as Montefiore's.

The command economy

The chief occupation of senior Party and government officials was running the command ('planned') economy. A flood of orders, regulations and directives rained down from Moscow on the heads of hapless provincial functionaries or enterprise managers. Most of them did their best to comply, not least from apprehension lest adverse consequences ensue, but compliance often went hand in hand with a variety of evasive tricks: building up unaccounted-for stocks or falsifying statistical data and the like. They would also commonly plead for unrealistic targets to be lowered, and involve some junior employees (engineers, foremen) in these practices, while others looked on suspiciously, eager to detect subversive leanings.

These informal relationships have been thoroughly studied in recent years by Western social historians (see Chapter 8, p. 128) whereas the economic aspects have rather gone out of fashion. This may partly be because socialist planning is no longer seen as a viable alternative to the 'free' market; partly it may stem from lack of the technical proficiency required to elucidate the rich documentary evidence that has now become available.

Another possible reason for neglect may be that in 1994 a team of (mainly) British specialists edited a work on the subject so authoritative as to deter emulators.[34] Buttressed by 61 statistical tables, this volume covered population, employment, agriculture, industry, transport and technological development. Davies argued here (pp. 151–2) that the Soviet leaders 'at least partly' achieved the main objectives they had set themselves in 1928/9: to catch up on the advanced capitalist countries in output per head and technical proficiency, doing so in conditions of enforced self-sufficiency, while 'progress also took place in . . . shift[ing] the location of industry' to the east; but he acknowledged the acute strain on consumers: between 1928 and 1937 real wages declined (according to one calculation by 43 per cent).

The Davies team's approach and statistics are endorsed by Manfred Hildermeier in his magisterial history,[35] although he gives greater weight to foreign technological input and is more critical of the planned economy's shortcomings: although 'the leap into the industrial age was achieved', the consumer remained a 'stepchild' of officialdom; this was an 'utopia gone awry', in which 'an entire generation was sacrificed to a vision that could not be realized in the short term, nor perhaps in the long term either' (p. 487).

For the non-specialist reader, the most accessible way of tackling the problems of the command economy is through study of the personalities of its 'commanders' and their often tragic fates. G.K. ('Sergo') Ordzhonikidze, the USSR's 'industrial tsar' until his suicide in 1937, is the subject of an article[36] by Francesco Benvenuti (Bologna), who notes that the Georgian's 'reformist inclinations' did not go very far and that he 'would change his opinions, or present them in different ways' to satisfy current political requirements (p. 153). Since then, three British authors have produced thorough studies of the economic decision-making process in a miscellany edited by another senior colleague, Paul Gregory, who contributes an article on Stalin's interventions.[37] This makes it clear that although the General Secretary's authority was a key factor he did not try to 'micro-manage' the economy, and that plan targets resulted from negotiation between institutions at different levels in the hierarchy. (One should add that there were important exceptions to this generalization.) The system was plagued by competition for scarce resources and tensions between centre and periphery.

This is much the same picture as one that emerged from an earlier miscellany (1997), edited by E.A. Rees.[38] Here the editor and Derek Watson dealt with decision-making in the Politburo, while Davies and Khlevniuk showed the strict limits within which Gosplan was obliged to operate; other articles dealt with the various people's commissariats, from Finance to Water Transport.

More recently, Davies, in tandem with Wheatcroft, has advanced new data on the reasons for the catastrophic famine of 1932–3 and official reactions to it.[39] They argue that, while the leadership cannot be absolved from responsibility (notoriously, it insisted on unrealistically high grain procurements from the starving), underlying agro-technical factors should not be forgotten: soil exhaustion due to over-cropping helps to explain why the 1932 harvest was much lower than expected; lack of traction power led to delays and crop losses; and last, but not least, the weather was bad. Government policy vacillated: first relatively 'soft' measures were adopted (the so-called 'neo-NEP') and even after it stiffened again there were 'important compromises and retreats' (p. 79). Later still, as the scale of the calamity could no longer be ignored, hitherto unknown secret orders were issued to release reserve grain stocks to the afflicted regions. In sum, the picture is 'more ambiguous and confused than is generally believed' (p. 89). This may well be true, but some of these revisionist arguments smack of special pleading and will scarcely shatter the 'traditional view' that Wheatcroft's volume sets out to 'challenge'.

Another recent article by Davies, once again together with the knowledgeable Russian scholar Oleg Khlevniuk, is less contentious and more plausible. They examine the very considerable shifts in investment policy that occurred during the so-called 'good years' of the Second FYP.[40] In 1935 there was a sharp increase (31.6 per cent up on the previous year, even higher in the defence sector), but from

August 1936 the authorities reverted to policies designed to lead to more balanced growth (pp. 875, 889). It was during the former phase that the leaders gave encouragement to the Stakhanov movement to boost labour productivity. Resistance to this at factory level provoked repressive measures by local zealots and the dismissal of many competent managers, and so in April 1936 it had to be toned down (p. 886). As regards the economic impact of Stakhanovism, it was relatively slight: it yielded no more than 'a quarterly blip in the general advance of productivity' that had begun well before the campaign started (p. 894). The authors buttress their analysis with a wealth of statistical data, while warning the reader of its imperfections.

Militarization and nationalism

What came to be called the Stalinist 'administrative-command system' had a strong military element. The desire to catch up on the Western ('imperialist') powers was a major motive behind the first FYP, with its (over-)rapid tempos of advance. Until quite recently, Soviet secrecy limited Westerners' ability to tackle this all-important 'defence component' of the plan, so that its significance was often underestimated. The situation has now improved and literature on this neglected topic is growing apace.

Roger Reese offers a general overview of the 'Soviet military experience' in which two chapters are devoted to the inter-war era and one to World War II.[41] The author draws on an earlier monograph (1996), based in part on materials in the military archive (RGVA), notably in regard to the Political Administration (PUR). Reese notes that this agency 'experienced a great failure in its efforts to lead soldiers in the socialist reconstruction of the countryside' and was unable to suppress the men's understandable hostility to forced collectivization. Indeed, by fostering basic literacy among the troops it actually engendered a potential backlash against the regime (pp. 75–7). Efforts to boost the number of humbly born officers also had disappointing results. Many of them were incompetent and 'criminal activity among officers manifested itself at an astoundingly high rate', notably in embezzlement of their men's pay; efforts to overcome such abuses were one reason for the shift to greater professionalization in the later 1930s (pp. 82–5). Reese is 'soft' on the impact of the Terror. He puts the number of military personnel arrested at 9,506, of whom 'several thousand were released and rehabilitated', while another 13,000 were discharged in disgrace, suggesting that the military purge was 'a less terrifying experience' than earlier writers thought – even though 'it left scars on the army's psyche' until the 1950s (pp. 86–9).

The equipment they got, apart from Lend-Lease deliveries after 1942, came from the defence-industry complex. This is the subject of a miscellany edited by two leading British specialists.[42] In an article on defence industry in the 1930s (pp. 70–95), Harrison and Davies conclude that in 1931–5, despite rapid rearmament, 'the burden on government resources did not grow because the government's share [of] national resources was now far larger than before' (which surely does not mean that the burden on the *population* did not increase?); but after 1936 real defence spending accelerated and 'its relative burden also grew markedly' as manpower and material resources were mobilized more intensively. (In the single key year of 1936, military expenditure rose by an estimated 60 per cent (pp. 92, 94).)

In a more detailed study of such matters during the First FYP era, David Stone offers a close, archive-based analysis[43] of the tug-of-war for resources between military and civilian planners, the latter backed notably by A.I. Rykov as CPC chairman. 'A shift towards radical rearmament' began in 1928, but yielded relatively little in the short term. The industrialization drive created a good deal of chaos, in which managers of defence plants took the blame, in a politically inspired campaign that had 'pernicious consequences', for failing to meet the expectations of the army leaders, who acquired a strong voice in policy-making. It was the Manchurian crisis of late 1931, however, that placed the economy 'on a permanent war footing'. Targets were drastically raised in a crash military build-up that did 'profound damage' to the economy. In particular, it produced a vast amount of equipment that would be out of date when disaster struck 10 years later. In an appendix, Stone offers figures for the defence budget from 1928 to 1932: it rose from 1.2 to 6.4 milliard roubles – five times higher than the figure officially published (p. 217) – which is a warning to anyone inclined to take Soviet statistics at face value.

This is not a volume readily accessible to the non-specialist, who would be well advised to lead off with a complementary work by the Swedish specialist Lennart Samuelson. This covers some of the same ground but has the advantage of focusing on the career of a cardinal decision-maker, Marshal M.N. Tukhachevsky.[44] By 1936, the armed forces' weapons procurements were over three times what they had been in 1933, but in the next critical year military industry could produce only two-thirds of the planned figure (pp. 180–2). Stalin's decapitation of the Red Army – here the estimated casualty figure is much higher than that put forward by Reese – had 'far-reaching consequences' in that it stifled debate on strategy and so undermined the country's war preparedness (pp. 185–8). Samuelson's main conclusions are that one should not speak of 'militarization' in the early 1930s (here he differs from Stone), and that subsequent contingency plans were realistic given the situation at the time, for no one could then reasonably have anticipated the events of 1939–41. Clearly, this is only the beginning of a fruitful debate that will long engage defence experts from many lands.

While purely military factors may be said to have determined the Soviet– German war's outcome, morale was clearly of major importance, and here the regime's appeal to Russian nationalism (thinly disguised as 'Soviet patriotism') played a decisive role. The shift of ideological values from Leninist 'proletarian internationalism' can be dated back at least to the NEP era, with Stalin's slogan of 'socialism in one country first'; it gathered force during the 1930s, when the modernization drive was hailed as bolstering the country's military might and great-power status. This topic is familiar territory to Western researchers, and historians today cannot add much unless they tap fresh archival sources. On the other hand, they cannot avoid reflecting contemporary concerns. The existence of powerful nationalist currents in the now independent Russian Federation have stimulated a quest for the origins of the phenomenon. A colloquium held at the University of London yielded a miscellany on *Russian Nationalism Past and Present*,[45] in which E.A. Rees provides a sensible, if not strikingly innovative, survey of Stalin's writing and thinking on the subject.[46] He notes the leader's prudence in introducing patriotic motifs into public discourse; thus in his speech of 7 November 1941 and later 'Stalin was careful not to associate himself too directly with this trend' (p. 89). One should not exaggerate the element of continuity with the official nationalism of the tsars, for the Soviet ruler never abandoned his commitment to revolutionary Marxism–Leninism. His conduct was shaped above all by tactical considerations: Russian patriotism was 'a force to be used and mobilized' in order to buttress the regime (p. 102). Few would dissent from this verdict, and Rees is also right to remind us that Leninism was never a cast-iron doctrine but 'embraced from the outset a diversity of opinion that included a certain nationalistic, messianistic current' (p. 97). After all, Marx, too, had his ethnic prejudices – a point brought out by Van Ree in the book discussed at the beginning of this chapter.

But how deeply were such prejudices shared by the populace? Sarah Davies, in her study of popular opinion in the late 1930s (to be considered more fully below, see p. 133), deals tangentially with this question. In Leningrad province (*oblast'*) the Terror, she contends, stimulated feelings of animosity toward Finns, although they comprised a mere 3 per cent of the inhabitants, and more particularly Jews (6.7 per cent), who were disliked because they were prominent in the privileged élite. Negative stereotypes abounded and particular leaders (for example, Ordzhonikidze) were identified as aliens whose 'defining characteristic [was their] non-Russianness'.[47] Davies may be reading too much here into the evidence of opinion surveys by the police, or *svodki*, and in the absence of polling data her findings should be regarded as provisional. Some other regions where the population's ethnic mix was greater may have manifested greater xenophobia, or so popular behaviour during wartime occupation suggests. On the other side of the coin, a positive sense of Russian identity, which according to Davies was weak in Leningrad in 1938–9 (p. 90), was surely far more prevalent once the enemy had been driven out, due to historical experience rather than to anything Authority said. The main point to emerge is that there was ample combustible material in the populace, which up to a point could be moulded in the direction the propagandists desired.

David Brandenberger presents a more positive view of popular 'Russo-centrism' on the eve of the war. Taking issue with Stephen Kotkin, who sees the regime as successfully forging a *Soviet* identity rather than a distinctly Russian one, he argues that the new patriotic line, as presented, for example, in Sergei Eisenstein's film *Alexander Nevsky*, evoked 'considerable resonance in Soviet society' and captured the general public's imagination. Educated people in particular were attracted, and half-consciously misconstrued it so as to exclude its 'Soviet' slant in favour of a more Russo-centric, indeed chauvinist, interpretation which officials tolerated even though they knew it deviated from what they really wanted, *étatisme*.[48] In an earlier article, written jointly with the Russian historian A.M. Dubrovsky, Brandenberger explored more closely 'the statist component of official ideology', focusing on its elaboration by pro-regime historians.[49] The two authors conclude (p. 883) that 'chauvinist, Russo-centric dimensions of the line are best understood as a consequence of the Party hierarchy's perhaps excessively cynical and calculating use of tsarist symbols and heroes, combined with a primitive understanding of history'. Stalin and his minions were not converts to Russian nationalism – on the contrary, they set out to destroy the hallmarks of Russians' national identity (Church, commune) as previously understood – but made a pragmatic calculation. Adapting one of the Leader's pet phrases, Brandenberger suggests that Soviet ideology was 'national in form, *étatiste* in content'.

A task for the future is to complement our knowledge of the re-emergence of Russian national feeling under Stalin's 'statism' with a deeper appreciation of contemporary developments among minority peoples, notably the Ukrainians. This large field has attracted a lot of attention from Western historians of ethnicity. Two of the leading authorities, Ronald Suny and Terry Martin, start out from the assumption (by now almost a cliché) that the Party's 'affirmative action' policy created problems that could not be contained by Soviet-style pseudo-federalism and ultimately brought the system down.[50] We shall touch on this topic only in the context of the repressions to which so many of these peoples, alas, fell victim (see Chapter 11).

Notes

1 Of the sources published in English, the most revealing is R.W. Davies *et al.* (eds), *The Stalin–Kaganovich Correspondence, 1931–1936* (New Haven, CT and London: Yale University Press, 2003; Russian edn, 2001), which supplements L.T. Lih (ed.), *Stalin's Letters to Molotov, 1925–1936* (New Haven, CT and London: Yale University Press, 1995). Another collection is P. Chinsky (ed.), *Staline: archives inédites, 1926–1936* (Paris: Berg International, 2001). Among the memoirs by senior personalities, the most rewarding on high politics in the Stalin era are those by N.S. Khrushchev, A.I. Mikoyan and G.K. Zhukov.

2 S. Sebag Montefiore, *Stalin: The Court of the Red Tsar* (London: Weidenfeld & Nicolson, 2003).

3 E. van Ree, *The Political Thought of Joseph Stalin: A Study in Twentieth-Century Revolutionary Patriotism* (London and New York: RoutledgeCurzon, 2002).

4 R.C. Tucker, *Stalin as Revolutionary, 1879–1929: A Study in History and Personality* (New York and London: Norton, 1973); *Stalin in Power: The Revolution from Above, 1928–1941* (New York and London: Norton 1990); cf. also his more recent article, 'Stalinism and Stalin: Sources and Outcomes', in M. Hildermeier (ed.), *Stalinismus vor dem II. Weltkrieg* (Munich: Oldenbourg, 1998), 1–16. Van Ree plays down Stalin's literary and aesthetic interests, whereas Montefiore sees him as 'a strangely literate dictator' (p. 310).

5 A.J. Rieber, 'Stalin, Man of the Borderlands', *AHR* 106 (2001), 651–91.

6 Rieber is not, evidently, a 'psycho-historian' such as Philip Pomper, author of *Lenin, Trotsky and Stalin: The Intelligentsia and Power* (New York: Columbia University Press, 1990), whose analysis is amplified by Eric Rhodes, 'Origins of a Tragedy: Joseph Stalin's Cycle of Abuse', *Journal of Psychohistory* (USA) 24 (1996/7), 377–89; he argues that his cruelty can be explained by the abuses he suffered as a child. Can these two approaches perhaps be reconciled?

7 H.-D. Löwe, *Stalin: der entfesselte Revolutionär* (Göttingen and Zurich: Muster-Schmidt, 2002); an English edition is anticipated.

8 'Leave [the physicists] in peace. We can always shoot them later,' he is said to have told Beria. See Chapter 10, p. 160.

9 Two recent biographies are as follows: (i) Miklos Kun, *Stalin: An Unknown Portrait* (Budapest and New York: Central European University Press, 2003), presumably by a descendant of the famous Hungarian revolutionary whom Stalin 'liquidated' in 1939; it is based in part on interviews and covers much the same ground as Montefiore's study (both volumes have excellent illustrations); (ii) R. Brackman, *The Secret File of Joseph Stalin: A Hidden Life*, London and Portland, OR: Frank Cass, 2001), who propounds the thesis that many of Stalin's actions can be explained by his embarrassment at the alleged discovery, in 1926, of documents on his earlier collaboration with the tsarist Okhrana. H. Rappaport, *Joseph Stalin: A Biographical Companion*, Santa Barbara, CA: ABC-CLIO, 1999) provides an alphabetic listing of persons and topics with some relationship to the Soviet leader. Recent work on his associates includes W. Hedeler, 'Neue Archivdokumente zur Biographie von G.Je. Zinowjev . . . ', *JHK* 1999, 297–316; K. Boterbloem, 'Young Zhdanov (1896–1918)', *CSP* 43 (2001), 281–96; and A. Graziosi, 'G.L. Piatakov, A Mirror on Soviet History', in idem, *A New Peculiar State: Explorations in Soviet History, 1917–1937* (Westport, CT and London: Praeger), 1–64 (first published in 1992). A biography of L.B. Kamenev is promised by Catherine Merridale.

10 Celebrated with pomp in December 1929; as is now known, Stalin was actually one year older than he claimed to be. Why he falsified the record has yet to be explained (see p. 32).

11 S. Davies, 'The Leader Cult: Propaganda and Its Reception in Stalin's Russia', in J. Channon (ed.), *Politics, Society and Stalinism in the USSR* (Basingstoke and London: Macmillan, 1998), 118, 122–4, 131.

12 J. Brooks, *'Thank You, Comrade Stalin!' Soviet Public Culture from Revolution to Cold War* (Princeton, NJ: Princeton University Press, 2000), 67.

13 B. Ennker, *Die Anfänge des Leninkults in der Sowjetunion* (Cologne: Böhlau, 1997); cf. D.L. Brandenberger, 'Sostavlenie i publikatsiia ofitsial'noi biografii vozhdia – katekhizis stalinizma', *VI*, 1997, no. 12, 141–50.

14 Idem, 'Politische Herrschaft und Stalinkult 1929–1939', in S. Plaggenborg (ed.), *Stalinismus: Neue Wege der Forschung* (Berlin: Arno Spitz), 151–82, here 181.

15 *'Thank You . . . '*, 60, 69ff. This volume is in a sense a sequel to Brooks's pioneering study *When Russia Learned to Read: Literacy and Popular Culture, 1861–1917* (Princeton, NJ: Princeton University Press, 1985).

16 M. David-Fox, *Revolution of the Mind: Higher Learning Among the Bolsheviks, 1918–1929* (Ithaca, NY and London: Cornell University Press, 1997).

17 C. Merridale, 'The Origins of the Stalinist State: Power and Politics in Moscow, 1928–1932', in Channon (ed.), *Politics, Society and Stalinism*, 69–92. The book was *Moscow Politics and the Rise of Stalin: the Communist Party in the Capital, 1925–1932* (Basingstoke: Macmillan, 1990).

18 The standard Western history of Moscow in the Soviet era, Timothy J. Colton, *Moscow: Governing the Socialist Metropolis* (Cambridge, MA and London: Belknap Press, 1995), provides a graphic picture of the Terror and also covers industrial expansion, social conditions and municipal politics.

19 S. Kotkin, *Magnetic Mountain: Stalinism as a Civilization* (Berkeley, CA: University of California Press, 1997). Kotkin has since written three books on the later Soviet and post-Soviet periods.

20 Hiroaki Kuromiya, *Freedom and Terror in the Donbas: A Ukrainian–Russian Borderland, 1870–1990s* (Cambridge and New York: Cambridge University Press, 1998); cf. also his 'Workers under Stalin: The Case of the Donbas', in Hildermeier (ed.), *Stalinismus*, 80.–97.

21 J.R. Harris, *The Great Urals: Regionalism and the Evolution of the Soviet System* (Ithaca, NY and London: Cornell University Press, 1999); cf. idem, 'Dual Subordination? The Political Police and the Party in the Urals Region, 1918–1953', *CMR* 42 (2001), 423–46.

22 E. Mawdsley and S. White, *The Soviet Elite from Lenin to Gorbachev: The Central Committee and Its Members* (Oxford and New York: Oxford University Press, 2000).

23 M.J. Carley, in *EAS* 55 (2003), 311–13.

24 S.G. Wheatcroft, 'From "Team-Stalin" to Degenerate Tyranny', in E.A. Rees (ed.), *The Nature of Stalin's Dictatorship: The Politburo, 1924–1953* (Basingstoke and New York: Palgrave Macmillan, 2004), 79–107, here 92. The data were first published in *IA*, 1994–8.

25 Rees's contribution, 'Stalin as Leader', is in two parts: 'From Oligarch to Dictator' (1924–37) and 'From Dictator to Despot' (1937–53), ibid., 19–58, 200–39.

26 D. Watson, *Molotov and Soviet Government: Sovnarkom, 1930–1941* (Basingstoke, London and New York, 1996); idem, 'The Politburo and Foreign Policy in the 1930s', in ibid., 134–67, stresses Molotov's decision-making role.

27 J.A. Getty in *SR* 53 (1997), 371–2.

28 Y. Gorlizki, 'Ordinary Stalinism: the Council of Ministers and the Soviet Neopatrimonial Elite, 1946–1953', *JMH* 74 (2002), 699–736; cf. also idem, 'Stalin's Cabinet: the Politburo and Decision-making in the Postwar Years', *EAS* 51 (2001), 291–312.

29 It is currently a research focus of the well-known Australian political scientist T.H. Rigby. Cf. also Gerald M. Easter, *Reconstructing the State: Personal Networks and Elite Identity in Soviet Russia* (Cambridge: Cambridge University Press, 2000).

30 S. Fitzpatrick, 'Intelligentsia and Power: Client-Patron Relations in Stalin's Russia', in Hildermeier (ed.), *Stalinismus*, 35–53; idem, 'Patronage and the Intelligentsia in Stalin's Russia', in S.G. Wheatcroft (ed.), *Challenging Traditional Views of Russian History* (Basingstoke: Palgrave, 2002), 92–111.

31 G. Gill, 'The Soviet Mechanism of Power and the Fall of the Soviet Union', in N.E. Rosenfeldt *et al.* (eds), *Mechanisms of Power in the Soviet Union* (Basingstoke, London and New York: Macmillan, 2000), 3–22.

32 Idem, *The Origins of the Stalinist Political System* (Cambridge and New York: Cambridge University Press, 1990); cf. also G. Gill and R. Pitty, *Power in the Party: The Organization of Power and Central-Republican Relations in the USSR* (London, 1997).

33 Other essays here by Russian scholars deal with the role of the intelligence services in decision-making (V.V. Pozdniakov); 'the transformation of extraordinary measures into a permanent system of government' (G.A. Bordiugov); propaganda in foreign policy-making (V.A. Nevezhin); and the decision to launch the war against Finland in 1939 (V.N. Baryshnikov). E.A. Rees thinks Rosenfeldt exaggerates the Secret Chancellery's role: 'Stalin as Leader' (see n. 25), 50–1.

34 R.W. Davies, M. Harrison and S.G. Wheatcroft (eds), *The Economic Transformation of the Soviet Union, 1913–1945* (Cambridge and New York: Cambridge University Press, 1994). Davies, a former director of the Centre for Russian and East European Studies at the University of Birmingham, is a leading authority on the Soviet economy whose work is notable for its professionalism, close attention to detail, and non-judgemental quality – in the tradition of E.H. Carr, whom Davies assisted in writing the later volumes of his monumental *History of Soviet Russia* (London: Macmillan, 1950–89). He is the author or co-author of numerous articles and papers. Mark Harrison (Warwick) is chiefly concerned with the Russian/Soviet economy during the two world wars. Stephen Wheatcroft (Melbourne) writes mainly on agriculture, demography and statistics. Other contributors to this volume were John Barber (Cambridge), Peter Gatrell (Manchester), Robert Lewis (Exeter) and the transport historian J.N. Westwood. On transport see now also M.J. Payne, *Stalin's Railroad: Turksib and the Building of Socialism* (Pittsburgh: University of Pittsburgh Press, 2001).

35 M. Hildermeier, *Geschichte der Sowjetunion 1917–1991: Entstehung und Niedergang des ersten sozialistischen Staates* (Munich: E.H. Beck), 480–7. For another recent survey see J. Sapir, 'L'économie soviétique: origine, développement, fonctionnement', in idem (ed.), *Retour sur l'URSS: histoire, économie, société* (Paris and Montreal: L'Harmattan, 1997), 99–144.

36 F. Benvenuti, 'A Stalinist Victim of Stalinism: "Sergo" Ordzhonikidze', in J. Cooper *et al.* (eds), *Soviet History, 1917–53: Essays in Honour of R.W. Davies* (Basingstoke and London: St Martin's Press, 1995), 134–57.

37 The other essays on this topic are by Rees and Davies. P.R. Gregory (ed.), *The Political Economy of Stalinism: Evidence from the Soviet Secret Archives* (Cambridge: Cambridge University Press, 2001), unavailable to the present writer, contains contributions by Harrison and several Russian specialists.

38 E.A. Rees (ed.), *Decision-making in the Stalinist Command Economy, 1932–1937* (London: Macmillan, and New York: St Martin's Press, 1997).

39 R.W. Davies and S.G. Wheatcroft, 'The Soviet Famine of 1932–3 and the Crisis in Agriculture', in Wheatcroft (ed.), *Challenging*, 69–91 (previously published in *OI*, 1998, no. 6, 94–131).

40 R.W. Davies and O. Khlevniuk, 'Stakhanovism and the Soviet Economy', *EAS* 54 (2002), 867–903. For more on Stakhanovism see Chapter 8, p. 126.

41 R.R. Reese, *The Soviet Military Experience: A History of the Soviet Army, 1917–1991* (London and New York: Routledge, 2000), 52–137. Cf. his *Stalin's Reluctant Soldiers: A Social History of the Red Army, 1925–1941* (Lawrence, KS: University of Kansas Press, 1996); and 'Red Army Opposition to Forced Collectivization, 1929–1930: the Army Wavers', *SR* 55 (1996), 24–45.

42 J. Barber and M. Harrison (eds), *The Soviet Defence-Industry Complex from Stalin to Khrushchev* (Basingstoke, London and New York: St Martin's Press, 2000). The two authors previously collaborated on a volume entitled *The Soviet Home Front, 1941–5: A Social and Economic History of the USSR in World War II* (London: Longman, 1991). Barber has written 'War, Public Opinion and the Struggle for Survival, 1941: the Case of Leningrad', *Annali . . . Feltrinelli*, 1998, 265–76 and other essays; Harrison is the author of two rather technical works: *Soviet Planning in Peace and War, 1938–1945* (Cambridge: Cambridge University Press, 1985); and *Accounting for War: Soviet Production, Employment, and the Defence Burden, 1940–1945* (Cambridge: Cambridge University Press, 1996). Both authors also have articles in the Cooper *et al.* collection (1995), 201–18, 219–42.

43 D.R. Stone, *Hammer and Rifle: The Militarization of the Soviet Union, 1926–1933* (Lawrence, KS: University of Kansas Press, 2000).

44 L. Samuelson, *Plans for Stalin's War Machine: Tukhachevsky and Military–Economic Planning, 1925–1941* (Basingstoke, London and New York: Macmillan, 2000). Cf. his *Soviet Defence Industry Planning: Tukhachevsky and Military–Industrial Mobilization* (Stockholm: Stockholm School of Economics, 1996) and 'The Red Army and Economic Planning, 1925–1940', in Barber and Harrison (eds), *The . . . Complex*, 47–69. Other related works include S.W. Stoecker, *Forging Stalin's Army: Marshal Tukhachevsky and the Politics of Military Innovation* (Boulder, CO: Westview, 1998) and (more briefly) A. Cristiani, 'Entre répression et reconstruction: l'armée soviétique dans la 2e moitié des années 30 . . . ', *CMR* 39 (1998), 221–32; D. Watson, 'STO (the Council of Labour and Defence) in the 1930s', *EAS* 50 (1998), 1203–28; J. Rohwer and M.S. Monakov, *Stalin's Ocean-Going Fleet: Soviet Naval Strategy and Shipbuilding Programmes, 1935–1953* (London: Frank Cass, 2001), of which D.C. Watt remarks (*TLS*, 17.5.02) that 'no portrait of Stalin lacking the element of his naval ambitions [is] adequate'.

45 Eds G. Hosking and R. Service (London: Macmillan, 1998). The collection is introduced by A.N. Sakharov. Another work that takes a long view is A.S. Tuminez, *Russian Nationalism since 1856: Ideology and the Making of Foreign Policy*, (Lanham, MD and Oxford, 2000); on Stalin's 'co-optation' of Russian national (and chauvinist) feeling see pp. 175–6.

46   E.A. Rees, 'Stalin and Russian Nationalism', 77–106. Rees has written an archive-based (but rather dry) account of the transport system in this period: *Stalinism and Soviet Rail Transport, 1928–1941* (Basingstoke and New York: Macmillan, 1995). See also Chapter 10, p. 161.

47   Sarah Davies, *Popular Opinion in Stalin's Russia: Terror, Propaganda and Dissent, 1934–1941* (Cambridge: Cambridge University Press, 1997), 85–8. Sarah Davies should not be confused with her namesake Robert W. Davies.

48   D.L. Brandenberger, 'Soviet Social Mentalité and Russo-centrism on the Eve of War, 1936–1941', *JGOE* 48 (2000), 388–406.

49   Idem, '"The People Need a Tsar": The Emergence of National Bolshevism as Stalinist Ideology, 1931–1941', *EAS* 50 (1998), 873–92. There is a further discussion of Stalinist historiography in Chapter 10.

50   R.G. Suny and T. Martin, *A State of Nations: Empire and Nation-making in the Age of Stalin* (New York and Oxford: Oxford University Press, 2001); Martin, *The Affirmative Action Empire: Nations and Nationalism in the Soviet Union, 1923–1991* (Ithaca, NY and London: Cornell University Press, 2001).

8 Adventures in social history

Peasants and workers

Collectivization and its sequels

A generation ago, an expert on the Soviet economy could treat the initial phase of collectivization almost entirely from the perspective of the Soviet authorities.[1] Such an approach now seems to be archaic, for the archival revolution and new methodologies have shifted the focus relentlessly toward the millions of peasant small-holders who were expropriated and either forced into the new *kolkhozy* or deported into exile. The same is true, *mutatis mutandis*, of the workers who toiled in the factories set up during the First Five-Year Plan (1929–32), some of them giant enterprises that symbolized the regime's hectic drive for modernity. In both cases, the emphasis is on the high social costs of Stalin's command economy: low wages, primitive working conditions, shortages of essential goods and, in 1932–4, even a catastrophic famine. Cultural historians go beyond such matters to inquire into the physical and mental world of ordinary folk, seeking to establish what meaning they attached to traditional customs or religious observances – and to property, the matter that so exercised contemporary political activists.

One should perhaps apologize for still speaking crudely of peasants and workers, as though these two elements of the subject population were not linked by a myriad ties. Lynne Viola (Toronto), a leading present-day authority on the period, points out that for a long time Western scholars, even those critical of the regime's policies, almost unthinkingly used Marxist–Leninist categories of class.[2] Yet the nature of stratification within the rural community in the 1920s was far from clear; differences were often based on gender or generation rather than ownership of property or the employment of hired labour; and when the village was threatened from outside, they were set aside in the common interest of all householders, rich and poor alike. Russian country folk had long memories, and just as they had once viewed tsarist tax collectors or 'non-toiling' landlords as enemies who infringed upon the village's 'moral economy' (James Scott's term), so in the post-revolutionary era those whom they pejoratively identified as 'kulaks' were more likely to be a profiteering miller, a White army veteran, or someone who cheated his neighbours – an outlook that was worlds away from that of class-obsessed Party members (pp. 442–5).

The gulf that separated such people from the bulk of the rural population has become vividly apparent from recently published documents. The first chapter of one such compilation, headed 'The Socialist Offensive', contains a selection of letters to leaders or the press, petitions, and similar material of popular origin, linked by an explanatory commentary.[3] The procedure adopted is open to the criticism that the sources chosen are mainly those showing conditions in an adverse light. Far more thorough is a five-volume series on collectivization and its aftermath (1927–38), edited by an international team including the eminent Russian specialist Viktor Danilov as well as Viola and Roberta Manning (Boston).[4] Viola has also published (but not yet in English) materials that illustrate the way collectivization was carried through in particular regions. This is especially welcome in that it highlights the decisive role played in implementing the measure by local officials. In the first of these volumes, on the initial assault on the village, Viola and Valerii Vasil'ev began with 'the view from the capitals' and proceeded down through various echelons of functionaries and activists to the level of a single village, Cherepashintsy (Vynnitsia province), which rebelled against being dragooned into joining the new *kolkhozy*. A sequel on Riazan' province contained 145 hitherto secret documents, mainly reports by police and other agencies, along with an introduction (by S.M. Zhuravlev) discussing the reliability of this information.[5]

Both volumes are essentially supplements to Viola's major work of 1996,[6] which focuses on the same initial period of mass collectivization but also contains a chapter on 'everyday forms of resistance' in the *kolkhoz* after 1930 (pp. 205–33). The author sees collectivization as a veritable civil war between town and country, a conflict of cultures in which the political authorities sought to establish their dominion over, to 'colonize', the countryside (pp. 44, 74) – terms that owe something to Foucault. Resistance began with the circulation of apocalyptic rumours that the end of the world was nigh – an effective mobilization device that 'provided peasants with a language of protest distilled through metaphor' that they readily understood. In PM terminology, 'rumour was a popular forum of social space in the abstract, in which peasants could create and maintain a political dialogue about soviet power, communism and the collective farm' (pp. 64–5). Thereupon, protest commonly took the form of what the authorities termed 'sabotage', as when potential victims sold off or ate their livestock – actually an entirely rational form of action. Others fled or wrote letters of complaint. Such missives might sorrowfully recount the writer's experiences, in a style that 'generally followed certain socio-political conventions'; the more skilful letter-writers employed and manipulated official jargon, 'calling upon the promise and rhetoric of the established order to justify their complaints' (pp. 96–7).

As the atmosphere darkened, aggrieved rural folk turned to more violent measures: riots, assaults on local officials, even murder. The OGPU reported nearly 13,800 'terrorist' acts in the full year 1930, the peak coming in March when 'the wild excesses of the collectivization campaign . . . touched off a major peasant conflagration' (p. 133). In response, Stalin published his duplicitous 'Dizziness from Success' article, scapegoating lower-level cadres, but this at first just provoked further unrest. Viola terms riots as being 'ritualized displays of rage . . . a specific genre in the peasant culture of resistance'. They were the outcome of genuine frustration and despair, but ultimately, as elsewhere in the world, 'peasant revolt

. . . only succeeded in contributing to the increasing centralization and repressive nature of the state' (pp. 154, 179). There is an archaic flavour to this account of a life-and-death struggle between two incompatible worlds, in which the much-touted advantages of modern mechanized farming scarcely figure – we must look to the earlier literature for discussion of such issues – but it abounds in gripping detail. Statistical tables are scattered through the text, but the author does not rely too heavily on such data, which are necessarily imprecise.

One noteworthy feature of Viola's book, anticipated in earlier work and taken up by other scholars, is the emphasis on the role of women in these outbursts, so putting gender studies in an unfamiliar light.[7] These *bab'ie bunty* – over a quarter of the total! – were often planned in advance and cleverly exploited officials' reluctance to penalize supposedly 'backward' village women who, they assumed, were incapable of taking such resolute action on their own initiative. Male villagers, appreciating the women's relative invulnerability, often chose to stand aside, and so these angry, pitchfork-wielding women in headscarves found themselves in the unlikely role of activists who led their community in resisting naked violence by outsiders.

Collectivization led to even greater suffering in national-minority regions. This point is stressed by Jörg Baberowski (Berlin) in an authoritative article on the deportation of the (so-called) kulaks. In Transcaucasia, he writes, 'collectivization was above all a campaign against cultural resistance to alien ways of life' and needs to be seen in the context of the intermittent warfare waged in 1930–3 along the USSR's eastern borders against bands of peasant and nomadic guerillas.[8] Another recent study of 'dekulakization' (a reprehensible term that one uses merely from convenience) deals with the Urals region.[9] James Harris, whose volume on this area has been noted in Chapter 7, supplements it with an article on the growth of forced-labour camps there in 1929–31, in which, using documents in the local archive, he shows that in this respect, too, the central and local authorities in effect outbid each other in their efforts to remedy a perceived shortage of labour by taking exceptional measures. These involved needless loss of life (p. 274) – as when, in January 1930, the Ural *obkom* organized the despatch of some 30,000 kulak households to forestry work: they were to be housed in camps and fed, but in practice instructions about their wellbeing were all too often ignored, since fulfilling the plan took priority. 'Central officials were well aware of conditions in the camps,' writes Harris, 'but took very little concrete action to improve them' (p. 278).

Harris's research complements that of James Hughes, who in 1996 published a comprehensive, exacting study of agrarian relations and policy-making in the Urals and western Siberia during the period. (This volume was in turn preceded by one on the 'crisis of NEP' there.)[10] Like Harris, he focuses on centre–periphery relations and stresses the radicalizing role played by local leaders (Syrtsov, Eikhe). The policy initially adopted towards 'kulaks', euphemistically termed one of 'social influence', was too crude to produce the results expected and so the authorities turned to more violent measures of expropriation. Another factor in this lurch to the left was the poor harvest obtained in 1928 from Ukraine and the Caucasus, which made the Ural–Siberian region seem to be the key source of agricultural supplies. Here, as elsewhere a year or so later, lynchings and forced loans led to 'sabotage' (that is, hiding the crop), flight to other areas, and riots. This tragic experience may be seen as a dress rehearsal for the wholesale collectivization to follow. Hughes's second volume, hailed by one reviewer as 'the best . . . analysis of the evolution of agricultural policy in the key years leading to collectivization', has been criticized for 'accept[ing] as real Stalinist categories of social and economic status'[11] – that is, the nature and extent of polarization within the village community. However this may be, we are offered a colourful and compelling picture of rural life before and during the 'great break' (another euphemism).

By and large, Western *agrarniki* are doing justice to their grim theme, and one hopes that further regional studies will follow. Returning for a moment to central policy, we have an interesting study, once again by the industrious Viola, of a top-level commission set up in 1930 to review appeals by exiled peasants who claimed, quite reasonably, that they had been deported to the North in error.[12] Within a matter of weeks, 23,360 applications (out of 35,000) had been reviewed and it was recommended that 2,341 and 2,863 families in two categories ('wrongly exiled' and 'doubtful cases') should be returned (p. 1453). The OGPU wanted the numbers reduced, but a 'liberal' commission member, V.N. Tolmachev, argued that 'these are living human beings, not crates of goods' (p. 1407) and that three-fifths of all those sent qualified for return. He was, naturally, overruled, in the last instance by Stalin. Viola acknowledges that Tolmachev deserves credit for speaking out against the intolerable conditions in which deportees had to live (overcrowded barracks, hunger, nearly all the children sick), but in the last resort a 'bureaucratic–institutional' struggle shaped the approach of both Tolmachev and his (younger, more ruthless) comrade, Bergavinov. The two men had much in common, and so we should beware of idealizing the one who seems more altruistic: 'both the regional and the human interests that Bergavinov and Tolmachev attempted to represent ran counter to Stalinist central state building and social engineering'. This sad verdict may be too deterministic, for there is other evidence that local officials could sometimes moderate harsh policies decreed by the centre.

If one escaped deportation, one could, as it were, 'deport oneself' by migrating to a precarious safety – if one was lucky, on a construction site or in some industrial enterprise; if unlucky, one might pass several years 'in unsettled wanderings', as Sheila Fitzpatrick puts it, engaged in a 'constant struggle to survive and maintain contact among deported family members'.[13] In the nature of things we can scarcely expect a full academic study of what was a largely spontaneous, self-directed movement[14] – one of the greatest anywhere in modern times. The rate of rural–urban migration, which stood at about 1 million a year in the late 1920s, leaped to 2.5 million in 1930 and to 4 million in 1931; the total transfer of population in 1928–32, including deportations, has been put at 12 million.[15] Some families fled in panic; in other cases one member might leave in search of a casual job and fail to return, his family perhaps joining him later; but on occasion it was a case of 'pull' rather than 'push', in so far as industrial expansion made better paid jobs available. By 1932, the onset of famine led the authorities to take firmer measures to control the flow, lest the rationing system break down under the strain. The fateful internal passport law (27 December) was 'intended to halt the peasant influx into the towns and at the same time purge them of socially undesirable and unproductive residents'.[16] It signalled a toughening of policy towards peasants in general, as distinct from just so-called 'kulaks', and led to a further wave of migration as surplus urban residents were rounded up and deported. Meanwhile, measures were taken to prevent peasants in famine-stricken areas from leaving their villages in search of food.

The terrible tale of the 1932–4 famine, the 'harvest of sorrow' as Robert Conquest memorably called it,[17] was the subject of a classic study that combined scholarly virtues with a strong indictment of the Soviet regime, not least for anti-Ukrainian prejudice. Much of the subsequent discussion revolved around this latter point, with critics pointing out that Russian ethnic areas suffered too, but this is really a secondary issue.[18] On the main problems – inflated grain procurements, governmental secrecy, the size of hidden reserves, the maintenance of grain exports, and especially the lack of timely, adequate relief – there is substantial agreement. The recent literature has filled in some of the 'blank spots'. In an article on the Don region, D'Ann Penner[19] estimates the total number of victims (1932–4) at no less than 6.7 million (rather than 5 million, as some post-Soviet historians have suggested) and goes on to argue that in one key region (northern North Caucasus *krai*) the insistence on pressing forward with inhuman measures led to a total breakdown in relations between the authorities and the rural population. The latter offered determined resistance, which was interpreted by those in charge as a declaration of war; in areas blacklisted as unco-operative the Party 'abet[ted] the process whereby shortage becomes famine, thereby making famine its partner in the subjugation of villagers' (p. 243). Peasants and cossacks in the region who had been fairly well disposed towards the government in 1927 were by 1933 completely disabused; OGPU reports mention that 'even loyalists [are] considering marching on Moscow, weapons in hand, with the aim of overthrowing the regime' (p. 54). Penner puts forward two explanations for the homicidal policy of blocking off famine-stricken areas: the sight of starving peasants would have undermined the activists' élan; and the authorities feared adverse publicity, or worse, in nearby Poland.

Stephen Wheatcroft has attempted to refine the statistical data on famine deaths, comparing the toll in the early 1930s with that during and after the civil war.[20] Elsewhere Wheatcroft, a keen debater, offers 'a further note of clarification' on the relationship between excess mortality due to famine and maltreatment in the Gulag, pointing to some contradictions in the NKVD data.[21] Discussion of this theme involves intricate calculations that are chiefly of specialist interest.

As for agricultural and other economic statistics in general, the French scholar Martine Mespoulet has given us a fine study[22] that begins with *zemstvo* workers in the late tsarist era and takes the story up to the later 1920s, when these ideal-istic and highly professional men and women were reduced to the lowly status of 'technicians of figures'. The 'promotees' (*vydvizhentsy*) who replaced them, at the Party's behest, were cast in a different mould and derived their legitimacy not from any professional qualifications but from their political reliability. Even so, they did try to preserve standards where they could, so long as a margin of liberty remained. By contrast, another group of professionals, local agricultural specialists, are said (by James Heinzen) to have favoured collectivization because they saw it as a means of regaining status vis-à-vis Party officials.[23] Mespoulet's monograph has since had a sequel, which unfortunately could not be examined here. The importance of statistics should be self-evident: without reliable, impartial data there could be no realistic economic planning, let alone socialism.

Keeping for the moment to the agricultural milieu, Stephen Merl and Gabor Rittersporn offer authoritative descriptions of the collectivized village that supplement Fitzpatrick's.[24] Merl points out *inter alia* that after 1933 the *kolkhoz* system had 'little in common' with its predecessor of the turbulent first years; that the concession of private plots allowed peasants at least to survive, even though at heavy cost; and that in 1937 a new campaign was launched against the last remaining entrepreneurs (*khutoriane*) and those farm chairmen deemed sympathetic to their interests. Thus, contrary to some other scholars' assertions, stability was *not* attained, for 'a system kept going by permanent force cannot be regarded as stable' (p. 126). The Soviet leaders fell victim to their own mendacity: wilfully ignoring the evidence, they assumed that the grain problem had been solved, whereas in fact the socialized farms, with their low (1:4) grain yields, merely 'perpetuated the backwardness' of traditional Russian agriculture. Although harvests were significantly larger than in the 1920s, and procurement agencies secured a greater share of them, the state was unable to meet increased consumer demand.

A positive feature of Merl's work is that he situates in an economic context the farmers' passive resistance and their efforts to protect their interests by 'playing the system', for instance by using the institutional structure to rid themselves of brutal farm chairmen during the Terror – practices on which Fitzpatrick supplies more detail.[25] Social historians are keen to stress the ability of the 'little man' to turn Soviet power to his own advantage, frustrating the intentions of authority, but Stephen Kotkin remarks justly that 'the trickier question is whether [peasants] imagined an alternative for realizing the hopes and values' stirred by the regime's pronouncements.[26] The answer is probably that they did not. Some embittered country folk yearned for foreign occupation, but this can scarcely be viewed as a viable option.

If the regime had supporters in the rural milieu, they were likely to be found among the élite of office holders, mechanizers and Stakhanovites. Mary Buckley (Cambridge) has prepared a major study of the last-named group, a foretaste of which is provided in several short studies where she explores the mixed motives for their show of zeal, as well as the various reactions they met with among ordinary *kolkhozniki*.[27] Only a minority of Stakhanovites shared the genuine commitment of their much-hailed standard bearer, Maria Demchenko.[28] Further light on this topic is shed by Lewis Siegelbaum, in an article devoted to a group of state dairy farmers who in 1934–5 participated in a contest to provide the best winter quarters for livestock.[29] A poll taken among the contestants 'affords a window on the living conditions and material culture' of peasants generally as well as on the relationships between various authorities (Party, union, *sovkhoz*). This showed, for instance, that of 108 respondents 23.2 per cent were literate and 54.6 per cent semi-literate, while about three-quarters reported that they were ill (pp. 120–2). 'I have been forgotten,' wrote one desperate complainant. The organizers tried to help by sending parcels of supplies, but simultaneously surveillance was reinforced. The authorities, Siegelbaum concludes, were inconsistent in distributing rewards and punishments; but those beneficiaries who became what he calls 'rural notables' acquired an enhanced sense of 'the importance of labour as self-validation'. Paternalistic power, he avers, aided in 'the formation of subjectivities'. A sceptic might query whether such farmers did not have some awareness of their place in the world as individuals *before* they came within the purview of the state; even so, one can appreciate that they gained greater self-esteem and so were better disposed toward the source of such patronage.

Relatively few recent Western scholars have tackled the problems of Soviet agriculture during the war and post-war years.[30] This is a field that merits more attention in future, especially to highlight the far from negligible achievements registered after 1953 under Khrushchev, which are deservedly more familiar.

The labour scene

For many years social history meant, where modern Russia was concerned, labour history, and there is a vast corpus of writing on the subject. Interest in this field has flagged recently as other issues have come to the fore. David Hoffmann points out that in the age of the Internet sociological studies of the world of labour have been superseded by investigations into semiotics and symbolic communication.[31] The last major conference devoted specifically to the *working class* seems to have been held at Michigan State University in 1990, while the USSR was still extant.[32] The editors of the miscellany that resulted jettisoned the once-popular quasi-Marxist approach. Influenced by the teaching of E.P. Thompson and others, they stressed the 'cultural paradigm of class' and saw class consciousness as the 'assertion of a particular kind of social identity'. The proletariat, like the nation, was an 'imagined community'. The historians' task was therefore not to document workers' exploitation, or their militancy in furthering their interests, but to explore 'individual and collective identities and their representation in language' and the way these operated 'to generate particular understandings of . . . collective behaviour or action'. In other words, no longer: how many Red flags were brought to the demonstration, but rather: what were the men thinking as they waved them?

Fitzpatrick, Rittersporn and Kotkin were among the leading contributors to this volume, and each had much of interest to say. The first discussed the Great Terror's impact on labour–management relations and found that reactions ranged widely, from indignation to selfish satisfaction ('they deserved what they got': pp. 312ff.). The second argued that Stalinism 'declassed' the work force, turning it into a 'mass' that had trouble absorbing the influx of unskilled peasants and so 'ruralizing' it (p. 260). The third described how workers lived in Magnitogorsk and found that political pressure produced conformism, quiescence and enthusiastic participation in campaigns to boost output. Kotkin took the same line in his later *magnum opus* on Magnitogorsk,[33] and inevitably provoked criticism that this showcase city was hardly typical. Some reviewers objected that Kotkin was too bold in claiming to have put forward a fundamentally original interpretation of Stalinism and that he arbitrarily heaped praise and (especially) blame on historians who had ploughed the same furrow earlier.[34]

If Siegelbaum's team aspired to 'set the agenda' for labour historians in the 1990s, they seem to have succeeded only in part, for much of the new writing on the Soviet thirties is fairly traditional in approach. Donald Filtzer (London) offers an overview[35] reminiscent of contemporary Trotskyist critiques in which he speaks of 'the atomization of the working class' during the First FYP (pp. 165, 170), designed to 'remove it as a potential source of opposition to the élite's political domination'; with 'the emergence of new production relations' the managerial bureaucracy did not, however, have its own way entirely but was obliged to develop 'an elaborate pattern of informal shop-floor bargaining' with the workers, forming 'a coherent system of mutual collusion . . . to evade the laws' and protect both partners against arbitrary repressive measures (p. 175). This arrangement, perpetuated until the 1980s, was something 'historically unique', neither capitalist nor socialist (p. 179). Most of this argument would be widely accepted today. Filtzer has since provided a thorough, balanced study of workers' lot in the last years of the Stalin era,[36] using archival evidence mainly from transport and coal-mining. One finding is that frequently 'managers and local legal officials /would/ circumvent restrictions on workers' freedom of action, for example by failing to prosecute those who left their jobs without permission' (p. 176). Food was desperately short, working conditions primitive, and sickness rates high, so that one can speak only of an 'attenuated recovery' before 1947/8, at which point the regime faced a 'genuine social crisis'. Thereafter it regained control. *Pace* Kotkin and others, Filtzer concludes that workers were *not* integrated into the political system; they merely accepted some of the dominant values, 'recognized their subordinate status, and reconciled themselves to the fact that they had few levers or outlets for effecting change' (p. 262).

The French (Toulouse) scholar Jean-Paul Depretto's thorough survey of Russian labour in the 1930s[37] was mainly written before the relevant archives had been opened. A sizeable chapter is devoted to the builders of the Kuznetsk industrial complex (pp. 187–251), and briefer sections to textile workers in the Moscow region, Leningrad metal workers, and Donbas coal miners (pp. 134–86). In evaluating attitudes towards the regime, Depretto engages with recent Russian studies and shows that discontent took many different forms, from slowdowns to strikes. He is perhaps on shakier ground where he pleads for continuity in the composition of the industrial labour force across the First FYP era and downplays the importance of the influx of rural recruits (pp. 352, 357).

In 1996 an American historian, David Shearer, published the second of two monographs[38] in which he set out to provide 'a political, economic and social history of the Stalinist industrial state during its formative period' and to describe 'how the Soviet industrial system actually worked, as opposed to how it was supposed to work' (pp. 13, 21). The bulk of the study is devoted to a close examination of the wrangles between administrative agencies during the First FYP era that highlights the roles played first by the so-called 'syndicates'[39] and then by Rabkrin, which by late 1930 had forced through its radical line, exemplified by Ordzhonikidze with his military style. The victory of this group created 'a culture of crisis' (p. 106), a veritable 'madhouse' characterized by needless purging of specialists, inter-bureaucratic rivalries, hoarding of resources and other forms of waste. More particularly, decisions were often taken at the level of the workshop rather than the factory; this was 'a world the regime could terrorize politically but could not control economically' (pp. 233–4).

Where Shearer is concerned with the industrial economy in general, Kenneth Straus is a structuralist whose research rests in part on close study of factories in one particular district (Proletarskii) of Moscow.[40] He argues that the most significant sociological development was 'the formation of a relatively homogeneous working class' with shared experiences of recent entry, crash training and work in brigades, all of which produced 'a sense of community' based on the enterprise where one was employed. This was a source of stability in a turbulent era and helps to explain the workers' conformism, or at least the relative lack of open protest at low wage levels or poor conditions. At the same time, they were able to take advantage of the shortage of skilled labour – a factor in the early 1930s and again after 1938, as the economy became more geared to military production – and learned to exercise leverage in such matters as food supply, housing or transport facilities.

Several critics found Straus's interpretation too benign vis-à-vis the regime – he had little to say about the role of Party organizations in the workplace, for example – and insufficiently sensitive towards the conflictual relationships that persisted beneath the surface calm. But even if Straus exaggerated the success of the 'Red directors' in overcoming such tensions, it was generally conceded that he had thrown light on an unusual and durable feature of the Soviet labour scene: namely, workers' tendency to identify with 'their own' factory.

Meanwhile other social historians emphasized the 'sore points' in management–labour relations, which they held had by no means lost their acuity under Stalin's draconian rule. Jeffrey Rossman has produced three archive-based studies of strikes that broke out among textile workers in the Ivanovo region in 1932. In the first two (1996–7), he focuses on the role played by two leading protesters: K. Klepikov, a committed anti-Communist who spent several years in the Gulag, and V. Khudiakov, a former tradesman. The demands put forward were purely economic (poor rations) and enjoyed public sympathy; although the strike leaders were arrested and punished, the authorities also responded positively by increasing food supplies. The affair was predictably kept secret but the relevant documents have survived in the local archive at Ivanovo. The third, at Vichuga, was the most violent, but the men 'stepped back from the precipice . . . after learning that the centre had apparently answered [their] plea for help'. In broader perspective, 'these events contributed to the social pressures that compelled the regime to soften its economic policies' ('Workers' Strike', pp. 80–1).[41]

Since textile workers were usually women, they have attracted interest among students of gender as well as labour historians. Gabriele Gorzka (Kassel) wrote on workers' clubs before turning to other cultural topics.[42] In two recent articles she deals with women workers at Yaroslavl', where she has conducted archival research. Zeroing in on the Krasnyi Perekop factory there, one of the oldest in the country (1722), she first describes the primitive physical conditions (no sewage pipes, for example) and then explores how urgent local problems were handled at general meetings of workers and managerial representatives. 'Resolutions were passed . . . , commissions established, those responsible removed, . . . but qualitative improvements were not achieved' (pp. 149, 152). Workers lost interest in such meetings and preferred to spend their leisure relaxing. Nevertheless, a minority 'became increasingly enthusiastic about education' and by the end of the decade 'about half the work force was receiving instruction to obtain further professional qualifications' (p. 156). In the second article, Gorzka provides more details on wages and prices, disciplinary measures, and social differentiation in this factory. Her principal finding is that 'the political authorities were unable to find the right approach to the masses. They did not concern themselves with everyday matters and, underestimating the workers' [intellectual] level and interests, offered them mere slogans. Only the educational facilities earned greater acceptance, whereas in the cultural–artistic field the Party's political strategies flopped' (p. 242).

Another German scholar, Dietmar Neutatz, has devoted a sizeable monograph to one of the 'great projects' of the First FYP era, the construction of the Moscow metro (Metrostroi).[43] In regard to labour problems, Neutatz concludes that the high rate of fluctuation was a typical worker strategy in conditions where genuine trade unionism and strike action were prohibited ('Enthusiasmus', p. 194); those who stuck with the job despite adverse conditions were often highly motivated, earned good wages, and ultimately made successful careers. Senior Party agencies continually interfered in matters of detail, raining down instructions to speed up the project, but as to what ordinary workers felt about this, the author is prudently non-committal.

One attribute of working-class culture to have received attention recently is alcoholic indulgence. Laura L. Phillips's entertaining book on this subject[44] only goes up to the 'great break' but is useful for background and method. Noting that the entrenched practice of 'ritual drinking' survived the revolution, since it embodied an important element in workers' masculine identity, she holds that 'labourers . . . demanded that their customs be treated with integrity and respect' and managed to force the state to back down over temperance policy (pp. 31, 44–6). This is all very well, but the argument would have been more convincing if Phillips had concerned herself with the physical consequences of insobriety or the liquor monopoly's contribution to state revenue, which was one reason why the temperance movement fared so badly under Stalin. To a cultural historian such matters seem too mundane.

Towards a new identity?

A more fundamental question that has been eagerly, and on the whole fruitfully, discussed of late is workers' (and others') attitudes towards the regime.[45] The debate is still in progress, and an interim report on it should begin by defining what is common ground. Everyone accepts that some (ex-)workers who for whatever reason rose up in the system, such as Party and Komsomol activists, were more likely to identify with the new order than those they left behind; and everyone agrees that peasants, who were harder hit, were more likely to be indifferent or disaffected; thus we are dealing essentially with manual workers and low-level employees. Another preliminary point: it is a misapprehension to believe that ordinary people are, or should be, consistently concerned about the politico-social order under which they live. Even in an open democratic polity most citizens are indifferent to public affairs and, when they do become involved, ambivalent in their opinions; their views on official policy will vary from topic to topic and change rapidly, influenced by a host of factors (personal well-being, influence of the media or rumours, current fashions); and their private opinions may well differ from those they express to pollsters or at the ballot box. In a closed society, people's views are even harder to track down.

Fundamental to contemporary investigations is the concept of identity (or 'social identity', as Steve Smith carefully qualifies it). The definition he offers is questionable in that it employs a derivative of the term to be explained, while another definition, by Volker Depkat, is more precise but suffers from prolixity.[46] It remains a vague, almost metaphysical concept – a bit like the soul for theologians, perhaps? But since the Stalinist state tried harder than virtually any other, then or since, to shape the way its citizens thought and acted, historians are quite naturally eager to find out, from newly available 'popular' sources, how far it succeeded in doing so.

In a critical analysis of the new archival sources,[47] Andrea Graziosi points out that 'the rapid contamination of secret reporting by the official lie' made police surveys of public opinion fallible. They were compiled according to a pre-set formula, with 'good' and 'bad' news recorded in appropriate dosages, so that 'the top Soviet leadership . . . ended up feeding on its own propaganda' (pp. 37–8). Donald Filtzer adds that *svodki* stressed extremes of behaviour: enthusiasm at one pole and subversion at the other.[48] Even if secret informers recorded some individual's opinions accurately, there is no guarantee that the words quoted reflected his or her 'true' views, that is, those held regularly, after reflection, and still less his or her 'identity'. For Soviet citizens developed the fine art of concealing their private doubts, or inner selves, behind a public façade of conformity. Many more were simply confused as to where they stood, which in the circumstances was perfectly understandable.

Petitions are similarly problematic in that the writer might well preface his or her particular complaint by complimentary flourishes about the virtues of the regime or its policies: how do we know whether these were a tactical device or sincere? Letters and diaries are more promising, but we need to guard against the writer's understandable reluctance to put down everything of importance that he or she thought, heard or experienced. Stepan Podlubnyi's now well-known diary had more of a 'confessional' character than most, but it seems risky to read as much into the text as does his translator/editor, Jochen Hellbeck, who advances his hypotheses more boldly than any of his colleagues.[49] Apparently this kulak's son felt guilty about his 'suspect' (from the regime's viewpoint) social origins and sincerely sought to conform to official norms by eradicating the 'reactionary' traits in his personality. In March 1935, on entering upon a medical career, he noted with satisfaction that 'I no longer fear my environment: I'm just like everybody else'; and although he suspected that Kirov's assassination had been engineered at top level, he felt ashamed of his doubts ('Fashioning', pp. 83, 89, 104). There may have been prosaic reasons for his ambivalence: in 1932 he agreed reluctantly to become a secret informer for the OGPU, who knew of his background and could exert pressure on him. It seems best to regard him in the first place as a victim of brain-washing, caught in a trap that deeply unsettled him (at one point he writes that his life is a lie *except* when he is speaking to his NKVD contacts). In 1937 his innocent mother was arrested and the injustice turned him against the regime. Yet he still 'could not challenge the legitimacy of the revolutionary process because he was personally implicated in it'; to have levelled a fundamental critique of the regime 'would have destroyed his positive sense of self' (pp. 110, 112).

Here, Hellbeck arguably strays beyond his evidence. Podlubnyi's diary reveals him to have been a contradictory character who tried, but failed, to adapt to new circumstances, but it is far from clear that his experience was typical, even among the upwardly mobile.[50] Yet on this slender basis, his editor maintains that 'illiberal revolutionary regimes [have] genuine appeal' ('Speaking Out', p. 76); both he and Stephen Kotkin see Soviet citizens as actively adopting Marxist–Leninist language and concepts in order to secure for themselves a psychologically acceptable niche within the system; if there were things about it they disliked (shortages, terror), they might grumble, but they were unable to articulate their grievances plainly and experienced 'their dissent as a crisis of the self' since they had 'internalized authority ... [and] cast themselves as revolutionary selves' (Fashioning', pp. 81, 84, 90). This contention has yet to be bolstered by sufficient empirical evidence.

At the other pole are those like Fitzpatrick and Sarah Davies – and still more so empiricist historians, with their traditional conceptual framework – who see Soviet citizens hiding their doubts from *fear* of the potential consequences, conforming outwardly but occasionally offering passive resistance to the regime's more outrageous demands. Summing up her observations on everyday life in the 1930s, Fitzpatrick points out that Soviet citizens had to take risks to survive, despite the dangers involved, but this 'did not mean that people were not frightened of the regime. Of course, they were frightened, given the regime's proven willingness to punish, the strength of its punitive arm, its long and vengeful memory, and the unpredictability of its outbursts. Hence the normal posture of a Soviet citizen was passive conformity and outward obedience'. People developed a 'we' and 'they' mentality, and strongly resented those who held political power and enjoyed the privileges this conferred. Yet the regime's self-identification with patriotism and progress won it the support of 'urban youth, or at least an impressive proportion of that group ... [who] seem to have assimilated Soviet values'. 'Many workers retained a residual feeling of connection with the Soviet cause', especially in cities with a strong revolutionary tradition, and 'this constituted passive support for the regime'. They looked on it as a provider of food, clothing and shelter – which did not mean that they felt a reciprocal obligation to work hard.[51]

Davies goes further than Fitzpatrick. Using police and Party reports from the Leningrad area in the main, she discerns a 'general hostility to the existing power structure'; 'many people acquired a whole new language and began to reflect on the absence ... of rights in the Soviet Union'; they disliked the new privileged caste (and outsiders generally, as we have seen) and took advantage of the Terror to avenge themselves on the most unpopular bosses.[52] Davies concentrates on the various issues over which the regime and the populace were liable to clash, remarking prudently that it is difficult to reach *quantitative* conclusions about the scale of dissent (p. 15). But this is precisely the Holy Grail that her more PM-oriented colleagues are seeking. Whether their goal is attainable or not, we are bound to learn much along the way.

Notes

1 R.W. Davies, *The Soviet Collective Farm, 1929–1930* (*The Industrialization of Soviet Russia*, vol. 2; Basingstoke: Macmillan, 1980).

2 L. Viola, 'The Peasants' Kulak: Social Identities and Moral Economy in the Soviet Countryside in the 1920s,' *Canadian Slavonic Papers* 42 (2001), 431–60, here 431–2.

3 L. Siegelbaum and A. Sokolov, *Stalinism as a Way of Life: A Narrative in Documents*, comp. L. Kosheleva *et al.* (New Haven, CT and London: Yale University Press, 2000), 28–102. Chapter 5, 'Bolshevik Order on the Collective Farm' (282–355), treats the period after 1935. Another such volume is A.G. Cummins (ed.), *Documents of Soviet History*, vol. 5: *Revolution from Above, 1929–1931* (Gulf Breeze, FL: Academic International, 2000); on collectivization, 189–216. This is the first of 12 volumes designed to cover the entire Soviet period to 1986, which includes official as well as new archival material.

4 V.P. Danilov, R. Manning, and L. Viola (eds), *Tragediia Sovetskoi derevni: kollektivizatsiia i raskulachivanie: dokumenty i materialy v 5 tt., 1927–1939 gg.*, vol. I: *mai 1927 – noiabr' 1929*; vol. II: *noiabr' 1929 – dekabr' 1930*; vol. III, *konets 1930 – 1938*, Moscow, 1999–2001: ROSSPEN). A five-volume English edition is in progress (New Haven, CT: Yale University Press), of which the first three volumes cover the years 1930–3; vols. 4 (1934–6) and 5 bear the publication dates 2001 and 2002 respectively. A condensed four-volume edition is also in preparation.

5 V. Vasil'ev and Viola, *Kollektivizatsiia i krest'ianskoe soprotivlenie na Ukraine, noiabr' 1929 – mart 1930 gg.* (Vinnitsa/Vynnitsia: Logos, 1997). Document 100 (390–400) is a report by the local Party regional committee (*okruzhkom*) with details of the numbers arrested and exiled; there were 416 incidents of resistance, the worst of which claimed eleven lives. Viola *et al.* (eds), *Riazanskaia derevnia v 1929–1930 gg.: khronika golovokruzheniia: dokumenty i materialy* (Moscow: ROSSPEN, 1998). A simultaneous outbreak in Viaz'ma guberniia is discussed in SERAP (Toronto) *Working Paper* no. 6 (2000, in Russian).

6 Viola, *Peasant Rebels under Stalin: Collectivization and the Culture of Peasant Resistance* (New York and Oxford: Oxford University Press, 1996; paperback edn 1999). Viola has since edited *Contending with Stalinism: Soviet Power and Popular Resistance in the 1930s* (Ithaca, NY: Cornell University Press, 2002), which contains her 'Popular Resistance in the Stalinist 1930s: Soliloquy of a Devil's Advocate', originally published in *Kritika*, as well as a close analysis by Tracy McDonald (Utah) of a revolt in Riazan' province in January 1930, which inspired Boris Mozhaev's story *Muzhiki i baby* (1988).

7 Viola, *Peasant Rebels*, 181–204; cf. *RR* 45 (1986), 23–42; W.Z. Goldman, 'Industrial

Politics, Peasant Rebellion and the Death of the Proletarian Women's Movement in the USSR', *SR* 55 (1996), 46–77, highlights the connection to the liquidation of the Party CC's women's department (*Zhenotdel*) in January 1930. For rural women in the later 1930s see R.T. Manning, 'Zhenshchina Sovetskoi derevni nakanune II-oi mirovoi voine', *OI* 5/01, 88–106.

8 J. Baberowski, 'Stalinismus "von oben": Kulakendeportationen in der Sowjetunion 1929–33', *JGOE* 46 (1998), 572–94, here 586–9, with five statistical tables. On Central Asia, A.L. Edgar, 'Genealogy, Class and "Tribal Policy" in Soviet Turkmenistan, 1924–1934', *SR* 60 (2001), 266–88, argues that the offensive actually reinforced kinship ties among the native peoples, so that in some areas resistance might well be organized by members of a single clan. On Belarus, for a longer period, see D. Siebert, *Bäuerliche Alltagsstrategien in der Belorussischen SSR 1921–1941: die Zerstörung patriarchalischer Familienwirtschaft* (Stuttgart: F. Steiner, 1998).

9 J.R. Harris, 'The Growth of Gulag: Forced Labour in the Urals Region, 1929–1931', *RR* 56 (97), 265–80. See also Y. Taniuchi, 'Decision-making on the Ural-Siberian Method', in J. Cooper *et al.*, *Soviet History, 1917–1953* (Basingstoke and London: Macmillan, 1995), 78–103; L. Viola, 'The Role of the OGPU in Dekulakization, Mass Deportations and Special Resettlement in 1930', *Carl Beck Papers* 1406 (2000), 1–52; idem, 'The Other Archipelago: Kulak Deportations to the North in 1930', *SR* 60 (2001), 730–55. See also Chapter 11.

10 J. Hughes, *Stalin, Siberia and the Crisis of the New Economic Policy* (Cambridge: Cambridge University Press, 1991); idem, *Stalinism in a Russian Province: A Study of Collectivization and Dekulakization in Siberia* (London and New York: Macmillan, 1996; idem, 'Capturing the Russian Peasantry: Stalinist Grain Procurement Policy and the "Ural-Siberian Method"', *SR* 53 (1994), 76–103; idem, 'Re-evaluating Stalin's Peasant Policy in 1928–1930', in J. Pallot (ed.) *Transforming Peasants: Society, State and the Peasantry . . .* (Basingstoke: Macmillan and New York: St Martin's Press, 1998), 238–58.

11 Viola, *RR* 57 (1998); D. Shearer, *EAS* 50 (1998), 181.

12 Viola, 'A Tale of Two Men: Bergavinov, Tolmachev and the Bergavinov Commission', *EAS* 52 (2000), 1449–66.

13 Fitzpatrick, *Stalin's Peasants: Resistance and Survival in the Russian Village after Collectivization* (New York and Oxford: Oxford University Press, 1994), 83–4. This major study will long remain the starting-point for future research into the peasant condition once the storm had blown its worst, but we must forego analysis of it here. Another earlier study of peasant migration was D.L. Hoffmann, 'Moving to Moscow: Patterns of Peasant Migration during the First Five-year Plan', *SR* 50 (1991), 847–57; his subsequent book, *Peasant Metropolis: Social Identities in Moscow, 1929–1941* (Ithaca, NY and London: Cornell University Press, 1994), tells us what happened to these migrants once they had arrived in an urban environment. For inter-republican migration trends, notably to Central Asia by Russians (1.3 million to 1937) in this period, see S. Maksudov, 'Migratsii v SSSR v 1926–1939 gg.', *CMR* 40 (1999), 763–96, an authoritative demographic study.

14 But see N. Moine's article in *CMR* 38 (1997), 587–600, 634, where the rather implausible argument is advanced that the 1932 passport law was not designed to regulate the population flux but was just a police measure.

15 Fitzpatrick, *Stalin's Peasants*, 80.

16 Ibid., 92.

17 R. Conquest, *The Harvest of Sorrow: Soviet Collectivization and the Terror-Famine* (New York and Oxford: Oxford University Press, 1986); Russian edn *Zhatva skorby* (Moscow, 1990).

18 On this point S. Merl, 'Golod 1932–33 gg. – genotsid ukraintsev dlia osushchestvleniia politiki russifikatsii?', *OI*, 1995, no. 1, 49–61, agrees that Stalin's failings are inex-cusable but points out that all areas had their delivery quotas raised to unacceptable

levels. He endorses the interpretation offered at the time by Otto Schiller and takes issue with Conquest and J.E. Mace (1983). For a more recent study from a Ukrainian perspective, see Graziosi, *Great Peasant War*. There are two recent works in French: P. Peretz, 'La Grande Famine ukrainienne de 1932–3: essai d'interprétation', *Revue d'études comparatives Est-Ouest* 30 (1999), 1, 31–52; G. Sokoloff (introd.), *1933, l'année noire: témoignages sur la famine en Ukraine*, trans. V. Bojczuk *et al.* (Paris: Albin Michel, 2000), based on interviews in seven regions of Ukraine in 1989–92. Sokoloff agrees with Merl.

19 D. R. Penner, 'Stalin and the *Italianka* of 1932–3 in the Don Region', *CMR* 39 (1998), 27–68. (Her dissertation on Party-peasant relations in the Don region, 1920–8, was presented at the University of California in 1995.) The article is based on archival research in Shakhty, Krasnodar and Rostov as well as in Moscow. The same issue of *CMR* contains other pertinent articles by the Russian scholars E.I. Osokina, G.A. Bordiugov and O.V. Khlevniuk.

20 S.G. Wheatcroft, 'Nutrition and Mortality in Famines, 1917–22, 1931–33', in 'Statistique démographique et sociale (Russie – URSS): politiques, administrateurs et société', *CMR* 38 (1997), 525–58; this issue contains other studies on harvests, prices and consumption (S. Adamets, 559–86), employment (C. Lefevre, 617–28) and suicides (G.A. Rittersporn, 511–24). In another article Wheatcroft makes the same claim in regard to *mortality* statistics after 1932, which he considers 'surprisingly complete and sensitive, given the enormous social crises that they [TsUNKhU statisticians] were recording and the political pressures they faced': idem, 'The Great Leap Upwards: Anthropometric Data and Indicators of Crises and Secular Change in Soviet [*sic*] Welfare Levels, 1880–1960', *SR* 58 (1999), 27–60, here 37.

21 *EAS* 49 (97), 503–5; see also Chapter 11, p. 183.

22 M. Mespoulet, *Statistique et révolution en Russie: un compromis impossible, 1880–1930* (Rennes: Presses universitaires, 2001), esp. 313–17. The sequel (by Mespoulet and A. Blum) is *L'Anarchie bureaucratique: pouvoir et statistique sous Staline* (Paris: La Découverte, 2003).

23 J.W. Heinzen, 'Professional Identity and the Vision of the Modern Soviet Countryside: Local Agricultural Specialists at the End of NEP, 1928–9', *CMR* 39 (1998) 9–26; cf. M. Wehner, 'The Soft Line on Agriculture: The Case of Narkomzem and Its Specialists, 1921–1927', in Pallot (ed.), *Transforming Peasants*, 210–37.

24 S. Merl, 'Bilanz der Unterwerfung: die soziale und ökonomische Reorganisation des Dorfes', in Hildermeier (ed.), *Stalinismus*, 119–45; G.A. Rittersporn, 'Das kollektivierte Dorf in der bäuerlichen Gegenkultur', in ibid., 147–67. Merl is the foremost German scholar specializing in Soviet agrarian history. His works are, however, not cited by Fitzpatrick. They include *Bauern unter Stalin: die Formierung des sowjetischen Kolchossystems 1930–1941* (Berlin: Ducker & Humblot, 1990); *Sozialer Aufstieg im sowjetischen Kolchossystem der 30er Jahre? Ueber das Schicksal der bäuerlichen Parteimitglieder, Dorfsowjetvorsitzenden, Posteninhaber im Kolchos, Mechanisatoren und Stachanovleute* (Berlin, 1990).

25 Fitzpatrick, *Stalin's Peasants*, 194–203; on peasant opinion at this time see also idem, 'Readers' Letters to *Krest'ianskaia gazeta*, 1938', *Russian History/Histoire russe* 24 (1997), 1–2.

26 S. Kotkin, '1991 and the Russian Revolution: Sources, Conceptual Categories, Analytical Frameworks', *JMH* 70 (1998), 384–425, here 420.

27 M.H. Buckley, '*Krest'ianskaia gazeta* and Rural Stakhanovism', *EAS* 46 (1994), 1387–1407; idem, 'Why be a Shock Worker or a Stakhanovite?', in R. Marsh (ed.), *Women in Russia and Ukraine* (Cambridge: Cambridge University Press, 1996), 199–213; 'Was Rural Stakhanovism a Movement?', *EAS* 51 (1999), 299–314; 'Categorizing Resistance to Rural Stakhanovism', in K. McDermott and J. Morison (eds), *Politics and Society* (Basingstoke and London: Macmillan, 1999), 160–88.

28 'Was Rural Stakhanovism . . . ?', 311.

29 L.H. Siegelbaum, '"Dear Comrade, You Ask What We Need": Socialist Paternalism and Soviet Rural "Notables" in the Mid-1930s', *SR* 57 (1998), 107–22.

30 John Channon provides a competent general overview in 'Stalin and the Peasantry: Reassessing the Post-war Years, 1945–1953', in idem (ed.), *Politics, Society and Stalinism*, 185–209. The wartime experiences of the peasantry are treated in J. Barber and M. Harrison, *The Soviet Home Front, 1941–1945: A Social and Economic History of the USSR in World War II* (London: Macmillan, 1991), 77–90, 137–8.

31 D.L. Hoffmann, in idem and Yu. Kotsonis (eds), *Russian Modernity: Politics, Knowledge, Practices*, (Basingstoke and New York: Macmillan, 2000), 258.

32 L.H. Siegelbaum and R.G. Suny (eds), *Making Workers Soviet: Power, Class and Identity* (Ithaca, NY and London: Cornell University Press, 1994). Two similar volumes were dedicated to the respected pioneer of Soviet social history, Moshe Lewin: W.G. Rosenberg and Siegelbaum (eds), *Social Dimensions of Soviet Industrialization* (Bloomington, IN: Indiana University Press, 1993), which contains articles by S. Fitzpatrick, S. Kotkin, R.W. Davies and other leading authorities; and N. Lampert and G.T. Rittersporn (eds), *Stalinism: Its Nature and Aftermath . . .* (Basingstoke and New York: Macmillan, 1992).

33 S. Kotkin, *Magnetic Mountain: Stalinism as Civilization* (Berkeley, CA and Los Angeles: University of California Press, 1995; pbk edn 1997). For a more recent picture of working conditions in the city (and the Donbas) in 1931–2 see D. Caroli, 'Bolshevism, Stalinism and Social Welfare, 1917–1936', *IRSH* 48 (2003), 27–54.

34 R.W. Davies, in RR 56 (1997), 140–1.

35 D. Filtzer, 'Stalinism and the Working Class in the 1930s', in J. Channon (ed.), *Politics, Society and Stalinism*, 163–84.

36 D. Filtzer, *Soviet Workers and Later Stalinism: Labour and the Restoration of the Stalinist System after World War II* (Cambridge: Cambridge University Press, 2002). Particularly important is Filtzer's coverage of the major contribution to post-war recovery of those he calls 'slave and indentured workers' (pp. 22–39).

37 J.-P. Depretto, *Les Ouvriers en URSS 1928–1941* (Paris: L'Atelier, 1997).

38 D.R. Shearer, *Industry, State and Society in Stalin's Russia, 1926–1934* (Ithaca, NY and London: Cornell University Press, 1996). His earlier work was narrower in scope: *Rationalization and Reconstruction in the Soviet Machine-Building Industry, 1926–1934* (Ann Arbor, MI: University of Michigan Press, 1992).

39 Sales and supply offices of industrial trusts, which attained a semi-autonomous status under NEP. Their ideas represented a 'middle way' more rational than the one eventually adopted.

40 K.M. Straus, *Factory and Community in Stalin's Russia: The Making of an Industrial Working Class* (Pittsburgh: University of Pittsburgh Press, 1997). The factory in question is the famous Hammer and Sickle works.

41 J.J. Rossman, 'Weaver of Rebellion and Poet of Resistance: K. Klepikov (1860–1933) and Shop-floor Opposition to Bolshevik Rule', *JGOE* 46 (1996), 374–408; idem, 'The Taikovo Cotton Workers' Strike of April 1932: Class, Gender and Identity Politics in Stalin's Russia', *RR* 56 (1997), 44–69; idem, 'A Workers' Strike in Stalin's Russia: The Vichuga Uprising of April 1932', in Viola, *Contending*, 44–83. For background to the region, see K. Gestwa, *Proto-Industrialisierung in Russland: Wirtschaft, Herrschaft und Kultur in Ivanovo und Pavlovo, 1741–1932* (Göttingen: Vandenhoeck & Ruprecht, 1999).

42 G. Gorzka, 'Work and Leisure among Textile-Workers in Soviet Russia: Iaroslavl' in the 1930s', in McDermott and Morison (eds), *Politics and Society under the Bolsheviks*, 140–60; idem, 'Krasnyi Perekop – Betriebsalltag und Arbeiterinteressen am Beispiel der Textilarbeiterschaft in Jaroslavl' in den 1930er Jahren', in Plaggenborg (ed.), *Stalinismus*, 209–42. Her earlier works include *Arbeiterkultur in der Sowjetunion: Industriearbeiterklubs, 1917–1929: ein Beitrag zur sowjetischen Kulturgeschichte* (Berlin: Arno Spitz, 1990).

43 D. Neutatz, *Die Moskauer Metro: von den ersten Plänen bis zur Grossbaustelle des Stalinismus, 1897–1935* (Cologne: Böhlau, 2001); idem, 'Zwischen Enthusiasmus und politischer Kontrolle: die Arbeiter und das Regime am Beispiel von Metrostroj', in Plaggenborg, *Stalinismus*, 185–208; idem, 'Arbeiterschaft und Stalinismus am Beispiel der Moskauer Metro', in Hildermeier, *Stalinismus*, 99–118. More recently, idem, "Schmiede des neuen Menschen" und Kostprobe des Sozialismus: Utopien des Moskauer Metrobaus' in W. Hardtwig (ed.), *Utopie und politische Herrschaft im Europa der Zwischenkriegszeit* (Munich: Oldenbourg, 2002), 41–56.

44 L.L. Phillips, *Bolsheviks and the Bottle: Drink and Worker Culture in St. Petersburg, 1900–1929* (DeKalb, IL: Northern Illinois University Press, 2000); one chapter appeared previously in *RR* 56 (1997), 25–43. See also K. Transchel, 'Liquid Assets: Vodka and Drinking in Early Soviet Factories', in W.B. Husband (ed.), *The Human Tradition in Modern Russia* (Wilmington, DE: Scholarly Resources, 2000), 129–42.

45 For the debate see *inter alia* S. Smith, 'Russian Workers and the Politics of Social Identity', *RR* 56 (97), 1–7; idem, 'Writing the History of the Russian Revolution after the Fall of Communism', in M. Miller (ed.), *The Russian Revolution: The Essential Readings* (Oxford and Malden, MA: Blackwell, 2001), 261–81; S.R. Davies, 'Us Against Them: Social Identity in Soviet Russia, 1934–1941', in Fitzpatrick (ed.), *Stalinism: New Directions*, 47–70 and her book *Popular Opinion* (see Chapter 7, p. 115); and works by J. Hellbeck cited in n. 49.

46 'It is a complex interaction of identifications based on age, ethnicity, gender, class, religion, whose unstable ordering is managed through language and representation: it involves processes of inclusion and exclusion, of negation and reinforcement. Crucially, it has a temporal dimension: identities are assembled through the meshing together of two types of historical time: the life history and the history of society.' 'Writing the History of the Russian Revolution', 275. Depkat defines identity as 'the bundle of perceptive and interpretative schemes, and sentiments of belonging, concepts and norms of value, orientations and loyalties, that allots an individual a place in a particular milieu, relates his/her own definition of self to those made by others, integrates the individual into larger groupings, and so enables him/her to function significantly in society': 'Autobiographie und die soziale Konstruktion von Wirklichkeit', *Geschichte und Gesellschaft* 29 (2003), 466.

47 A. Graziosi, 'The New Archival Sources: Hypotheses for a Critical Assessment', *CMR* 49 (1999), 13–64.

48 D. Filtzer, in *JMH* 33 (2001), 457.

49 J. Hellbeck, 'Fashioning the Stalinist Soul: The Diary of Stepan Podlubnyi, 1931–1939', in Fitzpatrick (ed.), *Stalinism: New Directions*, 77–116; idem, 'Feeding the Stalinist Soul: The Diary of Stepan Podlubnyi (1931–1939)', *JGOE* 46 (1996), 344–73; S.F. Podlubnyi, *Tagebuch aus Moskau 1931–1939*, tr. and ed. Hellbeck (Munich: Deutscher Taschenbuchverlag, 1996); idem, 'Speaking Out: Languages of Affirmation and Dissent in Stalinist Russia', *Kritika* 1 (2000), 71–96; 'Self-Realization in the Stalinist System: Two Soviet Diaries of the 1930s', in Hoffmann and Kotsonis, *Russian Modernity*, 221–42. Cf. also his and I. Halfin's responses to an interviewer in 'Thinking Theoretically About the Cultural and Linguistic Turn in Soviet Studies', *Ab imperio*, 2002, no. 3, 217–60.

50 This point is also made by Neutatz, *Moskauer Metro*, 244–5.

51 Fitzpatrick, *Everyday Stalinism: Ordinary Life in Extraordinary Times: Soviet Russia in the 1930s* (New York and London: Oxford University Press, 1999).

52 Davies, *Popular Opinion*, 106, 130–3; idem, 'Us and Them: Social Identity in Soviet Russia, 1934–1941', in Fitzpatrick (ed.), *Stalinism*, 47–70.

9 'It's a woman's world'

Gender studies and daily life

The politics of gender

Over the last two decades, feminist historiography has become a major sub-discipline, especially in the United States. It has found an echo in post-Soviet Russia, notably in the Moscow Centre for Gender Studies. The activists here are quite understandably concerned in the main with current developments. When they look back at the Stalinist era, the picture they see is unrelievedly grim. Olga Voronina, for example, writes of 'a masculinist assault on the women's move-ment' that was launched *c.* 1930, as a result of which women's right to work was transformed into 'a very powerful instrument for their enslavement'.[1] A certain exaggeration is perhaps to be expected among partisans of a (relatively) new cause that has to overcome deep-seated prejudices, and if pressed these writers would probably agree that other segments of Soviet society besides women were victims of Stalin's rule. Did women suffer proportionately more than men? This is an idle question that could be answered, if at all, only after examining specific 'gender issues'.

For this purpose, we first of all need more published sources. Here an important contribution has been made by the editors of the volume in which Voronina's article appeared. In co-operation with an American colleague, Anastasia Posadskaia mounted an oral history project that involved interviewing eight respondents, in Moscow and the Urals, about their experiences as wives and mothers as well as citizens.[2] Two of these women were members of so-called 'kulak' households that suffered expropriation; suddenly deprived of fathers and husbands, they found themselves homeless, without any means of support; if a relative took in a 'kulak' child, she might be subjected to repressive measures, too – as happened to Elena Dolgikh of Tomsk, who lost her job as a teacher for sheltering her refugee mother and was left in need, 'always . . . feeling vulnerable' (pp. 7, 157). Antonina Berezhnaia (Yekaterinburg) was more fortunate. Although her father had been an agronomist of gentry background, she 'embraced the values of her era', showed enthusiasm on her job administering a metallurgical plant, introduced several technical innovations in the face of (male) bureaucratic obstruction, and in 1940 graduated with a specialist degree that enabled her to become 'the chief refractory engineer in the Urals region'. Her social origin was no longer held against her and in later life she preferred to forget her difficult early years (pp. 101–16). Most respondents, however, remained in relatively low-status, ill-paid occupations. One such was Vera Malakhova (Tomsk). Of working-class background, she studied medicine, served four years at the front as a physician, took part in the battle of Stalingrad, was wounded twice and won several decorations. Yet when interviewed in 1994, she was practically destitute. Her frank recollections give a graphic picture of wartime realities, for instance soldiers' attitudes towards NKVD 'special section' operatives, as well as more immediate feminine concerns (pp. 175–218, esp. p. 202). These are all very human documents, which, as Engel notes with commendable honesty in her afterword, cannot readily be assessed 'within the framework of Western feminism . . . in terms of "advances" or "equality"'. The respondents resisted suggestions that women had enjoyed only a 'secondary' status under Soviet rule; almost all of them 'derived genuine satisfaction from their participation in public life', viewed work as intrinsically valuable, and despite the hardships endured were proud of what they had achieved (pp. 219–21).[3]

A far grimmer picture is conveyed by another volume of sources, Semen Vilensky's collection of memoirs by women who spent years in prison, camps or exile. This did not become available in an (abridged) English translation until a full decade had elapsed after its appearance in Russia.[4] Only half the sixteen survivors chosen for inclusion, nearly all of whom were arrested in the 1930s, lived to see their memoirs in print; some completed their manuscripts secretly while still behind barbed wire. John Crowfoot remarks that their testimonies

> offer a humanly approachable introduction to a horrific and alien world. The authors recount how, after the initial shock of imprisonment, maltreatment and loss, concern for the family and friends they had left behind was extended, in compassion, to those who now surrounded them – an assertion of human values in the face of an impersonal system of numbing scale and barely credible inhumanity.
>
> (p. 336)

Reading these tales of suffering, borne with amazing resilience, is a sobering and inspiring experience. Whether this information will have much impact on Western scholars' evaluations of the Stalin era it is still too early to say.

The earlier literature covered very fully the evolution of Party and government policy[5] on what earlier revolutionaries used to call the 'woman question', so that even with access to the archives it seems unlikely that anything strikingly novel could be said today about the changes in official attitudes between the 1920s and 1930s. There are, however, three articles of interest in the volume of essays edited by Stefan Plaggenborg.[6] Robert Maier argues that between 1932 and 1936 social pressure, in the form of the 'enormous discontent' felt by Soviet women at the human costs of the modernization drive, led Stalin to modify the regime's harsh policies and to introduce measures that could be interpreted as 'pro-women' (*frauenfreundlich*, p. 250). These pragmatically inspired concessions, part of what Nicholas Timasheff once memorably (but rather misleadingly) called the 'great retreat', had a spurious, demagogic character but did at least bring some benefits to a fortunate few and helped to stabilize the system. Official concern for family values, the pro-natalist policy with its honours for 'heroine mothers', limitations on divorce and abortion, and lastly the 'wives' movement' (to be considered below) all helped to bolster the regime's propagandist self-image and sometimes 'unleashed euphoric reactions' (p. 263). Maier cites the case of a female pig-herder in Siberia who, on receiving a sizeable sum for her maternal accomplishments, wrote to a local paper to express her pleasure at no longer having to queue in shops, adding 'how close I felt our dear Stalin was to me!'[7] At the same time the censors permitted the press to report realistically the cases of women who were destitute, sick and neglected. By these means 'the Stalinist leadership suggested convincingly that, unlike ignorant local functionaries, it *did* recognize many women's needs and took them seriously' – this at the height of the Terror. Motherhood and family life offered the hard-pressed citizenry a refuge where human values and socially responsible behaviour were cultivated (pp. 264–5).

Susanne Conze argues likewise that women should not be portrayed exclusively as 'passive victims': although they had limited opportunities to articulate their specific interests, the regime 'had to secure public acceptance of its social policies and offer people the chance to identify [with it]' (p. 294). She cites archival evidence of 'resistance behaviour by women, expressed in the context of prevailing norms and values'; for example, in 1947 a woman working in a Moscow motor-vehicle plant complained publicly about having to queue for hours to buy a cabbage, yet in the same breath assured her listeners that she and her comrades would over-fulfil their norms (pp. 316–17). Such action certainly took courage, but did it really amount to *resistance?* Conze deserves credit for tackling the neglected post-war years, but the picture she draws is rather remote from everyday realities – the famine of 1946–7, for instance, goes unmentioned.[8]

In the execution, if not the formulation, of the regime's social policies a prominent part was played by women Party members, who are the subject of a sociological study by a leading American writer on Russian women's history.[9] Barbara Clements (Kent, OH) has compiled a data base of prominent 'Bolshevik women' (*bol'shevichki*), 545 individuals who joined the Party before the revolution or during the civil-war years, most of whom were in a position to exercise authority in the Stalin era. Out of 384 for whom data are available as to their employment in 1929–1941, 108 were in education, 61 in the economy – and 67 in the Party *apparat*. Women in official jobs 'earned their promotion by dint of personal ability, qualifications, and ambition', but their chances of moving upwards in the bureau-cracy 'became even more circumscribed in the 1930s' than they had been earlier. In the Party, most female functionaries had 'concentrated on agitation and propa-ganda' in the 1920s; the Stalinist reorientation of values 'deeply disappointed' feminists such as Kollontai and Alexandra Artiukhina (last head of Zhenotdel),[10] yet neo-patriarchalism did not turn them against a regime from which they derived so many benefits. Most of them escaped arrest during the Terror, and one (Rozaliia Zemliachka), a Lenin associate from 1902, actually became 'an enthusiastic partici-pant in the atrocities committed by the Party' (pp. 17, 250–2, 261, 277–8, 286).

Women at work

Women's role in the labour force is familiar territory. A post-modernist view is offered by Carmen Scheide (Basle),[11] who sets herself the aim of 'making women visible as historical subjects . . . [and] describing how individuals perceived institutional structures and the interplay between various lifestyles and projects for social change'. Gender studies, she writes, should not be just an appendage to general history; instead the latter needs redefinition so as to give women their proper place (pp. 18–19, 21). The first two sections of her work are devoted to the Party's ideology and policy on the reform of everyday life (*byt*) and the relevant institutions; the third (pp. 197–346) looks more closely at the experiences of women workers in the Moscow region. Although Scheide does not go beyond the end of 1929, students of the 1930s will need to take account of her fresh data from 1929 on housing (p. 251), time budgets (p. 263), employment (p. 280), generational conflict at the workplace (p. 293), and alcoholism (pp. 338, 342).

Rather more traditional in approach is the study by the British social historian Melanie Ilič (Bristol), also based on archival sources, of labour protection policy and its practical implementation,[12] which takes us on through the 1930s. She shows that an administrative overhaul of the two inspectorates charged with this task in 1931 reduced their staffs and put the accent on fulfilment of production targets instead of the promotion of women workers' social and cultural interests. This was in effect a counterpart to the elimination in January 1930 of Zhenotdel[13] and the withering of the trade unions. Thereafter officials and managements frequently ignored regulations on, for example, the employment of pregnant women – but Ilič points out that this is not the whole story: 'women themselves often flouted the terms of the more restrictive elements of the laws' in order not to 'put at risk their continuation in employment or reduce wages' (pp. 77, 95). This conformism did not, however, extend to the increased obligation to carry heavy loads or to toil underground – abuses that often did much physical harm (pp. 92, 123, 167). Women learned to drive tractors and locomotives, or served as sailors on board cargo ships; on the credit side, toiling in such traditionally male jobs did at least prepare them to serve as equals of men in the armed forces during the war (p. 148).[14] Ilič makes no mention of women condemned to forced labour, and her conclusions are on the whole positive: women received 'unprecedented economic opportunities' (p. 175), even if equality between the sexes was not realized in practice and, indeed, sex segregation became entrenched. In the light of these findings one wonders whether the sub-title of her study is appropriately worded.

Rather more pertinent to feminist concerns is the solid work of Wendy Goldman, a leading US specialist, on gender conflict in industry.[15] She explores in detail, with a profusion of statistics, the influx of women into Soviet factories during the first FYP – by 1935 they comprised 45 per cent of total employed. This was in large part a consequence of inflation and the falling wages paid to their spouses. The Party's so-called 'regendering strategy', pursued over a whole range of occupations, provoked animosity among the newcomers' more prejudiced male comrades. Thus a certain Grivneva, employed at the Red Putilovets factory in Leningrad, 'spent the better part of a year "sharpening pencils". When she requested a transfer to more complex work, the master yelled, "you women can never be good lathe operators!"' ('Babas', pp. 80–1). Even adequately trained girls were allotted such jobs only under pressure. Conflicts arose when, for example, men were displaced to do heavier work, but deep-seated cultural bias was also involved. 'Men frequently expressed their resentment in a sexualized form, regarding women's very presence in the factory . . . as a sexual transgression'; the unfortunate girls were subjected to obscenities and unwanted advances, only to find themselves blamed for 'causing trouble'. Although the term 'sexual harassment' had yet to be invented, the phenomenon existed; women 'demonstrated a remarkable consciousness of gender . . . [and] had no trouble describing prejudice or expressing their anger at discrimination' (pp. 83–5). Such protests could bring little relief in the absence of effective institutions through which to articulate them.[16]

One (male) reviewer of Goldman's book complained that 'the voices of ordinary women labourers remain surprisingly muted'.[17] The more determined feminist writers include Claudia Kraft, of the 'Basle Initiative for Gender Studies', a workshop set up in 2001. She alleges that 'the old discourses about femininity' just trod water, accumulating factual material instead of contributing 'to the deconstruction of inherited images of gender'. Such works were too often bound up with the history of males (for example, at the workplace), whereas it should be recognized that ideas on (social) space were but constructs, which were generally made by men in any case.[18]

This broadside will probably provoke plenty of discussion. So far, the literature on women's lot under Stalin has not really gone very far in a radical feminist direction, to be sure. This would involve more emphasis on women's bodies. One of those who have tackled such issues is Frances Bernstein, who points to the 'biological determinism' that underlay scientific studies of endocrinology in the 1920s. This led to sexual stereotyping and a disregard of the cultural factors that lay behind prostitution, homosexuality, and other phenomena that were then (and later) deemed aberrant.[19] Elsewhere Bernstein turns to the problem of prostitution in particular, showing how official policy veered from rehabilitation in the 1920s to criminalization in the following decade, when most of the 'labour clinics' set up to shield 'fallen women' from 'negative influences', and train them for industry, were closed down. 'Gone was the faith in the possibility of transforming individual "human material" through education and consciousness-raising; in its place the authorities implemented a set of punitive policies aimed at forcing transformation on the entire population, willing and unwilling subjects alike.'[20]

At this point, we approach the important but neglected field of the history of medicine and public hygiene, which we cannot tackle here except to mention David Ransel's highly original study, *Village Mothers*, in which he compares health care and the survival of superstitious practices among Russians and Tatars. Greta Bucher, who teaches at the US Military Academy, highlights the plight of pregnant mothers in the post-war years. She places the blame for the poor state of maternity clinics firmly on 'bureaucratic manipulation of resources' without allowing for the very real shortages of skilled personnel, equipment and so forth, because of the war and the regime's overall priorities. This may unconsciously reflect an American rather than European approach to health care. But Bucher is undoubtedly correct to note that all too often women preferred dubious 'home remedies' to professional medical attention.[21]

Chris Burton agrees with Bucher about the critical state of post-war Soviet medicine, and points to the very damaging consequences for women's health of abortions performed illegally, outside state facilities. In 1951 and early 1952, abortions and miscarriages accounted for 18.8 per cent of total births – and the proportion was growing. Doctors were called on to engage in 'medical policing', a role they understandably resented on professional grounds, even though they had earlier (1936) played a role in the criminalization of abortion. By 1950 or so, everyone realized that changes in the law were needed, but so long as Stalin lived nothing could be done.[22]

The plight of children was, alas, only slightly less distressing than that of women, in so far as the state had any role in their upbringing, for example in institutions for homeless waifs. The French scholar Dorena Caroli, working on the archival fond of *Glavsotsvos* in the Education commissariat, usefully amplifies the work by Alan Ball mentioned above (p. 93) with a study of 'abandoned children' that goes up to 1931.[23] She modifies Bernstein's views as to the currency of biological determinism, showing that the theories of pedology developed by the psychologist A.B. Zalkind continued to be practised until 1935. In 1927 the Party began to abdicate its responsibilities for social protection. The process was taken further two years later, when orphans in institutional care were assigned to factory or farm work and 'total disorder' reigned (pp. 1310, 1315); many of these unfortunates fled. The repressive trend, she notes in fairness, was a pan-European one, but in the USSR it was concealed behind complacent official reports. The border between social assistance and the penal system became ever more fluid as even innocent waifs were put behind bars – as N.V. Krylenko admitted in an (unpublished) report of 1933, when there were 8,000 of them in prisons run by his commissariat (p. 1316).

The NEP era is seen as 'an age of anxiety' by the Canadian social historian Anne Gorsuch,[24] who deals extensively with the *besprizornye* (pp. 148–58) and what she calls 'discourses of delinquency' against the background of Bolshevik thinking and policies on young people in general, which led to embarrassing 'excesses of enthusiasm' among Komsomol members (pp. 80ff.). For Lisa Kirschenbaum Stalinism is 'a paradoxical mix of support for traditional gender and generational hierarchies with images of defiant, revolutionary youth'; young people were 'the revolutionary class *par excellence*, but only in the most conservative sense of devoting [themselves] to tasks laid out by the state' (pp. 4, 158).[25]

It would be good if such studies could be continued into the later Stalin era, about which little has been written so far. One scholar who *has* boldly tackled this era is Mark Edele. His general approach is post-modernist – there is talk of 'self-fashioning' and 'the construction of identity' among young people – but he argues that Hellbeck is wrong to see this process as coming about solely in response to *political* pressures: cultural reference points, he argues, could serve just as well.

This was how the 'style-chasers' (*stiliagi*) of the post-Stalin years originated: this movement, he stresses, took shape while Stalin was still alive.[26]

Everyday life

According to Lynne Attwood and Catriona Kelly,[27] Komsomol and Pioneer organizations did more than just shape children's outlook; they 'disseminated programmes for identity' by inculcating Communist morality (politeness, respect for one's elders, disciplined behaviour in school and so on) – values that were often questioned or negated in the home. We come here to studies of everyday life in Stalin's Russia – itself an extensive and growing field of study, in which these two authors are (along with Sheila Fitzpatrick) leading lights. 'Programmes for identity' embraced adults, too, of course. Acording to the 'culturalists', the fostering of better hygiene, the physical fitness (*fizkul'tura*) movement, and the development of organized sports should all be seen as part of *agitprop* in a broader sense. Athletes marched to the sound of heroic music and formed human pyramids in mass exercises 'intended as representations of the fit and healthy body politic' ('Programmes', p. 269) – their symbolic role being as important as their explicit one of encouraging physical well-being. Early Soviet culture, we are told, had a 'symbolic reality', whose various representations reveal its 'mythic signifieds . . . existing on a different level to daily conscious actions' (p. 276). In films and on posters, propagandists portrayed women in heroic roles, as 'strong, healthy and largely asexual . . . a tomboy whose femininity comes across as girlish vivacity' (p. 281). Women were 'used as signifiers of abstract ideas such as the Motherland, the People and morality'.

Elsewhere Attwood develops these arguments by dissecting the role of women's magazines, such as *Rabotnitsa* and *Krest'ianka*, as 'engineers of female identity'. She contends that 'women's images were reconfigured' to meet changing demands: thus in the 1930s, there was less emphasis than before on family problems and more on activist women's contributions to the country's economic and social progress; the roles assigned, she adds, were often contradictory.[28]

Practitioners of this approach are keen to get away from the 'totalitarian model', which in their opinion presented too simplified a view of Party and state bodies telling passive, obedient 'masses' what to think and how to behave. Stimulating as the 'new cultural history' is, it raises fresh problems in so far as these writers substitute images for reality or take refuge in obscurity at the critical juncture where we need concrete data as to how far people adapted their conduct to comply with official norms. Studies of everyday life have the merit of bringing history down to the popular level; they introduce us to the problems and experiences of common citizens whom we should otherwise never have heard of. In this way, our picture of society is made fuller, less abstract or élitist – a welcome corrective to the anonymity of much sociologically oriented research. On the other hand, there is a risk of confusing style with substance, of presenting a sanitized picture of reality by highlighting relatively trivial or superficial changes in popular lifestyles (*byt*) while neglecting power relationships, repression, economic hardship and other unpleasantnesses – all this in an effort to show what Kelly and Shepherd term the 'normality [of] the processes of everyday life' and their similarity to contemporary developments in Western countries, for instance, in the way homes were furnished.[29]

The *kul'turnost'* campaign of the later 1930s was certainly a fascinating and paradoxical phenomenon. At a time when the urban population was short of everyday necessities, regime spokesmen set out to promote more civilized standards of life and behaviour: personal cleanliness, refined speech, a more sophisticated diet, and (last but not least) domestic furnishings for the apartments that were springing up in lieu of the primitive factory barracks characteristic of earlier stages of urbanization. Women's journals featured illustrated articles on carpets, pictures, lampshades, dresses, stockings – even cosmetics (although Stalin personally seems to have disapproved of the use of perfume).[30] The appeal was addressed in particular to élite women – Stakhanovites as well as officials' wives with time on their hands. In addition to care of children, shopping and cooking, they were called on to provide a comfortable domestic environment for their menfolk. Such 'socially engaged wives' (the nearest English approximation to the term *obshchestvennitsy*) felt it their duty to apply their refined taste to improve the lives of their social inferiors, much as upper-class women had done before the revolution. The campaign had a charming old-fashioned ring to it, and some of the advice handed down from above had indeed featured in age-old books of etiquette. Mary Buckley notes that 'a certain tension pervaded ideology on the wives' movement'. They were supposed to be 'moral guides and promoters of decent values' in the home, yet 'some of their activities brought them into more assertive roles . . . drawing [them] out of the home into a wider social setting' and encouraging them to forsake traditional patterns of behaviour.[31] Their well-meant efforts were not always appreciated: 'the sentiment [among] workers that the wives were interfering busybodies looking for ways of filling their time appears to have been widespread . . . They were negatively viewed as snoopers who pried into other people's business' (pp. 162–3), and often received inadequate backing from local authorities which prevented them achieving their tasks (p. 168).

In the last resort, the successes of the wives' movement depended on greater availability of consumer goods. Fitzpatrick comments that 'the new orientation . . . involved a more fundamental shift away from the anti-consumerist approach of earlier years toward a new (and, in Marxist terms, surprising) appreciation of commodities', and cites a newspaper description of a Moscow grocery store that sold 38 types of sausage and kept fresh meat in a refrigerated glass case – a practice that would have been a luxury anywhere in Europe at the time. Advertisements showed consumer goods, although the tone of the messages was didactic, and so distinct from the crass commercialism of 'capitalist' countries. In large cities, restaurants started up again, dancing came back into fashion, and cinemas showed light-hearted romances along with more obviously propagandist films.[32] There is an air of artificiality about the *kul'turnost'* drive, for simultaneously the bulk of the population was going hungry, Terror was raging, and of course women in the Gulag inhabited a different world entirely. Writers on the subject are prone to play down its bogus character. The increased allocations to defence in the later 1930s, and then the war itself, would shortly bring consumerism to an end, but it would revive in new forms after 1953.

Another important aspect of everyday life to have received attention recently from Western cultural historians is the role of ritual, especially in forming a new 'Soviet' identity. The theme is not entirely new: earlier writers often noted the ritualistic element in elections where there was no choice of candidates, or in the procedure whereby Party members had to appear before 'purge commissions' and publicly acknowledge their errors.[33] Lorenz Erren has written a new study of the latter practice in which he argues that there were two strands in the development of this ritual, one involving criticism of others and the other of oneself.[34] Another German scholar to have worked on this theme is Malte Rolf (Berlin), who argues that the mass festivals held during the First Five-Year Plan era were an example of 'stage-managing the public sphere' to magnify the regime's support and so to legitimize it. The marchers observed a 'hierarchical order of space', yet often managed to gain a degree of autonomy from the organizers.[35]

This latter idea is the *leitmotif* of a work by an American historian, Karen Petrone.[36] Parades and celebrations of many kinds were utilized both by the organizers to promote the official myth and by humdrum participants to articulate an alternative view of things that was often implicitly subversive of authority. Petrone follows Foucault in maintaining that 'study of a particular discourse can reveal the operation of power in a society' but disagrees with him in 'see[ing] individual actors shaping discourse even as it shapes them' – in other words, we have a two-way process in which 'Soviet citizens employed the state's mandates for their own ends . . . to regain control over their lives' (p. 8).

To substantiate this thesis Petrone examines, not just formal parades such as that held to mark the twentieth anniversary of 'Great October', but also the celebrations marking heroic exploits by Arctic explorers and other technical feats, secular New Year festivities, and the 1937 Pushkin centennial. She adduces much interesting new material, for instance on the symbolism of the human body when displayed by athletes on parade (p. 33). Certain leading officials, notably P.P. Postyshev and A.V. Kosarev, are shown to have tried to depoliticize official festivals by encouraging a carnival-like atmosphere. A traditional-minded historian might see this simply as an example of a 'soft' tactical line prevailing over a 'hard' one, but a historian committed to PM methodology prefers to seek out latent symbolic meanings – even at the risk of losing his or her sense of proportion and going beyond the limitations of the evidence.[37]

For example, one may well agree that in 1937 some literary critics who wrote on Pushkin managed to convey thoughts that did not fit the Stalinist canon, and the use of such 'Aesopian language' certainly merits study. But can the centennial celebration *really* be said to have 'opened up spaces in which individual freedom could be both discussed and pursued'? Did 'the Soviet intelligentsia' *really* conduct 'debates . . . about artistic and political freedom . . . under threat of terror and in conditions of tight censorship' (pp. 137, 141). To elevate such cautious hints and a censor's oversight (or liberalism) into 'discourse' is surely misleading. Petrone concludes grandly as follows:

Soviet celebrations of the 1930s reveal the complexity of Stalinist political discourse and the myriad ways in which it could be *shaped by citizens*. Despite strict censorship, Soviet official discourse offered *a wide variety of opportunities* for Soviet citizens to think and talk about their lives in ways that did not conform to state dictates or intentions.

(p. 203: our italics)

Alas, engaging in such 'alternative discourse' would normally land one in very serious trouble. Obscured here is the essential, though familiar, point that in a modern 'mass mobilization' dictatorship (to use no more opprobrious term) officially sponsored ceremonies fill the gap left by the absence of normal politics. Those tempted to emulate Petrone's provocative (and in many ways excellent) study might do well to add a comparative dimension: how did Soviet public functions differ from, say, the funeral ceremonies in London for King George V or for that matter a New York ticker-tape parade? Here, too, there were elements of organization and spontaneity, but the flavour of the event was of course wholly different. Emphasis on the autonomy that Soviet citizens under Stalin arguably still possessed vis-à-vis the claims of authority can mislead unless we take the very peculiar political context into account.

Notes

1 O. Voronina, 'The Mythology of Women's Emancipation in the USSR as the Foundation for a Policy of Discrimination', in A. Posadskaya-Vanderbeck *et al.* (eds), *Women in Russia: A New Era in Russian Feminism*, trans. K. Clark (London and New York, 1994), 37–56, here 47.

2 B.A. Engel and Posadskaya-Vanderbeck (eds), *A Revolution of Their Own: Voices of Women in Soviet History*, trans. S. Hoisington (Boulder, CO and Oxford: Westview, 1998). The two editors eloquently express their gratitude 'for the serendipity that brought us together [which] . . . deepened our understanding of the lives and circumstances of the women whose stories unfold in these pages'. Engel continues her work on women's testimonies in 'The Womanly Face of War: Soviet Women Remember World War II', in Nicole A. Dombrowski (ed.), *Women and War in the Twentieth Century: Enlisted With or Without Consent* (London: Garland, 1999), 138–59.

3 For a similar collection, see S. Fitzpatrick and Y. Slezkine (eds), *In the Shadow of the Revolution: Life Stories of Russian Women from 1917 to the Second World War* (Princeton, NJ: Princeton University Press, 2000), hailed by a reviewer (K. Turton in *EAS* 53 (2001), 523–5) as 'an invaluable source for the feminist historian'. M. M. Leder, *My Life in Stalinist Russia: An American Woman Looks Back*, ed. L. Bernstein (Bloomington, IN: Indiana University Press, 2001) is an unpretentious autobiography by a woman who, as a factory worker in the 1930s, was briefly trained as a spy and later earned her living as a translator. C. Simmons and N. Perline offer a collection of sources on women's experiences during the war: *Writing the Siege of Leningrad: Women's Diaries, Memoirs and Documentary Prose* (Pittsburgh: University of Pittsburgh Press, 2002).

4 S. Vilensky, *Dodnes' tiagoteet: zapiski moei sovremennitsy* (Moscow, 1989); idem, *Till My Tale Is Told: Women's Memoirs of the Gulag*, trans. J. Crowfoot, prepared by Crowfoot and Z. Vesyolaya (Bloomington and Indianapolis: Indiana University Press, 1999). More recent is V. Shapovalov (ed. and trans.), *Remembering the Darkness: Women in Soviet Prisons* (Lanham, MD, 2001); cf. also E. Mason, 'Women in the Gulag in the 1930s', in M. Ilič (ed.), *Women in the Stalin Era* (Basingstoke and New York: Palgrave, 2001), 131–50.

5 The most recent account is W.Z. Goldman, *Women, the State and the Revolution: Soviet Family Policy and Social Life, 1917–1936* (Cambridge and New York: Cambridge University Press, 1993, repr. 1995). Earlier works include: D. Atkinson *et al.* (eds), *Women in Russia* (Stanford, CA: Stanford University Press, 1977); G.W. Lapidus, *Women in Soviet Society: Equality, Development and Social Change* (Berkeley, CA: University of California Press, 1978); A. McAuley, *Women's Work and Wages in the Soviet Union* (London and Winchester, MA: G. Allen and Unwin, 1981); M.H. Buckley, *Women and Ideology in the Soviet Union* (Ann Arbor, MI: University of Michigan Press, 1989).

6 R. Maier, '"Die Frauen stellen die Hälfte der Bevölkerung unseres Landes dar"': Stalins Besinnung auf das weibliche Geschlecht', in Plaggenborg (ed.), *Stalinismus*, 243–66; R. Sartori, '"Weben ist das Glück fürs ganze Land"': zur Inszenierung eines Frauenideals', ibid., 267–91; S. Conze, 'Stalinistische Frauenpolitik in den 40er Jahren', ibid., 293–320. The last two authors use archival sources. Maier's monograph *Frauen im Sozialismus: die Kolchosbäuerin in den 30er Jahren zwischen Anpassung und Mittäterschaft*, was not yet published at the time of writing. It is a sequel to his *Die Stachanow-Bewegung 1935–1938* (Stuttgart: F. Steiner, 1990).

7 Maier, 'Die Frauen', 264. The quotation exemplifies the problem of interpretation raised by such letters, which we have referred to in Chapter 6. B.E. Clements, *Bolshevik Women* (Cambridge and New York: Cambridge University Press, 1997); cf. her edition (with B.A. Engel and C. Worobec) of the miscellany *Russia's Women: Accommodation, Resistance, Transformation* (Berkeley, CA: University of California Press, 1991), most of which deals with the Soviet period.

8 Conze's dissertation has been published as *Sowjetische Industriearbeiterinnen in den 40er Jahren: die Auswirkungen des II. Weltkrieges auf die Erwerbstätigkeit von Frauen in der UdSSR, 1941–1950* (Stuttgart: F. Steiner, 2001). Cf. also idem, 'Women's Work and Emancipation in the Soviet Union, 1941–1950', in M. Ilič (ed.), *Women in the Stalin Era*, 216–34, and an article on gender problems in industry during the late Stalin era in C. Scheide and N. Stegman (eds), *Normsetzung und -überschreitung: Geschlecht in der Geschichte Osteuropas im 19. und 20. Jahrhundert* (Bochum: D. Winkler, 1999), 119–33.

9 B.E. Clements, *Bolshevik Women* (Cambridge and New York: Cambridge University Press, 1997). Clements was the biographer (1979) of Alexandra Kollontai.

10 For more on Artiukhina, see C. Scheide, '"Born in October": The Life and Thought of Aleksandra Vasil'evna Artiukhina, 1889–1969', in Ilič (ed.), *Women in the Stalin Era*, 9–28.

11 Scheide, *Kinder, Küche, Kommunismus: das Wechselverhältnis zwischen Frauenalltag und Frauenpolitik von 1921 bis 1930 am Beispiel Moskauer Arbeiterinnen* (Zurich: Pano, 2002, vol. 3 of Basler Studien zur Kulturgeschichte Osteuropas, ed. A. Guski and H. Haumann), with an excellent survey of the literature.

12 M. Ilič, *Women Workers in the Soviet Interwar Economy: From 'Protection' to 'Equality'* (London and New York, 1999). Ilič follows up this work in L. Edmondson (ed.), *Gender in Russian History and Culture* (Birmingham: CREES and New York: Palgrave, 2001), a miscellany that also contains articles on women's journals (L. Attwood) and women tractor drivers (S. Bridger), as well as by M.H. Buckley on women Stakhanovites.

13 *Zhenotdel* was superseded by relatively ineffective 'women's sections' (*zhensektory*) in Party bodies and later by 'women's councils' (*sovety zhen*). On the latter see R. Maier, '*Sovety zhen* as a Surrogate Trade Union: Comments on the History of the Movement of Activist Women in the 1930s', in McDermott and Morison (eds), *Politics and Society* . . . , 189–98.

14 On women in World War II see K.I. Cottam (ed. and trans.), *Defending Leningrad: Women Behind Enemy Lines* (Nepean, ON, 1998); R. Perrington, *Wings, Women and War: Soviet Airwomen in World War II Combat* (Lawrence, KS and London: University Press of Kansas, 2001), which opens 'an exciting new window into an area of Soviet military history that has received very little attention in the West', as S. Stoecker notes (*SR*

62 (2003), 192–3). A highly uncomplimentary view of Russian women in the rear is offered by a Polish deportee, K.R. Jolluck, '"You Can't Even Call Them Women" . . .', *Contemporary European History* 10 (2001), 463–80. For a more objective account see J. Hösler, 'Finis mundi im Hinterland: Erinnerungen russischer Frauen an die Kriegsauswirkungen in Jaroslavl 1941–1948', in idem and W. Kessler (eds), *Finis mundi: Endzeiten im östlichen Europa: Festschrift für Hans Lemberg zum 65. Geburtstag* (Stuttgart: F. Steiner, 1998), 189–208.

15 W.Z. Goldman, *Women at the Gates: Gender and Industry in Stalin's Russia* (Cambridge and New York: Cambridge University Press, 2002), anticipated in 'Babas at the Bench: Gender Conflict in Soviet Industry in the 1930s', in Ilič (ed.), *Women in the Stalin Era*, 69–88.

16 See also T.G. Schrand, 'The Five-year Plan for Women's Labour: Constructing Socialism and the "Double Burden", 1930–1932', *EAS* 51 (1999), 1455–78; idem, 'Soviet "Civic-Minded" Women in the 1930s: Gender, Class and Industrialization in a Socialist Society', *Journal of Women's History* 11 (1999), 126–50.

17 D. Raleigh, in *Journal of Interdisciplinary History* 34 (2003), 92.

18 C. Kraft, 'Wo steht die Frauen- und Geschlechtergeschichte in der Osteuropa-Forschung?', *JGOE* 50 (2002), 102–7.

19 F.L. Bernstein, '"The Dictatorship of Sex": Science, Glands and the Medical Construction of Gender Difference in Revolutionary Russia', in Hoffmann and Kotsonis (eds), *Russian Modernity*, 138–60. In another article, 'Panic, Potency, and the Crisis of Nervousness in Revolutionary Russia', in C. Kiaer and E. Naiman, *Everyday Subjects: Formations of Identity in Early Soviet Culture*, Ithaca, NY and London (Cornell University Press, forthcoming), Bernstein describes 'the sexual crisis atmosphere of NEP Russia'. Naiman is the author of *Sex in Public: The Incarnation of Early Soviet Ideology* (Princeton, NJ: Princeton University Press, 1997).

20 F.L. Bernstein, 'Prostitutes and Proletarians: The Soviet Labour Clinic as Revolutionary Laboratory', in W.B. Husband (ed.), *The Human Tradition in Modern Russia* (Wilmington DE: Scholarly Resources, 2000), 113–28, here 120, 127.

21 D.L. Ransel, *Village Mothers: Three Generations of Change in Russia and Tataria* (Bloomington and Indianapolis: University of Indiana Press, 2000); G. Bucher, 'Free and Worth Every Kopeck: Soviet Medicine and Women in Post-war Russia', in Husband (ed.), *Human Tradition*, 175–86; cf. idem, 'Struggling to Survive: Soviet Women in the Post-war Years', *Journal of Women's History* 12 (2000), 137–59.

22 C. Burton, 'Minzdrav, Soviet Doctors and the Policing of Reproduction in the Late Stalinist Years', *Russian History / Histoire russe* 27 (2000), 197–221.

23 D. Caroli, 'Socialisme et protection sociale: une tautologie? L'enfance abandonnée en URSS, 1917–1931', *Annales: Histoire, sciences sociales* 54 (1999), 1291–316. *Glavsotsvos* was the Main Department of Social Education. See also her article cited in Chapter 8.

24 A.E. Gorsuch, *Youth in Revolutionary Russia: Enthusiasts, Bohemians, Delinquents* (Bloomington, IN: Indiana University Press, 2000). Sections of this monograph appeared earlier in *SR* 55 (1996), 36–60; *RR* 56 (1997); and *Carl Beck Papers*, 1102.

25 L.K. Kirschenbaum, *Small Comrades: Revolutionizing Childhood in Soviet Russia, 1917–1932* (New York and London: RoutledgeFalmer, 2001). This author has also undertaken an analysis of women's wartime role as reflected chiefly in *Komsomol'skaia pravda*: '"Our City, Our Hearth, Our Families": Local Loyalties and Private Life in Soviet World War II Propaganda', *SR* 59 (2000), 825–47, in which she claims that 'feminized images of public service' helped to create a more 'bourgeois' outlook (846).

26 M. Edele, 'Strange Young Men in Stalin's Moscow: The Birth and Life of the *Stiliagi*, 1945–1953', *JGOE* 50 (2002), 37–61. This accords with the findings of J. Fürst, 'Prisoners of the Soviet Self: Political Youth Opposition in Late Stalinism', *EAS* 54 (2002), 353–75, who covers (355) the dissident Komsomol group at Voronezh (1947), and subsequent discussion (with H. Kuromiya) in ibid. 631–8 and 54 (2003), 353–75.

Edele has also written 'Paper Soldiers: The World of the Soldier Hero According to Soviet War-time Posters', *JGOE* 47 (1999), 91–108, in which he contends that the propagandists succeeded in adapting their line to the psychological needs of individual soldiers, so creating 'solidarity without consensus' and 'polyvalent icons' (e.g., of the Motherland) with 'a broad range of meanings' that they could interpret flexibly.

27 L. Attwood and C. Kelly, 'Programmes for Identity: The "New Man" and the "New Woman"', in Kelly and D. Shepherd (eds), *Constructing Russian Culture in the Age of Revolution, 1881–1940* (Oxford and New York: Oxford University Press, 1998), 259–90. Cf. Kelly and Shepherd (eds), *Russian Cultural Studies: An Introduction* (Oxford and New York: Oxford University Press, 1998); Kelly, *A History of Russian Women's Writing, 1820–1992* (Oxford and New York, 1994); idem, '*Kulturnost*' in the Soviet Union: Ideal and Reality', in G. Hosking and R. Service (eds), *Reinterpreting Russia* (London: Arnold, 1999); idem, *Reforming Russia: Advice Literature, Polite Culture and Gender from Catherine [II] to Yeltsin* (Oxford and New York: Oxford University Press, 2001).

28 L. Attwood, *Creating the New Soviet Woman: Women's Magazines as Engineers of Female Identity, 1922–1953* (Basingstoke: Macmillan and New York: St. Martin's, 1999); cf. her 'Women Workers at Play: The Portrayal of Leisure in the Magazine *Rabotnitsa* in the First Two Decades of Soviet Power', in Ilič (ed.), *Women in the Stalin Era*, 29–48. Another recent article by Attwood is 'Gender Angst in Russian Society and Cinema in the Post-Stalin Era', in Kelly and Shepherd, *Russian Cultural Studies*, 352–67.

29 *Constructing Russian Culture*, 5–7.

30 N. Akhgikhina and H. Goscilo, 'Getting Under Their Skin: The Beauty Salon in Russian Women's Lives', in Goscilo and B. Holmgren (eds), *Russia – Women – Culture* (Bloomington and Indianapolis: Indiana University Press, 1996), 98.

31 M.H. Buckley, 'The Untold Story of the *Obshchestvennitsa* in the 1930s', in Ilič (ed.), *Women in the Stalin Era*, 151–72, here 157–8; cf. R.B. Neary, 'Mothering Socialist Society: The Wife-Activists' Movement in the Soviet Culture of Daily Life, 1934–1941', *RR* 58 (1999), 396–412.

32 On entertainment, see R. Stites (ed.), *Culture and Entertainment in War-time Russia* (Bloomington: Indiana University Press, 1995), a follow-up to his *Russian Popular Culture: Entertainment and Society Since 1900* (Cambridge and New York: Cambridge University Press, 1992), and other works. For the consumerist phenomenon in general: Fitzpatrick, *Everyday Stalinism*, 156–61; C. Kelly and V. Volkov, 'Directed Desires: *Kul'turnost*' and Consumption', in Kelly and Shepherd (eds), *Constructing Russian Culture*, 291–313; R. Maier's article in the Hösler and Kessler miscellany mentioned in n. 15; S.E. Reid, 'Cold War in the Kitchen: Gender and De-Stalinization of Consumer Taste in the Soviet Union under Khrushchev', *SR* 61 (2002), 211–52; idem, 'All Stalin's Women: Gender and Power in Soviet Art of the 1930s', *SR* 57 (1998), 133–73, which is mainly on women artists' participation in an exhibition of 1939, but also deals with the wives' movement (161 ff.).

33 J.A. Getty, '*Samokritika* Rituals in the Stalinist Central Committee, 1933–1938', *RR* 58 (1999), 49–70.

34 L. Erren, 'Kritik und Selbstkritik in der sowjetischen Parteiöffentlichkeit der 30er Jahre: ein missverstandenes Schlagwort und seine Wirkung', *JGOE* 50 (2002), 186–94. Erren also contributed an article on this topic to J.C. Behrens, G.A. Rittersporn and M. Rolf (eds), *Zwischen inszenierten Massenfesten und kirchlichen Gegenwelten: Sphären von Oeffentlichkeit in Gesellschaften sowjetischen Typs* (Frankfurt, 2002).

35 M. Rolf, 'Feste der Einheit und Schauspiele der Partizipation: die Inszenierung von Oeffentlichkeit in der Sowjetunion um 1930', *JGOE* 50 (2002), 163–71; idem, 'Constructing a Soviet Time: Bolshevik Festivals and Their Rivals During the First FYP: A Study of the Central Black-Earth Region', *Kritika* 1 (2000), 447–73; idem, 'Feste des "Roten Kalenders": der grosse Umbruch und die sowjetische Ordnung der Zeit', *Zeitschrift für Geschichtswissenschaft*, 2 (2001), 101–18, on the rituals associated with

the revolutionary calendar. See also G.T. Rittersporn, 'Le régime face au carnival: folklore non-conformiste en URSS dans les années 1930', *Annales: Histoire, sciences sociales* 58 (2003), 471–98.

36 K. Petrone, *'Life has Become More Joyous, Comrades': Celebrations in the Time of Stalin* (Bloomington, IN: Indiana University Press, 2000).

37 An instance of such over-interpretation occurs where Petrone discusses a New Year *elka* (= fir-tree) fête for élite children (1937) at which toy telephones were displayed and the children were said to have carried on business-like conversations across the hall. 'The use of the adjective *delovoi* (= business-like) by the fir-tree organizers underlined the fact that real telephones were important tools used by the cadres who ruled the Soviet Union . . . The implication was that these children would become devoted Party and government officials . . . ' (97). But might not the implication have just been pride at their seemingly adult behaviour?

10 Captive minds

Faith, science, history

Religion and the churches

Cultural historians have not confined their attention to the lower orders of Soviet society. The efforts they have made to probe the minds of those in authority – Party leaders and functionaries in the main – return Marxist–Leninist ideology to centre stage, whence it was displaced by the revisionists. But in doing so, they explicitly dissociate themselves from the concept of totalitarian rule, seen as too simplistic: it assumed a polar opposition between the Stalinist Party–state and the 'atomized' individual, and placed too much weight on coercion as distinct from 'a process . . . of co-optation which drew the subject to self-destruction.'[1]

Igal Halfin, a pioneer of this 'culturalist' approach, differs from his forerunners in the 'grandfather generation' (see Chapter 6) in that he bases his critique of the 'Communist project' on (unstated) anthropological criteria instead of invoking 'Western values' (individualism rather than collectivism) derived ultimately from the Judaeo-Christian religious–philosophical tradition, as might have been argued 50 years ago. Yet he, too, prioritizes ethical concerns. 'Communist discourse', he affirms boldly, ' . . . was suffused with ethics' (p. 1). The struggle to create a socialist 'New Soviet Man' was perceived by its adepts in Manichean terms as one between Good and Evil. Party members (and others engaged in the great fight) constituted 'a messianic order', 'a brotherhood of the elect' who scoured their souls for traces of sinful backsliding, much like the religious zealots of old. Indeed, for Halfin, Soviet communism introduced a 'peculiar form of secularized Christianity characterized by an eschatological outlook according to which the faithful saw themselves as actors in a "salvational drama"', moving 'from darkness to light'. At the same time, he warns that the parallels with Christianity should not be vulgarized: although it is true that Bolshevism, too, had its saints, martyrs, heretics, sacred texts and so forth, it did not constitute a surrogate religion since it put 'science' in the place of God (pp. 12, 18–19, 25).

Halfin succeeds brilliantly in penetrating the mental world of the Stalinist fanatic, but leaves it unclear how widespread such messianic views were, even at the height of the Terror. The willingness to use massive violence against presumed enemies, and the fact that the intensity of repression varied greatly over time, can reasonably be explained in part by more humdrum non-ideological factors – a matter we shall examine further below (Chapter 11). For the moment, let us consider the atheist regime's no-holds-barred war against the religious values and practices that had defined Russian society before the revolution. Certainly, this onslaught, which got under way in earnest in 1922, had features of a crusade, one waged against all creeds in the name of 'enlightenment'.

The principal vehicle for atheist propaganda was the League of (Militant) Godless, or LMG, headed by E.M. Yaroslavsky, which operated under close Party supervision and often in conjunction with its youth organization, the Komsomol. Of several recent studies, Glennys Young's[2] reaches back to the late Imperial era and focuses on the 'parish question', which pitted the hierarchs against junior clergy eager for the Orthodox Church to engage itself more actively in public affairs in order to combat the spread of unbelief. During the NEP, the atheist movement's structure was 'fragile' and in rural areas even some Party members continued to go to church (pp. 86–8); the activists' campaigning style, marked by confrontation and debates with believers, actually damaged their cause, since the public response was overwhelmingly hostile. This was especially the case when violent measures were applied: they 'won the battle but lost the war' (pp. 100, 141–6). In her final chapter, 'Unexpected Resilience', Young claims that rural clergy and believers conducted an 'offensive' against the intruders, exercising 'wily ingenuity' (p. 180) by securing election to village soviets and using their position to promote parish interests. This interpretation seems to rest on too literal a reading of Party and OGPU sources (*svodki*), which continually deplored such 'counter-revolutionary infiltration', leaving one with the impression that the regime's renewed militancy after April 1929 (the 'storming of Heaven') was reactive, rather than a deliberate return to the coercive measures taken earlier by the more radical elements.

These 'interventionists', and their rivalry with the more moderately inclined 'culturalists' in the atheist movement, loom large in Daniel Peris's writings.[3] He is more concerned with the LMG as an institution than with the way its rhetoric and policies were translated into (sometimes violent) action at parish level. Using archival sources from the Pskov and Yaroslavl' regions to good effect, he takes the League's history on to 1941 (although most of the material is on the early 1930s). Membership reached its nadir in 1935 but recovered to three million two years later. Yet this 'revival' was half-hearted: the League's 'social militancy existed in name only' and although 'churches were again closed and clergy arrested . . . this was an exercise in power, not cultural transformation' (p. 220) – an explanation that surely would have seemed meaningless to the victims. A top-heavy bureaucratic edifice was created, for cells set up in provincial localities died out quickly. The underlying reason for the League's failure was its focus on combating external signs of religious belief (icons, festivals) rather than the core of the believers' world-view, which was beyond the ignorant activists' comprehension. And violent repression – forced church closures, the arrest and execution of clergy – only substantiated the Christians' view that they were faced with Evil in manifest form.

More recently, Sandra Dahlke has made similar points in an article on atheistic campaigning prior to 1933, in which she cites Peris's work approvingly.[4] She is at pains to locate the movement's place in 'public space' (*Oeffentlichkeit*) and makes use freely of PM terminology: we hear, for example, that 'the discursive construction of mass consent and participation [became] the most important means of the League's self-legitimation' (p. 175) – a point that would be self-evident to a traditionalist historian proceeding from the straightforward assumption that it was a quasi-autonomous organization under Party control, compelled to compete for resources. Rather more useful is Dahlke's documentation of the 'third stage' (post-1929) in the League's development, when it shifted to violent campaigning; Yaroslavsky's subsequent purge of the membership betrayed a 'paranoia' for which he had only himself to blame, since the leaders had authorized such practices as incorporating whole villages into the LMG without checking on the neophytes' anti-religious credentials (pp. 179–80).

The cultural studies approach is taken furthest by William Husband, who seeks to move away from 'the over-simplified terms of state oppression versus church resistance that have dominated much of previous historical discussion' and to treat the struggle in a broader context of 'the divergent cultural perceptions and aspirations that coexisted within Russian society'.[5] Not all religious believers resisted, he argues; there were others 'who acquiesced in Soviet programmes [to inculcate atheism] and still others who actively gave support'. The conflict, he believes, was decided by 'the critical mass who stood between the extremes', that is, citizens whose psyche contained elements both of piety and materialism. These individuals' priorities were 'conditional, even situational', and their behaviour 'possessed an internal logic that derived far more from variations on received experience than from direct attitudes toward ideologies old or new' (pp. xiii–xv, 124). One problem with this original approach is that non-commitment is intrinsically hard to document, although certainly it may be inferred from such practices as observing both religious and secular holidays – a popular way of increasing leisure time – or, in the case of adolescents, expressing religious belief within the family circle but denying God to one's friends outside the home (pp. 92, 126).

Husband has a great deal of interest to say about the social behaviour of people under stress, but his account leaves one dissatisfied, partly because it tails off after 1929, but chiefly because the author has deliberately blurred the basic issue over which the conflict was fought out, seeing in it, as behoves a cultural historian, just a clash of cultures; nor does he consider the alternatives offered by confessions other than Orthodoxy. In an epilogue, he correctly notes (p. 162) that the regime's objective was not just to replace 'one set of observances by another' but to ensure 'public acceptance of Soviet values as a belief system capable of providing the same range of functions and benefits as those grounded in the supernatural'. Yes indeed, but *why* could it not do so? Was it perhaps because the new 'secular religion' was fundamentally bogus, founded on deceit and violence rather than love and a profound understanding of human weaknesses? The cultural historian cannot very well raise such questions, since this would involve involve making traditional moral and religious judgements and taking us back to a dated, partisan, we-and-they approach. It is only fair to add that '*Godless Communists*' (the inverted commas are deliberate) has received enthusiastic reviews and that it represents a bold attempt to break free of stereotyped thinking about grave issues.

Where cultural historians seek to avoid any overt expression of religious commitment, and to adopt as far as possible a morally neutral stance, their more traditionally minded empiricist colleagues continue to explore sympathetically the sufferings of believers and the range of their responses, from forced accommodation (as in the case of the Orthodox hierarchs Patriarch Tikhon and Metropolitan Sergei) to the tenacity of the underground 'catacomb churches', the survival of religious belief among prisoners in the Gulag, and so on. Access to archival sources gives their work added authority. As the Canadian scholar Dmitri Pospielovsky points out, the unpublished materials do not radically change our view of what occurred but 'present documentary proof of what used to be scholarly hypotheses [and] shed light on formerly inexplicable twists and turns in Soviet policy'.[6] He has utilized these sources in a textbook, whose chapters on the years 1925–55 have an ecclesiastical emphasis.[7] They treat extensively the shifts in Soviet anti-religious policy, the Church's secret-police controllers, and its relations with Orthodox abroad. Pospielovsky characterizes as 'infamous' the loyalty declaration given under duress by Metropolitan Sergei in 1927 and attributes the LMG's decline unambiguously to 'a change of policy at the very top' (pp. 250, 265). As for the number of victims among the religious, he estimates that 'at least 40,000 members of the Orthodox clergy, a similar number of monks and nuns, and unknown millions of lay believers perished for their faith in the pre-war decades' (that is, since 1917: p. 258).[8]

Another prominent writer on modern Orthodoxy, Gregory Freeze (Brandeis), bases a recent study[9] in part on archival materials from Zhitomir. In this region, church closures in 1935–6 added momentum to the resistance movement; for example, parishioners invoked the new Constitution when submitting claims to use places of worship that had remained empty. The religious also put up clergy as candidates in the 1937 elections to the Supreme Soviet. Religious faith remained strong 'even [among] some segments of the urban inhabitants' and, contrary to a widespread assumption, males were prominent in church congregations (p. 224). Freeze concludes, perhaps a little too hastily, that 'secularization demonstrates the weakness, not the power, of the Soviet state', which could not restrain zealous activists; and that the ubiquity of resistance 'disproves the totalitarian theory' (p. 232). He does not consider the possibility that the authorities permitted discordant policies to operate simultaneously, so disorienting the targeted community.

The most substantial recent contribution to the study of anti-religious policy in the 1930s stems from the Finnish scholar Arto Luukkanen.[10] As its title indicates, this archive-based study focuses on a key central institution, the governmental 'Cult commission' set up in April 1929 when the frontal attack was launched on religion as part of the collectivization drive. This body was merely an auxiliary in the Politburo's 'war . . . to implement its strategic objectives in religious policy' (p. 57). It dealt, for example, with complaints about infractions of believers' rights. The annual figures show a 'low' of 1,248 in 1925 and 'highs' of 17,637 and 12,350 in 1930 and 1931 respectively (p. 59). In the campaign to remove bells, liquidate churches and arrest priests Luukkanen finds that the commission vacillated between the demands of the zealots and the pleas of believers (p. 104). Within narrow limits it was a force for moderation, but officials in the periphery would often ignore its instructions. During the Great Terror, the Cult commission, like the LMG, came under heavy fire for being 'too soft and ineffective' (p. 178). One could perhaps say that, with the ecclesiastical organizations all but destroyed, it had outlived its usefulness; but Luukkanen puts the point a little differently, insisting that 'the religious policy of the Stalinist state was not a diabolical phenomenon *per se*' since the Cult commission had tried to restrain local excesses; if it failed to do so, this was because the centre had too little bureaucratic clout in the provinces. He would have his readers 'comprehend the inner dilemmas of Soviet administration', put moral judgements aside, and take an intermediate position between the totalitarian and revisionist schools (pp. 187–8). This may sound attractive at first glance, but before we could do so we would need a fuller picture of *all* bureaucratic agencies charged with controlling the populace, and not just the relatively uninfluential body considered here – although this study might serve as a model for others of its kind.

We would also need more published documents. A beginning has been made here by Gerd Stricker, editor of the journal *Glaube in der zweiten Welt* (Zurich) and a historian of Russian Protestantism. He has compiled a useful two-volume selection of (previously published) documents on relations between the Orthodox Church and the Soviet state.[11] In English, there is a selection prepared by Felix Corley, of the Keston Institute (Oxford),[12] which includes translations of material from several provincial archives (including Chita, Novosibirsk, Kostroma, Vilnius and Erevan). The Stalin years are represented by 71 documents, which are often of considerable interest but offer only a foretaste of what one hopes will one day become available.[13]

On 4 September 1943, Stalin secretly summoned three Orthodox hierarchs to the Kremlin and agreed to their 'request' for a council (*sobor*) to elect a patriarch and a Synod to administer the Church; according to the terms of what some have called a 'Concordat', some seminaries were to be reopened and an official monthly publication issued. The bare facts of this strange encounter are generally familiar, whereas Stalin's motives are still a mystery. As well as the obvious one, the desire to impress Allied opinion, Anna Dickinson suggests that the dictator may have been influenced by the extent of the Church's popular support, but only with the aim of using it as a tool; as is now commonly agreed, the *rapprochement* had a bogus character, since the ecclesiastical establishment was kept under strict secret-police control. She criticizes the hierarchs present for failing to ask Stalin even to release ordinary priests from captivity.[14] The implication is that they behaved sycophantically towards the state and its leader, a charge often levelled against the hierarchy in subsequent years. There is ample room for more work on the Church in the post-war era, when it willingly or unwillingly co-operated in promoting Soviet influence abroad. The unhappy story of the Moscow patriarchate's forcible takeover of the Ukrainian Uniates (Greek Catholics) in 1945–6 is mentioned briefly by Pospielovsky (who points out that the move did at least save most ex-Uniate churches for worship: *Orth. Church*, pp. 301–2) and more extensively (and polemically) by the Ukrainian-Canadian scholar Bohdan Bociurkiw in a work of 1996.[15] For the later

Stalin years English-speaking readers will now turn first to a translation of Tatiana Chumachenko's recent study.[16]

The Armenian Church during the Stalin era is the subject of a study by Felix Corley,[17] but there is no equivalent for its Georgian counterpart. For the fate of the Protestant churches (which in 1944 were compulsorily merged into the Union of Evangelical Christians and Baptists), notably in the Baltic states after (re-)annexation, one must refer mainly to earlier literature.[18]

Education and culture

Western writers on Soviet literature and other arts quite naturally focus either on the formative NEP years or else the post-1953 'thaw', when cultural life recovered to some extent from the political regimentation that characterized the age of Stalin. Repression destroyed much of the country's creative talent and obliged intellectuals who survived to compromise their personal integrity. Here we shall simply point to a recent study which traces the fate of some of the most prominent among them (notably Vsevolod Meierhold and Sergei Eisenstein);[19] to attempt more would extend the scope of this survey beyond feasible limits.

Instead we may turn to the world of education, science and scholarship. Cultural historians display relatively little interest in the Soviet school system, which is rather surprising since recognition of the regime's achievements in spreading literacy and skills would substantiate the more balanced appraisal of the Stalin era that they aspire to. There are, however, some honorable exceptions. Thomas Ewing (Virginia) has written an excellent study of Soviet teachers in the 1930s[20] in which insights gleaned from PM theory are combined with a refreshingly direct approach to a wealth of evidence from archives and interviews: a happy marriage of methodologies, so to say. Teachers are represented as torn between their professional commitment and the 'behavioral restraints' imposed by the regime. Suffering acute material hardship, exposed to attacks from above and below, they nevertheless worked with a will to instil the rudiments of knowledge into their pupils, so playing 'a proactive role at the point of convergence between regime policies and community aspirations' (p. 82). While generally supportive of the drive to expand educational facilities, they were reserved about joining the Party: only one-third did so, far fewer than has hitherto been thought (p. 144). The switch to a more conventional system of instruction, with stricter discipline, examinations and so on, met with teachers' approval since it suited their professional preferences. Ewing is sensitive to regional and other nuances, pointing out that responses differed widely from one school to another: while some teachers responded enthusiastically, others 'evaded, ignored or challenged policies that restricted their range of actions' (p. 225). Moreover, the same diversity characterized their attitudes to the Terror in 1937–8, in which about 3 per cent succumbed (p. 243). A few stood up bravely, for example, by helping a child threatened by his father's arrest, but the majority tried to avoid becoming involved in witch-hunts and retreated into silence (in PM jargon, 'devised strategies to make their professional lives more tolerable and to pursue personal interests within dominant structures': pp. 227,

252). Such behaviour, Ewing notes, was typical in other contemporary dictator-ships, but for Soviet teachers things were worse: 'vast numbers' of them experienced 'an extraordinary degree of fear' (p. 274) that left lasting consequences.[21]

Moving up from the schools to higher (tertiary) education, Michael David-Fox makes the valid point that Stalin's so-called 'cultural revolution', while subjecting the populace to a series of 'mind-bending zigs and zags', did have a certain logic: among other things it promoted vocational training at the expense of pure research, a shift of effort that left lasting negative effects, especially in the provinces.[22] In this article, David-Fox amplifies the theme of his monograph on the Party schools discussed above (Chapter 7, p. 106), where he pointed out that political dictation in the social sciences was not just imposed on the learned community from outside but was to some extent actively self-inflicted.[23] But to what extent, for what reasons, and by whom in particular?

The natural sciences

Here a promising field of inquiry opens up. One of the scholars who has started to plough it is Vera Tolz (Salford).[24] Appropriately, she takes a long-term view, while focusing attention on a small group of individuals: 20 members of the Academy of Sciences elected to that august body before 1917. Of these men, she selects five for extended biographical profiles, presenting each as representative of a certain mental attitude and behaviour pattern. These individuals are as follows: the philolo-gist N.Ya. Marr (1864–1934), characterized here as a 'co-operator *extraordinaire*'; the orientalist (and permanent secretary of the Academy) S.F. Ol'denburg (1863–1934), a 'non-Communist co-operator'; the physiologist I.P. Pavlov (1849–1936), 'Bolshevism's sharpest critic'; the mathematician and shipbuilding engineer A.N. Krylov (1863–1945), 'a military man in academia'; and the founder of bio-geochemistry, V.I. Vernadsky (1863–1945), 'a within-system reformer'. At the crucial turning-point in the Academy's fortunes in 1929, five men compromised themselves politically, three took no definitive stand, but 12 opposed the proposed changes. The conformists' motives, predictably, were mixed: fear of persecution; an instinctive readiness to obey orders (most marked among those with a military background); desire to continue their professional work for the benefit of society; hopes that, thanks to their input, the regime would soften over time; and, last but not least, patriotic sentiment. Vernadsky, for example, drew satisfaction from the Bolsheviks' successful reconstitution of the old Russian empire; Marr was driven by lifelong chauvinistic sentiment (pp. 172–87). To their credit, several academi-cians (notably Vernadsky, Pavlov, and the physicist P.L. Kapitsa, 1894–1984), intervened to defend colleagues threatened with arrest during the Terror, and before this the entire Academy came out in support of N.N. Luzin (1883–1950), an eminent mathematician charged with the 'sin' of publishing his work abroad (p. 83).[25]

Tolz's work sets the agenda for further research into the phenomenon of accom-modation versus resistance among members of Russia's intellectual élite in various disciplines – a sensitive theme that, needless to say, should be approached with empathy for the individuals concerned, faced as they often were with life-threatening choices. Dietrich Beyrau, in his introduction to a useful miscellany devoted to professionals caught 'in the jungle of power',[26] notes that accommodation came more easily to natural scientists than to scholars in the humanities, because of the segmentation of scientific knowledge; that intellectuals occasionally took the initiative in forging the chains that bound them; and that the degree of autonomy permitted *faute de mieux* by the regime differed markedly between disciplines – and, one might add, institutions. In those branches of knowledge little affected by politics or ideology, a mixture of careerism, opportunism and naiveté led many scientists to set moral criteria aside and concentrate on their professional interests; 'but where ideological concerns invaded their discipline', as it did most crassly in agro-biology with T.D. Lysenko, 'men of learning defended themselves with all the means at their disposal, for the core of their professional interest was at stake. Here they showed a remarkable capacity for resistance that was lacking in the political sphere' (pp. 32–3).

These reactions are explored in greater depth by several historians of science with Soviet backgrounds now resident in the West, notably by Nikolai Krementsov, who begins his vigorously written and highly acclaimed *Stalinist Science*[27] by noting the paradox that 'many of the greatest triumphs . . . occurred exactly at the time of the greatest repression', when 'Gulag camps [were] overflowing' (p. 3). He takes issue with earlier writers who advanced explanations 'that relied on . . . the totalitarian nature of the Soviet state' and, identifying with the 'culturalists', presents us with a more complex picture: an 'interaction of institutions, professions, disciplines, interest groups and networks' – much as in Western countries. As elsewhere, science in the USSR developed not in conflict with the state but in symbiosis with it. Certainly, controls were much stricter there, but members of the scientific community found more elaborate ways to match, evade, and even exploit them. They cultivated political patrons, adopted the Party's militant rhetoric, and 'played intricate games and perform[ed] puzzling ceremonies . . . to advance their careers' (p. 6).

At this point, it may be useful to recall Lenin's formula *kto/kogo*: who was manipulating whom? Or to put the point crudely, when weighed in the scales of History, does the autonomy secured by Soviet physicists after Hiroshima outweigh their contribution to the development of nuclear weapons? It is probably too soon to say, but the achievements registered through covert oppositional activity, creditable though they are, need to be set against the services rendered to an oppressive state that (especially in Stalin's last years) threatened world peace.

Yet if Krementsov is inclined to minimize the latter and magnify the former, he places us in his debt for drawing a detailed picture of the means whereby, in the 1930s, science was mobilized by the regime, and how scientists responded to repression by forming countervailing interest groups that employed 'Party talk' in self-criticism sessions, ritually abasing themselves in order to undermine the system (pp. 31–53). During the war, the Soviet scientific–technological effort was crucial, which led to a 'sweet victory' for those responsible (p. 99).[28] The post-war years saw the reassertion of Party controls that climaxed in the *Zhdanovshchina*. Here the author's expertise in biology, and use of archival sources, enable him to give a fuller picture than we had hitherto of the charlatan Lysenko in his 'finest hour' – and the reverses he suffered at the hands of professional colleagues. In these debates, it was not the political leaders but the scientists themselves who called the tune (p. 193) – an acknowledgement that surely weakens the author's argument? Scientists went through the 'rituals'[29] of writing articles eulogizing 'the Party-mindedness of science', yet 'in covering their institutions with a Michurinist [that is, pro-Lysenko] veneer, top administrators . . . were also trying to camouflage their institutions and disciplines, hoping to immunize them from further Party encroachment' (p. 225). Their subversive intentions did not escape notice in the CC Secretariat, but these officials could not do much about it. Not until the 1960s, however, were scientists able to outmanoeuvre Lysenko and his followers.

The sad fate of Soviet biology in the Stalin and post-Stalin years does not bear out Krementsov's thesis very well, but in physics it was a different matter. Here the struggles between cliques became embroiled in the anti-Semitic campaign of the era. The brief account given here (pp. 275–9) is expanded in three articles by Peter Kneen (Durham) and the first chapter of Paul Josephson's highly readable study of the Soviet atomic project.[30] The Stalinists planned a follow-up conference to the one on biology in order to discipline errant physicists, but had to abandon it, partly because they had no physicist counterpart to Lysenko, partly because there was no alternative physics with which to challenge the academic variety (pp. 1201–2). Above all, in the atomic age physics was just too important to be allowed to become a plaything of scientific coteries or ideologists. Alexander Vucinich also deals with these issues in a work on the physics of relativity that ranges across the whole history of this discipline in Russia.[31]

Some of the less well-known scientific disciplines have also attracted sporadic attention of late. Christoph Mick offers figures for the number of geologists who fell victim to the Terror (pp. 340–9) and points out that many scientific struggles of the era were between theoretically inclined professionals and practical men ('Red cadres') rather than between cliques; those who bravely stood up to ideological pressure could do so because of alliances with certain Party 'high-ups' who needed their specialized knowledge to understand the problems they faced (p. 357).[32] The aspirations and experiences of engineers under NEP and later are studied by Susanne Schattenberg,[33] while Wim van Meurs (Munich) examines the ethnographers' contribution to the formulation of nationality policy.[34] Friedrich Bertrand argues that anthropologists successfully used their 'discourse' to legitimize their discipline, but at the price of compromising their scholarly integrity.[35] Finally, Kenneth Pinnow, whose dissertation (Columbia University, 1998) was on suicide in the Soviet 1920s, shows that doctors in forensic medicine, although they disagreed over the priority to be given to biological or sociological considerations, were keen to integrate into the system and thereby achieve greater 'self-definition' (p. 116).[36]

An exhaustive search of the specialized literature might yield further treasures of this kind, which we badly need to build up a comprehensive picture of Stalinist science in all its ramifications. In this rapidly growing field, there is also a place for old-fashioned institutional history. Lutz-Dieter Behrendt is engaged on a monograph about the key centre for training Bolshevik cadres, the Institute of Red Professors;[37] and Michael David-Fox has studied the Socialist (Communist) Academy, which was originally designed to replace the 'bourgeois' Academy of Sciences, but in 1936, to general surprise, found itself absorbed by the latter – one of those policy quirks that make the study of Stalinism so intriguing.[38]

The social sciences

The graduates of the Institute of Red Professors ('Ikapisty'), whose careers and influences Behrendt traces, were of course active in directing the social sciences as well. Some disciplines, such as sociology, political science and economics all but disappeared during the Stalin era, and their most prominent representatives, if they avoided physical repression, were obliged to change jobs. Here we may focus on the historians.

Three Western scholars – David Brandenberger (Harvard), Maureen Perrie (Birmingham) and Rainer Lindner (Constance) – have enlarged our understanding of the turn to a more nationalistic *Weltanschauung* after 1934. Brandenberger places the 'great retreat' in the broader context of 'national identity formation on the popular level'.[39] On the basis of archival evidence he concludes that even many educated people were confused as to how far they should go in 'embracing the rehabilitation of names from the Russian national past' such as Pushkin, Peter I, or Alexander Nevsky (p. 100). The authorities' intention was to bolster *étatisme* (statism), but in many cases 'a militant sense of national pride' engendered chauvinistic views and a patronizing attitude twowards the USSR's minorities. World War II reinforced this sense of 'Russian exceptionalism', which Stalin himself encouraged in his much-cited 1945 toast to the victors. By the late 1940s, 'a profound mythologization of the Russian people . . . was under way' in which historical references played a large part. By trying to mobilize Soviet society around 'national Bolshevik' themes, the regime, in part unwittingly, stimulated a 'maturation of Russian national identity' (pp. 231, 239).

Perrie's engaging and clearly written study of the curious cult of Ivan Groznyi ('the Terrible') under Stalin also explores the literary and artistic ramifications of the topic.[40] Even before the revolution Russian historians had been prone to search for 'contemporary relevance' in the historical themes they treated, including Ivan (p. 20). Under Soviet conditions of tight censorship, such parallels, if drawn too crudely, might involve unpleasantness, but if properly presented, they were welcomed by the ideological controllers, who on occasion even suggested how these themes ought to be dealt with. In the mid-1930s, the new Stalinist history textbooks contained markedly positive appraisals of the tsar; the analogy was 'in the air' but not until late 1940 did the cult get under way – touched off, not by the Terror (although here the parallel with Ivan's *oprichnina* was most obvious) but by annexation of the Baltic states (p. 89). The venerable Roman Vipper (1859–1954), an expert on the period who as an emigré had been close to the Eurasians, took things to an extreme: in a work of 1942, for which he was rewarded with the title of academician, he depicted the tsar as a great patriotic statesman whose wars had been purely defensive and whose terroristic measures wholly justified by treasonous plots among the boyars. These effusions were hard to square with conventional Marxist–Leninist notions. Already in 1944, Anna Pankratova, perhaps scenting the coming ideological shift, sought to moderate them in favour of a more 'orthodox' interpretation. However, the ensuing top-level discussion led nowhere since Zhdanov, the leader responsible for ideology, could not make up his mind. Stalin, as we know from the actor N.K. Cherkasov, thought that Ivan's repressive measures had not been carried through with requisite thoroughness. After the dictator's death, Soviet historians gingerly began to dissociate themselves from the praise they had lavished on both despots, but it was not until the late 1980s, with *glasnost'*, that the issue finally came out into the open. 'It was taken as self-evident proof of Stalin's monstrous character that he could have admired such a tyrant as Ivan Groznyi, and could even have regarded him as insufficiently resolute' (p. 2).

If the historians emerge with little credit from this study, the same is true of the novelists and playwrights who took up the theme. Sergei Eisenstein comes off best: his film on Ivan is rightly seen as 'a subversive parable'. 'It was part of Eisenstein's genius that, while providing an intellectual justification for state terror, he also showed the emotional toll which it exacted on the victor as well as on the victim' (p. 178). Perrie's analysis makes one hope for further work on the use of analogy as a form of 'Aesopian discourse', that is, as a critical device in Soviet scholarly publications and intellectual life generally.[41]

Perhaps there was more cliquishness among scholars in the humanities than in the natural sciences, or so one would supposes from reading Rainer Lindner's massive and wide-ranging study of the politics of historiography in Belarus.[42] This topic offers 'a promising chance to examine Stalinism as an "imperial phenomenon" with reference to a single [region] and to study the interaction between centre and periphery on an ideological, personal and Party level' (p. 20). In the 1920s, moderate nationalists such as V.I. Picheta and M.V. Dovnar-Zapolsky, who readily sought accommodation with the new regime, coexisted alongside national communists and diehard revolutionaries. Thereafter, the last group prevailed, but were likewise far from homogeneous, dividing into 'apologists for, sufferers from, and critics of the Bolshevik state' (p. 276); remarkably, there were no determined oppositionists. Three leading historians were killed or committed suicide. (Dovnar-Zapolsky, who was involved in the 'Academy case', avoided repression by dying in time!)

After 1944, a flood of literature poured out on the republic's fate during the war, in which the partisans' struggle was lionized (but nothing said about collaboration or the Holocaust!);[43] this was 'the third great myth in Soviet historiography, comparable only to the Lenin and Stalin cults' (p. 352). Immense efforts were made to produce a standard official history of Belarus since the earliest times, but the enterprise came to grief as time and again rival cliques detected ideological errors in each other's drafts. What was the proper dose of tribute to be paid to the Great Russian 'elder brother' vis-à-vis autochthonous national forces? As one would expect, when the text was published in 1954–8, after a 10-year delay, it was strongly biased against western (Polish, Catholic) influences on the White Russian past and involved outrageous massaging of the facts. 'Under the conditions of politicized criticisms by colleagues . . . no one could think of doing scholarly work', so that the exchanges of view among Stalin-era historians are best regarded as a 'ritual performance' (*Gesinnungsritual*, p. 330). This interpretation is akin to Krementsov's in regard to the scientists, although Lindner's view of these disputes is a good deal darker. His well-researched book, based on archives in Minsk, sets a high standard for Western writers on a region that has suffered unjust neglect.

The extension of Stalinist norms to historiography in Ukraine has also received attention from the Canadian-Ukrainian scholar Serhy Yekelchuk.[44] Basing his research in large part on regional archives, he contends that the 1947 ideological campaign against 'nationalist deviations' in Ukrainian scholarship was far less simple or successful than used to be assumed, since 'Stalinism as a system [sought] to achieve total control over society but in reality [was] often locked into a complex, if unequal, dialogue with its subjects' (the term 'dialogue', he carefully notes, being used in the Bakhtinian sense: 'Kaganovich', p. 579). Ukrainian historians succeeded in manipulating the official 'language' to resist Moscow's pretensions. When a conference was held in the spring of 1947 to condemn Hrushevs'kyi's 'bourgeois nationalist school', it was the historians, not the politicians, who did most of the talking; 'the argument ended in a stalemate [for] the historians had demonstrated their ability to fight back' (p. 587). Ordinary folk wrote letters to the press defending Hrushevs'kyi and other national heroes, which shows that they shared an 'alternative interpetation of the Ukrainian past [that] existed in the shadow of the official version, itself shaped by negotiations between the ideologues and the intellectuals' (p. 598). Yekelchyk concedes that the scholars and teachers concerned 'displayed attitudes that differed *only slightly* to very substantially from the Party line' (p. 594; our italics), and his argument would be stronger if he had shown how far the works put out between 1947 and 1953 reflected unorthodox nationalist or national-communist thinking. In short, while appreciating the achievement of those who resisted pressure we should not forget the 'accommodationists'.

Similarly, in an article of 2002, Yekelchyk shows that from 1939 to 1944 Ukrainian national-communist historians successfully developed 'a distinct national mythology' that was temporarily incorporated into the 'grand narrative', or 'imperial discourse', being constructed in Moscow, which portrayed the Ukrainians as 'lesser brethren' in the all-Union family (pp. 52, 55). Their impact was reflected in the praise lavished on heroes of early Ukrainian history such as the Cossack chieftain Bohdan Hmel'nyc'kyj and in use of the term 'the great *Ukrainian* people'. But from the end of 1943 onwards, Moscow, 'dissatisfied with the growth of Ukrainian mythology' (p. 74), intervened to check it and in Kyiv officials and intellectuals reluctantly fell into line. Notably, the author sees *both* 'mythologies' as just political constructs and not stemming from genuine historical research and reflection.

Anyone seeking to comprehend the restrictions under which scholars in the social sciences laboured before de-Stalinization needs to consider their situation afterwards as well, which is a more rewarding topic for their Western colleagues. Two important recent studies may be noted in passing.[45] Cultural historians are also sensitive to the way people's views of time (and space) evolved over the long term in changing circumstances. Klaus Gestwa, for example, notes that zealous Communists lived as much for the future as for the present, while disdaining the past; as a result the Soviet regime created 'landscapes of failure' that were ecological disaster areas. Furthermore, for a broader view of Stalinism's impact on the writing of history, we need to appreciate the difficulties experienced since 1991 by post-Soviet historians in freeing themselves from the burden of the past. This topic is treated below (Conclusions, pp. 219–20) and in Part I above. Among Western writers, general surveys are offered *inter alia* by Manfred Hildermeier and Elke Fein.[46] The latter discusses the treatment of Stalinism between 1953 and 1991, but the bulk of her work is devoted to the Yeltsin era. She concludes that attempts are only beginning to come to terms with the legacy of the Soviet past – a verdict that applies less to the historians than to those who read (or do not read) their works.

Notes

1   I. Halfin, *Terror in My Soul: Communist Autobiographies on Trial* (Cambridge, MA and London: Harvard University Press, 2003), 5. This is a sequel to his *From Darkness to Light: Class, Consciousness and Salvation in Revolutionary Russia* (Pittsburgh: University of Pittsburgh Press, 2000). See also David L. Hoffmann, *Stalinist Values: The Cultural Norms of Soviet Modernity, 1917–1941* (Ithaca, NY and London: Cornell University Press, 2003), esp. pp. 79–87 (on 'the internalization of values').

2   G. Young, *Power and the Sacred in Revolutionary Russia: Religious Activists in the Village* (University Park, PA: University of Pennsylvania Press, 1997).

3   D. Peris, *Storming the Heavens: The Soviet League of the Militant Godless* (Ithaca, NY and London: Cornell University Press, 1998). Two preliminary studies were published as 'The 1929 Congress of the Godless', *Soviet Studies* 43 (1991), 711–32 and 'Commissars in Red Cassocks: Former Priests in the League of Militant Godless', *SR* 54 (1995), 340–64; these priests who 'swapped religions' were deemed unreliable by the LMG leadership and phased out after 1929.

4   S. Dahlke, 'Kampagnen für Gottlosigkeit: zum Zusammenhang zwischen Legitimation, Mobilisierung und Partizipation in der Sowjetunion der 20er Jahre', *JGOE* 50 (2002), 172–85. Dahlke is the author of a monograph, *An der antireligiösen Front: Der Verband der Gottlosen in der Sowjetunion der 20er Jahre* (Hamburg: Dr. Kovac, 1998).

5   W.G. Husband, *'Godless Communists': Atheism and Society in Soviet Russia, 1917–1932* (DeKalb, IL: Northern Illinois University Press, 2000).

6   D. Pospielovsky, ' "The Best Years" of Stalin's Church Policy (1942–1948) in the Light of Archival Documents', *Religion, State and Society* [hereafter *RSS*] 25 (1997), 139.

7   Idem, *The Orthodox Church in the History of Russia* (Crestwood, NY: St Vladimir's Seminary Press, 1998; Russian edn Moscow, 1995). His other works include 'The Russian Church Since 1917 Through the Eyes of Post-Soviet Russian Historians', *RSS* 26 (1998), 357–66, a review of works by *proterei* V. Tsvinin and M.V. Shkarovsky. The last-named has an article, 'Russkaia tserkov' pri Staline v 1920-e – 1930-e gg.', in German translation, in Hildermeier (ed.), *Stalinismus*, 233–53. Pospielovsky taught in Canada and then at the Spiritual Academy, Sergiev Posad before moving beyond the Patriarchate's jurisdiction.

8   A. Dickinson, 'Quantifying Religious Oppression: ROC Closures and Repression of Priests, 1917–1941', *RSS* 28 (2000), 327–36, uses graphs and tables to represent the scale of repression from year to year. Executions of hierarchs peaked in 1925 (20), 1936

(20) and 1937 (50). R. Dzonkowski, 'The Fate of the Catholic Clergy in the USSR, 1917–1939', ibid. 26 (1998), 61–8, puts the minimum number of Catholic clergy arrested at 470, of those killed at 270; this study relies on French rather than Russian archival sources.

9   G.L. Freeze, 'The Stalinist Assault on the Parish, 1929–1941', in Hildermeier (ed.), *Stalinismus*, 209–32, esp. 225 ff.

10 A. Luukkanen, *The Religious Policy of the Stalinist State: A Case Study: The Central Standing Commission on Religious Questions, 1929–1938* (Helsinki: Societatis Historica Finlandiae, 1997); it contains an excellent bibliography. An earlier study by this author was *The Party of Unbelief: The Religious Policy of the Bolshevik Party, 1917–1929* (Helsinki: Societatis Historica Finlandiae, 1994). For an incisive review of the later work, see T. Martin in *EAS* 50 (1998), 1504–6.

11 G. Stricker, *Russkaia Pravoslavnaia Tserkov' v sovetskoe vremia (1917–1991): materialy i dokumenty po istorii otnoshenii mezhdu gosudarstvom i Tserkov'iu* (Moscow, 1995). This is based on an earlier work (with Peter Hauptmann), *Die Orthodoxe Kirche in Russland: Dokumente ihrer Geschichte, 860–1980* (Göttingen: Vandenhoeck and Ruprecht, 1988).

12 F. Corley, *Religion in the Soviet Union: An Archival Reader* (Basingstoke and London: Macmillan, 1996).

13 At this point, one may note a remarkable reference work: an alphabetical list of all Orthodox bishoprics with the names and dates of every known office holder (whether canonically appointed or not) and their dates of arrest. This list was originally compiled by a cleric while in detention – no easy task, to be sure, since arrests and disappearances were not generally reported in the media. See C. Patock OSA, 'Die Eparchien der Russischen Orthodoxen Kirche und die Reihefolge ihrer Hierarchie in der Zeit von 1893–1996', *Ostkirchliche Studien* (Würzburg), 46 (1997), 25–61 *et seq.*

14 A. Dickinson, 'A Marriage of Convenience? Domestic and Foreign Policy Reasons for the 1943 Church–State "Concordat"', *RSS* 28 (2000), 337–46.

15 B.R. Bociurkiw, *The Ukrainian Greek Catholic Church and the Soviet State, 1939–1950* (Edmonton: Canadian Institute for Ukrainian Studies, 1996); cf. Pospielovsky, '"Best Years"', 147, where he cites a Khrushchev memorandum to Stalin on 'measures to demoralize the Uniate Church'.

16 T.A. Chumachenko, *Church and State in Soviet Russia: Orthodoxy from World War II to the Khrushchev Years*, trans. and ed. E.E. Roslof (Armonk, NY and London: Sharpe, 2002).

17 F. Corley, 'The Armenian Church under the Soviet and Independent Regimes', *RSS* 24 (1996), 9–53 (1938–1954); for the sequel, see ibid. 26 (1998), 291–356.

18 Cf. esp. W. Sawatsky, *Soviet Evangelicals Since World War II* (Kitchener, ON, 1981). The Mennonites also take a keen interest in their denominational past and maintain a vigorous publishing programme.

19 K.B. Eaton (ed.), *Enemies of the People: The Destruction of Soviet Literary, Theater and Film Arts in the 1930s* (Evanston, IL: Northwestern University Press, 2002).

20 E.T. Ewing, *The Teachers of Stalinism: Policy, Practices and Power in Soviet Schools of the 1930s* (New York, Frankfurt, and Oxford: Peter Lang, 2002). Four related studies appeared in *East/West Education*, 18 (1997; on women teachers); *RR* 57 (1998; on teacher certification); *History of Education Quarterly* 41 (2001; on pedology); and *Gender and History* 13 (2002; on suicides).

21 For the World War II era, there is an excellent study by J. Dunstan, *Soviet Schooling in the Second World War*, Basingstoke, London and New York: Macmillan, 1997), which covers such matters as evacuation from threatened regions, enrolments, physical shortages, discipline and children's welfare, along with changes in official policy. L.E. Holmes, *Stalin's School: Moscow's Model School no. 25, 1931–1937* (Pittsburgh: University of Pittsburgh Press, 1999), studies a 'show-case' scholastic establishment attended *inter alia* by two of Stalin's offspring and explores the students' reactions to intense politicization.

22 M. David-Fox, 'The Assault on the Universities and the Dynamics of Stalin's "Great Break", 1928–1932', in idem and G. Péteri (eds), *Academia in Upheaval: Origins, Transfers and Transformations of the Communist Academic Regime in Russia and East Central Europe* (Westport, CT and London: Bergin & Garvey, 2000), 73–103.

23 Idem, *Revolution of the Mind*, 22.

24 V. Tolz, *Russian Academicians and the Revolution: Combining Professionalism and Politics* (Basingstoke and New York: Macmillan, 1997). Tolz is the granddaughter of the luminary Dmitrii Likhachev.

25 On the latter, see an earlier study by A.E. Levin, 'Anatomy of a Public Campaign: "Academician Luzin's Case" in Soviet Political History', *SR* 49 (1990), 90–108.

26 D. Beyrau (ed.), *Im Dschungel der Macht: Intellektuelle Professionen unter Stalin und Hitler* (Göttingen: Vandenhoeck & Ruprecht, 2000). An earlier work by Beyrau on this theme was *Intelligenz und Dissens: die russischen Bildungsschichten in der Sowjetunion 1917–1985* (Göttingen: Vandenhoeck and Ruprecht, 1993). Hildermeier notes pertinently: 'totalitarian states characteristically invested large sums [in science] to reach their overall socio-economic or technical goals and so tolerated areas of scientific autonomy (*Freiräume*) that could serve other purposes' (*Geschichte*, 580).

27 N.L. Krementsov, *Stalinist Science* (Princeton, NJ: Princeton University Press, 1997). Reviewed enthusiastically by P. Josephson in *SR* 57 (1998), 215–17 and J.T. Andrews in *RR* 57 (1998), 306–7. Cf. also the discussion between David Joravsky and A. Kojevnikov in ibid., 1–9, 455–9; also Josephson's reviews of several pertinent Russian works in *EAS* 52 (2000), 591–2. More critical is the stance taken by V.J. Birstein, *The Perversion of Knowledge: The True Story of Soviet Science* (Boulder, CO and Oxford: Westview, 2001).

28 Krementsov points out that we badly need a study of the achievements and deprivations of the scientific and other prisoners who toiled in the *sharashki* (103) – and indeed also of the attitudes taken by their more fortunate colleagues towards Gulag labourers.

29 For more on this point, see A. Kojevnikov, 'Rituals of Stalinist Culture at Work: Science and the Games of Intraparty Democracy circa 1948', *RR* 57 (1998), 25–52, esp. 32. An earlier study was 'Games of Soviet Democracy: Ideological Discussions in Soviet Science, 1947–1952', in Fitzpatrick (ed.), *Stalinism: New Directions*, 142–75.

30 P. Kneen, 'Physics, Genetics and the Zhdanovshchina', *EAS* 50 (1998), 1183–1202; 'De-Stalinization under Stalin? The Case of Science', *Journal of Communist Studies and Transition Politics* 16 (2000), 107–26, a follow-up to his 'Reconceptualizing the Soviet System: Pluralism, Totalitarianism and Science', ibid., 14 (1998). P.R. Josephson, *Red Atom: Russia's Nuclear Power Program from Stalin to Today* (New York: W.H. Freeman, 2000), 17–19. Among Josephson's more recent works are: *Totalitarian Science and Technology* (Atlantic Highlands, NJ: Humanities Press, 1996), which deals with Nazi Germany as well as the Soviet Union; *New Atlantis Revisited: Akademgorodok, the Siberian City of Science* (Princeton, NJ: Princeton University Press, 1997); 'Atomic-Powered Communism: Nuclear Culture in the Postwar USSR', *SR* 55 (1996), 297–324 (on Stalin's role, see esp. 312). On the dangers of large-scale projects see the Kendall Lectures delivered by a leading US historian of Soviet science, L.R. Graham, published as *What Have We Learned about Science and Technology from the Russian Experience?* (Stanford, CA: Stanford University Press, 1998). Still highly relevant is D. Holloway, *Stalin and the Bomb: The Soviet Union and Atomic Energy* (New Haven, CT: Yale University Press, 1994), esp. 224–52.

31 A. Vucinich, *Einstein and Soviet Ideology* (Stanford, CA: Stanford University Press, 2001).

32 C. Mick, 'Wissenschaft und Wissenschaftler im Stalinismus', in Plaggenborg (ed.), *Stalinismus*, 321–61. By the same author: 'Deutsche Fachleute in der sowjetischen Rüstungsforschung nach 1945', in Beyrau (ed.), *Im Dschungel*, 378–92.

33 S. Schattenberg, 'Die Sowjetunion als technische Utopie: die alten Ingenieure und das neue Regime', *FOIZ* 5 (2001), 2, 241–69; idem, *Stalins Ingenieure: Lebenswelten zwischen Technik und Terror in den 1930er Jahren* (Munich: Oldenbourg, 2002).

34 W. van Meurs, 'Soviet Ethnography: Hunters or Gatherers?', *Ab imperio* (Kazan'), 2001, no. 3, 8–42.

35 F. Bertrand, *L'anthropologie soviétique des années 20–30: configuration d'une rupture* (Bordeaux: Presses universitaires, 2002).

36 K.M. Pinnow, 'Cutting and Counting: Forensic Medicine as a Science of Society in Bolshevik Russia, 1920–1929', in Hoffmann and Kotsonis (eds), *Russian Modernity*, 115–37.

37 For a foretaste, see L.-D. Behrendt, 'Der Nachlass der Roten Kaderschmiede: die Lebensläufe der Absolventen des Instituts der Roten Professur', in Beyrau (ed.), *Im Dschungel*, 157–69.

38 M. David-Fox, 'Symbiosis to Synthesis: the Communist Academy and the Bolshevization of the Imperial/Soviet Academy of Sciences, 1918–1929', *JGOE* 46 (1998), 219–43.

39 D.L. Brandenberger, *National Bolshevism: Stalinist Mass Culture and the Formation of Modern Russian National Identity, 1931–1956* (Cambridge, MA and London: Harvard University Press, 2002). In an appendix the author analyses efforts in the late 1930s to produce an acceptable history textbook for school and university use; the winning draft, by A.V. Shestakov (1937), was actually written in large part by Zhdanov, and most of those associated with it perished in the purges (259).

40 M. Perrie, *The Cult of Ivan the Terrible in Stalin's Russia* (Basingstoke and New York: Palgrave, 2001); previous articles on the theme in *SEER* 56 (1978), 275–86 and in two miscellanies edited by Geoffrey Hosking and Robert Service: *Russian Nationalism: Past and Present*, (London: Macmillan, 1998), 107–27; *Reinterpreting Russia* (London: Arnold, 1999), 156–69. For a briefer study of the Groznyi/Stalin relationship: K.M.F. Platt and D. Brandenberger, 'Terribly Romantic, Terribly Progressive, or Terribly Tragic: Rehabilitating Ivan IV under Stalin', *RR* 58 (1999), 635–54.

41 However, J. Neuberger complains that Perrie exaggerates the degree to which artists or others deviated from the official line and does not distinguish sufficiently between the varied quality of the works concerned. *SR* 62 (2003), 190–1.

42 R. Lindner, *Historiker und Herrschaft: Nationsbildung und Geschichtspolitik in Weissrussland im 19. und 20. Jahrhundert* (Munich: Oldenbourg, 1999); cf. idem, 'Nationalhistoriker im Stalinismus: zum Profil der akademischen Intelligenz in Weissrussland, 1921–1946', *JGOE* 47 (99), 187–209, a study of five leading historians' 'biographical paradigms'.

43 On this point, see S. Cholawski, 'The Holocaust and Armed Struggle in Belorussia as Reflected in Soviet Literature and Works by Emigrés in the West', in Z. Gitelman (ed.), *Bitter Legacy: Confronting the Holocaust in the Soviet Union* (Bloomington and Indianapolis: Indiana University Press, 1997), 214–29.

44 S. Yekelchuk, 'How the "Iron Minister" Kaganovich Failed to Discipline Ukrainian Historians: A Stalinist Ideological Campaign Reconsidered', *Nationalities Papers* 27 (1999), 579–604; idem, 'Stalinist Patriotism as Imperial Discourse: Reconciling the Ukrainian and Russian "Heroic Pasts", 1939–1945', *Kritika* 3 (2002), 51–80. Other relevant articles by Yekelchuk appeared in *SR* 59 (2000), 597–624; *EAS* 50 (1998), 1229–44; and in D.J. Raleigh (ed.), *Provincial Landscapes: Local Dimensions of Soviet Power, 1917–1953* (Pittsburgh: University of Pittsburgh Press, 2001), 255–75.

45 J. Hösler, *Die sowjetische Geschichtswissenschaft 1953 bis 1991: Studien zur Methodologie- und Organisationsgeschichte* (Munich: Otto Sagner, 1995); Roger D. Markwick, *Rewriting History in Soviet Russia: The Politics of Revisionist Historiography, 1956–1974* (Basingstoke and New York: Macmillan, 2001). On the significance of Stalin's *Short Course*, see Markwick, 42–7, and for an appreciative review by G. Enteen: *SR* 61 (2002), 357–63.

46 K. Gestwa, 'Sowjetische Landschaften als Panorama von Macht und Ohnmacht: Historische Spurensuche auf den "Grossbauten des Kommunismus" und in dörflicher Idylle', *Historische Anthropologie* 11 (2003), 72–100. Raleigh (ed.), *Provincial Landscapes*, contains essays on various regional issues. J. Plamper, 'The Spatial Poetics of the

Personality Cult: Circles Around Stalin', in E. Dobrenko and E. Naiman, *The Landscape of Stalinism: The Art and Ideology of Soviet Space* (Seattle and London: University of Washington Press, 2003), 19–50 breaks new ground, e.g.: 'the circle was, I believe, the seminal Stalinist shape used to structure space' (30).

46 M. Hildermeier, 'Der Stalinismus im Urteil russischer Historiker', in N. Frei *et al.* (eds), *Geschichte vor Gericht: Historiker, Richter: die Suche nach Gerechtigkeit* (Munich: Beck, 2000), 93–102; idem, 'Interpretationen des Stalinismus', *Historische Zeitschrift* 264 (97), 660–74; E. Fein, *Geschichtspolitik in Russland: Chancen und Schwierigkeiten einer demokratisierenden Aufarbeit der sowjetischen Vergangenheit am Beispiel der Gesellschaft 'Memorial'* (Hamburg: Lit-Verlag, 2000).

11 'Koba the Dread'

Repression and terror

Logic of violence

Among the successive cohorts of Western students of Stalinism, there do not appear to have been any historical revisionists of the calibre of those who, like David Irving, questioned the reality of Hitler's Holocaust, provoking a storm of violent controversy and ostracism from the scholarly community. However, several critics have discerned an apologetic tendency in earlier revisionist literature, when the eagerness to rewrite Soviet history 'from below' led to a downplaying of the more coercive, malign aspects of Stalinist rule so strongly stressed by traditionalists. The 'new cohort' saw them as politically biased. The charge was not wholly unfounded, but in refuting it, certain enthusiasts were inclined to throw out the proverbial baby with the bath water.

In lieu of the familiar Stalin as an epitome of centralized dictatorial rule,[1] readers were confronted with a fearful, hesitant leader who had been obliged to react *ad hoc* to successive crises, since he had but a tenuous control over a chaotic administration, staffed by inefficient, potentially disloyal functionaries; seen in this light, it was only rational for 'the centre' to try to bring these men to heel, and if the degree of coercion applied had been excessive, one had to remember that there was a real threat of dissidence weakening the state when it was seriously menaced from abroad. In any case, so the reasoning went, the excesses that occurred were in large part due to misinterpretation of commands from above by ignorant or over-zealous careerists; moreover, in creating a witch-hunt atmosphere the general public had also played a key role by denouncing official malfeasance, so widening the circle of victims beyond the limits originally intended. This might be termed a 'circumstantialist' interpretation of the Great Terror as distinct from an 'intentionalist' one that saw Stalin and his cronies as the key decision-makers, who bore a heavy moral responsibility for crimes they either deliberately willed or had failed to check in good time.

Revelations from the archives since 1991, and the work done by Russian historians such as Viktor Zemskov and Oleg Khlevniuk, have shown that both the traditionalist and revisionist views need modification. While there are still differences in interpreting the evidence, they pertain to nuances rather than essentials. Over the last decade or so, the parameters of the debate have narrowed and the more extreme opinions now find little favour.[2] In this 'normalization' of historical discourse co-operation with colleagues in the FSU has been a major factor, for the latter are closer to the documentary material and better placed to deliver fresh insights. Happily, much literature on this grim topic now appears in books or miscellanies written by scholars in various countries, who broadly speaking share a common approach.[3]

It is, for example, generally accepted that the violence of the Stalin years had its origins in the turbulent era of revolution. The three-year civil war, marked by famine and epidemic disease, cost some 10 million lives, mostly of non-combatants. This epic struggle was the principal formative experience of those who in the 1930s found themselves in positions of responsibility. After 1921, Party propaganda idealized the heroism of the Reds and stressed the inexorability of class conflict; young people were encouraged to prepare for future wars; and the destruction of the traditional social order destabilized them psychologically. For many, the normal problems of adolescence became much more difficult to solve without resorting to violence. Hundreds of thousands of vagrant waifs eked out a living on the margin of the law. When Stalin launched his first campaigns against domestic enemies after 1928, some disoriented youngsters joined in with gusto, while others rallied to the official viewpoint because they hoped a strong 'socialist' state would offer them greater security.

These are some of the findings of an international team, based in Basle, which has studied the problem of youth violence 'between revolution and resignation'.[4] The title of the resulting volume reflects the complex and paradoxical nature of this theme, for as Gabor Rittersporn puts it, young people 'were mostly at the receiving end of violence' rather than its perpetrators (p. 70), as may be seen from the frequency of suicide among teen-agers and the high mortality rate in homes for juveniles, where conditions were as a rule primitive and discipline barbaric. These studies usefully illuminate the 'sub-culture of violence' that existed in Soviet Russia before 1929, but in the nature of things they cannot offer much more than generalities by way of explaining the scale and intensity of state-sponsored violence in the following years. The reasons for this have to be sought elsewhere, in the more familiar realms of politics and ideology.

Several general accounts have appeared lately which distinguish the main stages undergone by Stalinist 'repression' (to use a neutral term), the chief groups targeted, and the various forms it took; they also offer provisional estimates of the number of victims. Markus Wehner offers a brief survey,[5] in which he argues that the terror was 'functional', given the regime's objective of eliminating 'class enemies' and compelling the population to abide by the 'socialist' norms it prescribed; the relevant policies were devised at the centre, with junior officials ('little Stalins') play-ing an auxiliary role; popular input into the process was even less important. This is the familiar 'intentionalist' interpretation, updated by reference to recent Russian work, although Wehner takes pains to dissociate himself from 'the old totalitarian theory' (pp. 388–9).

Similar in approach is the work by Jörg Baberowski (Berlin), *Red Terror* – a general survey of Stalin's rule stressing repression, which rests on close study of newly available published and unpublished documents.[6] In another useful article Stephen Wheatcroft (Melbourne) examines the statistical evidence on mass killings in successive phases; he modestly calls this an 'attempt to move closer to laying the basis' for an explanation of the 'short-term shifts and oscillations'.[7] Nicolas Werth, a leading French specialist on the USSR, offers two articles in a miscellany that includes comparative material on the Nazis.[8]

These encapsulate the findings of a much longer essay that appeared in the controversial *Black Book of Communism*.[9] Critics of the latter charged the editors with concentrating on the repressive aspects of Communist rule wherever in the world it was practised, without sufficiently considering the contexts in which the various regimes operated. They did not seriously contest the facts or arguments adduced by Werth as regards the USSR. His piece has since been published in book form and can stand on its own merits.[10]

The first of the two articles of 1999 expands on earlier analyses by Moshe Lewin (and Richard Löwenthal) that saw the Stalinist state of the 1930s as a battle-ground between two 'logical systems': personal despotic rule by the dictator, as head of a distinct 'clan culture', versus the regular (routinized) bureaucratic administration needed for effective government in any modern state, especially a socialist one aspiring to manage a nationalized economy. Werth accepts the earlier revisionists' point that this bureaucracy was in chaotic condition, due largely to the impossible demands made on officials by the Party's successive campaigns, conducted in an atmosphere of perpetual emergency, so that their actions escaped the centre's control; hence Stalin's efforts to limit the local bosses' autonomy and ultimately to purge them in a wave of *spetsofagiia* ('specialist-eating'), driven by fear of sedition. To counter the revisionist argument that it is facile to attribute the terror to the quirks of a single leader, Werth offers the term 'institutionalized paranoia', a mental state he sees as afflicting an entire group: those who composed the dictator's 'clan' and were ensconced in the Party and police apparatuses. The Great Terror, 'a final radical attempt at social cleansing', signalled the triumph of the despotic principle; officialdom was cowed into submission, although paradoxically the *nomenklatura* expanded in size, so that the leader's personal power remained insecure. After the war, Stalinism became 'routinized', the bureaucracy more stable and professional – characteristics that were enhanced after 1953. Werth is not much concerned (either here or in his book) with the post-war era, which he dismisses as 'second Stalinism', although in our view it would be better to see it as an internationalization of the phenomenon. What he supplies is a middle-of-the-road explanation of the circumstances in which terrorist violence climaxed during the 1930s.

In the second article, Werth zeroes in on this violence, distinguishing between four 'repressive logics'[11] that operated jointly to drive it forward. These were: (a) the leadership's paranoia; (b) its centralizing proclivities; (c) the criminalization of routine economic activities essential to survival; (d) the rise of (Great) Russian chauvinism. Another key feature was the combination of extra-legal with regular legal methods, stress being placed on one or the other as expedient, the line between them being left obscure. Accordingly, state violence was applied unpredictably, with 'variable geometry' as it were, to shifting targets at different levels of intensity.

Successive campaigns

We may summarize these campaigns here before looking at them chronologically. 'Dekulakization' was an effort to destroy the rural élite, 'an immense plundering and gigantic settling of accounts'; carried through by hasty improvisation, it led to considerable loss of life and a vast expansion of the forced-labour system. In 1932 some of those arrested were released, but the stage set for man-made famine in the south. This second phase caused greater mortality than any other. Simultaneously, and especially after 1934, the police were authorized to conduct successive 'sweeps' of marginal ('socially dangerous') elements from the towns: people with dubious political 'biographies', infringers of passport regulations, mendicants and petty criminals.

The techniques developed in this operation served the NKVD well when it came to Stage Four. This comprised action on two levels: (a) at the top against political foes (ex-Oppositionists in the Party, military chiefs), an aspect that, with the 'show trials', has hitherto received the lion's share of attention; (b) about a dozen secret 'mass operations' directed against various categories of humdrum suspects: residents of frontier regions, for instance, along with the aforementioned 'marginals'. In these operations, a key feature, though not a novel one, was the arrest of people according to previously compiled lists; another was the establishment of quotas (*limity*) specifying how many 'enemies' local functionaries were to arrest. They were classified into two categories: the first were to be shot, the second sent to the Gulag. Late in 1938, the Great Terror was brought to an end by central *diktat*, although sporadic violence continued in various localities.

The fifth stage, which began during the fourth, was predominantly one of 'ethnic cleansing'. The targeted groups comprised Polish deportees and other inhabitants of the western areas annexed in 1939–40, most of whom were deported but some shot (the Katyn Forest massacre); later, during the war, it was the turn of the Volga and other Germans (after 1941) and several non-Slavic 'ethnies', mainly in the north Caucasus (1943–4). Treason, actual or potential, was stated as the cause; trials were dispensed with; and most victims were deported as 'special settlers'.

Building on Werth's classification, what may be termed the sixth (international) phase concerns two groups of war captives: (a) repatriated Soviet soldiers or civilian deportees, who were treated as collaborators; (b) enemy POW, plus enemy nationals taken from occupied Germany or Austria after 1945, politically suspect citizens of the east European 'people's democracies', and last but not least those who resisted reimposition of Soviet control in the Baltic states or western Ukraine. Repression continued on a reduced scale until Stalin's death, when the total population in custody (camp inmates and exiles) was about 5.3 million, roughly half in each major category; some nine-tenths of the exiles were non-Russians, and another 300,000 were in jail.

Each of these phases and target groups has, or deserves to have, its historians, working from the documentary record. Here we shall first indicate the main lines of current inquiry, keeping to the chronology outlined above, and then consider the perpetrators, popular complicity and the Gulag, concluding with some observations on the legal context. Of particular value is the work being done on the basis of local archival material. When these findings are put together, there will be a much fuller picture of what transpired. Whether the wealth of new information will fundamentally alter the Western view of Stalinism, either at the academic or popular level, remains to be seen.

'De-kulakization'

Recent studies of the mass deportation of peasant farmers that began in the early months of 1930 have shown that the central and local authorities must share the blame for the inhuman way in which this 'operation' was conducted. James Harris, in the article referred to in Chapter 8, gives the impression that the functionaries in the Urals, with their insistent requests for the despatch of more labour to toil in the local forests and mines, were primarily responsible for the growth of the Gulag there. Jörg Baberowski, on the other hand, stresses Moscow's role: 'the Stalinist leadership', he writes, 'made its terrorist intentions abundantly plain [and] was only secondarily concerned with economic considerations or local initiatives'.[12] The leadership was ideologically motivated and 'had no need for demands from below'; he does, however, acknowledge 'a congruence of interest between the centre and certain regional Party leaders' (p. 579). Elsewhere Baberowski cites from the minutes of a secret conclave (February 1930) at which Molotov first mentioned the possibility of drowning or shooting kulaks *en masse* before turning to the option of exile, 'to concentration camps, if Eikhe [in Siberia] has any'; only then did he suggest that 'we must consider what kind of work we can send them to, perhaps [felling] timber'.[13] In short, the initial decision to deport was taken to remove undesirables rather than to exploit the resources of distant regions; efforts to 'rationalize' the exile system came later, after thousands of unfortunates had already died of cold, hunger, disease and sheer neglect.

We know (from Zemskov) that 1.8 million peasants were deported and 31,000 sentenced to death; these figures, Baberowski notes, exclude those shot without any proceedings or who died en route. As for mortality in the reception areas, the figure for the Northern region of 16.8 per cent by 1 December 1930 gives some idea of its scale; (we do not yet have a trustworthy total). As Lynne Viola notes, 'it is likely that children accounted for a disproportionate percentage of these deaths'.[14] Her study, based on papers in Vologda as well as central archives, details the callous negligence that was the rule among officials at all levels, although some intermittent efforts were made to alleviate the worst abuses. In April 1930, families were permitted to send their offspring home to live with relatives (typically, at their own expense); even this concession was later suspended for six months. Viola chronicles the grim conditions in hastily built 'special villages': water-logged huts, nettle soup as food, lethal hygienic conditions, schooling (rarely) and the various work assignments, which all, even young children, had to perform. Interviews with the now elderly survivors lend a human note to what might otherwise have been a dry study of (mal)administration. As to *why* children were treated so harshly, Viola supplies a convincing explanation: the Party believed that class attributes were inherited and so sought 'to tear up the evil by its roots', regardless of the human cost.[15]

The next wave comprised various marginalized groups. Essential background to their fate is supplied by Golfo Alexopoulos (Tampa), who unearthed in Siberia an archive containing some 100,000 files on *lishentsy*, or disfranchised persons.[16] Numbering some 4 million at their peak, these impoverished folk, often aged and sick, received neither ration cards nor medical care, but were allowed to apply for reinstatement of their civic rights. The author scrutinizes a cross-section of these pathetic petitions (1928–31), but as a post-modernist is less concerned with the writers' actual situation than with their perceptions of it ('refashioning of the self'): their subsequent persecution is only touched on briefly (pp. 180–3). David Shearer (Delaware) and Paul Hagenloh (Austin) pick up the story.[17] They make it clear that the 'socially dangerous elements' included many peasants fleeing starvation in search of food and employment, who as a rule lacked valid internal passports (obligatory since November 1932), and the police would conduct periodical sweeps to round up such vagrants, sometimes on the basis of lists compiled from data supplied by informers. Among those detained were people whose political 'biographies' (that is, the information supplied on questionnaires (*ankety*) when applying for residence or a job) revealed them to be of 'class-alien' background or former members of other political parties.

An initial drive in August 1933 led to some 7,000 convictions, a relatively small fraction of the 24,000 cases summarily adjudicated. Two years later, a second campaign yielded a larger human 'harvest': 266,000, most of whom were probably sent to camps, but for five years instead of the previous three.[18] The operation was conducted under the authority of an NKVD order (no. 00192) of 9 May 1935. The total sentenced that year by *troiki* (three-man commissions) was 116,159, and in the following year 141,318 (p. 527). These figures need to be set beside those for sentences by the NKVD's Special Board for major anti-state crimes: 118,465 and 119,159, of which 24.9 and 15.9 per cent respectively were for 'counter-revolution'.[19] In the light of these findings it is no longer plausible to see the mid-1930s as a time when repression eased. This view placed too much weight on decrees ordering the release of prisoners or forbidding *troiki* to pass death sentences. The impact of such reformist measures was offset by other ordinances promulgated in secret. It was a feature of Stalinist governance to send out 'mixed signals' (McLoughlin), and to pursue contradictory policies simultaneously, as a means of throwing opponents off guard.

Purges and 'mass operations'

Kirov's assassination (1 December 1934) intensified the paranoia at the top and led to spectacular actions against ex-oppositionists in the Party, notably in Leningrad. The former capital was seen as a hotbed of potential disloyalty. A round-up there in March 1935 led to 11,072 convictions, of which some five thousand may have been of *byvshie liudi* or old-regime holdovers. Lesley Rimmel (Stillwater), who has investigated this episode,[20] places it in the context of the earlier struggle against violators of the passport regulations. In 1933–4, over 75,000 such individuals had been expelled (p. 530); the post-Kirov assault was, however, more lethal, and involved 'quotas' (*limity*) and mass executions. Nine-tenths of the 'former people' were condemned to death, a proportion 'which approached the target figures' (p. 534). In this article, Rimmel is principally concerned with the public reaction to the arrests, which ranged from sympathy with the victims ('how can they be harmful if they're over eighty?') through apprehension ('today they're going for princes and barons, [soon] they'll strike at humble folk') to opportunism or *Schadenfreude* ('why were [the accused] allowed to go free until now?') – a point we shall come back to below.

On the Kirov assassination itself, Western researchers have had little novel to add. In 1999 Amy Knight, well known as biographer of Beria and an authority on Soviet police matters, published a book with a sensational title[21] that presented a rather positive account of the subject's earlier career; as regards his murder, after carefully reviewing the evidence, she inclined to the hypothesis of Stalin's implication, but this remains unproven.[22] It seems unlikely that conclusive evidence on this point will emerge and so it is still open to speculative inference. Baberowski is non-committal, but evidently leans towards Alla Kirilina's interpretation. He stresses the consequence: it 'changed the atmosphere' in the leadership: death now cast its shadow on the Party' (p. 144).

On the show trials of prominent Bolsheviks, the same author notes that their purpose was to persuade the populace, and above all Party members, of the need for constant vigilance (p. 150). On this topic, the focus of much earlier Western literature, including Robert Conquest's magisterial study, a monumental and well-documented 'chronicle' is presented by Wladislaw Hedeler (Berlin). Although not entirely free of factual errors and redundancies, it has the merit of showing clearly how these monstrous judicial farces were staged, and what public reactions they evoked.[23] In 1993 Sheila Fitzpatrick wrote a stimulating article on the show trials staged in the provinces towards the end of 1937 in which she stressed the element of 'popular carnival', that is, a festival licensed by authority at which ordinary folk took pleasure in humiliating their local bosses now under arrest. Recently, she has been taken to task for this interpretation by Michael Ellman (Amsterdam), who calls it 'forced' and 'one-sided'. Far from these trials being carnivalesque affairs, they were most sinister; instead of being 'worlds apart' from the trials in Moscow, they were initiated in response to a Stalin order of 3 August, the text of which Ellman reproduces. They should therefore be seen as designed to win peasant support for the terror that was being launched across the country.[24]

Toilers in the archives have uncovered a good deal of material on the fate of Comintern cadres,[25] but in general, attention has shifted away from the purges of élite elements to the several so-called 'mass operations' unleashed in secrecy from July 1937 onward. These remained enshrouded in obscurity until 1992, when a newspaper (*Trud*, 4 June) first published the NKVD's now notorious operational order no. 00447 of 31 July 1937, which set the lethal campaign in motion. Hitherto the extension of the terror to the lower ranks of society had been generally seen as a spontaneous, even unplanned, development: it was reasoned that the 'high-ups' charged with Trotskyism and other offences had incriminated their associates under pressure, and so the net had automatically widened; many people had been denounced by embittered colleagues or underlings who exploited the wave of hysteria for their own purposes. Both these things did indeed occur, but we now know that impulses from the centre were at the core of the process. The discussion on this point is worth looking at in detail.

In these debates, now conducted with more restraint than formerly, the key figure is J. Arch Getty (Riverside), a leading US authority on the Soviet 1930s. His *Origins of the Great Purges* (1985) became a bible of revisionism and a subject of keen controversy. Getty argued inter alia for a dispassionate approach to Stalinist repression and focussed attention on the machinery whereby it was put into effect, that is, on 'input from below' rather than the will of the leader(s) – an approach resembling that of the 'functionalists' among historians of the Third Reich. In particular, Getty saw the earlier Party purges as a drive to reassert central control over errant and inefficient officials, which ought to be sharply distinguished from the terror wave that followed. Important though this issue is, the arguments for and against it have now been thoroughly ventilated and so need not be discussed here. In the 1990s, having gained access to the archives, Getty produced what he and his co-authors prudently called a 'first approach' to calculating the number of Stalin's victims.[26] This likewise provoked controversy, but has not yet been superseded by a final reckoning.

More recently, Getty has co-operated with the Russian scholar Oleg Naumov in bringing out a notable volume in Yale's 'Annals of Communism' series, in which 199 documents are linked by an extensive commentary, as well as several articles exploring the Terror from various angles.[27] In the last of these, the notion of 'social input' into the purging process is again advanced, but less stridently than before. On the 'intentionalist' side of the discussion are scholars such as Barry McLoughlin (Vienna) and especially Rolf Binner (Amsterdam) and Marc Junge (Bochum). The two last-mentioned have produced what is currently the most thorough study of the 'mass operations', based on archival records as well as the extensive literature that has appeared in various parts of the FSU in recent years.[28] Even so, research into this question is only in its initial stages and many questions are still obscure. In particular, it is not yet clear just what relationship the 'mass operations' had to the political machinations at the top.

Another obvious question is the immediate reason for launching the campaign so abruptly. The generalities are familiar: 'institutionalized paranoia' (Werth); previous elaboration of ideological justifications for social cleansing; fear of German and Japanese attack; evidence of successful 'fifth column' subversion in Spain; confidence in the NKVD's technical 'expertise' in such actions; the continued need for more Gulag labour. But what weight should be apportioned to each motive? The operation was launched within two weeks of Stalin's annihilation of the Red Army command, which suggests linkage – but precisely what? Getty points out that Party officials were concerned at the prospect of elections to the Supreme Soviet under the new Constitution, with ostensibly free balloting, and made their worries known to the centre. 'It is hard to avoid the conclusion that in return for forcing the local Party leaders to conduct an election, Stalin chose to help them win it by giving them license to kill or deport hundreds of thousands of "dangerous elements"' ('Excesses', p. 126). Since their fears could have been dispelled more cheaply, by hints as to the fraudulent electoral procedure eventually adopted, this was surely at best a subsidiary motive. McLoughlin advances it as one of three possible reasons ('Vernichtung', pp. 59–60), the others being fear of (especially ethnic) disloyalty in a two-front war and coping with economic sabotage. There is no sign of long-term planning. An extremely nervous leadership acted in panic, indifferent to the operation's broader consequences (let alone the cost in lives).

On 2 July, the Politburo adopted a resolution giving the Party's subordinate territorial agencies five days in which to draw up, with the aid of the local NKVD, lists of 'saboteurs' (that is, potential victims), who were to be divided into two categories, the first to be shot and the second deported; they were also to nominate the members of local three-man tribunals (troiki). The proposed totals were duly reported by each agency and approved, as were the triumvirates. On 16 July, NKVD leaders conferred with regional officials and issued instructions about the simplified pseudo-judicial procedure to be applied, and procuracy officials were told by Vyshinsky to comply with them. On 31 July, the Politburo approved these arrangements, whereupon Yezhov communicated order no. 00447 to the local NKVD bosses. The operation was scheduled to start on 5 August, but some over-eager locals jumped the gun.[29]

Getty detects in this process 'input from below', for 'understanding the kulak operation [sic] purely as planned and centrally directed violence, without taking account of power contests between central and regional bodies, tells only half the story' ('Excesses', p. 115). Undoubtedly, centre–periphery relations were, as he suggests, complex; but do these tussles amount to 'power contests' or are we dealing here with seniors and juniors in the hierarchy trying to outbid each other in harshness? Is it right to speak here, in PM terms, of 'implicit (and sometimes explicit) dialogue and negotiation' (p. 116)? Some local functionaries tried to restrain the centre's zeal, but others 'helped to instigate and shape' the operation; in particular, it was they, rather than the chiefs in Moscow, who decided which individuals should be included in either of the two categories, so that they literally exercised powers of life and death over their subjects. They could and did petition for additional quotas, and these requests were more often granted than refused (p. 130; Binner and Junge, p. 579). For instance, in Omsk the troika chairman asked for the limit to be raised from 5,000 to 8,000 and Stalin minuted: 'Yezhov, I'm in favour'. (Stalin and Yezhov usually decided such matters in tandem, without reference to the full Politburo.) Many NKVD chiefs just filled up the local prisons and then cited overcrowding as the reason for requesting a higher quota (especially for Category I). In January 1938, the centre granted 48,000 more of these, and 9,200 more in Category II, in 22 territorial units where repression was fiercest (p. 582). Getty correctly shows that provincial Chekists displayed a great deal of energy and initiative, for none of them seems to have objected to the operation, but the principal conclusion must surely be that the centre uncaringly gave local officials carte blanche.

Getty's last-ditch effort to demonstrate input from below fails to convince, for the evidence he cites bears out an intentionalist interpretation.

Binner and Junge break new ground by offering details of the 'special actions' undertaken in prisons and Gulag camps (pp. 586–90), which were covered by separate instructions; the 'target figure' for deaths in the Gulag was 10,000. The two authors also provide a composite table showing the quotas originally suggested and approved, and successive additions to them, for *each* territorial unit (pp. 593 ff.), together with a 'final reckoning'. This reveals that 767,397 individuals were convicted, of whom 356,105 were in Category I (killed).

This figure relates only to the operation conducted under order no. 00447. But from spring 1938 onwards the purge was increasingly directed against ethnic minorities. This aspect has been treated most fully by Terry Martin;[30] there are also specialized studies of particular groups, to which we shall turn in a moment. Martin arrives at a total figure of 335,513 such convictions (July 1937 – November 1938), of which 247,157 were 'Category I' ('Origins', p. 858). Non-Russians were more likely to be put to death than others arrested. In Belarus 83 per cent of those arrested were shot, and in Khakassia (southern Siberia) the percentage was even higher (94 per cent) (p. 76). In support of the 'centralist' interpretation, McLoughlin makes the point that 'the way executions were carried out was prescribed exactly': by night, in a cellar or forest, without victims' families being informed; he identifies some executioners by name and specifies the location of certain burial sites. In conclusion, he directs a few barbs at the 'circumstantialists': 'the fundamental theses and assertions of the social-history oriented "revisionists" are in my view no longer tenable', for this was 'a comprehensive programme of mass destruction' that owed a good deal to Russian national chauvinism as well as to *raison d'état* (pp. 84–7).

Eric Weitz (Minnesota) has since taken this view further by calling the national-minority purges 'racial politics without the concept of race'.[31] He questions earlier scholars' practice of using the term 'ethnicity' in preference to 'race' lest they should appear to be inferring parallels with Nazi genocide (p. 10). After citing N. Bugai's estimate of 3 to 3.5 million people, from 58 ethnies, who were deported under Stalin, he states that 'the manner of deportations bears all the character of other ethnic cleansings in the twentieth century, including the Holocaust' (p. 14). The heart of Weitz's argument is that the authorities acted on the principle that anti-Soviet sentiment *inhered* in the group targeted and was transmitted from one generation to the next – as we have seen in connection with 'kulak' children. In the author's view, this amounted to 'racializing': dedicated as it was to the total recasting of society (social engineering), and not respecting any legal or moral constraints upon its power, the Stalinist state is said to have operated a 'racial logic' (p. 18). Although the biological concept of race had been disowned in theory (1931), it was applied in practice; from the victims' standpoint 'ultimately it mattered little whether the characteristics ascribed to ['disloyal' minorities] were understood to be transmitted by biology or culture' (p. 23).

Weitz's critics have countered that the distinction did indeed matter; that minorities had the option of assimilation to the dominant culture; that the regime sought to eradicate certain minorities' 'territorial identity', rather than their physical existence; and that exiles could at least appeal against their fate as individuals (pp. 41, 46, 48). The debate on this issue is productive and likely to continue.

The vexing question of ethnic cleansing, rendered topical by recent tragedies in the Balkans, is examined in a general work by Norman Naimark, who deals *inter alia* with the Soviet experience.[32] Another overview, by Alfred Rieber, pleads for use of the term 'repressive population transfer' as more accurate and less prone to political manipulation. After briefly discussing the fate of Poles, Balts, Germans and north Caucasians, he points out that we still know too little about the reception given to these involuntary migrants by the peoples of the host territories, and how many succeeded in integrating into them.[33] Otto Pohl, an independent scholar in Germany who publishes in North America, has compiled two statistical volumes which tabulate the findings of post-Soviet writers for Westerners unable to read the originals.[34] In the first of these, he offers 76 tables covering such topics as sentences by the security organs, the number of prisoners in Gulag camps, colonies, and settlements, and the demographics of exile; the bibliography goes up to 1994. Since Otto Pohl did not himself have archive access, he was unable to verify his sources first-hand. The tone is more restrained than in the second volume, which crudely denounces revisionist scholars for 'whitewashing Stalin's crimes' (p. xiii). Here the arrangement is different, with separate chapters for each of 13 ethnic groups. There is much material on Germans but curiously nothing on Ukrainians or the three Baltic peoples.

An excellent brief survey of repression in Ukraine is given by Dieter Pohl (Berlin); but most of the literature on this republic is, perhaps rightly, concerned with the nation-building process.[35]

The Baltic states, especially Lithuania, were the scene of a ferocious guerilla and counter-guerilla struggle after the war. The methods used by the NKVD in repressing this movement are explored by Arvydas Anušauskas (Vilnius), who supplies references to the extensive literature in Lithuanian.[36] The part played by Suslov in master-minding these operations has also been examined, on the basis of Party records, by Donal O'Sullivan of Eichstatt (Germany).[37]

Some years ago, the leading Western specialist on the history of the Crimean Tatars, Edward Allworth (New York), published a documentary miscellany devoted to that people's 'return to the homeland' containing five articles on 'the ordeal of forced exile' after 1944 – valuable in that exiles' fate in their new territories is so far little studied. The editor concludes that 'both practical political and ideological motivations' were involved in the decision to deport this ethnic group and underlines the point that such destructive actions 'constitute[d] a normal aspect of Soviet nationality policies' (p. 204).[38] More recently, Brian Williams (Dartmouth, MA) has published a well-informed, if strongly partisan, account, based on interviews with survivors as well as archival documents, of the deportation of this group. Mortality during transport is put at 7,900, another 40–44,000 dying in the first four years of exile.[39] For the Transcaucasian peoples we now have the first of two studies by Jörg Baberowski, which focuses on Azerbaijan.[40]

Foreigners, too, fell victim to the terror. Among the first groups were Poles, Koreans, Finns – and Germans. There is a growing literature on all these groups, especially the last, of which we can offer only a glimpse here.[41] Treatment of ethnic repression under Stalin has been somewhat disjointed, but this defect will no doubt be corrected in years to come.

Perpetrators and denouncers

At this point, we may interrupt the catalogue of wickedness and woe to consider two inter-related problems: what has been learned of late about the perpetrators of these deeds, and how far were ordinary people their willing or unwilling accomplices?

For cultural historians, these are not the questions we should be asking. Since many victims were themselves victimizers, it would be better, they argue, to inquire into the ways such persons made sense of their experiences. Susanne Schattenberg, whose work on early Soviet engineers was noted in Chapter 10, seeks to 'reconceptualize' the Terror:

> If we proceed from the assumption, not that an omnipotent state maltreated a powerless (*ohnmächtiges*) population of victims, but that each individual was also subject and actor, then it is relevant to ask what the criteria were according to which each thought and acted, and how these criteria were influenced and changed. The subjective view of the historical actors would then become the key to [understanding] the objective history of violence and [solving] the question as to how such deeds could come to pass. The new cultural history can help to explain . . . how an idea can be translated into violent acts. It establishes the nexus between the state's plans and aims on one hand and the behaviour of various segments of the population on the other, by focussing on the point that each 'system' is conditioned by the other, and studies this interaction. In this way culture appears as the transmission belt, so to speak, whereby the Politburo, appealing to pre-existing patterns and traditions, managed to influence [the actors'] view of reality, their norms, values, and motives for doing what they did.[42]

Whatever may be said for such an approach, it sidesteps the problem of ascertaining the historical actors' responsibility for their deeds, or at least postpones this until such time as we would have a complete picture of the behaviour of each and every member of the community.

Eric Weitz notes 'an enormous deficit of research on the perpetrators' in Stalin's realm as compared with Hitler's and argues for a high degree of popular complicity.[43] With the first of these statements few would disagree, but credit should go to the Russian scholars who have done much of late to fill the gaps in our knowledge. Nikita Petrov, whose work is available in French,[44] offers data on the size and composition of the security organs which show that, for instance, they became increasingly 'russified' during the 1930s. A Ukrainian colleague, writing in the same volume, points out that many 'Chekists' began their careers as secret informers.[45]

Other (Western) researchers explore relations between the NKVD and the Party at local level (James Harris) and with the regular police, or militia (Paul Hagenloh). Harris's study is part of his work on government and administration in the Urals, which as we have seen focusses on centre–periphery tensions. He sees the leaders of the two bodies as working closely together until the Terror, when their 'collusion' was exposed by Yezhov's men; thereafter 'the centre chose all local political police agents and carefully monitored their activities'.[46] Hagenloh, supplementing an earlier article noted above, shows that the militia, too, became involved in selecting target groups during the 1937–8 'mass operations', for it was they who kept records of social misfits; they likewise had their *troiki*, which passed (non-lethal) sentences of up to five years' detention.[47] Further studies of particular localities would be helpful, but they will need more liberal access to provincial archives than is granted at present.

It is a little easier to study the NKVD's organizational structure and leadership. Among Western writers, Michael Parrish, who back in 1992 gave us a biographical dictionary of members of the security establishment, identifies many senior officials in his description of what he calls the 'lesser terror' after the war.[48] In a major biography of 'Stalin's loyal executioner', based on hitherto closed papers of the security organs, Marc Jansen (Amsterdam) and Nikita Petrov explain Yezhov's rise to power in part by the 'almost hypnotic' power exercised over him by the leader, as well as his 'great organizational talents'; he was 'a product of Stalin's totalitarian, terrorist and bureaucratic system, [who] had one essential shortcoming: he did not know where to stop' (pp. 20, 203, 209).[49] Another Western biographer, Arch Getty, in a preliminary sketch[50] likewise stresses his ordinariness and compares him to Eichmann in Germany: Yezhov was a 'skilled bureaucrat' of a type that the system needed to function as it did. Getty goes on to suggest rather incautiously that 'the more we learn about him the less he seems like a monster' (p. 173), a remark that can surely apply only to the initial stages in his career – although his close colleague Gabor Rittersporn uses a similar term for *all* the executants of the terror.[51]

A biographical approach 'from above' can and should be supplemented by sociologically inspired investigations into popular attitudes. Sarah Davies, in her study of what passed for public opinion under Stalin, sees the Terror as 'in part a populist strategy designed to mobilize subordinate groups against those in positions of responsibility, thereby deflecting discontent away from the regime itself'.[52] There seems to be no documentary evidence of such an intention, but it may have been an unconscious motive – and certainly was one of the results. As she shows, many people were sceptical about official charges against former oppositionists ('the newspapers are lying'); nevertheless support for repressive measures, at least in the Leningrad area, was 'widespread' (pp. 118–19). Some expressed sympathy for those arrested, and there was even the odd protest, but such reactions were confined mainly to the intelligentsia (p. 123) – a conclusion that may reflect the limitations of the source base of the study; however, in 1935 the public mood in the city was not dissimilar, as Rimmel showed in the article cited above.[53]

A fine line distinguishes citizens' routine complaints about official neglect or incompetence, which the writer blamed for his or her predicament, from letters of denunciation in the narrower sense, which were expected or calculated to injure the person targeted. Sheila Fitzpatrick's stimulating investigation of this topic (1996) has encouraged emulation, notably by Jörg Baberowski.[54] Fitzpatrick examined 200 denunciations in 12 central and regional archives. The practice was encouraged by authority and informants were more likely to be 'regulars' than ordinary citizens acting spontaneously. There were four characteristic targets: (1) erring comrades, denounced either 'from loyalty' or from malice; (2) social aliens, seen as having fraudulently crept into positions of power; (3) superiors, deemed to have abused their office; (4) family members or neighbours, for brutal or immoral behaviour – a category that includes what the author calls 'apartment denunciations' prompted by the housing shortage.

Baberowski's classification is broadly similar, although he distinguishes a separate 'ethnic' category, which in Azerbaijan, for instance, led to an epidemic of denunciations as members of various nationalities accused each other of incorrect behaviour or opinions: in the last five months of 1937, Molotov received no fewer than 1,477 such letters from this republic alone (178). Baberowski goes on to examine the symbolic meaning of the vocabulary used by such letter writers. Unlike Kotkin and others, he sees the adoption of official jargon as just a tactical device, not as a reflection of the writer's convictions.

As to the outcome, Fitzpatrick views such letters as means of assuaging feelings of social envy and correcting specific injustices ('Signals', p. 115), whereas Baberowski is more attuned to the aspect of political manipulation: the letter writers, he argues, 'deprived themselves of every chance to influence their own fate; both those denounced and those who denounced others placed themselves in the hands of the political leaders, who decided which side would win' (p. 189). He goes on to argue that the practice of denunciation acquired such dynamism that it led to the self-destruction of the government apparatus in Azerbaijan – and by implication in other localities as well.

Thus we are led back here to the traditional view of 'popular input' as an important but only an *auxiliary* reason for the Terror's vast scope: in their desperation people naively responded to intimations from above and ventilated their grievances on local bosses, which served the centre's purposes. This is the very concept that Fitzpatrick had originally challenged as 'privileging the regime perspective'. In her view, complaining was a natural social phenomenon and any abuse of it for political ends incidental; most denouncers were paranoids or busybodies such as one might find anywhere.

It might move the controversy forwards if one distinguished more clearly between periods of normal and heightened tension: in the First FYP era 'accusatory practices' did little harm beyond the immediate local level, whereas in 1937–8 they became a major political factor, albeit of lesser account than the decisions taken on high. We also need to remember that denunciations for political 'heresy' are more likely to be found in (closed) police archives than complaints filed for, say, wasting resources or bullying subordinates (to say nothing of wife-beating). Research into what Stefan Plaggenborg calls the 'accomplices' (*Mittäter*) of Stalinism is still just beginning and we ought not to rush to judgement, especially since ideally each individual case should be evaluated on its merits.

The Gulag and post-war Terror

The heart of the Stalinist repressive system was of course the network of camp and settlement complexes that we commonly speak of, following Solzhenitsyn but a little inaccurately, as 'the Gulag'. Not until 2003 did Westerners have at their disposal a comprehensive scholarly study of this hidden world, all the more remarkable for being written by a non-academic.[55] Anne Applebaum (Washington) has visited the sites of many camp complexes, talked to survivors, and scoured provincial archives as well as the abundant memoir literature, a source used with due care. The first part (pp. 27–124) surveys the administrative background and the main phases in the expansion of the prisoner population to 1941, stressing the system's economic rationale but taking a firm intentionalist position on the reasons for the Terror (p. 105). The main body of the work (pp. 127–370) offers a detailed picture of the inmates' experiences. The arrangement is thematic, recalling Solzhenitsyn's work, but the tone here is restrained, without the great writer's heavy sarcasm. Applebaum shows that reality diverged greatly from the official image: regulations specified a minimum of welfare but were disregarded in practice; survival depended on arbitrary decisions by criminals (*urki*) and guards, who displayed a 'stupid, lazy' form of cruelty, seeing their charges as sub-human detritus. The use of food as a means of control; camp hierarchies; the fate of women and children – these are but a few of the topics explored here. Applebaum then shows that World War II brought prisoners even greater hardship: rations were cut and 2 million died. The losses were made up by the influx of new categories of captive, such as enemy prisoners of war (who came under different branch of the administration, GUPVI, which would deserve another book). In Stalin's last years, the Gulag reached its zenith, with the setting up of 'special' camps and increased resort to forced labour (*katorga*), while officials struggled for control against gangs of professional criminals (*vory v zakone*), desperadoes who hated and exploited the other groups. But 'the Gulag's masters . . . by tightening the repressive noose . . . made their task more difficult. The rebelliousness of the politicals and the wars of the criminals hastened the onset of an even deeper crisis' as the authorities (but not Stalin) came to realize how unprofitable the system was (p. 423). In an appendix, Applebaum offers some thoughts on prisoner numbers (28.7 million, including exiles?) and casualties. Precision is scarcely feasible here, given the prevalence of statistical error at lower levels. Nor have post-Stalin regimes gone far in acknowledging the enormity of the crimes committed, let alone making reparation, for in Russia 'the past is a bad dream to be forgotten . . . like a great unopened Pandora's box, it lies in wait for the next generation' (p. 512).

Next to this mammoth work, other recent contributions, despite their importance, look rather puny. Federico Varese is illuminating on the criminal prisoners, whose role has been downplayed in the literature in favour of the politicals.[56] Others have examined particular regions, such as Magadan in the Far East, with the notorious Kolyma gold-mining camps. David Nordlander brings out the remarkable degree of central control exercised over this remote area and adjusts downwards earlier estimates of the number of prisoners.[57] In three articles, Nick Baron (Manchester) scrutinizes Karelia and the North, tracing the camps' evolution and stating roundly that deaths from hardship and brutality were their 'defining characteristics' ('Conflict', p. 646).[58] For western Siberia, we may go back to a 1991 study by Alain Brossat and colleagues.[59] The camps set up in post-war Germany are the subject of a continuing documentary series sponsored by an international editorial board and other studies.[60] Much more work of this kind is needed before we have an adequate picture of the archipelago's manifold ramifications.

Space limitations preclude detailed examination here of recent Western literature on post-war terror, which is much thinner than material on the 1930s, partly because archival access for this period is more difficult.[61] Some categories of victims have been referred to above, but Soviet Jewry is a conspicuous exception. The anti-Semitic measures of Stalin's last years were more than just an expression of security concerns and reflected deep-seated prejudice. The investigation, trial and judicial murder of members of the Jewish Anti-Fascist Committee (JAFC), and the Stalin-sanctioned assassination of Solomon Mikhoels that preceded it, have been the subject of several well-documented studies. Arno Lustiger, who in 1994 published a German translation of Vasilyi Grossman's and Ilya Ehrenburg's *Black Book*, followed up four years later with a *Red Book* in which he argued that the JAFC affair exemplified the late Stalin regime's substitution of 'Russian imperial ideology' for the earlier internationalism.[62] Most writers on the subject repeat the story that in the wake of the 1953 'doctors' plot' affair Stalin intended to deport Soviet Jews eastward *en masse*, much as he had the Chechens and others in 1943–4. But Samson Madiewski (Aachen) points out that the evidence for this is inconclusive.[63] Central Committee records do not confirm the existence of such a plan. Vladimir Naumov points out that the incriminating documents (notably for construction of a giant new camp complex) may have been destroyed, so that for the present the question should be left open.

If the projected anti-Jewish terror wave remained 'unconsummated', so to speak, by the happy coincidence of Stalin's demise, this was not the case for another batch of post-war victims, the two million or so repatriated Soviet prisoners of war. This question has been dealt with at length by Russian writers, but not as yet by Westerners – partly perhaps because it raises the painful problem of Allied governments' complicity in the return of these unfortunates from potential sanctuary abroad, a point forcefully made some years ago by Nikolai Tolstoi.[64] The leading Russian authority on this matter is Pavel Polian, whose work of 1996 has since been translated into German.[65]

Another glaring gap in Western scholarship on Stalinist repression is the lack of professional juridical assessments of what, by later international standards at any rate, were massive crimes against humanity. There are several reasons for this neglect. One is surely the regime's skill in providing a quasi-legal camouflage for many of its actions. It was able to combine 'mass operations' by NKVD *troiki*, in which there was no pretence of due process, with other campaigns that to some degree did involve regular courts or special tribunals. To the end of the Soviet regime's existence, law was seen as a political instrument. The leading North American expert in this domain, Peter Solomon Jr. (Toronto), in his standard work on criminal justice under Stalin (1996), is concerned with the routine administration of justice rather than extraordinary quasi- or pseudo-judicial measures. He shows the paradoxical situation that resulted from the fact that in the 1930s efforts were made to build a more professional legal system, for example, by preventing local officials from interfering with court decisions, while simultaneously penal policy was being made more punitive, with heavy sanctions for petty offences, and police arbitrariness reached its peak.[66] It is good to be reminded here that some courageous jurists (and for that matter, even Chekists) resisted orders to commit illegal acts and paid for this with their lives. But what one might call the 'non-judicial aspect of socialist legality' under Stalin is deliberately played down here,[67] even though members of the procuracy and 'people's judges' were often closely involved in committing totally unjustified acts of repression. In this way we are left with an overall impression that is a little misleading. In similar spirit, Yoram Gorlizky argues[68] that after 1947 the rigid bureaucracies that had by then come into being, staffed by professionals of conservative temperament, acted as a brake on campaign-style justice in 1930s style (p. 1247), even though at this time penal sanctions were being made more severe. Certainly, there is something to this argument; yet if the Stalin clique had resolved to overcome such obstruction, can we doubt that it was strong enough to get its way?

A balanced approach is attempted by Gabor Rittersporn in an article devoted to the very question of 'extra-judicial repression and the courts'.[69] He states (p. 218) that, of the 1.5 million 'counter-revolutionary' offences dealt with between 1940 and 1952, 78.5 per cent were tried by the courts – but among these he includes military tribunals. These surely ought rather to be seen as 'irregular' or quasi-judicial bodies like the 'special boards' or *troiki*.

A definitive treatment of this issue is still outstanding. Oleg Khlevniuk has a surer sense of historical realities where he speaks of the Stalin regime's 'flirtation with legality';[70] but we shall probably have to await more specialized studies of various aspects of the repressive system before some jurist could deliver a 'final verdict' – if such is ever possible.

Notes

1 The title of this chapter is borrowed from M. Amis, *Koba the Dread: Laughter and the Twentieth Century* (London: Jonathan Cape, 2002).

2 This applies in particular to the extravagant arguments advanced by Robert W. Thurston, in *Life and Terror in Stalin's Russia, 1934–1941* (New Haven, CT and London: Yale University Press, 1996), that the Soviet regime had not intervened greatly in the lives of ordinary people, so that 'vast numbers' did not experience fear; that Trotsky's agents had formed a bloc with Party dissidents, giving Stalin grounds to mount the show trials; and that Yezhov drove the purge forward, while Stalin reacted to information as it came to him (pp. xviii, 25, 51). Markus Wehner commented: 'Thurston's book is annoying in its ignorance of the facts and cynical when one considers the victims': *JGOE* 47 (1999), 291.

3 Cf. notably J.A. Getty and O.V. Naumov, *The Road to Terror: Stalin and the Self-Destruction of the Bolsheviks* (New Haven, CT and London: Yale University Press, 1999); articles in *CMR* 42–43 (2001, 2002, with contributions by O.V. Khlevniuk, N.V. Petrov and colleagues in Kiev and Vilnius) and especially B. McLoughlin and K. McDermott

(eds), *Stalin's Terror: High Politics and Mass Repression in the Soviet Union* (Basingstoke and New York: Palgrave Macmillan, 2003), which takes a strongly 'intentionalist' approach to the events of 1937–8 and (a valuable feature) presents to Anglo-Saxon readers some recent research by German and Russian specialists.

4   C. Kuhr-Korolev *et al.* (eds), *Sowjetjugend 1917–1941: Generation zwischen Revolution und Resignation* (Essen: Klartext, 2001), esp. articles by H. Haumann (25–61), Rittersporn (63–82), and Plaggenborg. For more by Kuhr, see n. 15 and by Plaggenborg: 'Gewalt und Militanz in Sowjetrussland', *JGOE* 44 (1996), 409–30; 'Gewalt im Stalinismus: Skizzen zu einer Tätergeschichte', in Hildermeier (ed.), *Stalinismus*, 193–208.

5   M. Wehner, 'Stalinismus und Terror', in Plaggenborg (ed.), *Stalinismus*, 365–90. Wehner is the author of a study of agrarian policy under NEP: *Bauernpolitik im proletarischen Staat: die Bauernfrage als zentrales Problem der sowjetischen Innenpolitik 1921–1928* (Cologne, Weimar and Vienna: Böhlau, 1998).

6   J. Baberowski, *Der rote Terror: Geschichte des Stalinismus* (Munich: DVA, 2003).

7   S.G. Wheatcroft, 'Towards Explaining the Changing Levels of Stalinist Repression in the 1930s: Mass Killings', in idem (ed.), *Challenging Traditional Views of Russian History* (Basingstoke: Palgrave, 2002), 112–46.

8   N. Werth, 'Staline et son système dans les années 1930' and 'Logiques de violence dans l'URSS stalinienne', in H. Rousso (ed.), *Stalinisme et nazisme: Histoire et mémoire comparées* (Brussels: Eds Complexe, 1999), 45–78, 99–128.

9   S. Courtois and N. Werth (eds), *Le Livre noir du communisme: crimes, terreur et répression* (Paris: Robert Laffont, 1997); Eng. edn: *The Black Book of Communism: Crimes, Terror, Repression*, trans. J. Murphy and M. Kramer (Cambridge, MA: Harvard University Press, 1999). For a balanced review, see D. Beyrau, 'Die korrekte Moral und die historische Profession: ein Kommentar', *JGOE* 47 (1999), 254–62; cf. also the extensive discussion in *Osteuropa* 2000, 6, 585–729 and H. Weber, 'Zur Rolle des Terrors im Kommunismus', *JHK* 1999, 39–62.

10   N. Werth, *Ein Staat gegen sein Volk*, trans. Bertold Galli (Munich: Piper, 2002).

11   *Logique* in the sense of conformity to law, or *zakonomernost'*?

12   J. Baberowski, 'Kulakendeportationen' [see ch. 8, n. 8], 576.

13   Idem, '"Entweder für den Sozialismus oder nach Archangel'sk!" Stalinismus als Feldzug gegen das Fremde', *Osteuropa* 2000, 6, 617–37, here 618–19.

14   L. Viola, '"Tear Up the Evil from the Root": The Children of the *Spetspereselentsy* of the North', *Studia Slavica Finlandensia* 17 (2000), 34–72, here 63; cf. also idem, 'The Other Archipelago: Kulak Deportations to the North in 1930', *SR* 60 (2001), 730–55.

15   Corinna Kuhr discusses the fate of children in the later 1930s in 'Kinder von "Volksfeinden" als Opfer des stalinistischen Terrors 1936–1938', in Plaggenborg (ed.), *Stalinismus*, 391–417 and, more briefly, 'Children of "Enemies of the People" as Victims of the Great Purges', *CMR* 39 (1998), 209–20.

16   G. Alexopoulos, *Stalin's Outcasts* (Ithaca, NY and London: Cornell University Press, 2003).

17   P.M. Hagenloh, '"Socially Harmful Elements" and the Great Terror', in Fitzpatrick (ed.), *Stalinism*, 286–308; D.R. Shearer, 'Crime and Social Disorder in Stalin's Russia: A Reassessment of the Great Retreat and the Origins of Mass Repression', *CMR* 39 (1998), 119–48; idem, 'Social Disorder, Mass Repression and the NKVD During the 1930s', *CMR* 42 (2001), 505–34. Shearer updates his findings in 'Social Disorder, Mass Repression and the NKVD During the 1930s', in McLoughlin and McDermott (eds), *Stalin's Terror* (see n. 3), 85–117. Sarah Davies uses records in Novosibirsk (and St Petersburg) in her 'The Crime of "Anti-Soviet Agitation" in the Soviet Union in the 1930s', *CMR* 39 (1998), 149–57.

18   Shearer, 'Social Disorder', 521, 524–5: thus in western Siberia, which Shearer has studied closely, 9,000 arrests had been made by November 1935, half of which led to convictions by *troiki*, while the others were handed over to the courts.

19 G.T. Rittersporn states that the 260,000 convictions by *troiki* in 1934–6 represented 8.7% of the total number of convictions. 'Extra-Judicial Repression and the Courts: Their Relationship in the 1930s', in P.H. Solomon Jr. (ed.), *Reforming Justice in Russia, 1864–1996* (Armonk, NY and London, 1996), 211.

20 L.A. Rimmel, 'A Microcosm of Terror, or Class Warfare in Leningrad: The March 1935 Exile of "Alien" Elements', *JGOE* 48 (2000), 528–51 (first published in Bulletin no. 3 of the Stalin-Era Research and Archive Project (SERAP), Toronto, 1998). Cf. idem, 'Another Kind of Fear: The Kirov Murder and the End of Bread Rationing in Leningrad', *SR* 56 (1997), 481–99, based on *svodki* compiled by local Party officials, where she shows that ordinary folk connected the assassination in various ways with anticipated improvements in food supply, which had been announced a few days earlier. For more on this angle see O.V. Khlevniuk and R.W. Davies, 'The End of Rationing in the Soviet Union, 1934–1935', *EAS* 51 (1999), 557–610.

21 A.W. Knight, *Who Killed Kirov?: The Kremlin's Greatest Mystery* (New York: Hill and Wang, 1999). Knight saw Kirov's personal papers but not those from the former NKVD. Her earlier works were as follows: *Beria: Stalin's First Lieutenant* (Princeton, NJ: Princeton University Press, 1993); *The KGB: Police and Politics in the Soviet Union* (Boston: Unwin Hyman, 1988).

22 A. Kirilina, author of *Neizvestnyi Kirov* (St Petersburg, 2001), takes the now more generally accepted view that Stalin did not actually arrange the assassination but just exploited it for political ends. Her earlier work on this topic has appeared in French as *L'Assassinat de Kirov: destin d'un stalinien, 1888–1934* (Paris: Du Seuil, 1995). This view is shared by M. Lenoe, 'Did Stalin Kill Kirov and Does It Matter?', *JMH* 74 (2002), 352–80, who comments (378) that 'the Kirov case will never be closed'.

23 W. Hedeler, *Chronik der Moskauer Schauprozesse 1936, 1937 und 1938: Planung, Inszenierung und Wirkung* (Berlin: Akademie-Verlag, 2003); cf. idem (ed.), *Stalin'scher Terror 1934–1941: eine Forschungsbilanz* (Berlin: BasisDruck, 2002) (neither volume currently available; reviewed in *Neue Zürcher Zeitung*, 25 February 2004). In the McLoughlin and McDermott volume noted above (n. 3) Hedeler has an article on the third Moscow trial (34–55), in which he compares the published proceedings with the original stenographic report. R. Conquest's magisterial study of 1968 was revised as *The Great Terror: A Reassessment* (London and New York: Hutchinson, 1990).

24 M. Ellman, 'The Soviet 1937 Provincial Show Trials: Carnival or Terror?', *EAS* 53 (2001), 1221–33; Fitzpatrick's article appeared in *RR* 52 (1993), 299–320. In a sequel, 'The Soviet 1937–1938 Provincial Show Trials Revisited', *EAS* 55 (2003), 1305–21, Ellman examines the 'reversal of verdicts' and releases of prisoners in 1939 and sharpens his criticism of Fitzpatrick: 'the danger of focussing on the Potemkin aspect . . . rather than the real side is that it can lead to prettifying the Terror' (1312). A 'culturalist' approach to the topic is taken by J.A. Cassiday, *The Enemy on Trial: Early Soviet Courts on Stage and Screen* (DeKalb, IL: Northern Illinois University Press, 2000), who sees the proceedings as a 'civic ritual'.

25 There is much on this theme in *JHK*; see also W.J. Chase, *Enemies Within the Gates? The Communist International and the Stalinist Repression, 1934–1939* (New Haven, CT and London: Yale University Press, 2001), which contains many important documents in English translation (by V.A. Staklo); see especially Document 45 (309), which reproduces lists compiled in 1939 of arrested ECCI officials. Chase sees these men as 'instruments of their own downfall' (227) because until their arrest they had willingly promoted the vigilance campaign. See also B. Studer and B. Unfried, *Der stalinische Parteikader: identitätsstiftende Praktiken und Diskurse in der Sowjetunion der 1930er Jahre* (Cologne and Vienna: Böhlau, 2001) and idem, articles cited in Chapter 12, n. 33.

26 J.A. Getty *et al.*, 'Victims of the Soviet Penal System in the Prewar Years: A First Approach on the Basis of Archival Evidence', *AHR* 98 (1993), 1017–49 (and later correspondence).

27 Getty and O.V. Naumov, *The Road to Terror: Stalin and the Self-Destruction of the Bolsheviks, 1932–1939* (New Haven, CT and London: Yale University Press, 1999); Getty, 'Afraid of Their Shadows: The Bolshevik Recourse to Terror, 1932–1938', in Hildermeier (ed.), *Stalinismus*, 169–91; idem, 'Mr. Ezhov Goes to Moscow: The Rise of a Stalinist Police Chief', in Husband (ed.), *Human Tradition* [see Chapter 8, n. 44], 157–74; idem, '"Excesses Are Not Permitted": Mass Terror and Stalinist Governance in the Late 1930s', *RR* 61 (2002), 113–38.

28 B. McLouglin, '"Vernichtung des Fremden": der "Grosse Terror" in der USSR, 1937–1938', *JHK* 2000/2001, 50–88; R. Binner and M. Junge, 'Wie der Terror "gross" wurde: Massenmord und Lagerhaft nach Befehl 00447', *CMR* 42 (2001), 557–614, 43 (2002), 181–228. In the *Stalin's Terror* volume (n. 3), McLoughlin sums up the current state of knowledge on these matters in 'Mass Operations of the NKVD, 1937–8: A Survey', 118–52. Two Russian authors, N. Petrov and A. Roginsky, deal here (153–72) with the 'Polish operation' in an article first published in L.S. Yeremina (ed.), *Repressii protiv poliakov i pol'skikh grazhdan* (Moscow, 1997), 22–43. See also M. Ilič, 'The Great Terror in Leningrad: A Quantitative Analysis', *EAS* 52 (2000), 1515–34, also in Wheatcroft (ed.), *Challenging Traditional Views*, 147–70.

29 The text (abbreviated) is in Getty and Naumov, *Road to Terror*; a complete version may be found in R. Kokurin and N.V. Petrov (eds), *Gulag 1917–1960* (Moscow: Mezhdunar. fond Demokratiia, 2000), 96–104.

30 T. Martin, 'The Origins of Soviet Ethnic Cleansing', *JMH* 70 (98), 812–61 (for 1937–8, 852 ff.); idem, 'Terror gegen Nationen in der Sowjetunion', *Osteuropa* 50 (2000), 6, 606–16 and 'Stalinist Forced Relocation Policies: Patterns, Causes, Consequences', in M. Weiner and S. Russell (eds), *Demography and National Security* (New York: Berghahn Books, 2001), 305–39, where he constructs an original typology of deportations (309). Martin has also written a standard account of Soviet nationality policy in general: *The Affirmative Action Empire: Nations and Nationalism in the Soviet Union, 1923–1939* (Ithaca, NY and London: Cornell University Press, 2002).

31 E.D. Weitz, 'Racial Politics Without the Concept of Race: Re-evaluating Soviet Ethnic and National Purges', *SR* 61 (2002), 1–29, with comments by F. Hirsch, A. Weiner and A. Lemon, 30–61 and Weitz's reply, 62–5.

32 N.M. Naimark, *Fires of Hatred: Ethnic Cleansing in Twentieth-Century Europe* (Cambridge, MA: Harvard University Press, 2001), 85–107. Naimark is best known for his *The Russians in Germany: A History of the Soviet Zone of Occupation, 1945–1949* (Cambridge, MA: Belknap Press, 1995), and has also co-edited *The Establishment of Communist Regimes in Eastern Europe, 1944–1949* (Boulder, CO and London: Westview, 1997).

33 A.J. Rieber, 'Repressive Population Transfers in Central and Eastern Europe, 1939–1950', in idem (ed.), *Forced Migration in Central and Eastern Europe, 1939–1950* (London: Frank Cass, 2000). This volume contains in translation an important article (28–45) by N.S. Lebedeva on the deportation of the Polish population in 1939–41 and the Katyn' massacre.

34 J.O. Pohl, *The Stalinist Penal System: A Short History of Soviet Repression and Terror, 1935–1953* (Jefferson, NC and London: McGarland, 1997); idem, *Ethnic Cleansing in the USSR, 1937–1949* (Westport, CT and London: Greenwood, 1999); see the review by M. Gelb in *RR* 59 (2000), 472–4.

35 D. Pohl, 'Stalinistische Massenverbrechen in der Ukraine 1936–1953: ein Ueberblick', *JHK* 1997, 325–37. He points to 'significant uncertainties' in establishing a total figure for convictions or deportations (336). S. Yekelchyk, whose historiographical studies were referred to in Chapter 10, gives a detailed picture of a police sweep in Kiev in 1934, which was directed against nationalists as well as social marginals: 'The Making of a "Proletarian Capital": Patterns of Stalinist Social Policy in Kiev in the Mid-1930s', *EAS* 50 (1998), 1229–44, here 1233–6. See also, for the later years, Jeffrey Burds, 'Gender and Policing in Soviet Western Ukraine, 1944–1948', *CMR* 42 (2001), 279–320.

36 A. Anušauskas, 'La composition et les méthodes des organes de sécurité soviétiques en Lituanie, 1940–1953', *CMR* 42 (2001), 321–56 (translated); cf. idem (ed.), *The Anti-Soviet Resistance in the Baltic States* (Vilnius: Vilspa, 1999), the first such study to be based on documentary sources; cf. V. Kasauskiane's 'Deportations from Lithuania under Stalin, 1940–1953', *Lithuanian Historical Studies* (Vilnius) 3 (1998), 73–82; H. Strods and M. Kott, 'The File on Operation "Priboi": A Reassessment of the Mass Deportations of 1941', *Journal of Baltic Studies* 33 (2002).

37 D. O'Sullivan, 'Reconstruction and Repression: The Role of M.A. Suslov in Lithuania, 1944–1946', *Forum OIZ*, 2000, 175–208. O'Sullivan is an editor of this journal.

38 E.A. Allworth (ed.), *The Tatars of the Crimea: Return to the Homeland*, 2nd rev. edn (Durham, NC: Duke University Press, 1998).

39 B.G. Williams, 'The Hidden Ethnic Cleansing of Muslims in the Soviet Union: The Exile and Repatriation of the Crimean Tatars', *Journal of Contemporary History* 37 (2002), 323–48. Williams is the author of *The Crimean Tatars: The Diaspora Experience and the Forging of a Nation* (Leiden: Brill, 2001).

40 J. Baberowski, *Der Feind ist überall: Stalinismus im Kaukasus* (Munich: DVA, 2002).

41 On Poles, see J.W. Borejsa, 'La Russie moderne et l'Union soviétique dans l'historiographie polonaise après 1989', *CMR* 40 (99), 529–46; and on Finns and Koreans, see M. Gelb, 'An Early Soviet Ethnic Deportation: The Far Eastern Koreans', *RR* 54 (1995), 389–412; idem, "Karelian Fever": The Finnish Immigrant Community During Stalin's Purges', *EAS* 45 (1993), 1091–1116; idem, 'The Western Finnic Minorities and the Origins of the Stalinist Nationalities Deportations', *Nationalities Papers* 24 (1996), 237–67; idem, 'Ethnicity During the Ezhovshchina: A Historiography', in J. Morison (ed.), *Ethnic and National Issues in Russian and East European History: Selected Papers from the Fifth World Congress of Central and Eastern European Studies, Warsaw, 1995* (Basingstoke and New York: Macmillan, 1999), 192–213. Cf. also A. Kostiainen (Turku), 'The Finns of Soviet Karelia as a Target of Stalin's Terror', ibid., 214–29, who shows that this group were 17 times more likely to be repressed than Russians in Karelia (226) and gives tentative figures for each 'ethnic'; half the *c.* 15,000 Finns killed were from this autonomous republic. The German contingent was massively reinforced in 1941, and again after 1943 with the advent of Axis prisoners of war. For an introduction to this last problem, see A. Hilger *et al.* (eds), *Sowjetische Militärtribunale*, vol. I, *Die Verurteilung deutscher Kriegsgefangener, 1941–1953* (Cologne: Böhlau, 2001). On the Japanese, see: T. Kato, 'Biographische Anmerkungen zu den japanischen Opfern des stalinistischen Terrors in der UdSSR', *JHK* 1998, 330–43 and an unpublished dissertation (Zurich, 2001) by R. Dähler.

42 S. Schattenberg, 'Die Frage nach den Tätern', *Osteuropa* 50 (2000), 638–55, here 641–2.

43 Weitz, 'Racial Politics', 26.

44 N.V. Petrov, 'Les transformations du personnel des organes de sécurité soviétique, 1922–1953', *CMR* 42 (2001), 375–96 (an article in *Forum OIZ* 5 (2001), 2, 91–120 covers much the same ground); cf. also D.R. Shearer in ibid., 513, for the number of such personnel: a slow growth from 124,000 in late 1934 to 182,000 in 1938 and 213,000 in 1940, including militia and railway police.

45 V. Semystiaha, 'The Role and Place of Secret Collaborators in the Informational Activity of the GPU-NKVD in the 1920s and 1930s (on the basis of materials of the Donbass region)', ibid., 231–44.

46 J.R. Harris, '"Dual Subordination"? The Political Police and the Party in the Urals Region, 1918–1953', ibid., 423–46. He provides more detail in 'The Purging of Local Cliques in the Urals Region, 1936–1937', in Fitzpatrick (ed.), *Stalinism*, 262–85.

47 P.M. Hagenloh, '"Chekist in Essence, Chekist in Spirit": Regular and Political Police in the 1930s', ibid., 447–76, esp. n. 92 (474). For the earlier article, see n. 13 above.

48   M. Parrish, *Soviet Security and Intelligence Organizations, 1917–1990: A Biographical Dictionary and Review of Literature in English*, foreword by R. Conquest (New York: Greenwood, 1992); idem, *The Lesser Terror: Soviet State Security, 1939–1953* (Westport, CT and London: Praeger, 1996), esp. 100, 116, 167, 170, 174. On the organs' activities abroad, the documents collected by V. Mitrokhin are revealing. C. Andrew and V. Mitrokhin, *The Sword and the Shield: The Archive and the Secret History of the KGB* (London and NewYork: Basic Books, 1999), has seven chapters on the Stalin era.

49   M. Jansen and N. Petrov, *Stalin's Loyal Executioner: People's Commissar Nikolai Ezhov, 1895–1940* (Stanford, CA: Hoover Institution Press, 2002).

50   Getty, 'Mr. Ezhov Goes to Moscow: The Rise of a Stalinist Police Chief', in Husband (ed.), *Human Tradition* [see Chapter 8, n. 44], 157–74.

51   Rittersporn, 'Between Revolution and Daily Routine: Youth and Violence in the Soviet Union in the Interwar Period', in Kuhr-Korolev *et al.*, *Sowjetjugend* (see n. 4), 80.

52   Davies, *Popular Opinion*, 113.

53   Rimmel, 'Microcosm' [see n. 20], 537–50.

54   S. Fitzpatrick, 'Signals from Below: Soviet Letters of Denunciation of the 1930s', in idem and R. Gellately (eds), *Accusatory Practices: Denunciation in Modern European History, 1789–1989* (Chicago and London: University of Chicago Press, 1997), 85–120 (previously in *JMH* 65 (1996), 831–66); J. Baberowski, '"Die Verfasser von Erklärungen jagen den Parteiführern einen Schrecken ein": Denunziation und Terror in der stalinistischen Sowjetunion 1928–1941', in F. Ross and A. Landwehr (eds), *Denunziation und Justiz: historische Dimensionen eines sozialen Phänomens* (Tübingen: diskord, 2000), 165–98. Cf. also G. Alexopoulos, 'Exposing Illegality and Oneself: Complaint and Risk in Stalin's Russia', in P.H. Solomon Jr. (ed.), *Reforming Justice* [see n. 19], 168–89; idem, 'Victim Talk: Defense Testimony and Denunciation under Stalin', in Hoffmann and Kotsonis, *Russian Modernity*, 204–20; F.-X. Nérard, 'Les organes de contrôle d'état et les journaux dans l'URSS de Stalin: des auxiliaires de la police politique?', *CMR* 42 (2001), 263–77. For surveillance in the regime's early years: P. Holquist, '"Information is the Alpha and Omega of Our Work": Bolshevik Surveillance in Its Pan-European Context', *JMH* 69 (1997), 415–50; cf. also idem, 'State Violence as Technique: The Logic of Violence in Soviet Totalitarianism', in A. Weiner (ed.), *Landscaping the Human Garden . . .* (Stanford, CA: Stanford University Press, 2002), 23–32. O. Khakhordin stresses (and perhaps over-stresses) the importance of denunciation in *The Collective and the Individual: A Study of Practices* (Berkeley and Los Angeles: University of California Press, 1999), 73.

55   A. Applebaum, *Gulag: A History of the Soviet Camps* (New York and London: Allen Lane, 2003). Ralf Stettner's comprehensive study, *'Archiepel GULAG': Stalins Zwangslager: Terrorinstrument und Wirtschaftsgigant: Entstehung, Organisation und Funktion des sowjetischen Lagersystems 1928–1956* (Paderborn: F. Schöningh, 1996) suffered from lack of archival access. See also E. Bacon, *The Gulag At War: Stalin's Forced Labour System in the Light of the Archives* (Basingstoke and New York: Macmillan, 1994, 2nd rev. edn 1996); G. Ivanova, *Gulag v sisteme totalitarnogo gosudarstva*, (Moscow: Mosk. obshchestvennyi nauchnyi fond, 1997); trans. C. Flath, ed. D. Raleigh as *Labor Camp Socialism: the Gulag in the Totalitarian System* (Armonk, NY and London: M.E. Sharpe, 2000). A moving photographic record of the Gulag has been compiled by a Polish ex-inmate: T. Kizny, *Goulag*, ed. D. Roynette, trans. L. Dyèvre (Paris: Acropole, 2003).

56   F. Varese, 'The Society of the *Vory v zakone*, 1930s–1950s', *CMR* 39 (1998), 515–38. Varese is an authority on the present-day Russian mafia.

57   D.J. Nordlander, 'Origins of a Gulag Capital: Magadan and Stalinist Control in the Early 1930s', *SR* 57 (1998), 791–812; in a later article on this subject, 'Magadan and the Evolution of the Dalstroi Bosses in the 1930s', *CMR* 42 (2001), 649–65, he argues that the earlier 'utopian' (or 'liberal') chiefs gave way in the later 1930s to pragmatists who presided over 'an unyielding camp regimen'. Cf. also J.A. Bone (Chicago), 'A la

recherche d'un Komsomol perdu . . .' (on the substitution of forced labourers in the building of Komsomol'sk-na-Amure), *Revue d'études slaves* 71 (1999), 59–92; M.J. Bollinger, 'Did 12,000 Gulag Prisoners Die on the *Dzhurma*?', *Russian History/Histoire russe* 29 (2002), 65–78 – about an incident on the Northern Sea Route in 1933–4: the answer is 'no', but this finding does not detract from 'the injustice, horror and death' of millions (78).

58 N. Baron, 'Conflict and Complicity: The Expansion of the Karelian Gulag, 1923–1933', *CMR* 42 (2001), 615–47; idem, 'Production and Terror: The Operation of the Karelian Gulag, 1933–1939', ibid., 43 (2002), 139–80. (Baron's thesis (Birmingham, 2001) was on Karelia, 1920–1937.) For the region to the east see Judith Pallot, 'Forced Labour for Forestry in the Twentieth Century: History of Colonization and Settlement in the North of Perm *Oblast*', *EAS* 54 (2002), 1055–83. Baron also covers the construction of the Belomor canal, the subject of a study by the 'culturalist' Cynthia Ruder, *Making History for Stalin: The Story of the Belomor Canal* (Gainesville, FL: University Press of Florida, 1999), which has a very different emphasis. On Gorky's role in 'Belomor', see now D. Tolczyk, *See No Evil . . .* (New Haven, CT and London: Yale University Press, 1999).

59 A. Brossat *et al.* (eds), *Ozerlag, 1937–1964: le système du Goulag: traces perdues, mémoires réveillées d'un camp stalinien* (Paris: Eds Autrement, 1991).

60 S.V. Mironenko, L. Niethammer *et al.* (eds), *Soujetische Speziallager in Deutschland 1945–1950.* Vol. II: R. Possakel (ed.), *Soujetische Dokumente zur Lagerpolitik* (Berlin: Akademie-Verlag, 1998). (Russian edn Moscow, 2001.)

61 M. Parrish, *The Lesser Terror* . . . (see n. 48).

62 A. Lustiger, *Rotbuch: Stalin und die Juden: die tragische Geschichte des Jüdischen Antifaschistischen Komitees und der soujetischen Juden* (Berlin: Aufbau-Verlag, 1998); cf. J. Rubenstein and V.P. Naumov (eds), *Stalin's Secret Pogrom: The Postwar Inquisition of the JAFC*, trans. L.E. Wolfson (New Haven, CT: Yale University Press, 2001); S. Feinstein, *Staline, Israel et les Juifs* (Paris: PUF, 2001).

63 S. Madiewski, '1953: la déportation des juifs soviétiques était-elle programmée?', *CMR* 41 (2000), 561–8.

64 N. Tolstoi, *Victims of Yalta* (London: Hodder and Stoughton, 1977); cf. N. Bethell, *The Last Secret: Forcible Repatriation to Russia, 1944–1947* (London and New York: Hodder and Stoughton, 1987).

65 P.M. Polian, *Deportiert nach Hause: soujetische Kriegsgefangene im 'Dritten Reich' und ihre Repatriierung* (Kriegsfolgen-Forschung ed. S. Karner, vol. 2) (Munich and Vienna: Oldenbourg, 2001). Polian has since supplied details of the (more humane) French role in the return of 10,000 prisoners: 'Le repatriement des citoyens soviétiques depuis la France et les zones françaises d'occupation en Allemagne et Autriche', *CMR* 41 (2000), 165–90.

66 P.H. Solomon Jr., *Soviet Criminal Justice under Stalin* (Cambridge and New York: Cambridge University Press, 1996); cf. also his 'The Bureaucratization of Criminal Justice under Stalin' in idem (ed.), *Reforming Justice* [see n. 19], 228–55.

67 For example, the few pages devoted to the Military Collegium of the USSR Supreme Court (235, 261–3) do not mention the number of sentences it passed or the abbreviated procedure it employed.

68 Y. Gorlizky, 'Rules, Incentives and Soviet Campaign Justice after World War II', *EAS* 51 (1999), 1245–65.

69 Rittersporn, 'Extra-Judicial Repression' (see n. 19), 207–27.

70 O.V. Khlevniuk in ibid., 201.

12 No longer a riddle?

Aspects of Soviet foreign policy

From Munich to Barbarossa

The diplomatic origins of World War II are well-trodden ground. Now that the Soviet archives are (in principle) open to Western researchers, one naturally asks whether major new insights have been gleaned on Moscow's policy towards other European powers during and after the 1938 Munich crisis. (The earlier 1930s deserve separate treatment, as does Soviet wartime diplomacy.) To answer the question summarily, fresh light has indeed been thrown on Soviet conduct at crucial junctures, but the inner recesses of Stalin's mind (and it was he who took the decisions) still invite speculation. First, we may outline the parameters of contemporary scholarly thinking and then look at what has been written of late on the main 'landmarks' in chronological order.

What may be termed the 'classical' interpretation sees Stalin's policy as pragmatic, ambivalent and flexible: options were kept open for as long as possible before a final decision was taken, and this was based on sober calculation of the 'balance of forces' and state interest. The 'collective security' line, long identified with Litvinov, was not definitively abandoned until mid-August 1939, two weeks or so before signature of the Molotov–Ribbentrop pact. The chief reason why it was held to for so long was the leadership's recognition of the USSR's relative military weakness vis-à-vis Germany and Japan, the most likely aggressor states, which would take several years to overcome; in the interim, provocation had to be avoided and allies sought among the Western democracies. Yet Moscow had no illusions about Anglo-French leanings toward appeasement and with some justification suspected these powers of seeking to drive Hitler eastward while they remained neutral. Meanwhile, Stalin kept in reserve, so to speak, the policy option of 'self-sufficiency', that is, leaving the 'imperialist' powers to fight it out among themselves while the USSR remained neutral, with the prospect of intervening when hostilities were over to recast Europe in a socialist mould; this option could be stretched to encompass territorial expansion westward at the expense of the USSR's smaller neighbours. However, the argument runs, this course was only taken at the last moment, under duress and in desperation.

In recent scholarship, the 'classical' view is best represented by Geoffrey Roberts (Cork, Ireland), while Jonathan Haslam (Cambridge) offers a more nuanced variant of it.[1] At the other end of the spectrum are those sometimes called 'revisionists' (a term best avoided since it is used in a contrary sense in regard to Soviet domestic affairs; 'realists' might be a better label). Realists pay greater heed to the ideological foundations of Stalin's thinking and his fondness for Machiavellian tactics; the more extreme see the *Vozhd'* as harbouring a deeply ingrained antagonism towards Anglo-French capitalism that drew on the experience of Allied intervention in the Russian civil war, while remaining alert to the chance of an (albeit temporary) accommodation with the Nazis, whose 'petty-bourgeois' social base made them vulnerable to revolutionary forces abetted by Soviet armed might. In this perspective, the Soviet military build-up in the 1930s assumes a more sinister, potentially offensive character. This interpretation is reflected to a greater or lesser degree in works by Robert Tucker, Richard Raack and (an extreme view) Joachim Hoffmann.[2]

This attempt to indicate the main lines of the argument is admittedly an over-simplification. It would be wrong to draw the conclusion that the field is polarized; on the contrary, there is much common ground. Just as most realists would shrink from backing the 'Suvorov hypothesis' (see below), so classicists would reject as naïve the benign view of Stalin's intentions commonly held at the time by anti-appeasers in the West. Fortunately, all writers on the topic can now draw upon the exceptionally well-documented, indeed magisterial, study by Gabriel Gorodetsky (Tel Aviv), *Grand Delusion*,[3] in which British policy-makers are indicted for short-sightedness almost as vehemently as are the familiar follies of the two dictators. This hefty volume concentrates on the two years between the Nazi-Soviet pact and the invasion; particularly welcome is the attention devoted to lesser players in the drama such as Romania, Turkey and even Vichy France, whose role is usually overlooked.

Over the last decade, Russian historians have produced more than 60 volumes of documents on pre-war Soviet foreign policy.[4] Against this background, the Western contributions look thin,[5] but Georgii Dimitrov's correspondence with Stalin has been published in English with a knowledgeable commentary by Alexander Dallin.[6] Among the eight documents from our period is one (pp. 153–63) containing Stalin's oral remarks on 7 September 1939, which have been taken by realists as his 'genuine' (that is, Machiavellian) reasons for concluding the pact. (This document appeared in Russia already in 1989.) Another important source, published for the first time in English in 2002, is the verbatim minutes of the Central Committee meeting held on 14–17 April 1940, with military commanders present, to review the (mediocre) results of the Winter War against Finland.[7]

Anyone embarking on research in this field might well begin with the highly competent general survey by Caroline Kennedy-Pipe (Durham),[8] who begins her chapter on 'the search for security' by noting that there were two rival orien-tations in Moscow: collective-security advocates and those who 'favoured a tactical rapprochement with Germany' (p. 36), such as Molotov. (Kaganovich, Zhdanov and Vyshinsky should be added to make up the 'group of four' discerned by Albert Resis of DeKalb, IL).[9] As a classicist, Kennedy-Pipe believes that 'the story of the 1930s is the story of the USSR under siege'; the fragility of the political and economic system meant that the USSR badly needed allies, yet Stalin mistrusted them unduly. It is perhaps not by chance that she sees him wanting 'buffer states' in the Baltic but omits to mention the 1940 annexations in their chronological context; when they are referred to incidentally later, it is just to note the 'positive' effect they had on Soviet security (pp. 48, 53).

Everyone agrees that the USSR was aggrieved at being excluded from the Munich conference (September 1938), at which the Western powers (in)famously sacrificed the Czechs to Hitler's appetite. Zora Steiner (Cambridge) traces the development of Soviet policy towards its ally in Prague from the beginning of that year, making use of Litvinov's (recently published) letters to Stalin as well as diplomatic correspondence. Her conclusions are unsurprising: the USSR had no intention of helping the putative victim militarily unless France took concerted action, adhering literally to the terms of the two 1935 pacts; since the French, hamstrung by their British ally, were unwilling to commit themselves, these particular 'chestnuts' (to use Stalin's celebrated later term) were left to perish in the fire. This scenario was foreordained: 'the Soviet leaders . . . never considered taking independent action to assist Czechoslovakia, nor did they anticipate that the French would come to their ally's assistance should the Germans invade' (p. 769). Probably Stalin never decided what to do if the French reacted strongly. As it was, Moscow did at least remonstrate with the Poles when they menaced their unfortunate neighbours, and the military moves made during the crisis served as 'a demonstration of Soviet resolve' (p. 770). Steiner concludes modestly that her study just adds detail on internal Moscow politics and that final certainty must await examination of *all* the relevant archives. With regard to the military preparations, Hugh Ragsdale (formerly Alabama), who has scrutinized the Romanian records, adduces evidence that, despite that country's generally anti-Soviet stance, it *was* willing to allow the passage of sizeable Soviet ground forces and aircraft overflights.[10]

Hitler's march into Prague led Britain to guarantee the security of Romania, Greece – and Poland. This unilateral move was regarded askance in Moscow, which again had not been consulted, and led indirectly to the fall of Litvinov (3 May), a topic on which more information has recently become available. On its symbolic effect, all agree. Roberts[11] contests the prevailing view that the (Jewish) commissar's dismissal was due to his identification with a 'soft' line favouring the Western democracies; he points out that it was 'not followed by any shift whatsoever in policy towards Germany' since Molotov, on succeeding him, displayed 'the utmost vigour in pursuing negotiations with the Western allies' ('Alliance', p. 397). Jonathan Haslam agrees with the last point but considers Roberts's explanation 'most implausible' ('Soviet–German Relations', pp. 793–4). There is good evidence (notably in Ambassador Maisky's memoirs) that, when Litvinov was summoned to the Kremlin meeting (27 April) that sealed his fate, Stalin and especially Molotov were extremely hostile (the two ministers had clashed on several occasions). The NKVD is known to have been preparing a 'case' against Litvinov (which in the event was not pursued), and Haslam suggests that this body may have served as a 'back channel' for communication with Berlin. Donal O'Sullivan points out that the Foreign Affairs commissariat (NKID) was in eclipse at the time, when policy was actually made by the Politburo (essentially, Stalin and Molotov); Litvinov was no 'Westerner' but 'an example of the orthodox Leninist–Stalinist influence in the NKID', who could decide nothing independently of his boss.[12] Albert Resis drives the point home: Litvinov had 'irreparably discredited himself with his masters' by his willingness to accept the feeble Anglo-French proposals as a basis for negotiation and, above all, 'had committed an unforgivable offence against Stalinist *Realpolitik*' by recommending that the putative allies should agree 'to bar separate negotiations with Germany on matters affecting east European states'.[13]

This did not mean definitive abandonment of the collective-security approach, only that the USSR would henceforward insist irrevocably on stiff conditions (a minimal five-year term and specific military commitments) for a triple alliance, which the Western powers could and would not meet. The final sticking point was whether the future allies should effectively restrict the sovereignty of the intermediate east European states by imposing security guarantees they did not all want, especially where this meant permitting transit of Soviet troops. Roberts provides a convincing blow-by-blow account of the diplomatic exchanges and the actual talks ('Alliance', pp. 399 ff.). As he puts it, 'the wonder is not that the negotiations failed but that they got so far' (p. 408). The crucial decision in favour of a pro-Axis orientation was taken on or about 11 August – some three days before Voroshilov, on 14 August, faced the Allied mission with a demand he expected to be answered in the negative. Thus already before the talks collapsed the die had been cast, when Moscow opted for 'a security policy based on expansion into eastern Europe and friendship with Hitler's Germany' (p. 409). Roberts sees Stalin acting with reluctance ('Alliance', p. 384), but if so it was an emotion tinged with *Schadenfreude* that the old foes of 1918–20 had been humiliated and skilfully outwitted.

Enough ink has been spilled on the moral iniquities of 'the Pact'. Judged more pertinently by the criteria of *Realpolitik*, it proved to be a giant miscalculation for the Soviet leader who (like most others, to be sure) reckoned that, having turned Hitler's designs westward, he would enjoy a lengthy interlude in which to consolidate Soviet defences. This was to overestimate France's ability to resist the Nazi onslaught when launched in earnest (May 1940). What for the West was the 'phoney war' era saw much of eastern Europe carved up between the signatories to the Pact and its secret protocols.

On 17 September, Soviet troops embarked on the 'liberation' of western Belarus and Ukraine. This action is viewed by the Russian historian Sergei Sluch as having *de facto* involved the USSR in World War II.[14] Purists will object to such a formulation (was the United States 'at war' with the Axis before Pearl Harbor?), but he provides Western readers with interesting detail on German-Soviet military co-operation in occupied Poland. Anglo-Saxon authors have shown less interest in this theme recently, perhaps because it was dealt with so thoroughly some years ago by Jan Gross.[15]

A rather different picture obtains in regard to the Baltic states and Finland. A recognized authority on the history of the region, David Kirby (London) contributes an article to a general miscellany which stresses the differences between the three republics' fate.[16] Whereas the Western democracies could (or would) do little to help the Balts, the Finns at least won their moral support. The British are criticized by P.W. Doerr for taking a 'frigid but unprovocative' line towards the Soviets during the first months of the Finnish Winter war: placing *Realpolitik* before ideology, they tried to salvage at least a degree of economic co-operation and did not allow sympathy for the Finns to endanger relations with Moscow.[17] Some Finnish historians, not surprisingly, express distaste (to use no stronger expression) at such prudence. Timo Vihavainen of Helsinki, whose views are available in Russian, has no doubt about exclusive Soviet responsibility for the 'great tragedy' of the Winter War; the Finns were quite justified in rejecting Stalin's territorial demands and their vigorous defence of their country's independence spared it the cruel fate meted out to fellow neutrals on the Baltic's southern shore.[18]

In the documentary volume on Moscow's post-war analysis (see n. 7), Harold Shukman notes that 'Stalin quickly tired of negotiation and resolved to settle the matter by force', gravely underestimating his adversaries' determination and ability to resist; when it was all over he blamed the Red Army's failures on defective intelligence and other technical shortcomings in 'a conspiracy to deflect criticism' from the political leadership, which the senior officers who participated in the discussion were too scared to mention.[19] According to the US military historian Carl Van Dyke, 'the war revealed many deficiencies in the Red Army's ability to conduct contemporary warfare'; Soviet casualties, officially put at 48,745 killed and 158,863 wounded, may understate reality by half. Diplomatically, the Winter War led to a rapprochement between Helsinki and Berlin that eventuated in a further round of armed struggle in 1941–4.[20] This latter conflict and its sequel have so far received inadequate attention in English, but Ruth Büttner argues plausibly that Stalin respected Finnish politicians' skill and feared adverse Western reactions to a takeover of that country.[21]

Despite the initial setback, 1940 was 'a happy year for Stalin', or so at least two German historians contend.[22] He had consolidated his personal rule and augmented Soviet territory in key strategic regions. But these successes were superficial, for in reality industrial production was in decline – even the privileged defence sector was having problems. Yet these difficulties were concealed by vainglorious propaganda, which deceived the leaders themselves as much as the population.

Soviet–German relations

This 'snapshot' view can be substantiated by glancing at the uneasy course of Soviet–German relations. In Moscow, the unexpectedly rapid fall of France elicited a dual response: further annexations in the Baltic and the south-western border region (northern Bukovina, Bessarabia) and a more active policy to frustrate German expansionism in south-eastern Europe. Rivalry over Bulgaria and the Straits led Ribbentrop to invite Molotov to Berlin, with the idea of concluding a second Nazi–Soviet pact that would associate the USSR more closely with the Axis powers and Japan. Molotov, acting on Stalin's instructions, dug in his heels in his incomparable fashion. The Soviet leader wanted a change in the Straits regime, along with bases, to avert a supposed British threat from that quarter, and a mutual assistance pact with Bulgaria, whose government was veering towards the Axis. Angered by this obstructionism, Hitler upped the priority for the attack on Russia, now code-named 'Barbarossa'; this 'became the focal point of a new aggressive strategy . . . the intransigence of the Russians stiffened Hitler's resolve to resort to force'. The crucial directive for the operation was issued on 18 December, one day after the Soviets had made plain their intention to maintain control of the Danube delta.[23] Gorodetsky stresses the importance of these traditional power-political concerns in bringing about the calamitous invasion. He plays down the ideological aspect (which became operative later) but acknowledges that 'the economic advantages were taken into consideration'.

The economic aspects of Soviet–German relations during this period have been closely studied by Karl Heinz Blumenhagen.[24] He reconstructs in minute detail the flow of goods (by type) in each direction, along with the pertinent financial arrangements, and offers new figures for their total value (p. 386). A significant amount of arms and military equipment reached the Soviets, but (despite the book's title) the author does not investigate the role this played in enhancing Soviet military preparedness. A sequel is promised, but this too seems likely to deal with what the Axis powers, rather than the Soviets, gained from the relationship.

As is well known, the USSR kept up deliveries of oil and other essentials until the eve of the invasion. Stalin repeatedly refused to heed warnings about German intentions and the military build-up that he received from Soviet intelligence and diplomatic sources, as well as foreign ones (not least, from Churchill) – a failing so remarkable as to prompt fantastic speculations. Was he just a simpleton? Gorodetsky thinks not, and points to a number of possible explanations:[25] intelligence data were 'massaged' to conform to the leader's presuppositions and their meaning was ambiguous; Stalin expected Hitler to delay an attack until he had defeated Britain, so as to avoid a two-front war; he thought 'moderates' in the German army would prevail over the hard-liners; he expected the Germans to present an ultimatum with limited demands that could be satisfied, rather than to launch all-out war without warning; he was eternally suspicious, and never more so than after the Hess affair, of Britain's willingness to make peace with Germany and send Hitler's legions marching east. The last of these reasons seems to have been the overriding one. In addition, Stalin remembered the lessons of 1914, when a premature Russian mobilization had helped to unleash hostilities, but overlooked the lessons of 1939–40 which showed the Reichswehr's potential for conducting a *Blitzkrieg*.

Did he plan a preventive strike? What Teddy Uldricks in a recent article calls 'the Icebreaker controversy'[26] was set in motion over ten years ago by Viktor Rezun ('Suvorov'), a former security official, who propounded the theory – advanced at the time by none other than Hitler – that the invasion had been a response to preliminary offensive moves on the Soviet side. The extensive literature generated on this topic in Russia and elsewhere, based on close examination of the relevant sources, has shown that the theory lacks justification. Uldricks believes that Stalin's speech of 5 May 1941, in which he urged military academy graduates to adopt an offensive posture, was deliberately leaked in the hope of deterring the Germans from attacking. He warns against the tendency 'to diabolize the Kremlin' and to ignore the ambiguities in Soviet policy, which 'was a complex and frequently shifting balance of elements involving both appeasement and resistance'.[27] As chief of the general staff (since January), Zhukov took the speech as a signal to plan for a pre-emptive strike; but the army's ideas (for a limited operation) were turned down. Gorodetsky brings out the institutional deficiencies that harmed the ultra-secretive process of Soviet decision-making: the army chiefs were not told about the 'great game' of diplomacy that the *Vozhd'* was playing.[28] His detailed account bolsters the traditional picture of a leader who vastly overestimated his own 'genius' and underestimated his adversary's guile. (Had Hitler *not* invaded, Stalin might have launched a strike *later*, but this is to enter the realm of hypothesis.)

Two authors of a popular but well-referenced study of Soviet intelligence speak of Stalin's 'unfettered *hubris*': he believed in his own infallibility and 'unmatchable political flair'; he insisted on serving 'as his own intelligence analyst'; plenty of reliable information came in but it was not properly integrated into policy formulation.[29] They provide fascinating details of the deception (disinformation) operations conducted on both sides, and mention the sorry fate that awaited many loyal Soviet agents. The principal conclusion is that the intelligence services played an unusually large role in the conduct of foreign relations which ultimately proved to be self-defeating, due to the ultra-personalized nature of the system.

Less crucial perhaps, but nonetheless worthy of scholarly attention, is Soviet propaganda (or 'information policy', to use a less loaded term), at home and abroad – a topic on which V.A. Nevezhin is the leading Russian authority. Western writers include Sarah Davies, who in her book on popular opinion in Leningrad (see Chapter 7), examines this aspect in regard to the domestic audience. The efforts to influence foreigners were scrutinized many years ago by David Caute and Paul Hollander.[30] There is more to be said on this now that the archives are accessible. A recent general study of French opinion about the USSR, by Sophie Coeuré,[31] discusses *inter alia* the mechanisms for manipulating travellers and projecting a fallacious view of the system, called here rather portentously 'the most tragic misconception of our age' (p. 290). To a Europe that was 'fatigued and in despair', the Soviet land seemed 'a distant saviour wearing a confusing halo'. Then and later, French intellectuals were reluctant to debate seriously the repressive aspects of Stalinism.

A comparative study of the way public opinion was moulded throughout Western Europe would be of interest, however slight its impact may have been on policy makers. This would involve looking at the role of local Communist parties. Exemplary in this respect is Andrew Thorpe's study of the CPGB,[32] which uses relevant Russian archives and brings out the complexities of its relationship with its Moscow overlords. Although the latter took the major decisions, member parties did have a certain leeway in interpreting them that led to debate and schism. This point is also made by Kevin McDermott and Jeremy Agnew in their general history of the Communist International,[33] in which they argue against 'a crude teleological rendition of Comintern history' and plead for due attention to the 'various socio-political national contexts in which Communist parties worked' (pp. xxiv–xxv). The organization's importance was now greatly reduced; indeed, to please Berlin, Stalin would have dissolved it earlier than he eventually did. On some issues at least 'strict Stalinist discipline . . . coexisted with limited autonomous responses to diverse national and local situations' (p. 191), so that we should be ever alert to the nuances. This is also apparent from 319 coded telegrams sent by the Comintern to its member parties in western Europe between August 1939 and December 1941, now available in French translation.[34]

Even after the Comintern had been formally dissolved in 1943 it continued to exist in secret as 'Institutes 99, 100 and 205', located in the same premises as the old ECCI. Clearly, Stalin intended them to play a role in countries liberated from Nazi rule in eastern Europe and elsewhere.

Stalinism and Cold War origins

For nearly half a century after 1945, most of the world, and Europe in particular, learned to live with the prospect of mass annihilation by nuclear weapons in the event of some miscalculation by the masters of bipolar global politics. The term 'Cold War' scarcely does justice to this long drawn-out confrontation between the two blocs, with its moments of crisis and détente, but is too convenient to discard; here we are concerned solely with the initial phases.[35] Studies of the phenomenon entered upon a new age after 1991 when political passions cooled and, more importantly, research became possible in Russian archives; hitherto the limited amount of information available on Soviet intentions and actions had led to value judgements that were too often clouded by prejudice or ignorance.

The orthodox or 'classical' view blamed the conflict on Stalin's ambitions, the Marxist–Leninist ideological heritage, and the Red Army's predominance in post-war Europe; in some quarters an image was created of overpowering menace that called for resolute counter-measures, and these were then credited with having halted a supposed drive for world hegemony. Subsequently, a revisionist school took shape, whose spokesmen argued that the Kremlin had pursued limited goals, not least on account of the country's post-war economic weakness; this had led the leadership to expect generous aid from its Western allies in reconstruction and collaboration in averting the threat of renewed German aggression; but these legitimate aspirations had been rebuffed, so that blame for the post-war schism rested equally, if not primarily, on the United States as the premier capitalist power. Both these interpretations came under critical scrutiny from post-revisionists (notably, John L. Gaddis) who shifted the focus of debate away from culpability to the inter-relationship of fallacious threat perceptions: governments on both sides had misconstrued each other's intentions and responded to challenges by ill-considered counter-moves that had accelerated the cycle of distrust.

Meanwhile the conventional diplomatic-history approach had been challenged by partisans of international relations theory (IR), political scientists such as M. Kaplan or K. Waltz who applied to this field precepts drawn from US 'behavioral studies', and more particularly the sociology of large organizations. They viewed the global struggle as a process 'managed' by rival geopolitical systems, each of which followed scientifically ascertainable logical rules in mobilizing and projecting its power. IR 'discourse' had much to say about the structure of international politics but left little place for ideas or the human beings who held them. Some of the bolder theorists[36] claimed a predictive power for their analyses, while others were more cautious. The unanticipated collapse of the eastern bloc in 1989–91 dealt a heavier blow to scientific *hubris* than it did to the relatively tentative hypotheses of humanists, who made a comeback. They were aided by the emergence from the shadows of actual Soviet policy makers: the venerable Molotov (d. 1986) was no more, but he had at least given interviews (to Feliks Chuev), while Gromyko and many lesser lights wrote memoirs or engaged in face-to-face contact with journalists and scholars. All this, together with the declassification of most of the long secret sources, opened up the enticing prospect that maybe 'We Now Know' (the title of a work by Gaddis) what, for instance, Stalin's true intentions had been in the post-war world: what opportunities had existed for continued co-operation between the 'Big Three' and why were they not realized?

'The greatest surprise to have come out of the Russian archives', writes Vojtech Mastny, 'is that there was no surprise.'[37] By and large, the private thoughts of the Soviet leaders had conformed to what they had said in public; there was no 'hidden agenda'; neither had there been a well-oiled machine to implement some grand design. Extrapolating, one might add that Soviet foreign policy had evolved by trial and error, in response both to domestic needs and to actions by (potential) adversaries. Although there was less input from below than in other administrations, there had been rivalries between individuals and institutions,[38] so that the tale is one of fumbling and ambivalence, of goals not clearly specified, of awkward decisions put off, of problems 'solved' in contradictory fashion – much as happens anywhere. This finding is reassuring, for it takes us back to the familiar world of human agency with all its limitations. The Stalin who emerges from the archive records is still a paranoid despot, but an ageing one who often finds it hard to make up his mind.

This has become almost a consensus view among a bevy of writers, east and west, whose work appeared more or less simultaneously in the 1990s. Among them are two Moscow State University graduates, Vladislav Zubok and Constantine Pleshakov, whose jointly authored monograph has been published in Russian and English editions, the latter with encouragement from the prestigious Cold War International History Project in Washington, DC.[39] Another research centre that actively fosters such studies is the Norwegian Nobel Institute (Oslo), which sponsored a symposium on the topic in 1998; the papers delivered there have been edited by Odd Arne Westad (London), a specialist in Sino-Soviet relations.[40] On this topic a major international conference was held in Washington in 1996.[41]

Mastny is thus not alone in tracing Cold War origins to Stalin's 'insatiable craving for security': he neither intended nor expected his actions to lead to a prolonged confrontation with the Western allies, yet this outcome was 'predetermined' since his fundamental assumptions lay so far apart from theirs. For Hannes Adomeit, a specialist on Soviet German policy, Stalin's conduct was governed by an 'imperial and ideological paradigm' which involved 'a close interrelationship between power and ideology in domestic politics and between imperial and revolutionary purposes in foreign policy'.[42] The Soviet leader reckoned that he had been, or soon would be, granted a free hand within the Soviet sphere of influence; however, this contravened the basic interests of the Western powers, as well as notions of freedom and justice that were taken seriously by their governments (and still more so by their publics). But even mild expressions of concern at high-handed Soviet actions, for example over Polish elections or German reparations, were construed by Moscow as malignant interference and rebuffed. This was a major error, explicable in ideological terms: first, 'bourgeois' governments were by definition deemed to be insincere in uttering such sentiments; secondly, one could afford to disregard them because the impending 'crisis of capitalism' would force them to yield under pressure from below, orchestrated from Moscow. The Stalin of 1945–7 did not necessarily expect fully fledged 'proletarian revolution' in the Western democracies; but he did count on their state order being enfeebled by social strife, which would oblige them to adhere to the soft, pliable line they had taken during the war, while the United States would relapse into isolationism and withdraw from Europe.

Western acquiescence was the precondition for forward Soviet policies in the contiguous borderlands of central-eastern Europe, where Stalin initially sought to establish, not the satellite states that eventually came into being there, but 'people's democracies' with an overtly pluralistic form of government, in which pro-Soviet elements would call the tune.[43] This policy applied equally to Hungary, Romania and Bulgaria. In south-eastern Europe Stalin was prepared to urge restraint on local hotheads so as not to provoke the West. Such restraint did not preclude probes against Turkey or Iran, but these were low-level adventures, which could be called off if and when local resistance stiffened.

On the cardinal problem of occupied Germany, 'Stalin seemed peculiarly reluctant to commit himself to any definite course in dealing with so unpredictable a country lest it again misfire', and allowed his agents there to pursue contradictory policies.[44] On one hand he condoned atrocities against civilians in the Soviet occupation zone and fleeced it of resources in the guise of reparations; on the other hand, when elections were held in 1946, he seems to have genuinely expected the population to vote massively in favour of the Socialist Unity party (SED), the proto-communist party forcefully created by his satraps. When they did not, tougher policies were taken which subverted the Allied Control Commission and deepened the division between the two halves of the country. Hannes Adomeit argues plausibly that this 'occurred by default rather than by design' (p. 59); Stalin, who had a healthy respect for the potential of German nationalism, recognized that division would be unacceptable to the people in the long run, and so prejudicial to the USSR's best interests, but thought that in the short term it was a lesser risk to concentrate on consolidating the Soviet hold on the eastern zone. This did not preclude demands for a share of Ruhr coal, loud protests at 'divisive' Western measures, and (once the Federal Republic had come into being) attempts to lure it into the Soviet sphere; but all this had a lower priority than building up the future

GDR. Adomeit quotes evidence by Vladimir Semenov, political counsellor to the Soviet military administration in Germany (SMAG), that Stalin personally decided policy at regular meetings with Soviet and German communist functionaries (p. 79);[45] nevertheless, taken as a whole, 'Stalin may never really have had a clear conception how to approach, let alone solve, the German problem . . . The division [of Germany] occurred as a consequence of a process of interaction [with the West] which in turn was driven in large measure by the pressures and requirements generated by the ideological and imperial paradigm' (p. 71).

For Mastny, Moscow's actions had by mid-1947 made the Cold War 'inevitable'; what made it 'irreversible' was the negative Soviet reaction to the Marshall Plan – or, as Robert Bideleux adds, at least to the proposed inclusion in it of the future Federal Republic.[46] For this spelled West European (and particularly West German) economic recovery and integration under capitalist auspices, an end to hopes of obtaining reparations from that quarter or of successfully inciting disorders in Italy or France. Initially, Moscow cautiously welcomed Marshall's initiative, since it offered east Europeans, too, the prospect of financial assistance in reconstruction and development, and accordingly Molotov encouraged them to stake their claims; but when he came to the Paris meeting of prospective participants, as head of the Soviet delegation, he quickly came round to the rejectionist view, especially because the plan provided for US control over all disbursements. Warnings from several quarters reinforced his inner conviction that the scheme was basically anti-Soviet, and he led his delegation out of the talks; subsequently, after emitting some mixed signals, Moscow compelled the east Europeans (and Finns) to forego the opportunity to participate, in this way reinforcing the economic and political partition of the continent.[47]

Was this another of Stalin's 'blunders'? If one takes the view that he had *already* decided on a strategy of consolidation, then it was not, for an eastward extension of the Marshall plan would indeed have undermined Soviet control over what were fast becoming its satellites. Rather more dubious was the wisdom of setting up the Cominform, which as Anna Di Biagio notes was much more than a mere reaction to the Paris decisions; springing from domestic needs, it was designed to halt centrifugal tendencies within the emerging bloc and to ensure that the east European states synchronized their policies in isolation from the West. Announced with militant flourishes, the organization proved counter-productive, since Moscow's clumsy centralizing policies provoked dissent, which had to be repressed by staging political trials, and ultimately the open rift with Yugoslavia.[48] Zubok and Pleshakov add new details on Zhdanov's role in establishing this body: its proximate causes had much to do with independent moves by Dimitrov and Tito. The two authors agree that it signalled an effort to build up a cohesive bloc in the east of the continent instead of trying to win over its western half.[49] Examining the implications for Italy, Silvio Pons notes that 'the stakes were not raised above a certain level'; despite all the bluster he detects a residue of the former more co-operative attitude towards the West.[50] As for the French party (PCF), accused of lack of militancy at the Cominform's inaugural meeting, its leader Maurice Thorez went to confess his errors to Stalin in person, only to be comforted. Stalin told him 'we are all Communists and that's what matters', and on a more practical level promised additional weaponry, urging that it be well hidden. But did he really expect a repeat performance of the 1944 insurrection, as Stéphane Courtois implies here?[51]

In central Europe, the most dramatic Soviet response to Western integration was the Berlin blockade, designed to force the Allies to abandon their presence in the western sectors of the former German capital and so to bolster the homogeneity of what was shortly to become the GDR. Adomeit suggests that the blockade was seen as both a defensive and offensive measure, and that Stalin (once again) did not make up his mind in advance what his precise goals were; this would have been good Leninist tactics, which allowed him to back down when the Western powers unexpectedly showed, by the airlift, their ability to resist Soviet pressures. This was indeed another of Stalin's errors: a 'risky venture' which further accelerated the very counter-moves that it was hoped to frustrate: the foundation of the Federal Republic and the introduction of a separate currency.[52] Even harsher in his judgement is the Russian historian Mikhail Narinsky, who, citing archival sources, speaks of it as 'a gamble' and 'fundamental mistake', in that 'the Soviet leadership . . . underestimated the resolution of the Western Powers' and failed to seize the chance of a reasonable compromise solution in time.[53] Mastny, not to be outdone, chronicles 'a harvest of blunders' between June 1948 and April 1949 (when the blockade was called off as NATO was formed). The other major mistake was the bullying of Tito, which provoked the first successful schism in Communist history and undermined 'Stalin's credibility as the undisputed master of eastern Europe'.[54]

On 29 August 1949, Soviet scientists succesfully tested an atomic device, so putting an end to the US nuclear monopoly. Though still in a position of stark inferiority to its adversary (which had some fifty bombs to the Soviets' initial two, and far better means of delivery), the USSR received a psychological boost that was soon translated into offensive action – in Asia, where the 'correlation of forces' was becoming far more favourable to Soviet designs.

The Far East

In the Far East, Moscow's policy had at first been relatively cautious. As Pleshakov puts it, 'Stalin's strategy in China was basically colonial in the traditional European sense. He wanted to get physical control over Chinese natural resources and communications, to create a Soviet protectorate in Manchuria and if possible in Xinjiang.'[55] The brief Manchurian campaign in 1945 brought the USSR a considerable accretion of territory and power in the region, avenging the humiliation inflicted by the Japanese on Imperial Russia 40 years earlier: not just the Kuriles and southern Sakhalin, but also strongholds on the Liaodong peninsula which, with the access routes, could serve as a launching pad for eventual further expansion, but the immediate priority was to consolidate these gains; moreover, US nuclear hegemony in the north Pacific called for prudence. At that time the possibility of a Communist-ruled China seemed remote, and anyway Stalin did not trust Mao Zedong. It was symptomatic that, as Eva-Maria Stolberg notes in her close study of this relationship, the amount of arms obtained by the CCP from Soviet sources in the summer of 1945 was slight by comparison with deliveries to the Nationalists (Guomindang) during the war – and had to be paid for; aid on an extensive scale was granted only from 1947 onward.[56]

This monograph is part of a rich body of literature that has grown up over the last decade, based on newly declassified Chinese and Soviet documentary sources, under the aegis of the research institutes referred to above. Sino-Soviet relations and the diplomacy of the Korean War, once all but a closed book for outside observers, have now been illuminated more authoritatively than almost any other field of Soviet affairs during the Stalin era.[57] These studies amplify, without fundamentally altering, the judicious treatment provided in 1993 by Sergei Goncharov and others.[58] Nin Jun writes that since we have obtained first-hand evidence of the two parties' 'motivations and patterns of action, . . . we are getting closer to seeing the issues of the Sino-Soviet relationship from within, and not only through Western lenses'.[59]

We cannot examine here the evolution of Chinese policy; so far as the Soviet side is concerned, the first signs of serious interest in the CCP as potential partner came in February 1949, when Mikoian visited its headquarters in northern China; the breakthrough did not, however, come until the summer, when Stalin privately admitted his earlier errors (while clinging to Soviet privileges in northern China) and promised to support an 'all-China democratic coalition government' as soon as one was established.[60] As this formula shows, he was still hedging his bets and reckoned on a compromise of sorts with Nationalist elements, according to the formula being tried out in eastern Europe. Suspicious as ever, and mindful of earlier disagreements with the CCP, he feared that a Maoist regime might turn out to be a Titoist one writ large, and China too large a country to accommodate into his simplistic bipolar view of East–West relations – a view that in a sense later history would bear out. It is no wonder that the Soviet leader 'forgot' to congratulate Mao when recognizing the CCP government on its establishment (1 October 1949).

Dieter Heinzig devotes no less than two hundred pages to the tortuous negotiations, marked by successive affronts to the dignity of the 'two oriental emperors', held before the friendship treaty was concluded. This provided for (phased) evacuation of Manchuria and (modest) economic aid to the new Chinese regime, but in Mao's eyes was still all too reminiscent of the 'unequal' treaty that Moscow had concluded four years earlier with the Guomindang.[61] Stalin had now satisfied himself that Mao would take a sufficiently strong anti-American line, yet his anxiety to cling for a time to the Liaodong bases shows that he was preparing for the last war as well as for the next.

The Korean War of 1950–3, as we now know, was as much 'made in Moscow' as it was in Pyongyang, for on 30 January 1950 the North Korean (PDRK) leader Kim Il Sung, whom Stalin had at first kept on a tight leash, was given a green light to proceed with long-held plans to attack his southern neighbour. This shift to a more offensive stance was an immediate product of the new relationship with Beijing and, seen in wider context, of the stalemate in Europe and the Soviets' new self-confidence after the successful atomic test. Stalin was also misled by Acheson's speech (12 January) which seemed to indicate that the US would not resist an invasion militarily. Typically, 'Filippov' (as the Soviet leader styled himself in radio communications with Mao; to Kim he used the pseudonym Fyn Si) did not fully inform his new ally of his intentions.[62] Perhaps he hoped that Mao might 'refus[e] to play along, [which] would have given Stalin a chance to back out of the Korean challenge with his revolutionary credentials intact, while chastening Mao's bothersome vigour on regional issues'.[63] He did, however, warn Kim that the Soviet Union intended to stay out of the conflict, which they both assumed would be a walkover. A Soviet military mission was sent to advise on the 'technical' arrangements, but it appears that the actual timing of the attack was left to the North Koreans.

It was the Chinese rather than the Soviets who provided additional muscle for the invaders; but when the Americans counter-attacked and pushed them back beyond the thirty-eighth parallel, the Chinese leader served notice on Stalin that he was unwilling to intervene in force to save Kim. 'It took a direct request from Stalin to Mao, as well as a series of meetings between the Soviet leader and a Chinese delegation . . . in the Crimea on 9–10 October, to get the Chinese to change their minds'.[64] For a brief moment, Stalin was even prepared to write off the whole adventure and to accept US troops on the Soviet border; but the danger passed, and once the Chinese had committed their troops the Soviets found themselves willy-nilly drawn indirectly into the war. Stalin, as a master of 'dosage', was careful to limit their involvement and left China to bear the brunt of the fighting – a strategy that would lead to recrimination later.

Western military historians have not dealt at length (at least in public) with the engagements between Soviet and UN forces, mainly in the air, and few Russian historians have gained access to the pertinent archives.[65] There is rather more information (from Chinese sources) about Sino-Soviet military collaboration in the field, which seems to have been 'rather harmonious' (Westad), perhaps because the PLA was willing, like Mao himself at this stage, to defer to Soviet experience.

Stolberg does not pursue her subject into the two years or so of stalemate in Korea (and Heinzig's ends even before the war began), so that here too there is room for further detailed studies. They would need to encompass Stalin's entire *Weltpolitik* in this final phase of his career, when he tried to balance embroilment in the Far East with 'peaceful' overtures to the West over Germany, while forcing the Soviet bloc's military build-up. 'At no previous juncture of the Cold War', writes Mastny, 'had the stakes been so high yet the outcome so dependent upon forces beyond Stalin's control', for in Korea a turn for the better depended on the Chinese, while in Europe it depended on the Germans and Americans. Both Moscow and Washington expected war within two years. 'There was a danger of a self-fulfilling prophecy' in these common beliefs, but happily neither side 'was willing, much less eager, to go over the brink'.[66]

The German question

It was in this sinister setting, while inconclusive manoeuvres were undertaken to bring about an armistice in the simmering Korean conflict, and ever more east European leaders were vanishing into the dungeons, that Stalin launched his last major foreign-policy initiative, the proposal of 10 March 1952 for a German peace treaty that would make that country 'united, independent, democratic and peace-loving'. The objective was clearly to prevent the Western powers from proceeding with their plan to end the Federal Republic's occupied status and to integrate its renascent armed forces into those of the projected European Defence Community. As seen from Moscow, such an arrangement would give Bundeswehr generals with dubious pasts (and contempt for the Oder-Neisse line) a leading role in NATO's operational decision-making.[67] The first draft of the Soviet plan, prepared under Gromyko's auspices, was so unaccommodating as to suggest that the aims were purely propagandist; it was then revised, but even this version 'was still not good enough to be sent out', and so the final text of the 'Peace Note' consisted merely of general principles.[68] Contrary to the original intention, the future united Germany was to have its own armed forces, within narrow limits laid down by the four powers; 'independent' meant that it could not join NATO or any other alliance the Soviets deemed prejudicial to their interests; and 'democratic' was construed according to the Leninist 'dialectical' understanding of the term – this at least is the majority view, which merits closer examination.

Did Stalin really envisage sacrificing the GDR for a dubious greater gain? Hannes Adomeit thinks not. He lists (pp. 90–1) seven points that buttress the traditional view of 'the manipulative and instrumental character of the initiative'. The most convincing of these is that it was not 'embedded in an overall change of Soviet ideology, domestic politics and foreign policy' (a sort of Gorbachev-style 'new thinking') but on the contrary was accompanied by repressive measures to tighten bloc discipline.[69] Seen in this light, the Note's rejection, first by the Bonn government and then by the Western allies, was a foregone conclusion that needs no apology.

For the dissidents, the leading spokesman today is Wilfried Loth (Essen). In 1994, he argued that the GDR was 'Stalin's unwanted child',[70] which he would indeed have been willing to jettison in order to establish Soviet security on a sounder basis; the 1952 initiative was part of a consistent strategy on the German question pursued since 1945. This study, written without access to the Russian documents and relying heavily on Wilhelm Pieck's notes on the preparatory discussions, has now been superseded by the same author's close analysis of the way the 1952 notes were elaborated in the Foreign Affairs ministry and other policy-making bodies, accompanied by 15 relevant documents in translation.[71]

This puts the inner-German debate on a sounder footing but does not settle it. Loth evidently still believes that an opportunity to reunite the country was missed, but does not weigh up the arguments *pro* and *contra* here; instead he is at pains to show that the offer was meant seriously and had been carefully designed to make it palatable to German and European opinion. He acknowledges that 'Stalin's interventions in [preparing] the project harmed it', because he first delayed it for months and then made corrections that weakened its credibility; the initiative suffered from 'the general ponderousness of a political system in which all major decisions had to be made by the dictator himself' (p. 61). Nevertheless, Stalin did 'reach out in significant measure to the Germans' by offering terms that embodied 'what he was really aiming at: implementation of the anti-fascist core of the Potsdam decisions' (p. 55). A month later (7 April) he told GDR leaders that the Western reaction had destroyed his last illusions about Allied co-operation in solving the German question and so 'you must organize your own state; the demarcation line . . . must be treated as . . . a very dangerous frontier, whose defence needs enhancing' (p. 59).

Was this moment a post-war equivalent of the fateful decision of 11 August 1939? Loth's critics contend that the wily Stalin never seriously envisaged an alternative to consolidating his east European gains. For Hermann Graml[72] the archival documents 'tell us nothing about Stalin's actions . . . [or] plans and motives' (p. 121); he sees no evidence that, as Loth suggests, he hesitated before endorsing the proposal lest his prestige suffer; as for his anti-fascism, had he not already in 1947 wanted ex-Nazis in the eastern zone to have their own party, and did he not now propose that they might participate in the political life of a neutralized Germany (p. 123)? The documents, he insists, show that (1) the initiative originated with the SED leaders, not in Moscow; (2) its terms, far from being tailored to meet Western susceptibilities, clearly envisaged extending the GDR's economic and social order westwards. In short, 'Molotov and Stalin were not concerned with elaborating an acceptable basis for a four-power conference, but purely with maximizing [the notes'] propagandist effect' (p. 131).

Perhaps the debate needs to be steered away from Moscow's intentions towards the practicalities of a hypothetical neutral united Germany, even though this involves some counter-factual reasoning. In judging the Western Powers' negative response, one needs to know (1) whether such a state (with minimal armed forces, no legitimate 'anti-Soviet' civic bodies, and still suffering from post-war trauma) could have defended itself against Communist infiltration; (2) whether NATO could have functioned with Germany neutral. If the answer to either question is 'no', rejection was the right course, however generous Stalin's motives. One also needs to look beyond Germany to neighbouring neutral European states (Finland, Sweden, Yugoslavia; from 1955, Austria), all of which successfully resisted the threat of sovietization. To this it will be said that Germany's size and history put it in a different category. In any case, however self-interested the proposal was, it should not be reckoned among Stalin's foreign-policy blunders, like the Berlin blockade or the Korean War, since to have offered greater concessions than he did would have meant dismantling his empire.

In support of this judgement, we may note that a few years later the post-Stalin leadership tried to resolve the issue in similar fashion, with no greater success: the Cold War battle lines had been too firmly drawn. For this, the Soviet dictator, and the logic of his system, must indeed be held largely responsible. His death, on 5 March 1953, removed a major impediment to détente and reduced the imminent threat of armed conflict between the two blocs. But it was not in itself sufficient to end the Cold War, which had acquired an institutional dynamic of its own.

Notes

1 G.K. Roberts, *The Soviet Union and the Origins of the Second World War: Russo-German Relations and the Road to War, 1933–1941* (Basingstoke: Macmillan, 1995); cf. idem, 'The Alliance That Failed: Moscow and the Triple Alliance Negotiations, 1939', *European History Quarterly* 29 (1996), 383–414. Jonathan Haslam, 'Soviet–German Relations and the Origins of the Second World War: The Jury is Still Out', *JMH* 69 (1997), 785–97. Other important studies include T.J. Uldricks, 'Soviet Security Policy in the 1930s', in G. Gorodetsky (ed.), *Soviet Foreign Policy, 1917–1991* (London: Frank Cass, 1994); idem, 'Debating the Role of Russia in the Origins of the Second World War', in G. Martel (ed.), *The Origins of the Second World War Reconsidered: A.J.P. Taylor and the Historians* (London and New York: Allen & Unwin, 1999), 135–54.
2 R. Tucker, *Stalin in Power* (see Chapter 7, n. 1), 341–50, 409–15, 513–25, 592–607. R.C. Raack, *Stalin's Drive to the West, 1938–1945: The Origins of the Cold War* (Stanford, CA: Stanford University Press, 1995); idem, 'Stalin's Plans for World War II Told by a High Comintern Source [i.e., Walter Ulbricht]', *Historical Journal* 38 (1995), 1031–6; Joachim Hoffmann, *Stalins Vernichtungskrieg 1941–1945: Planung, Ausführung und Dokumentation*, 5th edn (Munich: Herbig, 1999), reviewed critically by B. Bonwetsch: *JGOE* 48 (2000), 453–4. S. Pons, *Stalin and the Inevitable War* (London and Portland, OR: Frank Cass, 2002; Italian edn Turin, 1995) endeavours to break free from these categories, arguing that elements of both ideology and realism were involved in each of the two contradictory strategies adopted, collective security and isolationism (ix–xi). This work appeared too late to be considered here.
3 G. Gorodetsky, *Grand Delusion: Stalin and the German Invasion of Russia* (New Haven, CT and London: Yale University Press, 1999).
4 Usefully listed by Sergei Slutsch [= Sluch], 'Die Aussenpolitik der UdSSR und die sowjetisch-deutschen Beziehungen in der Zwischenkriegszeit in der russischen Historiographie des letzten Jahrzehnts', *JHK* 2000, 289–98.
5 In H.-G. Linke (ed.), *Quellen zu den deutsch-sowjetischen Beziehungen 1917–1945*, 2 vols, (Darmstadt: Wissenschaftliche Buchgesellschaft, 1998, 2001), some two-fifths are drawn from Soviet sources but they are based on translations rather than the originals. More useful, though narrower in scope, is Gerd Ueberschär and Lev A. Bezymensky (eds), *Der deutsche Angriff auf die Sowjetunion* (Darmstadt: Wissenschaftliche Buchgesell-schaft, 1998, repr. 1999), which contains 13 Soviet and an equal number of German documents on planning for the invasion, with a commentary indicating the gaps in our knowledge. Klaus Meyer analysed Western and Russian writing from 1989 to the mid-1990s in 'Zwei Wege nach Moskau: vom Pakt bis zum Ueberfall: Neuere Literatur zur Geschichte der deutsch-sowjetischen Beziehungen von 1939 bis 1941', *Zeitschrift für Ostmitteleuropa-Forschung* 47 (1998), 215–30.
6 A. Dallin and F.I. Firsov (eds), *Dimitrov and Stalin, 1934–1943: Letters from the Soviet Archives* (New Haven, CT and London: Yale University Press, 2000), Russian docu-ments trans. Vadim A. Staklo; I. Banac (ed.), *The Diary of Georgi Dimitrov, 1937–1949*, trans. J.T. Hedges *et al.* (New Haven, CT: Yale University Press, 2003).
7 A.O. Chubarian and H. Shukman (eds), *Stalin and the Soviet-Finnish War, 1939–1940*, trans. T. Sokokina (London and Portland, OR: Frank Cass, 2002; Russian edn Moscow, 2002).
8 C. Kennedy-Pipe, *Russia and the World, 1917–1991*, London and New York: Arnold, 1998), 36–56.
9 A. Resis, 'The Fall of Litvinov: Harbinger of the German–Soviet Non-Aggression Pact', *EAS* 52 (2000), 33–56, here 46.

10 H. Ragsdale, 'Soviet Military Preparations and Policy in the Munich Crisis: New Evidence', *JGOE* 47 (1999), 210–26; idem, 'The Munich Crisis and the Issue of Red Army Transit Across Romania', *RR* 57 (1998), 614–17. This point is also made by Steiner (764).

11 Roberts, 'Fall of Litvinov'; idem, *Soviet Union*, 71–4; idem, 'Alliance', 397.

12 D. O'Sullivan, 'The Role of the Narkomindel in Formulation and Implementation of Soviet Foreign Policy, 1939–1941', *Forum OIZ* 1999, 1, 115–36, here 119. The leading French student of the NKID is Sabine Dullin, whose *Des Hommes d'influences: les ambassadeurs de Staline en Europe, 1930–1938* (Paris: Payot, 2001) was preceded by articles in *Communisme* 40 (1995), 4, 76–80, *Les Cahiers de l'ITHP* 55 (1996), 29–41, *Relations internationales* 91 (1997), 339–55 and in S. Pons and A. Romano (eds), *Russia in the Age of Wars, 1914–1945* (Milan: Annali Feltrinelli, 2000).

13 Resis, 'Fall of Litvinov', 45–6, 51.

14 S. Slutsch [= Sluch], '17. September 1939: der Eintritt der Sowjetunion in den zweiten Weltkrieg: eine historische und völkerrechtliche Bewertung', *Vierteljahresschrift für Zeitgeschichte* 48 (2000), 219–54. Sluch first advanced this argument to a domestic audience: cf. his articles in *OI* 5 (2000), 46–58 and 6, 10–28.

15 J.T. Gross, *Revolution from Abroad: The Soviet Conquest of Poland's Western Ukraine and Western Belorussia* (Princeton, NJ: Princeton University Press, 1988, pbk edn 2002).

16 D Kirby, 'Incorporation: the Molotov-Ribbentrop Pact', in G. Smith (ed.), *The Baltic States: The National Self-determination of Estonia, Latvia and Lithuania* (Basingstoke and New York: Macmillan, 1994, 2nd edn, 1996), 41–68. Geoffrey Roberts's article 'Soviet Policy and the Baltic States, 1939–1940: A Reappraisal', *Diplomacy and Statecraft* (London, 1995), 6, has not been available.

17 P.W. Doerr, '"Frigid but Unprovocative": British Policy Towards the USSR from the Nazi–Soviet Pact to the Winter War, 1939', *Journal of Contemporary History* 36 (2001), 423–39. A specialist in British foreign policy, Doerr characterized it in a study (Manchester, 1998) as 'hope for the best, prepare for the worst'.

18 T. Vihavainen, *Stalin i finny*, trans. N.A. Kovalenko, ed. F.M. Kovalenko (St Petersburg, 2000; Finnish edn Otava, 1998), 120–64, here 122; on the Continuation War see 165–95.

19 Chubarian and Shukman (eds), *Stalin and the Soviet-Finnish War*, xxi–xxv, 263–74.

20 C. Van Dyke, *The Soviet Invasion of Finland, 1939–1940* (London and Portland, OR: Frank Cass, 1997), 190, 214 (citing V.O. Apteker's estimates), 221–2. Two earlier studies by D.W. Spring (Nottingham) should be noted: 'Stalin and the Winter War', *Yearbook of Finnish Foreign Policy* (Helsinki: Finnish Institute of International Affairs, 1990), 37–42 (cf. *Soviet Studies* 38 (1986), 107–26).

21 R. Büttner, *Sowjetisierung oder Selbständigkeit? Die sowjetische Finnlandpolitik 1943–1948* (Hamburg: Dr Kovac, 2001).

22 W. Hedeler and S. Dietzsch, '1940: Stalins glückliches Jahr: eine mentalitäts-geschichtliche Momentaufnahme', *Forum OIZ* 1999, 2, 153–66.

23 Gorodetsky, *Grand Delusions*, 83–6.

24 K.H. Blumenhagen, *Die deutsch-sowjetischen Handelsbeziehungen 1939–1941: ihre Bedeutung für die jeweilige Kriegswirtschaft* (Hamburg: Dr Kovac, 1998); laudatory reviews in *JGOE* 47 (99), 445–6, *Geschichte in Wissenschaft und Unterricht* 51 (2000), 619. Blumenhagen makes exensive use of German documents, including those of private firms, but not the Soviet counterparts or even post-Soviet scholarship.

25 Gorodetsky, *Grand Delusions*, 136, 139, 141, 151, 246–7 et passim.

26 T.J. Uldricks, 'The Icebreaker Controversy: Did Stalin Plan to Attack Hitler?', *SR* 58 (1999), 626–43; cf. also idem, 'Soviet Security Policy' (see n. 1) and earlier works. Viktor Rezun ('Suvorov') followed up his *Ledokol* (Icebreaker) with a work of 1996 that has been translated into German by Winfried Böhme as *Stalins verhinderter Erstschlag: Hitler erstickt die Weltrevolution* (Selent, Germany, 2000). For other repudiations

of Rezun, see C.A. Roberts, 'Planning for War: The Red Army and the Catastrophe of 1941', *EAS* 47 (1995), 1293–1326, with comments by S.J. Main in 48 (1996), 837–9.

27 Uldricks, 'Icebreaker', 639–40; cf. Haslam, 'Soviet–German Relations', 797 and Gorodetsky, *Grand Delusion*, 208.

28 Gorodetsky, 238–41.

29 J. Barros and R. Gregor, *Double Deception: Stalin, Hitler and the Invasion of Russia* (DeKalb, IL: Northern Illinois University Press, 1995), 223–4.

30 D. Caute, *The Fellow Travellers: Intellectual Friends of Communism* (rev. edn New Haven, CT: Yale University Press, 1988); P. Hollander, *Political Pilgrims: Travels of Western Pilgrims to the Soviet Union, China and Cuba, 1928–1978* (New York and Oxford: Oxford University Press, 1981).

31 S. Coeuré, *La Grande Lueur à l'est: les Français et l'Union Soviétique, 1917–1939* (Paris: Du Seuil, 1999).

32 A. Thorpe, *The British Communist Party and Moscow, 1920–1943* (Manchester and New York: Manchester University Press, 2000); on the party's volte-face in 1939, 256–64.

33 K. McDermott and J. Agnew, *The Comintern: A History of International Communism from Lenin to Stalin* (Basingstoke and London: Macmillan, 1996); cf. McDermott, 'Stalinist Terror in the Comintern: New Perspectives', *Journal of Contemporary History* 30 (1995), 111–30. The Swiss historian Brigitte Studer (Bern) has written 'At the Beginning of History: Visions of the Comintern after Opening of the Archives', *IRSH* 42 (1998), 419–46 and 'Private Matters Become Public: Western European Communist Exiles and Emigrants in Stalinist Russia in the 1930s', *IRSH* 48 (2003), 203–23 (both with Berthold Unfried, the latter previously published in *Historische Anthropologie*, 1999, 7, 83–108); cf. also her article in *JHK* 1995, 306–21.

34 B.H. Bayerlein *et al.* (eds), *Moscou – Paris – Berlin: télégrammes chiffrés du Komintern, 1939–1941* (Paris: Tallandier, 2003).

35 A recent general treatment is G. Roberts, *The Soviet Union in World Politics: Coexistence, Revolution and Cold War, 1945–1991* (Basingstoke and New York: Macmillan, 1999); on the late Stalin era see 13–41. C. Kennedy-Pipe, *Stalin's Cold War: Soviet Strategies in Europe, 1943–1956* (Manchester and New York: Manchester University Press, 1995) discerns six successive Soviet strategic objectives, from ensuring *survival* in 1943 to *denial* of territory to potential adversaries, *occupation* of neighbouring lands deemed essential to Soviet security, and the *consolidation* of these gains to phases of renewed *confrontation* and, finally, *stabilization* along a finite border. Roberts hails this work, which uses Soviet archives, as 'the best single monograph on the Soviet role in the Cold War': *EAS* 49 (1997), 1527.

36 For the subtle distinctions between these standpoints, see A. Murray, 'Reconstructing the Cold War: The Evolution of a Consuming Paradigm', in A.P. Dobson *et al.* (eds), *Deconstructing and Reconstructing the Cold War* (Aldershot and Brookfield, NY: Ashgate, 1999), 25–43. R. Bideleux, 'Soviet and Russian Perspectives on the Cold War', ibid., 226–50, updates the 'liberal' revisionist interpretation.

37 V. Mastny, *The Cold War and Soviet Insecurity: The Stalin Years* (New York and Oxford: Oxford University Press, 1996), 4. The Czech-born US scholar is the leading Western authority on the topic and makes fuller use than most of east European sources. His earlier monograph, *Russia's Road to the Cold War: Diplomacy, Warfare and the Politics of Communism, 1941–1945* (New York: Columbia University Press, 1979), took a more 'hawkish' view of Soviet intentions than the later one.

38 One thinks here primarily of the military establishment and the economic ministries, but Yoram Gorlizky, who has studied Politburo records for the period, makes the case that, although this body was 'still further adapted to the leader's ... requirements' after 1945, it nevertheless had a distinct role to play which included control of foreign affairs: Y. Gorlizky, 'Stalin's Cabinet: The Politburo and Decision-Making in the Post-

War Years', *EAS* 52 (01), 291–312, here 291. Rees, 'Stalin as Leader', (cf. Chapter 7, n. 25) thinks Gorlizki's analysis of post-war Politburo politics 'too subtle' (232).

39 V.M. Zubok and C. Pleshakov, *Inside the Kremin's Cold War: From Stalin to Khrushchev,* (Cambridge, MA and London: Harvard University Press, 1996). Zubok lives in Washington, Pleshakov in Moscow. Cf. F. Gori and S. Pons (eds), *The Soviet Union and Europe in the Cold War, 1943–1953* (Basingstoke: Macmillan, and New York: St Martin's Press, 1996), esp. the paper by A.M. Filitov, 'Postwar Construction and Foreign Policy Conceptions', 3–22.

40 O.A. Westad (ed.), *Reviewing the Cold War: Approaches, Interpretations, Theory* (London and Portland, OR: Frank Cass, 2000).

41 Westad (ed.), *Brothers in Arms: The Rise and Fall of the Sino-Soviet Alliance, 1945–1963* (Washington, DC: Woodrow Wilson International Center for Scholars, 1998). The Cold War International History Project, based in this institute, has published since 1991 a *Bulletin* and a series of Working Papers that contain much new information gleaned from former Soviet and Chinese archives <http://cwihp.si.edu/default. htm>; in 2000 the *Bulletin* became a journal, *Cold War History* (London and Portland, OR). Two other relevant institutions are: (i) the Harvard Project on Cold War Studies, which publishes the *Journal of Cold War Studies,* ed. M. Kramer (e-mail: hpcws @fas.harvard.edu), and (ii) the Project on the Cold War as Global Conflict, in the International Center for Advanced Studies of New York University (e-mail: icas@ nyu.edu), which currently focuses on the reflection of the conflict in everyday life and culture. Much of the traffic between these institutions is carried on over the Internet.

42 H. Adomeit, *Imperial Overstretch: Germany in Soviet Policy from Stalin to Gorbachev: An Analysis Based on New Archival Evidence, Memoirs and Interviews* (Baden-Baden: Nomos, 1998), 51–2.

43 On Soviet policy in Poland see J.J. Kulczycki, 'The Soviet Union, Polish Communists, and the Creation of a Polish Nation-State', *Russian History/Histoire russe* 29 (2002), 251–76. This volume contains papers from a conference held in Chicago in May 2002.

44 Mastny, *Cold War,* 19, 24.

45 This point is also stressed by S. Creuzberger, *Die sowjetische Besatzungsmacht und das politische System der SBZ* (Cologne and Weimar: Böhlau, 1996), who provides details of the financial and material assistance supplied, mainly through the SMAG, to the SED. Creuzberger has since co-operated with M. Görtemaker in editing a documentary study on this theme with a broader geographical coverage: *Gleichschaltung unter Stalin? Die Entwicklung der Parteien im östlichen Europa 1944–1949* (Paderborn: Schöningh, 2002), which amplifies the earlier studies in N. Naimark and L. Gibianskii (eds), *The Establishment of Communist Regimes in Eastern Europe* (Boulder, CO: Westview, 1997).

46 Mastny, *Cold War,* 27; Bideleux, 'Soviet and Russian Perspectives', 240.

47 G. Roberts, 'Moscow and the Marshall Plan: Politics, Ideology and the Onset of the Cold War, 1947', *EAS* 46 (1994), 1371–86; S.D. Parish and M.M. Narinsky, 'New Evidence on the Soviet Rejection of the Marshall Plan, 1947', *CWIHP Working Paper* 9 (1994); Narinsky, 'Soviet Foreign Policy and the Origins of the Cold War', in G. Gorodetsky (ed.), *Soviet Foreign Policy, 1919–1991: A Retrospective* (London: Frank Cass, 1994), 105–10.

48 A. Di Biagio, 'The Marshall Plan and the Founding of Cominform, June – September 1947', in Gori and Pons (ed.), *Soviet Union and Europe,* 208–21.

49 The chief documentary source is now the Russian scholar G.M. Adibekov, *Das Kominform und Stalins Neoordnung Europas,* ed. B.H. Bayerlein *et al.,* trans. B.Höhne *et al.* (Frankfurt, Oxford and Vienna: P. Lang, 2002), which supplements the same author's *The Cominform: Minutes of the Three Conferences, 1947–1948–1949,* ed. G. Procacci *et al.* (Milan: Feltrinelli, 1994). Adibekov usefully examines the organization of the new body in 'Der Apparat des Kominforms', *JHK* 1998, 219–53 (trans. from Russian). For more on Stalin's attitude to the territorial conflicts in the Balkans, see G.P. Murashko and

A.F. Noskova (eds), 'Stalin and the National–Territorial Controversies in Eastern Europe, 1945–1947', *Cold War History* 1 (2000), 161–72 (the sequel deals with Poland and Hungary); R.C. Nation, 'Balkan Union? South-eastern Europe in Soviet Security Policy', in Gori and Pons (eds), *Soviet Union and Europe*, 125–43 (for the 1947 situation, see 133). A follow-up to Cominform was Comecon, or the Council for Mutual Economic Relations; on this see L.K. Metcalf, 'The Creation of a Socialist Trading System', *East European Quarterly* 29 (1995), 465–86.

50 S. Pons, 'A Challenge Let Drop: Soviet Foreign Policy, the Cominform and the Italian Communist Party, 1947–8', in Gori and Pons (eds), *Soviet Union and Europe*, 246–63.

51 S. Courtois, 'Thorez, Stalin und Frankreichs Befreiung im Lichte der Moskauer Archiven', *JHK* 1998, 77–85, here 84–5. This article also deals with the two leaders' earlier meeting in November 1944.

52 Adomeit, *Imperial Overstretch*, 80–3.

53 M.M. Narinsky, 'The Soviet Union and the Berlin Crisis, 1948–9', in Gori and Pons (eds), *Soviet Union and Europe*, 57–75, here 67, 71.

54 Mastny, *Cold War*, 47, 53–4, 62.

55 C. Pleshakov, 'Studying Soviet Strategies and Decision-making in the Cold War Years', in Westad (ed.), *Reviewing the Cold War*, 232–41, here 234.

56 E.-M. Stolberg, *Stalin und die chinesisichen Kommunisten, 1945–1953: eine Studie zur Entstehungsgeschichte der sowjetisch-chinesischen Allianz vor dem Hintergrund des Kalten Krieges* (Stuttgart: F. Steiner, 1997), 99–103.

57 Westad (ed.), *Brothers in Arms*, 314–35, publishes in English translation five documents (in APRF) from this period, four of which relate to Mao's visit to Moscow in the winter of 1949–50 that eventuated in the friendship treaty of 14 February, notably two records of conversations between him and Stalin (16 December, 22 January), which give an unparalleled insight into their personal relationship. Stolberg publishes in German translation 21 documents from August 1945 to September 1952: *Stalin*, 276–92. Heinzig (see n. 61) prints 15 documents from 5 January to 22 March 1950 (655–74). Earlier top-level exchanges are documented in CWIHP *Bulletin* 6–7 (1995–6), 7, 27–9; this issue also includes A. Mansourov, 'Stalin, Mao, Kim and China's Decision to Enter the Korean War: September 16 – October 15, 1950: New Evidence from the Russian Archives' (94–107); K. Weathersby, 'New Russian Documents on the Korean War' (30–84).

58 S.N. Goncharov *et al.*, *Uncertain Partners: Stalin, Mao and the Korean War* (Stanford, CA: Stanford University Press, 1993). A related work that appeared at this time was Westad, *Cold War and Revolution: Soviet–American Rivalry and the Origins of the Chinese Civil War* (New York: Columbia University Press, 1993). See also P. Wingrove, 'Mao in Moscow, 1949–1950: Some New Archival Evidence', *Journal of Communist Studies and Transition Politics* (London), 11 (1995), 309–34.

59 Nin Jun, 'The Origins of the Sino-Soviet Alliance', in Westad (ed.), *Brothers in Arms*, 47–89, here 47.

60 Westad (ed.), *Brothers in Arms*, 10; cf. Stolberg, 162, who makes the point that his chief concern at this juncture was still to keep China free from American influence.

61 For a comparison, see Stolberg, *Stalin*, 53–4, 186–92. D. Heinzig, *Die Sowjetunion und das kommunistische China 1945–1950; der beschwerliche Weg zum Bündnis* (Baden-Baden: Nomos, 1998), 429–626. Heinzig was for many years a senior analyst of Sino-Soviet relations at the Bundesinstitut für ostwissenschaftliche Studien, Cologne.

62 Stolberg, *Stalin*, 221–2, citing Weathersby: 'it would have been hard to win Mao over to support North Korea when he simultaneously opposed an invasion of Taiwan'.

63 Westad (ed.), *Brothers in Arms*, 13. For an account by a well-informed US sinologist, see R.C. Thornton, *Odd Man Out: Truman, Stalin, Mao and the Making of the Korean War* (Washington, DC: Brassey's, 2001). (The 'odd man out' is Mao.) Also now available in English is A.N. Lankov, *From Stalin to Kim Il Sung: The Formation of North Korea, 1945–1960* (London: C. Hurst, 2003).

64 Loc. cit.; cf. Stolberg, 220–3.
65 For a partial account of the air war, see Yu.N. Semin and S.N. Ruban, 'Uchastie SSSR v koreiskoi voine: novye dokumenty', *VI*, 1994, no. 11, 3–20.
66 Mastny, *Cold War*, 113–15.
67 Among recent works are R. van Dijk, 'The 1952 Stalin Note Debate: Myth or Missed Opportunity?', CWIHP Working Paper 14 (1996); G. Wettig, 'The Soviet Union and Germany in the Late Stalin Period, 1950–1953', in Gori and Pons (ed.), *Soviet Union and Europe*, 356–74; idem, *'Bereitschaft zur Einheit in Freiheit?' Die sowjetische Deutschlandpolitik 1945–1955* (Munich: Olzog, 1999), 200–26. L. Castin-Chaparro, *Puissance de l'URSS, misères de l'Allemagne: Staline et la question allemande, 1941–1955* (Paris: Eds de la Sorbonne, 2002), 351–3, follows the arguments of H. Graml (see below).
68 Mastny, *Cold War*, 136. More precisely, 'Notes', since identical notes were sent to each Western power.
69 According to J. Gaddis, in *We Now Know: Rethinking Cold War History* (Oxford: Clarendon Press, 1997, 1998), 127, citing Filitov, Vladimir Semenov later recalled Stalin asking him whether the Americans were certain to turn the note down; only when assured that they would do so did he give the go-ahead. This is of course anecdotal evidence that needs corroboration. Thanks for this reference to M. Trachtenberg, <http://www.fas.harvard.edu/hpcws/comment8.htm>, 2.
70 W. Loth, *Stalin's Unwanted Child: The Soviet Union, the German Question and the Founding of the GDR*, trans. R.F. Hogg (London: Macmillan and New York: St. Martin's Press, 1998; German edn 1994).
71 Idem, 'Die Entstehung der "Stalin-Note": Dokumente aus Moskauer Archiven', in J. Zarusky (ed.), *Die Stalin-Note vom 10. März 1952* (Munich: Oldenbourg, 2002), 19–115 (documents 63–115).
72 H. Graml, 'Eine wichtige Quelle – aber missverstanden: Anmerkungen zu Wilfried Loths "Die Entstehung . . ."', ibid., 117–38.

Conclusions

Wilfried Loth has since published a reply to his critics[1] that testifies to his determination, but he seems to be fighting a losing battle against the consensus view. This extends beyond Stalin's line on Germany to broad areas of Soviet foreign policy in general, both before and after World War II, as we have seen. Future contributions to historical understanding may well be concerned with lesser players in world affairs such as Turkey or Japan, although certainly we still need to know more about the way Soviet strategists developed the underlying ideological concepts concerning East–West relations, that is, how various goals were prioritized.

The consensus among Western historians is somewhat shakier as regards the USSR's domestic affairs: the nature of the regime, the extent of its popular support, its economic and social policies – and even repression, although so far as the Great Terror is concerned it is perhaps less a matter of revisionists challenging the 'totalitarian stereotype' with a radically novel approach than of their leaving such issues aside in pursuit of knowledge in other, more congenial fields. It is sometimes asserted that the academic 'cold warriors' concentrated unduly on such matters in order to discredit the ideological enemy; that the basic facts about the purges and the Gulag are by now familiar, so that little intellectual profit is to be gained by elaborating on them further; that the post-Stalin leaders tried to make amends for the grossest abuses, even if the rehabilitation process was uncertain, reluctant and self-interested; and finally, writers who go on and on about the horrors of Stalinism engage in tedious moralizing: why inveigh against ancient evils when what we really need are studies of the way the system worked, how it managed to involve so many ordinary people in vicious actions, and what their motives were?

There is force in these arguments; yet there is a risk here of 'normalizing' a phenomenon that by any normal standards was monstrous. Even if it is banal to say so, licensed and arbitrary violence was the principal characteristic of Stalinist rule, and in so far as scholars avoid the Terror or minimize its significance, they risk being suspected of apologetic tendencies, however pure their intentions. Moreover, only by investigating such matters can one hope to assist the new post-Soviet Russia in coming to terms with its past, a matter on which more will be said in a moment. It might be objected that Egyptologists do not waste time condemning the pharaohs for gross misuse of human resources but get on with the job of analysing that civilization's surviving artefacts. But 'Stalinist civilization' (Stephen Kotkin's term) is a phenomenon of our own age and has to be judged by contemporary criteria of right and wrong, of success and failure.

At this point some would query the propriety of using the term 'Stalinism', as has been done in these pages: should one not rather speak of 'Communism', of which Stalinism was but one, if the most influential, variant? This takes us back to the controversy surrounding the *Black Book*,[2] which has been settled – provisionally at least, for such issues never die – in a sense unfavourable to its principal author's designs. The book's critics argue that we should be specific in passing judgement on the Communist movement, and the regimes to which it gave rise, since they took on different contours in various lands, shaped largely by the particular situations they faced; at best we should speak of 'communisms' instead of lumping together like and unlike indiscriminately, and take due note of the major changes that took place over time in each country. For example, the Leninism practised in Soviet Russia until the mid-1920s was substantially different from what followed, even if the latter was born out of the former and could not have existed without its Leninist foundations. Similarly, North Korea is today often referred to appropriately as 'Stalinist', whereas such an appellation would not fit either the Chinese People's Republic or Vietnam. As in the study of any other phenomenon, one has to be alert to the nuances without losing sight of the whole.

In an appreciation of the literature on world Communism over the last decade, Hermann Weber notes that 'considerable progress' has been made, thanks to the use of a variety of methodological approaches; the many discussions that have been held have yielded rich fruit. But he goes on to warn that 'inflationary' use of the term Stalinism 'serves to divert [the public] from Communist reality and to make it appear less harmful than it was'. Empirical research should continue to be encouraged, and not become overlaid by argument over abstract concepts such as modernization; 'finally, one must be aware of the dangers that stem from the *Zeitgeist*, from following current intellectual fashions.[3]

There is much to endorse here when considering the more limited field of Stalin's USSR. The first point to make is that, given the fact that only a decade or so has elapsed since the archives were opened, a vast corpus of original scholarly work has seen the light. If at first some writings were unduly sensation-seeking, the historical literature has since become more specific and concrete, more firmly based on documentary (and oral) sources. Second, both traditionalist (empiricist) historians and those employing PM concepts have made valuable contributions. The former approach has most merit in the study of state policy, ideology and administration; the latter approaches have enlarged our understanding of how Soviet society actually worked in the 1930s, behind the façade of imposed conformity; how, for example, the upwardly mobile 'constructed' for themselves a new identity that combined official values with others of a more traditional or individual kind; how subordinate officials on the 'periphery' had a hand in shaping the way policies conceived on high were implemented in practice; or how humble folk used the language of the powerful to advance their own interests. We have learned that there was much more disaffection among the general populace than earlier observers generally supposed; that horizontal group loyalties might be more substantial than vertical ones; that even in the Party's ranks there was a good deal of ambivalence and double-thinking – which tragically was all too often mis-construed as subversion and served to rationalize the purges. Others, by contrast, suppressed their inner doubts and, swayed by all-pervasive official propaganda, went along with their comrades in perpetrating violence against those they saw as 'internal enemies'. As a rule, they acted as they did under heavy societal pressures that it seemed pointless to resist.

The term 'complicity' has a rather sinister ring to it, as does the German *Mittäterschaft*, but is useful for our purposes, in that a great many people were induced by ambition and/or fear (mingled in proportions that varied from one individual to another as well as over time) to engage in activities ordained from above. These activities ranged from the inoffensive (improving one's physique, planting bushes in a neighbourhood park) to the malign (publicly charging a col-league with disloyalty at a 'criticism and self-criticism' meeting). Stefan Plaggenborg is certainly right that we need to know more about the nature and extent of such complicity:[4] its intensity in various social strata and the like. This is part and parcel of efforts to explore the interstices in the power structure, the 'grey areas' between those at the apex of the power pyramid and the commonality of citizens. In pursuing such investigations, we are aided by the numerous 'ego-documents' that have been published and studied, from which we can reconstruct their authors' *Lebenswelt*. This calls for an intuitive sympathy for the individuals concerned. We should never forget that, since Soviet society from 1929 onward was almost entirely insulated from external influences and the media were under strict control, ordinary people lacked the knowledge to make informed decisions, and so were easily swayed by prejudice or rumour.

These remarks apply to the Western writings that are considered in Part II of this book. Alter Litvin concludes that in Russia today the phenomenon of Stalinism remains a topical issue because the present ruling élite has so many links with the Soviet past. Although the KPRF is not in government, it has considerable influence and openly recognizes Stalin as an honoured former leader. Yet the task facing the country in the twenty-first century is to modernize both its political and economic structure: to promote the development of a mature civic society, democracy and the rule of law, and to make industrial enterprises more efficient and internationally competitive, for in today's globalized world market increased trade (preferably not just in raw materials) and foreign investment are the surest means of improving popular living standards.

But did not Stalin in his day also speak of modernizing a backward agrarian society? Did not his forced development of the industrial infrastructure accord with a global trend? Certainly this was so, but Soviet Russia's misfortune was that Stalin-style state socialism led to the creation of a powerful military–industrial complex while impoverishing the population, not least in the countryside. And pursuit of this idea of progress led to abuse of human rights on a massive scale, indeed to crimes that, as has been argued above, are devoid of any justification, moral or otherwise. Mass terror and the widespread use of slave labour, far from serving the cause of modernity, represented a giant step backward into barbarism.

'Modernization rather than democratization': this was the title of an article in *Izvestiia* in March 2004, just after President Putin's electoral triumph.[5] The authors speculated that the state's role in economic life would increase further, and that the ruling élite would contain an even greater proportion of officers from the armed forces, police, or other elements in the 'power structures'. If these writers are correct, will the Stalinist precedent be invoked or will its lessons be heeded? Given the fact that one third of the population is nostalgic for the Soviet era, while another third dreams of Russia taking a national, non-Western road to her destiny, it is hard to be optimistic. In any case, it is clear that members of the political class, not just historians, are interested in finding out how Stalin's Party–state functioned and manipulated opinion. Meanwhile, on the positive side, there are still many people who cherish the memory of the dictators' victims. Recently a website was created containing the names of over one million inmates of the Gulag, which their relatives or descendants may freely consult.[6]

In the Western world, fewer people are tempted to seek a silver lining in Stalin's dictatorial system. Even so, empiricist historians who take a long-term view of the 'Soviet experiment' cannot but recall that for many centuries the criteria applied in assessing a leader's merits were very different from those of today. At a time when human rights were little regarded, even by theologians or political philosophers, it was common to acclaim past or present rulers who had built mighty states, led their armed forces to victory, and provided firm government: Carolus Magnus, Akbar the Great, Frederick the Great, Peter the Great – the list is long (although some 'great' monarchs were seen less as empire builders than as models of piety and moral probity).

Iosif Vissarionovich fits neatly into this pattern: although not of royal blood, he and his minions skilfully reoriented revolutionary doctrine towards *étatiste* principles, papered over social divisions by the 1936 constitution, preached ethnic harmony and national grandeur, and redirected the people's resources to military purposes. After defeating the invaders in World War II, he ended his days as the world's most powerful ruler, master of an empire that stretched across two continents and outlasted him for two generations. These were indeed signal accomplishments of the traditional type. If that were all to be said about Stalin, we could confidently range him alongside his prototypes (including Ivan Groznyi, with whom as we know he felt a peculiar affinity) in the gallery of history's 'remarkable men'. But there are obvious blemishes in such a favourable picture. Stalin's claims to have organized victory in 1945 ring hollow. Such talents as he may have displayed as commander-in-chief or as an 'integrating figure' on the home front are outweighed by his arbitrary interventions in military appointments and operations, and especially by the homicidal purge of the Red Army leadership in 1937–8, the product of his overweening paranoia. And if Stalin was no military genius, the results of his dictatorial rule in the economic and political realms were equally woeful: bureaucratic inefficiency, shortages of essential goods, intellectual atrophy and so on. In defence of the *Vozhd'*, one might point to the rights granted on paper to (certain) national minorities, which allowed them to maintain or develop a sense of nationhood under the mask of 'Soviet patriotism'. But this was not the General Secretary's aim and he would have been horrified by the results to which it eventually led. Similarly, if Stalin is credited with the expansion of educational facilities and the sponsorship of research in certain branches of science and technology, one has to set these attainments against the blighting of creativity in so many other fields of culture by censorship and terror. In short, even leaving out of consideration the cost of Stalinist rule to human life and liberty, the record is bleak indeed.

As bad as Hitler's? For the reputed historian of ideas Alain Besançon, it was even worse,[7] although that is probably a minority view. Going beyond the more obvious criteria used when comparing Europe's most extreme twentieth-century dictatorships, Besançon argues that Stalinism, as a modern variant of the early Christian heresy of Gnosticism, did incalculable *invisible* damage to the ethical sense of the peoples over whom it ruled, by corrupting the values of the Enlightenment for which it claimed to stand and on which its popular appeal was based: 'the aim is not noble, it merely clothes itself in the colours of nobility' (pp. 33, 46–9, 51). Nazis and Bolsheviks both controlled the flow of information and spread lies, but the latter 'incit[ed] the population to be [their] accomplices', whereas the former tried to conceal their crimes. In Stalin's USSR, everyone was a potential target, not just people in limited categories, as in the Third Reich; paradoxically, the Gulag was the only place where freedom of thought could precariously survive (pp. 57–60).

This is strong meat, and many of Besançon's readers will feel he overstates his case. This is less historical analysis than a polemic (originally a lecture) rooted in an unfashionably rigorous theological position. Other Western historians, working on a less elevated plane, have sought rather to compare the Hitlerite and Stalinist systems as regimes (or, less convincingly, as societies).[8] Here much more work needs to be done, but the outlines are fairly clear: both grew out of post-war chaos and despondency; both pursued utopian goals with fanaticism; both held to a *Führerprinzip* but applied it differently; both relied on would-be monolithic parties; both engaged in propagandist manipulation of the popular mind; both interfered in the economy (the Hitlerites less ambitiously) and stood for 'guns before butter'; both dehumanized real or potential adversaries. The numbers of victims are roughly comparable (Stalin leading, but over a longer time span); Hitler's were mainly exogenous, Stalin's indigenous; extermination policies were more 'intentionalist' (deliberate) under the Nazis, whereas Stalin relied more on liquidation through purposeful neglect, although these might be distinctions without a difference and, as we have seen above (Weitz), both regimes applied ethnic criteria.

This catalogue is by no means exhaustive (both leaders were devotees of the cinema and grandiose architecture). But more remarkable than the shared features is the fact that each dictator remained publicly indifferent to the other's 'expertise' in repression: there is little hard evidence, for instance, that Stalin's terror owed much to the example of Hitler's 1934 putsch of the SA, or that the latter was impressed by the former's efficiency in destroying so many 'enemies' in 1937–8. The two regimes were so self-sufficient ideologically that, so to speak, they passed one another by in mutual ignorance.

Comparative studies of this kind need to be conducted with a feeling for the differences as well as the similarities. It is misleading to limit the exercise to the two most horrendous examples, and to forget that at this time Europe as a whole was prey to the lure of mechanistic thinking and total power. Few countries escaped it entirely, and so to arrive at a rounded evaluation one would need to situate the two extreme 'specimens' in the context of authoritarian regimes generally. The Western democracies also dishonoured themselves during World War II by state-sponsored violence on an uncalled-for scale (Hamburg and Dresden, Hiroshima and Nagasaki). Ute Frevert has argued for a 'Europeanization of memory'.[9] Ultimately, what matters is less the wickedness of particularly doctrinaire totalitarian regimes than the temptation for any modern government, whatever its colour, to abuse the vast power that advanced technology places in its hands.

Coming to terms with Stalinism

It is against this general background that one should try to evaluate the efforts made since 1953 to 'come to terms' with the legacy of Stalinism. There is no adequate English equivalent for the ponderous German word *Vergangenheitsbewältigung* (literally, 'overcoming the past'), which in recent years has given way to the less moralistic term *Aufarbeitung der Vergangenheit* ('working up the past').[10] The latter suggests scholars dispassionately sifting data and presenting the evidence to the broader public in such a way as to stimulate reflection and moral self-examination. As Barahona de Brito points out, it is only when repressive regimes are overthrown by war or revolution that we can expect a thorough-going break from earlier unjust practices, along with a purge of evil doers from positions of responsibility, followed by their trial and conviction according to *Rechtsstaat* principles. Far more common are 'negotiated transitions' in which people with compromised pasts continue to hold some power and/or exercise influence behind the scenes. This leads to an uneasy equilibrium between them and human rights advocates, which determines the extent to which victims are rehabilitated and compensated, as well as the scale of efforts to reshape a nation's collective memory by erecting memorials, holding remembrance ceremonies and so on. Alas, it is precisely 'in countries where lies have triumphed the longest and where repression has . . . claimed the most victims' that the democratic institutional structure is most fragile (pp. 11–17). The need to build a new polity based on a degree of consensus inhibits the authorities from taking judicial action against officials of the *ancien régime*.

There can scarcely be legal accountability in a 'shocked society' where sudden revelations of past injustices have led to 'feelings of guilt, shame and disgrace'.[11] The 1992 trial of former CPSU functionaries before the Russian Constitutional Court led to a verdict that reflected the balance of political power in the country at that moment and effectively exempted members of the successor party, the KPRF, from the obligation to 'work up' their past.[12] Certainly, there has been some progress: the 1991 law on the rehabilitation of victims of repression led to modest compensation grants for hundreds of thousands, but there was no 'lustration' or purge of the security service or other such bodies, and some of its old functionaries, such as V.S. Abakumov, have been rehabilitated. Adler sums up justly that 'no institutional way has been found to judge the crimes of Soviet rule' (p. 301).

This means that the task of 'working up the past' has to be shouldered by activists in civic bodies such as Memorial, often in the face of official disparagement, and in particular by historians. The latter's efforts, described in Part I of the present work, are most creditable and deserve more appreciation from their Western *confrères* than they usually get. The German historian Horst Schützler notes that most of the scholars concerned are people who suffered personally under Stalin or later, whereas their Western counterparts are as a rule younger 'outsiders'.[13] This helps to explain why the former are generally better at documentation and description, the latter at analysis.

Here post-modernism, and more particularly the 'cultural turn', which have been so influential of late, particularly in the United States, are unfortunately of limited help. Holocaust scholars have justly complained that historians who look on the Shoah as a cultural phenomenon have produced 'ethically compromised' work, by blurring the line between perpetrators and victims.[14] The same is true in regard to Stalinism. One should certainly give credit to the practitioners of PM for many often brilliant insights into social life and cultural patterns. But in her *Everyday Stalinism*, Sheila Fitzpatrick duly acknowledges that 'the state can never be kept out, try as we may'. Indeed, it has to be close to the heart of any narrative on the USSR after 1929. Social processes and cultural adaptations, interesting topics though they are, cannot *explain* the Stalinist phenomenon, and it is risky if Soviet citizens are represented as going about their daily rounds much as contemporaries did abroad when in the background there lurked a 'coercive ideocratic power' that most people would call, for want of a better term, 'totalitarian'.[15] In so far as the use and abuse of power demands the historian's attention, he or she is probably better off with well-tried methods of investigation. It is perfectly legitimate to inquire into the average citizen's mind, to explore imaginatively the dreams and fantasies that motivated their ambitions or relieved their anxieties, but we should not let these 'images' obscure reality – which is still worth hunting for, however hard it may be to apprehend.

Notes

1 Wilfried Loth, 'Das Ende der Legende', *Vierteljahresschrift für Zeitgeschichte* 50 (2002), 653–64; more recently, T. Schroeder in ibid. 52 (2004), 99–118.

2 See Chapter 11, n. 9.

3 Hermann Weber, 'Zehn Jahre historische Kommunismusforschung: Leistungen, Defizite, Perspektiven', ibid., 50 (2002), 611–34, here 626, 629, 631.

4 'Research into Stalinism ought to habituate itself to describing the various forms of social collusion': S. Plaggenborg, 'Stalinismusforschung: wie weiter?', in ibid. (ed.), *Stalinismus*, 443–52, here 446.

5 *Izvestiia*, 16 March 2004.

6 Ibid., 26 March 2004.
7 Alain Besançon, *Le malheur du siècle: sur le communisme, le nazisme et l'unicité de la Shoah* (Paris: Fayard, 1998); German trans. (used here) by Bodo Schulze, *Ueber die Shoah, den Nationalsozialismus und den Stalinismus* (Stuttgart: Klett-Cotta, 2001), 62.
8 For a good exposé of the problem of comparison, see D. Schmiechen-Ackermann, *Diktaturen im Vergleich* (Darmstadt: Wiss. Buchgesellschaft, 2002), esp. 78–82, who provides a thorough review of earlier historiography; on the *Black Book*, 120–3. Sir Alan Bullock, 'Has the Role of Hitler and Stalin Been Exaggerated?', *Government and Opposition* 32 (1997), 65–83, predictably answers the question in the negative (this lecture is a follow-up to an earlier monograph on the two leaders). Ian Kershaw and Moshe Lewin (eds), *Stalinism and Nazism: Dictatorships in Comparison* (Cambridge: Cambridge University Press, 1997), contains useful articles on the USSR by R. Suny, M. Lewin, B. Bonwetsch and others, but does not delve very deeply into the comparative aspect. Ian Kershaw argues plausibly that there are only 'superficial similarities' between the two regimes: 'Hitler and the Uniqueness of Nazism', *Journal of Contemporary History* 39 (2004), 239–54, here 241.
9 *Neue Zürcher Zeitung*, 30–1 August 2003.
10 On the two terms: A. Langenohl, *Erinnerung und Modernisierung: die öffentliche Rekonstruktion politischer Kollektivität am Beispiel des neuen Russland* (Göttingen: Vandenhoeck and Ruprecht, 2000), 281. On the process in Germany: P. Reichel, *Vergangenheitsbewältigung in Deutschland: die Auseinandersetzung mit der NS-Diktatur von 1945 bis heute* (Munich: C.H. Beck, 2001). There is now a vast literature on the 'construction' of collective memory and the problem of making atonement and restitution to the victims of repressive regimes: see notably *History and Memory* (Tel Aviv). Most relevant to our theme: N. Adler (Amsterdam), 'In Search of Identity: The Collapse of the Soviet Union and the Recreation of Russia', in B. de Brito *et al.* (eds), *The Politics of Memory: Transitional Justice in Democratizing Societies* (Oxford and New York: Oxford University Press, 2001), 275–302; cf. also C. Merridale, *Night of Stone: Death and Memory in Russia* (London: Granta, 2000; New York: Viking, 2001); K.E. Smith, *Mythmaking in the New Russia: Politics and Memory During the Yeltsin Era* (Ithaca, NY: Cornell University Press, 2002).
11 Adler, 'In Search of Identity', 277.
12 E. Fein, lecture, Basle, 2002; a monograph by this author on the topic is scheduled.
13 H. Schützler, 'Einblicke: zur "Totalitarismus"-Sicht und -Diskussion in der russischen Historiographie', in A. Loesdau and H. Meier (eds), *Zur Geschichte der Historiographie nach 1945: Beiträge eines Kolloquiums zum 75. Geburtstag von Gerhard Lozek* (Berlin: Trafo-Verlag Weist, 2001), 115–42, here 136. Cf. M. Hildermeier, 'Der Stalinismus im Urteil russischer Historiker', in N. Frei *et al.* (eds), *Geschichte vor Gericht: Historiker, Richter und die Suche nach Gerechtigkeit* (Munich: C.H. Beck, 2000), 93–102.
14 See N. Berg, *Der Holocaust und die westdeutschen Historiker: Erforschung und Erinnerung* (Göttingen: Wallstein, 2003).
15 M. Malia, 'Revolution Fulfilled', *Times Literary Supplement*, 15 June 2001, with correspondence on 20 July, 18 August 2001. Malia here attacks Fitzpatrick with unwarranted ferocity.

Glossary

Agitprop CC department for ideological work (agitation and propaganda)

agrarnik historian specializing in agricultural history

anti-cosmopolitanism campaign (1946–) to consolidate ideological controls at the expense of non-Russians, esp. Jews

apparat administrative officials (Party and/or state)

bunt spontaneous riot

byvshie liudi lit. 'people from the past': members of the former 'possessing classes'

Chekist familiarly, an official of the security police

collectivization drive (1929–) to expropriate independent peasant smallholders and to make them join collective farms

Cominform Communist Information Bureau (1947–56): body to co-ordinate activities of certain European Communist parties

Comintern Third (Communist) International (1919–43): agency promoting proletarian solidarity and revolution directed from Moscow

'cult of the individual' euphemistic term for Stalin's personal dictatorship, contrasted with the ideologically more respectable 'collective leadership'

dacha suburban cottage (rarely, villa), usually with garden allotment

dvoiki groups of two (cf. *troiki*)

Eurasians school of historians and philosophers, founded by emigrés in 1920s, who stress Russia's oriental affiliations in a generally positive sense

fond archival unit, roughly equivalent to a collection, containing several files (*dela*)

Gosplan State Planning Commission

'great break' Stalin's term for ending NEP and moving ahead with 'socialist construction', i.e. collectivization, forced-drive industrialization, and tougher repression of suspected domestic enemies

'Great Terror' popular term for waves of repression (1937–8) launched against alleged hidden enemies of the regime

Gulag popular term for Soviet penal system under Stalin, administered by the GULag (Main Administration of Labour Camps of the NKVD), which ran ITK, ITL and supervised 'special settlers' (*q.v.*)

katorga exile with forced labour under a particularly harsh regime

kolkhoz collective farm

kolkhoznik collective-farm worker

kompromat material collected or fabricated by security organs to discredit or harm a suspected person

Komsomol Young Communist League: the CPSU's chief organization for adolescents and young adults

kulak under Stalin, derogatory term for relatively well-to-do smallholder, suspected of 'capitalist' tendencies and slated for 'liquidation as a class'

kul'turnost' civilized, decent standards of everyday behaviour

limit quota, i.e. for tribunals (*troiki*) passing sentences during 'mass operations'

lishinets (pl. *lishentsy*): persons, e.g. members of former 'possessing classes', deprived of civil rights under the 1918 RSFSR Constitution

'mass operations' during the 'Great Terror' and later, drives to arrest and 'liquidate' (by shooting or exile to the Gulag) members of suspect social or ethnic groups

Memorial civic organization for defence of human rights which *i.a.* assists victims of repression during the Soviet era

Military Collegium special tribunal of USSR Supreme Court (and some lower courts) for judging certain political cases under a simplified procedure; in (post-Soviet) Russia, also concerned with rehabilitation of political offenders under Soviet rule

'neo-NEP' term given by some scholars to a temporary easement of domestic policy (1932–4)

NEPmen entrepreneurs or traders permitted to exist during NEP (1921–7/8), but later suppressed

nomenklatura properly, list of official positions to which holders were appointed by a Party organization at the appropriate level; popularly, Party or state officials enjoying hidden privileges

obkom Party committee in an *oblast'*

obkomsec first secretary of an *oblast'* Party committee

oblast' province, subdivided into districts (*raiony*)

Okhrana popular term for political police during last decades of tsarist era

oprichnina reign of terror against suspect boyars and dependants under Ivan IV ('the Terrible'), 1564–72

Party, the the ruling party in Soviet Russia/ USSR, known successively as RCP(b) (1918–25), AUCP(b) (1925–52), CPSU (1952–91)

people's commissariat chief executive organ in Soviet government (1917–46), thereafter more conventionally termed ministry

people's democracy Soviet term for political and social order in certain east European satellite countries after 1945, in which a limited degree of pluralism was permitted to exist

Politburo (Political Bureau): senior decision-making body in Communist Party

Procurator-General (1935–): chief legal official in USSR

Secretariat organ of CC CPSU which, with its departments, supervised the administration of the Party, and by extension of the country

security police popularly, 'the organs': agency for control of the population and repression of political offences; known successively as Vecheka, GPU, OGPU (1923–34), NKVD (1934–46), MVD and MGB (1946–54), KGB (1954–91); succeeded in post-Soviet Russia by FSB

seksot   under-cover informer

sharashka   colloquial term for special camp within Gulag for scientists and engineers assigned to work on top-priority projects

SMERSH   (literally, 'death to spies!'): counter-intelligence force during World War II

sovkhoz   State farm, organized on more thorough 'socialist' principles than a collective farm (*kolkhoz*)

Sovnarkom   acronym for Council of People's Commissars, formally the senior governmental decision-making body

special settlers   (*spetspereselentsy*): exiles, a category of prisoners assigned by NKVD to a particular zone of residence and labour tasks

spetskhran   in archive or library, special repository for politically sensitive material

Stakhanovite   participant in Party-directed competitive campaign to boost output (1935–41)

Supreme Soviet   the two-chamber legislature (1936–)

svodki   reports submitted by security police operatives and Party functionaries on the political situation and popular mood in a given locality

troika   group (commission) of three set up for action on an emergency task, esp. quasi-judicial tribunal for rapid sentencing and disposal of accused during 'Great Terror'

urka   criminal convict in Gulag

vory v zakone   members of criminal gangs in Gulag effectively allowed temporary control over certain camps

Vozhd'   'the Leader', term used in laudatory sense of Stalin

vydvizhentsy   lit. 'promotees': predominantly working-class youngsters who moved up to hold administrative jobs under Stalin

Zhdanovshchina   campaign for greater political conformity in literature and the arts (1946–), generally associated with A.A. Zhdanov

Zhenotdel   Department for Work among Women in Party CC (1919–30)

Bibliography

This bibliography is limited to monographs and miscellanies published since 1997. Collective volumes are where possible entered under the name of the editor or compiler.

Russian-language works

Abramkin, V. and Chesnokova, V. *Tiuremnyi mir glazami politzakliuchennykh, 1940–1980-e gg.* (Moscow: Muravei, 1998).

Afanas'ev, Yu.N. *Opasnaia Rossiia: traditsii samovlastiia segodnia* (Moscow: RGGU, 2001).

—— *et al.* (eds) *Sovetskoe obshchestvo: vozniknovenie, razvitie, istoricheskii final* (Moscow: RGGU, 1997).

Allilueva, S.I. *Dvadtsat' pisem drugu* (Moscow: Zakharov, 2000).

'Al'met'evskoe delo': tragicheskie stranitsy iz istorii krest'ianstva Al'met'evskogo raiona (konets 20-kh – nachalo 30-kh gg.): sbornik dokumentov i materialov (Kazan', 1999).

Al'tman, I.A. *Zhertvy nenavisti: Kholokost v SSSR, 1941–1945 gg.* (Moscow: Fond Kovcheg, 2002).

Antonov-Ovseenko, A.V. *Teatr Iosifa Stalina* (Moscow: AST, 2000).

Artizov, A. and Naumov, O. (comps) *Reabilitatsiia: kak eto bylo: dokumenty Prezidiuma TsK KPSS i drugie materialy. Vol. I: mart 1953–fevral' 1956. Vol. 2: fevral' 1956–nachalo 80-kh gg.* (Moscow: Mezhdunarodnyi fond 'Demokratiia', 2000).

—— (comps) *Vlast' i khudozhestvennaia intelligentsiia: dokumenty TsK RKP(b)–VKP(b), VChK–OGPU–NKVD o kul'turnoi politike, 1917–1953 gg.* (Moscow: Mezhdunarodnyi fond 'Demokratiia', 1999).

Bagavieva, S.S. *Politicheskie repressii v sovetskom Tatarstane (1918–nachalo 50-kh gg.): analiz i kharakteristika istochnikov.* Thesis abstract. (Kazan', 2003).

Balandin, R. and Mironov, S. *'Klubok' vokrug Stalina: zagovory i bor'ba za vlast' v 1930-e gg.* (Moscow: Veche, 2002).

Berezhkov, V.I. *Piterskie prokuratory: rukovoditeli VChK–MGB, 1918–1954* (St Petersburg: Blits, 1998).

—— and Pekhtereva, S.V. *Zhenshchiny–chekisty* (Moscow: Olma-press, 2003).

Bezverkhiy, A.G. *et al.* (eds) *SMERSH: istoricheskie ocherki i arkhivnye dokumenty* (Moscow: Glavnoe arkhivnoe upravlenie Moskvy, 2003).

Biriukov, A. *Kolymskoe triedinstvo. Part I. Poslednyi Riurikovich* [Prince D.P. Sviatopolk-Mirsky] (Magadan: Maobti, 2001).

Bobrenov, V.A. *'Doktor smerti', ili varsonof'evskie prizraki* (Moscow: Olimp, 1997).

Bokhanov, A.N. *et al.* (eds) *Rossiia i mirovaia tsivilizatsiia: k 70-letiiu chlena–korrespondenta RAN A.N. Sakharova* (Moscow: IRI RAN, 2000).

Bugai, N.F. and Gonov, A. *Kavkaz: narody v eshelonakh, 20-e–60-e gg.* (Moscow: Insan, 1998).

Buldakov, V.P. *Krasnaia smuta: priroda i posledstviia revoliutsionnogo nasiliia* (Moscow: ROSSPEN, 1997).

Cherushev, N.S. (comp.) *'Dorogoi nash tovarishch Stalin!' . . . i drugie tovarishchi: obrashcheniia rodstvennikov i repressirovannykh komandirov Krasnoi armii k rukovoditeliam strany* (Moscow: Zven'ia, 2001).

Chubar'ian, A.O. *et al.* (eds), *Stalin i 'kholodnaia voina': sbornik dokumentov* (Moscow: IRI RAN, 1998).

Chuev, F.I. *Molotov, poluderzhavnyi vlastelin* (Moscow: Olma-press, 1999).

—— *Soldaty imperii: besedy, vospominaniia, dokumenty* (Moscow: fond Kovcheg, 1998).

Chukovsky, K.I. *Dnevniki, 1926–1934* (Moscow: Nauka, 2001).

Danilov, V.P. *et al.* (eds) *Tragediia soveskoi derevni: kollektivizatsiia i raskulachivanie: dokumenty i materialy v 5 tomakh, 1927–1939* (Moscow: ROSSPEN, 1997 – in progress).

D'iakov, Yu.L. *et al.* (eds) *« Sovershenno sekretno »: Lubianka–Stalinu o polozhenii v strane, 1922–1934 gg.* (Moscow, 2001 – in progress).

Dienko, A. *et al.* (comps) *Razvedka i kontrrazvedka v litsakh: entsiklopedicheskii slovar' rossiiskikh spetssluzhb* (Moscow: Russkii mir, 2002).

Fel'shtinsky, Yu.G. (ed. and comp.) *Byl li Stalin agentom okhranki?: sbornik statei, materialov i dokumentov* (Moscow: Terra, 1999).

Fradkin, V. *Delo Kol'tsova* (Moscow: Vagrius, 2002).

Frolov, N.S. *Tragediia naroda: iz istorii Cheremshenskogo raiona Tatarstana* (Kazan', 1999).

Fursenko, A.A. (ed.) *Istoricheskaia nauka na rubezhe vekov* (Moscow: Nauka, 2001).

Gaiduk, I.V. *et al.* (eds), *Stalinskoe desiatiletie kholodnoi voiny: fakty i gipotezy* (Moscow: Nauka, 1999).

Gorodetsky, G. *Mif 'Ledokola' nakanune voiny* (Moscow: Progress-Akademiia, 1995).

—— *Rokovoi samoobman: Stalin i napadenie Germanii na Sovetskii Soiuz* (Moscow: ROSSPEN, 1999).

Gorshkov, M.K. *et al.* (eds) *Krainosti istorii i krainosti istorikov: sbornik statei* (Moscow: RNISiNP, 1997).

Got'e, Yu.V. *Moi zametki* (Moscow: Terra, 1997).

Gromov, E. *Stalin: vlast' i iskusstvo* (Moscow: Respublika, 1998).

Gur'ianov, A.E. (comp.) *Repressii protiv poliakov i pol'skikh grazhdan* (Istoricheskie sborniki Memoriala, fasc. 1.) (Moscow: Zven'ia, 1997).

Gusliarov, E. *Stalin v zhizni: sistematizirovannyi svod vospominanii sovremennikov, dokumentov epokhi, versii istorikov* (Moscow: Olma-press, 2003).

Heinemann, M. and Kolchinsky, E.I. (eds) *Za 'zheleznym zanavesom': mify i realii sovetskoi nauki* (St Petersburg: Dm. Bulanin, 2002).

Ilizarov, B.S. *Tainaia zhizn' Stalina: po materialam ego biblioteki i arkhiva: k istoriosofii stalinizma* (Moscow: Veche, 2002).

Istoriia politicheskikh repressii i soprotivleniia nesvobode: kniga dlia uchitelei (Moscow: Mosgorarkhiv, 2002).

Ivanov, V.A. *Mekhanizm massovykh repressii v Sovetskoi Rossii v kontse 20–40-kh gg.: na materialakh Severo-zapada RSFSR.* Thesis abstract (St Petersburg, 1998).

Ivanova, G.M. *GULAG v sisteme totalitarnogo gosudarstva* (Moscow: Moskovskii obshch-estvennyi nauchnyi fond, 1997).

Karpov, V.V. *Generalissimus.* 2 vols (Kaliningrad: Yantarnyi skos, 2002).

Katalog vystavki '1953 god: mezhdu proshlym i budushchim' (Moscow, 2003).

Khaustov, V.N. *Deiatel'nost' organov gosudarstvennoi bezopasnosti NKVD SSSR, 1934–1941 gg.* Thesis abstract (Moscow, 1998).

—— *et al.* (eds) *Lubianka: Stalin i VChK–GPU–OGPU–NKVD: sbornik dokumentov: ianvar' 1922–dekabr' 1936* (Moscow: Mezhdunarodnyi fond 'Demokratiia', 2003).

Khlevniuk, O.V. *et al.* (comps) *Politbiuro TsK VKP(b) i Sovet ministrov SSSR, 1945–1953* (Moscow: ROSSPEN, 2002).

—— (eds) *Stalin i Kaganovich: perepiska, 1931–1936 gg.* (Moscow: ROSSPEN, 2001).

Khlusov, M.I. (comp.) *Ekonomika GULAGa i ee rol' v razvitii strany, 1930-e gg.: sbornik dokumentov* (Moscow: IRI RAN, 1998).

Khrushchev, N.S. *Vospominaniia: izbrannye fragmenty* (Moscow: Vagrius, 1997).

—— *Vremia: liudi: vlast'.* 4 vols (Moscow: Moskovskie Novosti, 1999).

Kirilina, A. *Neizvestnyi Kirov* (St Petersburg: Neva, 2001).

Kokurin, A.I. and Petrov, N.V. (comps), Shostakovsky, V.N. (ed.), *GULAG (Glavnoe upravlenie lagerei), 1918–1960: dokumenty* (Moscow: fond 'Demokratiia', 2002).

—— (comps) *Lubianka: organy VChK–OGPU–NKVD–NKGB–MGB–MVD–KGB, 1917–1991: spravochnik* (Moscow: Materik, 2003).

Kondakova, I.A. and Chernobaev, A.A. *'Istoricheskii arkhiv', 1919–2001 gg.: ukazatel' opublikovannykh materialov* (Moscow: ROSSPEN, 2002).

Kornienko, G.M. *'Kholodnaia voina'. Svidetel'stvo ee uchastnika* (Moscow: Olma-press, 2001).

Kostyrchenko, G.V. *Tainaia politika Stalina: vlast' i antisemitizm* (Moscow: Mezhdunarodnye otnosheniia, 2001).

Kozlov, V.P. *Obmanutaia, no torzhestvuiushchaia Klio: podlogi pis'mennykh istochnikov po rossiiskoi istorii v XX v.* (Moscow: ROSSPEN, 2001).

—— *Rossiiskoe arkhivnoe delo: arkhivno-istochnikovedcheskie issledovaniia* (Moscow: ROSSPEN, 1999).

Kumanev, G.A. *Riadom so Stalinym* (Moscow: Bylina, 1999).

Kvashonkin, A.V. *et al.* (eds), *Sovetskoe rukovodstvo: perepiska, 1928–1941 gg.: sbornik dokumentov* (Moscow: ROSSPEN, 1999).

Lebedeva, N.S. *Katyn', mart 1940 – sentiabr' 2000 g.: rasstrel: sud'by zhivykh: ekho Katyni: dokumenty.* Ed. V.P. Kozlov *et al.* (Moscow: Ves' mir, 2001).

Leushin, M.A. *Dokumenty VKP(b) (KPSS) kak istochnik po istorii istoricheskoi nauki v SSSR, 1945–1955.* Thesis abstract. (Moscow: RGGU, 2000).

Liparteliani, G.L. *Stalin velikii* (St Petersburg: Roza, 2001).

Litvin, A.L. (ed.) *Genrikh Yagoda: narkom vnutrennikh del SSSR, general'nyi komissar gosbezopasnosti: sbornik dokumentov* (Kazan', 1997).

—— *Men'shevistskii protsess 1931 g.: sbornik dokumentov.* 2 bks. (Moscow: ROSSPEN, 1999).

Livshin, A.Ya.and Orlov, I.B. *Pis'ma vo vlast', 1917–1927* (Moscow: ROSSPEN, 1998).

Lobanov, M. *Stalin: v vospominaniiakh sovremennikov i dokumentakh epokhi* (Moscow: Algoritm, 2002).

Manning, R. *Bel'skii raion, 1937 god* (Smolensk: SGPU, 1998).

Markov, Ye.V. *et al.*, *Gulagovskie tainy osvoeniia Severa* (Moscow: Stroiizdat, 2002).

Medvedev, Zh. and R. *Neizvestnyi Stalin* (Moscow: Folio, 2002).

Mel'tiukhov, M.I. *Upushchennyi shans Stalina: Sovetskii Soiuz i bor'ba za Yevropu, 1930–1941: dokumenty, fakty, suzhdeniia* (Moscow: Veche, 2002).

Mlechin, L.M. *Predsedateli KGB: rassekrechennye sud'by* (Moscow: Tsentrpolitgraf, 1999).

Mukhin, Yu.I. *Ubiistvo Stalina i Beriia* (Moscow: Forum, 2002).

Naumov, V.P. *et al.* (comps) *Lavrentii Beriia: 1953: stenogramma iiul'skogo plenuma TsK i drugie dokumenty* (Moscow: Mezhdunarodnyi fond 'Demokratiia', 1999).

Ostrovsky, A.V. *Kto stoial za spinoi Stalina?* (St Petersburg: Neva, 2003).

Papchinsky, A.A. and Tumshis, M.A. *Shchit, raskolotyi mechom: NKVD protiv VChK* (Moscow: Sovremennik, 2001).

Papkov, S.A. *Stalinskii terror v Sibiri, 1928–1941* (Novosibirsk, 1997).

Pavlov, D.B. *Otechestvennye i zarubezhnye publikatsii dokumentov rossiiskikh partii* (Thesis) (Moscow, 1998).

Pavlova, I.V. *Mekhanizm vlasti i stroitel'stvo stalinskogo sotsializma* (Novosibirsk: SO RAN, 2001).

Peregudova, Z.I. *Politicheskii sysk Rossii, 1890–1917* (Moscow: ROSSPEN, 2000).

Petrov, N.V. and Skorkin, K.V. *Kto rukovodil NKVD, 1934–1941: spravochnik* (Moscow: Zven'ia, 1999).

Piankevich, V.L. *Vosstanovlenie ekonomiki SSSR (seredina 1941 g. – seredina 1950-kh gg.): istoriografiia* (St Petersburg: Nestor, 2001).

Piatnitsky, V. *Zagovor protiv Stalina* (Moscow: Sovremennik, 1998).

Pikhoia, R.G. *Sovetskii Soiuz: istoriia vlasti, 1945–1991* (Moscow: RAGS, 1998).

—— *et al.* (eds) *Katyn': plenniki neob'iavlennoi voiny : dokumenty i materialy* (Moscow: Fond 'Demokratiia', 1997).

Pokaianie: martirolog. 4 vols (Sytkyvkar, 1998–2001).

Polian, P. *Ne po svoei vole . . . Istoriia i geografiia prinuditel'nykh migratsii v SSSR* (Moscow: OGI-Memorial, 2001).

Poliansky, A.I. *Yezhov: istoriia 'zheleznogo' stalinskogo narkoma* (Moscow: Veche, 2001).

Poliansky, M.M. *Narkom Yagoda* (Moscow: Veche, 2002).

Politicheskii sysk v Rossii: istoriia i sovremennost': sbornik (St Petersburg: Gosudarstvennyi universitet, 1997).

Pyzhikov, A.V. *Khrushchevskaia 'ottepel''* (Moscow: Olma-press, 2002).

Radzinsky, E. *Stalin* (Moscow: Vagrius, 1997).

Rapoport, Ya.L. *Na rubezhe dvukh epokh: delo vrachei 1953 g.* (St Petersburg: Pushkinskii fond, 2003).

Repressii protiv rossiiskikh nemtsev (Moscow, 1998).

Riutta, U. and Togi, I. *Osuzhdennyi po 58-i stat'e: istoriia cheloveka, proshedshego ural'skie lageria* (St Petersburg: Bibliia dlia vsekh, 2001).

Rogovin, V.Z. *Konets oznachaet nachalo* (Moscow: Shcherbinskaia tipografiia, 2002).

—— *Partiia rasstreliannykh* (Moscow: Vadim Rogovin, 1997).

Rokitiansky, Ya.G. *et al.* (comps) *Sud palacha: Nikolai Vavilov v zastenkakh NKVD: biograficheskii ocherk: dokumenty* (Moscow: 1999).

Sakharov, A.N. *et al.* (eds) *Obshchestvo i vlast': rossiiskaia provintsiia, 1917–1980-e gg.: po materialam Nizhegorodskikh arkhivov.* Vol. I: *1917 – seredina 30-kh gg.* Ed. A.A. Kulakov (Moscow: IRI RAN, 2002).

Semenov, A.V. *et al.* (eds) *Zabveniiu ne podlezhit: kniga pamiati zhertv politicheskoi repressii Omskoi oblasti,* 8 vols (Omsk: Omskoe knizhnoe izdatel'stvo, 2000–3).

Sevost'ianov, G.N. *et al.* (eds) *Etot protivorechivyi XX vek: k 80-letiiu so dnia rozhdeniia akademika RAN Yu.A. Poliakova* (Moscow: ROSSPEN, 2001).

Shalamov, V. *Vospominaniia* (Moscow: Olimp, 2001).

Shnol', S.E. *Geroi i zlodei rossiiskoi nauki* (Moscow: Kron-press, 1997).

Sipols, V.Ya. *Tainy diplomaticheskie: kanun Velikoi Otechestvennoi, 1939–1941* (Moscow: IRI RAN, 1997).

Smirnov, M.V. *et al.* (comps), *Sistema ispravitel'no-trudovykh lagerei v SSSR, 1923–1960: spravochnik* (Moscow: Zven'ia, 1998).

Sobolev, V.A. *et al.* (eds) *Lubianka 2: iz istorii otechestvennoi kontrrazvedki* (Moscow: Mosgorarkhiv, 1999).

Soifer, V.N. *Vlast' i nauka: razgrom kommunistami otechestvennoi intelligentsii* (Moscow: CheRo, 2002).

Sokolov, A.K. *Kurs sovetskoi istorii, 1917–1940: uchebnoe osobie dlia VUZov* (Moscow, 1999).

Sokolov, B.V. *Narkom strakha: Yagoda, Yezov, Beriia, Abakumov* (Moscow: AST-press-kniga, 2001).

Solov'ev, B.G. and Sukhodeev, V.V. *Polkovodets Stalin* (Moscow: Eksmo-press, 2001).

Solzhenitsyn, A.I. (comp.) *Pozhivshi v GULAGe* (Moscow: Russkii put', 2001).

Spetssluzhby i chelovecheskie sud'by (Moscow: Olma-press, 2000).

Stepashin, S.V. and A.P.Bykov (eds) *Organy gosudarstvennoi bezopasnosti SSSR v Velikoi Otechestvennoi voine: sbornik dokumentov.* Vol. I in 2 bks: *Nakanune.* Vol. 2 in 2 bks. *1941 god: dokumenty* (Moscow: A/O Kniga i biznes, 1995, 1998).

Stetsovsky, Yu. *Istoriia sovetskikh repressii.* 2 vols (Moscow: Obshchestvennyi fond Glasnost', 1997).

Stoliarov, K.A. *Palachi i zhertvy* (Moscow: Olma-press, 1997).

Stoliarova, L.V. *et al.* (comps), Shmidt, S.O. (ed.), *U istochnika: sbornik statei v chest' chlena–korrespondenta RAN S.M. Kashtanova,* 2 pts (Moscow: MPU Signal, 1997).

Sudoplatov, A.P. *Tainaia zhnizn' generala Sudoplatova: pravda i vymysly o moem ottse.* 2 bks (Moscow: Olma-press, 1998).

Sudoplatov, P.A. *Spetsoperatsiia: Lubianka i Kreml', 1930–1950 gg.* (Moscow: Olma-press, 1997).

Sukhomliknov, A.V. *Vasilii, syn vozhdia* (Moscow: 'Sovershenno sekretno', 2001).

Suvenirov, O.F. *Tragediia RKKA, 1937–1938* (Moscow: Terra, 1998).

Suvorov [Rezun], V. *Ochishchenie: zachem Stalin obezglavil svoiu armiiu?* (Moscow: AST, 1998).

—— *Zachem Gitler napal na Sovetskii Soiuz?* (Moscow: AST, 2000).

Sysoev, N.G. *Zhandarmy i chekisty: ot Benkendorfa do Yagody* (Moscow: Veche, 2002).

Tagirov, I.R. (ed.) *Neizvestnyii Sultan-Galiev: rassekrechennye dokumenty i materialy* (Kazan': Tatarskoe knizhnoe izdatel'stvo, 2002).

Tkachenko, V.G. and K.V. [Enko, K. and T.] *Chastnaia zhizn' vozhdei: Lenin, Stalin, Trotskii* (Moscow: Tsentrpoligraf, 2000).

Torchinov, V.A. and Lentiuk, A.M. *Vokrug Stalina: istoriko–biograficheskii spravochnik* (St Petersburg: Filologicheskii fakul'tet St Peterburgskogo gosudarstvenngo universiteta, 2000).

Ulanovskaia, N. and M. *Istoriia odnoi sem'i: memuary* (St Petersburg: Inapress, 2003).

Vaksberg, A.I. *Gibel' burevestnika: M. Gor'kii: poslednie 20 let* (Moscow: Terra, 1999).

Vasil'ev, V. and Viola, L. (eds) *Kollektivizatsiia i krest'ianskoe soprotivlenie na Ukraine, noiabr' 1929 – mart 1930 gg.* (Vinnitsa/Vynnitsa: Logos, 1997).

Vihavainen, T. *Stalin i finny.* Tr. N.A. Kovalenko, ed. F.M. Kovalenko (St Petersburg: Neva, 2000).

Viola, L. *et al.* (eds) *Riazanskaia derevnia v 1929–1930 gg.: khronika golovokruzheniia: dokumenty i materialy* (Moscow: ROSSPEN, 1998).

Yakovlev, A.N. *Krestosev* (Moscow: Vagrius, 2000).

—— *Omut pamiati: ot Stolypina do Putina.* 2 vols (Moscow: Vagrius, 2001).

—— *Postizhenie* (Moscow: Vagrius, 1998).

—— *Sumerki* (Moscow: Materik, 2003).

—— *Svoboda – moia religiia: k 80-letiiu so dnia rozhdeniia: sbornik statei* (Moscow: Vagrius, 2003).

Yazhborovskaia, I.S. *et al.*, *Katynskii sindrom v sovetskso–pol'skikh i rossiisko–pol'skikh otnosheniiakh* (Moscow: ROSSPEN, 2001).

Yemel'ianov, Yu.V. *Stalin: put' k vlasti* (Moscow: Veche, 2002).

Yesakov, V.D. *et al.* (comps) *Akademiia nauk v resheniiakh Politbiuro TsK RKP(b) – VKP(b), 1922–1991.* Vol. I. *1922–1952* (Moscow: ROSSPEN, 2000 – in progress).

Zalessky, K.A. *Imperiia Stalina: biograficheskii entsikopedicheskii slovar'* (Moscow: Veche, 2000).

Zdanovich, A.A. *et al.* (eds) *Rossiiskie spetssluzhby: istoriia i sovremennost': materialy istoricheskikh chtenii na Lubianke 1997–2000 gg.* (Moscow: X-History, 2003).

Zen'kovich, N.A. *Tainy ukhodiashchego veka – 3* (Moscow: Olma-press, 1999).

Zhukovsky, V.S. *Lubianskaia imperiia NKVD, 1937–1939* (Moscow: Veche, 2001).

Zima, V.F. *Golod v SSSR 1946–1947 gg.: proiskhozhdenie i posledstviia* (Moscow: IRI RAN, 1996; 2nd edn Lewiston NY, 1999).

Zubkova, E.Yu. *Poslevoennoe sovetskoe obshchestvo: politika i povsednevnost', 1945–1953 gg.* (Moscow: ROSSPEN, 2000).

Zuskina-Perel'man, A. *Puteshestvie Veniamina: razmyshleniia o zhizni i sud'be evreiskogo aktera Veniamina Zuskina* (Moscow: Mosty kul'tury and Jerusalem: Gesharim, 2002).

Works in Western languages

Adibekov, G.M. *Das Kominform und Stalins Neuordnung Europas*, ed. B.H. Bayerlein *et al.* (Frankfurt, Oxford and New York: P. Lang, 2002).

Adler, N. *The Gulag Survivor: Beyond the Soviet System* (New Brunswick, NJ: Rutgers University Press, 2002).

Adomeit, H. *Imperial Overstretch: Germany in Soviet Policy from Stalin to Gorbachev: An Analysis Based on New Archival Evidence, Memoirs and Interviews* (Baden-Baden: Nomos, 1998).

Alexopoulos, G. *Stalin's Outcasts: Aliens, Citizens and the Soviet State, 1926–1936* (Ithaca, NY and London: Cornell University Press, 2003).

Andrew, C. and Mitrokhin, V. *The Sword and the Shield: The Mitrokhin Archive: The KGB in Europe and the West* (New York and London: Basic Books, 1999).

Anušauskas, A. *et al.* (eds) *The Anti-Soviet Resistance in the Baltic States* (Vilnius: Vilspa, 1999).

Applebaum, A. *Gulag: A History of the Soviet Camps* (New York and London: Allen Lane, 2003).

Attwood, L. *Creating the New Soviet Woman: Women's Magazines as Engineers of Female Identity, 1922–1953* (Basingstoke: Macmillan, 1999).

Baberowski, J. *Der Feind ist überall: Stalinismus im Kaukasus* (Munich: DVA, 2003).

Baberowski, J. *Der rote Terror: Geschichte des Stalinismus* (Stuttgart: DVA, 2003).

Banac, I. (ed.) *The Diary of Georgi Dimitrov, 1933–1948*. Trans. J.T. Hedges *et al.* (New Haven, CT: Yale University Press, 2003).

Barahona de Brito, A. *et al.* (eds) *The Politics of Memory: Transitional Justice in Democratizing Societies* (Oxford and New York: Oxford University Press, 2001).

Bayerlein, B.H. *et al.* (eds) *Moscou – Paris – Berlin: télégrammes chiffrés du Komintern, 1939–1941* (Paris: Tallandier, 2003).

Bertrand, F. *L'anthropologie soviétique des années 20–30: configuration d'une rupture* (Bordeaux: Presses universitaires de Bordeaux, 2002).

Besançon, A. *Ueber die Shoah, den Nationalsozialismus und den Stalinismus*. Trans. B. Schulze (Stuttgart: Klett-Cotta, 2001).

Beyrau, D. (ed.) *Im Dschungel der Macht: intellektuelle Professionen unter Hitler und Stalin* (Göttingen: Vandenhoeck & Ruprecht, 1999).

Birstein, V.J. *The Perversion of Knowlege: The True Story of Soviet Science* (Boulder, CO and Oxford: Westview, 2001).

Blum, A. and Mespoulet, M. *L'anarchie bureaucratique: pouvoir et statistique sous Staline* (Paris: Ed. de la Découverte, 2003).

Blumenhagen, K.H. *Die deutsch-sowjetischen Handelsbeziehungen 1939–1941: ihre Bedeutung für die jeweilige Kriegswirtschaft* (Hamburg: Kovac, 1998).

Bogle, L.L. (ed.) *The Cold War*. 5 vols (New York: Routledge, 2001).

Boobbyer, P. *The Stalin Era* (London and New York: Routledge, 2000).

Brandenberger, D.L. *National Bolshevism: Stalinist Mass Culture and the Formation of Modern Russian National Identity, 1931–1956* (Cambridge, MA: Harvard University Press, 2002).

Brent, J. and Naumov, V.P. *Stalin's Last Crime: The Plot against the Jewish Doctors* (New York: HarperCollins, 2003).

Brooks, J. *Thank You, Comrade Stalin! Soviet Public Culture from Revolution to Cold War* (Princeton, NJ: Princeton University Press, 1999).

Bullard, J. and M. (eds) *Inside Stalin's Russia: The Diaries of Reader Bullard, 1930–1934* (Charlbury, UK: Day Books, 2000).

Büttner, R. *Sowjetisierung oder Selbständigkeit? Die sowjetische Finnlandpolitik 1943–1948* (Hamburg: Kovac, 2001).

Carley, M.J. *1939: The Alliance That Never Was and the Coming of World War II* (Chicago: Ivan R. Dee, 1999).

Cassiday, J.A. *The Enemy on Trial: Early Soviet Courts on Stage and Screen* (DeKalb, IL: Northern Illinois University Press, 2000).

Castin-Chaparro, L. *Puissance de l'URSS, misères de l'Allemagne: Staline et la question allemande, 1941–1955* (Paris: Publications de la Sorbonne, 2002).

Caute, D. *The Dancer Defects: The Struggle for Cultural Supremacy during the Cold War* (London and New York: Oxford University Press, 2003).

Channon, J. (ed.) *Politics, Society and Stalinism in the USSR* (Basingstoke and London: Macmillan, 1998).

Chase, W.J. *Enemies Within the Gates? The Comintern and the Stalinist Repression, 1934–1939*. Russian documents trans. V.A. Staklo (New Haven, CT and London: Yale University Press, 2002).

Chinsky, P. *Staline: archives inédites, 1926–1936* (Paris: Berg International, 2001).

Chubarian, A.O. and Shukman, H. (eds) *Stalin and the Soviet-Finnish War, 1939–1940*. Trans. T. Sorokin (London and Portland, OR: Frank Cass, 2001).

Chumachenko, T.A. *Church and State in Soviet Russia: Orthodoxy from World War II to the Khrushchev Years*. Trans. and ed. E.E. Roslof (London and Armonk, NY: M.E. Sharpe, 2002).

Clements, B.E. *Bolshevik Women* (Cambridge and New York: Cambridge University Press, 1997).

Cottam, K.J. (ed. and trans.) *Defending Leningrad: Women Behind Enemy Lines* (Nepean, ON: New Military Publishers, 1998).

Courtois, S. *et al. The Black Book of Communism: Crimes, Terror, Repression* (Cambridge, MA: Harvard University Press, 1999).

Cummins, A.G. (ed.) *Documents of Soviet History*, vol. 5: *Revolution from Above, 1929–1931* (Gulf Breeze, FL: Academic International, 2000).

Dahlke, S. *'An der antireligiösen Front': der Verband der Gottlosen in der Sowjetunion der zwanziger Jahre* (Hamburg: Kovac, 1998).

Dallin, A. and Firsov, F.I. (eds) *Dimitrov and Stalin, 1934–1943: Letters from the Soviet Archives*. Trans. V.A. Staklo (New Haven, CT: Yale University Press, 2000).

David-Fox, M. *Revolution of the Mind: Higher Learning among the Bolsheviks, 1918–1929* (Ithaca, NY and London: Cornell University Press, 1997).

David-Fox, M. and Peteri, G. (eds) *Academia in Upheaval: Origins, Transfers and Transformations of the Communist Academic Regime in Russia and East Central Europe* (Westport, CT: Bergin and Garvey, 2000).

Davies, R.W. *et al.* (eds) *The Stalin-Kaganovich Correspondence, 1931–1936.* Russian documents trans. S. Shabad (New Haven, CT: Yale University Press, 2003).

Davies, S. *Popular Opinion in Stalin's Russia. Terror, Propaganda and Dissent, 1934–1941* (Cambridge: Cambridge University Press, 1997).

Depretto, J.-P. *Les ouvriers en URSS, 1928–1941* (Paris: Institut d'études slaves, 1997).

—— *Pour une histoire sociale du régime soviétique, 1918–1936* (Paris, Budapest and Turin: L'Harmattan, 2001).

—— *Pouvoirs et société en Union Soviétique* (Paris: Ed. de l'Atelier, 2002).

Dimitroff, G. *Tagebücher 1933–1943*, ed. B.H. Bayerlein, trans. W. Hedeler *et al.* (Berlin: Aufbau-Verlag, 2000).

Dobrenko, E. and Naiman, E. *The Landscape of Stalinism: The Art and Ideology of Soviet Space* (Seattle and London: University of Washington Press, 2003).

Donger, E. *et al.* (eds) *'Ihr verreckt hier bei ehrlicher Arbeit': Deutsche im Gulag 1936–1956: Anthologie des Erinnerns* (Graz and Stuttgart: Stocker, 2000).

Dullin, S. *Des hommes d'influences: les ambassadeurs de Staline en Europe, 1930–1939* (Paris: Payot, 2001).

Duskin, J.E. *Stalinist Reconstruction: The Confirmation of a New Elite, 1945–1953* (Lanham, MD: University Press of America, 1999; Basingstoke: Palgrave, 2001).

Easter, G.M. *Reconstructing the State: Personal Networks and Elite Identity in Soviet Russia* (Cambridge and New York: Cambridge University Press, 2000).

Eaton, K.B. (ed.) *Enemies of the People: The Destruction of Soviet Literary, Theater and Film Arts in the 1930s* (Evanston, IL: Northwestern University Press, 2002).

Edmondson, L. (ed.) *Gender in Russian History and Culture* (Basingstoke: Palgrave, 2001).

Engel, B. and Posadskaya-Vanderbeck, A. (eds) *A Revolution of Their Own: Voices of Women in Soviet History* (Boulder, CO: Westview, 1998).

Engelstein, L. and Sandler, S. (eds) *Self and Story in Russian History* (Ithaca, NY: Cornell University Press, 2000).

Ewing, E.T. *The Teachers of Stalinism: Policy Practices and Power in Soviet Schools of the 1930s* (New York: P. Lang, 2002).

Fein, E. *Geschichtspolitik in Russland: Chancen und Schwierigkeiten einer demokratisierten Aufarbeitung der sowjetischen Vergangenheit am Beispiel der Tätigkeit der Gesellschaft Memorial* (Hamburg: Lit-Verlag, 2000).

Filtzer, D. *Soviet Workers and Late Stalinism: Labour and the Restoration of the Stalinist System after World War II* (Cambridge: Cambridge University Press, 2002).

Fitzpatrick, S. (ed.) *Stalinism: New Directions* (London and New York: Routledge, 2000).

Fitzpatrick, S. *Everyday Stalinism: Ordinary Life in Extraordinary Times: Soviet Russia in the 1930s* (New York and London: Oxford University Press, 1999).

Fitzpatrick, S. and Gellately, R. *Accusatory Practices: Denunciation in Modern European History* (Chicago: University of Chicago Press, 1997).

Fitzpatrick, S. and Slezkine, Y. (eds) *In the Shadow of the Revolution: Life Stories of Russian Women from 1917 to the Second World War* (Princeton, NJ: Princeton University Press, 2000).

Gassenschmidt, C. and Tuchtenhagen, R. (eds) *Politik und Religion in der Sowjetunion 1917–1941* (Wiesbaden: Harrassowitz, 2001).

Getty, J.A. and Naumov, O.V. *The Road to Terror: Stalin and the Self-Destruction of the Bolsheviks* (New Haven, CT: Yale University Press, 1999).

Gitelman, Z. (ed.) *Bitter Legacy: Confronting the Holocaust in the Soviet Union* (Bloomington and Indianapolis: Indiana University Press, 1997).

Goldman, W.Z. *Women at the Gates: Gender and Industry in Stalin's Russia* (New York and Cambridge: Cambridge University Press, 2002).

Gooding, J. *Socialism in Russia: Lenin and His Legacy, 1890–1991* (Basingstoke and New York: Palgrave, 2002).

Gorodetsky, G. *Grand Delusion: Stalin and the German Invasion of Russia* (New Haven, CT: Yale University Press, 1999).

Gorsuch, A.E. *Youth in Revolutionary Russia: Enthusiasts, Bohemians, Delinquents*. Ed. A. Rabinowitch and W.G. Rosenberg (Bloomington and Indianapolis: Indiana University Press, 2000).

Graham, L. *What Have We Learned About Science and Technology from the Russian Experience?* (Stanford, CA: Stanford University Press, 1998).

Graziosi, A. *A New, Peculiar State: Explorations in Soviet History, 1917–1937* (Westport, CT and London: Praeger, 2000).

Gregory, P.R. (ed.) *Behind the Façade of Stalin's Command Economy: Evidence from the Soviet State and Party Archives* (Stanford, CA: Hoover Institution Press, 2001).

Grimsted, P.K. (ed.) *Archives of Russia: A Directory and Bibliographic Guide to Holdings in Moscow and Saint Petersburg* (Armonk, NY: M.E. Sharpe, 2000).

Gross, J.T. *Revolution from Abroad: The Soviet Conquest of Poland's Western Ukraine and Western Belorussia*. Expanded edn (Princeton, NJ and Oxford: Princeton University Press, 2002).

Halfin, I. (ed.) *Language and Revolution: The Making of Modern Political Identities* (London and Portland, OR: F. Cass, 2002).

Halfin, I. *From Darkness to Light: Class, Consciousness and Salvation in Revolutionary Russia* (Pittsburgh: University of Pittsburgh Press, 2000).

Halfin, I. *Terror in My Soul: Communist Autobiographies on Trial* (Cambridge, MA: Harvard University Press, 2003).

Hanson, P. *The Rise and Fall of the Soviet Economy: An Economic History of the USSR from 1945* (London and New York: Pearson Education, 2003).

Harris, J.R. *The Great Urals: Regionalism and the Evolution of the Soviet System* (Ithaca, NY and London: Cornell University Press, 1999).

Hildermeier, M. *Geschichte der Sowjetunion 1917–1991* (Munich: Oldenbourg, 2001).

Hildermeier, M. and Müller-Luckner, E. (eds) *Stalinismus vor dem II. Weltkrieg: Neue Wege der Forschung* (Munich: Oldenbourg, 1998).

Hilger, A. *Deutsche Kriegsgefangene in der Sowjetunion, 1941–1956: Kriegsgefangenenpolitik, Lageralltag und Erinnerung* (Essen: Klartext, 2000).

Hilger, A., Schmeitzner, M. and Schmidt, U. *Sowjetische Militärtribunale*. 2 vols (Cologne, Weimar and Vienna: Böhlau, 2001–03).

Hoffmann, D.L. (ed.) *Stalinism: The Essential Readings* (Oxford: Blackwell, 2003).

Hoffmann, D.L. and Kotsonis, Y. (eds) *Russian Modernity: Politics, Knowledge, Practices* (New York and Basingstoke: Macmillan, 2000).

Holmes, L.E. *Stalin's School: Moscow's Model School No. 25, 1931–1937* (Pittsburgh: University of Pittsburgh Press, 1999).

Holmgren, R. (ed.) *The Russian Memoir: History and Literature* (Evanston, IL: Northwestern University Press, 2003).

Husband, W.B. *'Godless Communists': Atheism and Society in Soviet Russia, 1917–1932* (DeKalb, IL: Northern Illinois University Press, 2000).

Husband, W.B. (ed.) *The Human Tradition in Modern Russia* (Wilmington, DE: Scholarly Resources, 2000).

Ilič, M. *Women Workers in the Soviet Interwar Economy: From 'Protection' to 'Equality'* (London: Macmillan and New York: St Martin's Press, 1999).

Ilič, M. (ed.) *Women in the Stalin Era* (Basingstoke: Palgrave, 2002).

Ivanova, G.M. *Labor Camp Socialism: The Gulag in the Soviet Totalitarian System.* Trans. C. Flath. Ed. D. Raleigh (Armonk, NY: M.E. Sharpe, 2000).

Jansen, M. and Petrov, N. *Stalin's Loyal Executioner: People's Commissar Nikolai Ezhov, 1895–1940* (Stanford, CA: Hoover Institution Press, 2002).

Jolluck, K.R. *Exile and Identity: Polish Women in the Soviet Union during the Second World War* (Pittsburgh and London: University of Pittsburgh Press, 2002).

Josephson, P.R. *New Atlantis Revisited: Akademgorodok, the Siberian City of Science* (Princeton, NJ: Princeton University Press, 1997).

Josephson, P.R. *Red Atom: Russia's Nuclear Power Program from Stalin to Today* (New York: W.H. Freeman, 2000).

Kennedy-Pipe, C. *Russia and the World, 1917–1991* (London: Arnold, 1998).

Kelly, C. *Refining Russia: Advice Literature, Polite Culture and Gender from Catherine to Yeltsin* (Oxford and New York: Oxford University Press, 2001).

Kelly, C. and Shepherd, D. (eds) *Constructing Russian Culture in the Age of Revolution, 1881–1940* (Oxford and New York: Oxford University Press, 1998).

Kelly, C. and Shepherd, D. (eds) *Russian Cultural Studies: An Introduction* (Oxford and New York: Oxford University Press, 1998).

Kershaw, I. and Lewin, M. (eds) *Stalinism and Nazism: Dictatorships in Comparison* (Cambridge: Cambridge University Press, 1997).

Kharkhordin, O. *The Collective and the Individual in Russia: A Study of Practices* (Berkeley and Los Angeles: University of California Press, 1999).

Kirschenbaum, L.K. *Small Comrades: Revolutionizing Childhood in Soviet Russia, 1917–1932* (New York and London: RoutledgeFalmer, 2001).

Klein-Gousseff, C. (ed.) *Retour d'URSS: les prisonniers de guerre et les internés français dans les archives soviétiques, 1945–1951* (Paris: CNRS, 2001).

Knight, A. *Who Killed Kirov? The Kremlin's Greatest Mystery* (New York: Hill and Wang, 1999).

Krementsov, N.L. *Stalinist Science* (Princeton, NJ: Princeton University Press, 1997).

Krone-Schmalz, G. *Strasse der Wölfe: zwei junge Frauen erleben Russland in den dreissiger Jahren* (Cologne: Kiepenhauer & Witsch, 1999).

Kuhr-Korolev, C. *et al.* (eds) *Sowjetjugend 1917–1941: Generation zwischen Revolution und Resignation* (Essen: Klartext, 2001).

Kun, M. *Stalin: An Unknown Portrait* (Budapest and New York: Central European University Press, 2003).

Küntzel, K. *Von Niznij Novgorod zu Gor'kij: Metamorphosen einer russischen Provinzstadt: die Entwicklung der Stadt von den 1890er bis zu den 1930er Jahren* (Stuttgart: F. Steiner, 2001).

Lahusen, T. *How Life Writes the Book: Real Socialism and Socialist Realism in Stalin's Russia* (Ithaca, NY and London: Cornell University Press, 1997).

Laine, A. and Yikangas, M. (eds) *Rise and Fall of Soviet Karelia: People and Power* (Helsinki: University of Helsinki, 2002).

Lankov, A.N. *From Stalin to Kim Il Sung: The Formation of North Korea, 1945–1960* (London: C. Hurst, 2002).

Leder, M.M. *My Life in Stalinist Russia: An American Woman Looks Back.* Ed. L. Bernstein (Bloomington, IN: Indiana University Press, 2001).

Lindner, R. *Historiker und Herrschaft: Nationsbildung und Geschichtspolitik in Weissrussland im 19. und 20. Jahrhundert* (Munich: Oldenbourg, 1999).

Loth, W. *Stalin's Unwanted Child: The Soviet Union, the German Question and the Founding of the GDR.* Trans. R.F. Hogg (London: Macmillan, 1997).

Loth, W. *Overcoming the Cold War: A History of Détente, 1950–1991* (Basingstoke: Palgrave, 2002).

Lovell, S. *The Russian Reading Revolution: Print Culture in the Soviet and Post-Soviet Eras* (Basingstoke: Macmillan, 2000).

Lowe, N. *Mastering Twentieth-Century Russian History* (Basingstoke and New York: Palgrave, 2002).

Luukkanen, A. *The Religious Policy of the Stalinist State: The Central Standing Commission on Religious Questions, 1929–1938* (Helsinki: Societas Historica Finlandiae, 1997).

Mäder, E. and Lohm, C. (eds) *Utopie und Terror: Josef Stalin und seine Zeit* (Zurich: Chronos, 2003).

Martin, T. *The Affirmative Action Empire: Nations and Nationalism in the Soviet Union, 1923–1991* (Ithaca, NY and London: Cornell University Press, 2001).

Mawdsley, E. *The Stalin Years: The Soviet Union, 1929–1953* (Manchester and New York: Manchester University Press, 1998).

Mawdsley, E. and White, S. *The Soviet Elite from Lenin to Gorbachev: The Central Committee and Its Members* (Oxford and New York: Oxford University Press, 2000).

McCannon, J. *Red Arctic: Polar Exploration and the Myth of the North in the Soviet Union, 1932–1939* (New York: Oxford University Press, 1998).

McDermott, K. and Morison, J. (eds) *Politics and Society under the Bolsheviks: Selected Papers from the Fifth World Congress of Central and East European Studies, Warsaw, 1995* (Basingstoke and London: Macmillan, 1999).

McLoughlin, B. and McDermott, K. (eds) *Stalin's Terror: High Politics and Mass Repression in the Soviet Union* (Basingstoke: Palgrave, 2003).

Merridale, C. *Night of Stone: Death and Memory in Russia* (London: Granta, 2000; New York: Viking, 2001).

Mespoulet, M. *Statistique et révolution en Russie: un compromis impossible, 1880–1930* (Rennes: Presses universitaires, 2001).

Miner, S.M. *Stalin's Holy War: Religion, Nationalism and Alliance Politics, 1941–1945* (Chapel Hill, NC and London: University of North Carolina Press, 2003).

Mironenko, S. *et al.* (eds), *Sowjetische Speziallager in Deutschland 1945–1950*, vol. 2: *Sowjetische Dokumente zur Lagerpolitik*, ed. R. Possekel (Berlin: Akademie-Verlag, 1998).

Montefiore, S.S. *Stalin. The Court of the Red Tsar* (London: Weidenfeld & Nicolson, 2003).

Müller, K.-D. *et al.* (eds), *Die Tragödie der Gefangenschaft in Deutschland und der Sowjetunion 1941–1956* (Cologne and Weimar: Arendt-Stiftung, 1998).

Naimark, N.M. *Fires of Hatred: Ethnic Cleansing in Twentieth-Century Europe* (Cambridge, MA: Harvard University Press, 2001).

Naimark, N.M. and Gibiansky, L. (eds) *The Establishment of Communist Regimes in Eastern Europe, 1944–1949* (Boulder, CO: Westview, 1997).

Neutatz, D. *Die Moskauer Metro: von den ersten Plänen bis zur Grossbaustelle des Stalinismus, 1897–1935* (Cologne, Weimar and Vienna: Böhlau, 2001).

Nieckau, G. *Im Gulag: aus der Kriegsgefangenschaft ins sowjetische Arbeitslager* (Hamburg, Berlin and Bonn: E.S. Mittler, 2003).

Osokina, E. *Our Daily Bread. Socialist Distribution and the Art of Survival in Stalin's Russia, 1927–1941.* Ed. K. Transchel. Trans. K. Transchel and G. Bucher (Armonk, NY: M.E. Sharpe, 2001).

Payne, M.J. *Stalin's Railroad: Turksib and the Building of Socialism* (Pittsburgh: University of Pittsburgh Press, 2001).

Peris, D. *Storming the Heavens: The Soviet League of the Militant Godless* (Ithaca, NY and London: Cornell University Press, 1998).

Perrie, M. *The Cult of Ivan the Terrible in Stalin's Russia* (Basingstoke: Palgrave, 2001).

Perrington, R. *Wings, Women and War: Soviet Airwomen in World War II Combat* (Lawrence, KS: University Press of Kansas, 2002).

Peter, E. (ed.) *Von Workuta bis Astrachan: Kriegsgefangene aus sowjetischen Lagern berichten* (Graz: L. Stoecker, 1998).

Peter, E. and Jepifanov, A.E. *Stalins Kriegsgefangene: Ihr Schicksal in Erinnerungen und nach russischen Archiven* (Graz: L. Stoecker, 1997).

Petrone, K. *'Life Has Become More Joyous, Comrades!': Celebrations in the Time of Stalin* (Bloomington: Indiana University Press, 2000).

Phillips, L.L. *Bolsheviks and the Bottle: Drink and Worker Culture in Saint Petersburg, 1900–1929* (DeKalb, IL: Northern Illinois University Press, 2000).

Plaggenborg, S. (ed.) *Stalinismus. Neue Forschungen und Konzepte* (Berlin: Arno Spitz, 1998).

Pohl, J.O. *The Stalinist Penal System: A Short History of Soviet Repression and Terror, 1930–1953* (Jefferson, NC and London: McGarland, 1997).

Pohl, J.O. *Ethnic Cleansing in the USSR, 1937–1949* (Westport, CT and London: Greenwood, 1999).

Polian, P. *Deportiert nach Hause: Sowjetische Kriegsgefangene im 'Dritten Reich' und ihre Repatrierung* (Munich and Vienna: Oldenbourg, 2001).

Pons, S. *Stalin and the Inevitable War, 1936–1941* (London and Portland, OR: F. Cass, 2003).

Pospielovsky, D. *The Orthodox Church in the History of Russia* (Crestwood, NY: St. Vladimir's Seminary Press, 1998).

Raleigh, D.J. (ed.) *Provincial Landscapes: Local Dimensions of Soviet Power, 1917–1953* (Pittsburgh: University of Pittsburgh Press, 2001).

Ransel, D.L. *Village Mothers: Three Generations of Change in Russia and Tataria* (Bloomington and Indianapolis: Indiana University Press, 2000).

Rappaport, H. *Joseph Stalin: A Biographical Companion* (Santa Barbara, CA, Denver, CO and Oxford: ABC-CLIO, 1999).

Read, C. *The Stalin Years: A Reader* (Basingstoke: Palgrave, 2002).

Rees, E.A. (ed.) *Decision-Making in the Stalinist Command Economy, 1932–1937* (London: Macmillan and New York: St. Martin's Press, 1997).

Reese, R.R. *The Soviet Military Experience: A History of the Soviet Army, 1917–1991* (London: Routledge, 2000).

Rieber, A.J. (ed.) *Forced Migration in Central and Eastern Europe, 1939–1950* (London and Portland, OR: F. Cass, 2000).

Rogovin, V.Z. *1937: Stalin's Year of Terror* (Oak Park, MI: Mehring, 1998).

Rogovin, V.Z. *Die Partei der Hingerichteten* (Essen: Arbeiterpresse, 1999).

Rogovin, V.Z. *Vor dem grossen Terror: Stalins Neo-Nöp* (Essen: Arbeiterpresse, 2000).

Rogovin, V.Z. *Weltrevolution und Weltkrieg* (Essen: Arbeiterpresse, 2001).

Rohwer, J. and Monakov, M.S. *Stalin's Ocean-going Fleet: Soviet Naval Strategy and Shipbuilding Programme, 1935–1953* (London and Portland, OR: F. Cass, 2003)

Rosenfeldt, N.E. *et al.* (eds) *Mechanisms of Power in the Soviet Union* (Basingstoke and New York: Macmillan, 2000).

Rosenthal, B.G. *New Myth, New World: From Nietzsche to Stalinism* (University Park, PA: Pennsylvania State University Press, 2004).

Rousso, H. (ed.) *Stalinisme et nazisme: histoire et mémoire comparées*. Textes de N. Werth *et al.* (Brussels: Editions complexe, 1999).

Rubenstein, J. and Naumov, V.P. *Stalin's Secret Pogrom: The Postwar Inquisition of the Jewish Antifascist Committee*. Trans. L.E. Wolfson (New Haven, CT: Yale University Press, 2001).

Rucker, L. *Staline, Israel et les Juifs* (Paris: PUF, 2001).

Ruder, C.A. *Making History for Stalin: The Story of the Belomor Canal* (Gainesville, FL: University Press of Florida, 1998).

Sandle, M. *A Short History of Soviet Socialism* (London and Philadelphia: UCL Press, 1999).

Sapir, J. (ed.) *Retour sur l'URSS: économie, société, histoire* (Paris and Montreal: L'Harmattan, 1997).

Schattenberg, S. *Stalins Ingenieure: Lebenswelten zwischen Technik und Terror in den 1930er Jahren* (Munich: Oldenbourg, 2002).

Scheide, C. *Kinder, Küche, Kommunismus: das Wechselverhältnis zwischen sowjetischen Frauenalltag und Frauenpolitik von 1921 bis 1930 am Beispiel Moskauer Arbeiterinnen* (Zurich: Pano, 2002).

Scheide, C. and Stegmann, N. (eds) *Normsetzung und Normüberschreitung: Geschlecht in der Geschichte Osteuropas im 19. und 20. Jahrhundert* (Bochum: D. Winkler, 1999).

Schmiechen-Ackermann, D. *Diktaturen im Vergleich* (Darmstadt: Wissenschaftliche Buchgesellschaft, 2002).

Service, R. *A History of Twentieth-Century Russia* (Cambridge, MA and London: Harvard University Press, 1998).

Shapovalov, V. (ed.) *Remembering the Darkness: Women in Soviet Prisons*. Trans. V. Shapovalov (Lanham, MD: University Press of Maryland, 2001).

Shcherbakowa, I. *Nur ein Wunder konnte uns retten: Leben und Ueberleben unter Stalins Terror*. Trans. S. Scholl (Frankfurt: Campus, 2000).

Siebert, D. *Bäuerliche Alltagsstrategien in der Belarussischen SSR, 1921–1941* (Stuttgart: F. Steiner, 1998).

Siegelbaum, L.H. and Sokolov, A. *Stalinism as a Way of Life: A Narrative in Documents*. Documents compiled by L. Kosheleva *et al.* Trans. T. Hoisington and S. Shabad (New Haven, CT and London: Yale University Press, 2000).

Simmons, C. and Perline, N. *Writing the Siege of Leningrad: Women's Diaries, Memoirs and Documentary Prose* (Pittsburgh: University of Pittsburgh Press, 2002).

Smith, J. (ed.) *Beyond the Limits: The Concept of Space in Russian History and Culture* (Helsinki: SHS, 1999).

Smith, K.E. *Mythmaking in the New Russia: Politics and Memory during the Yeltsin Era* (Ithaca, NY and London: Cornell University Press, 2002).

Sokoloff, G. (Introduction) *1933: l'année noire: témoignages* [by L. Kovalenko and V. Maniak] *sur la famine en Ukraine*. Trans. V. Bojczuk *et al.* (Paris: Albin Michel 2000).

Solomon, P.H. Jr. (ed.) *Reforming Justice in Russia, 1864–1996: Power, Culture and the Limits of Legal Order* (Armonk, NY: M.E. Sharpe, 1997).

Stark, M. *'Ich muss sagen, wie es war': Deutsche Frauen des GULags* (Berlin: Metropol, 1999).

Straus, K.M. *Factory and Community in Stalin's Russia: The Making of an Industrial Working Class* (Pittsburgh: University of Pittsburgh Press, 1997).

Studer, B. and Unfried, B. *Der stalinische Parteikader: identitätsstiftende Praktiken und Diskurse in der Sowjetunion der 1930er Jahre* (Cologne, Weimar and Vienna: Böhlau, 2001).

Studer, B., Unfried B. and Herrmann, I. (eds) *Parler de soi sous Staline: la construction identitaire dans le communisme des années trente* (Paris: Musée de l'Homme, 2003).

Suny, R.G. (ed.) *The Structure of Soviet History: Essays and Documents* (New York and Oxford: Oxford University Press, 2003).

Suny, R.G. *The Soviet Experiment: Russia, the USSR, and the Successor States* (New York and Oxford: Oxford University Press, 1998).

Suny, R.G. and Martin, T. (eds) *A State of Nations: Empire and Nation-Making in the Age of Lenin and Stalin* (New York and Oxford: Oxford University Press, 2001).

Thornton, R.C. *Odd Man Out: Truman, Stalin, Mao and the Making of the Korean War* (Washington, DC: Brassey's, 2001).

Thorpe, A. *The British Communist Party and Moscow, 1920–1943* (Manchester and New York: Manchester University Press, 2000).

Toker, L. *Return from the Archipelago: Narratives of Gulag Survivors* (Bloomington: Indiana University Press, 2000).

Tolczyk, D. *See No Evil: Literary Cover-Ups and Discoveries of the Soviet Camp Experience* (New Haven, CT and London: Yale University Press, 1999).

Tolz, V. *Russian Academicians and the Revolution: Combining Professionalism and Politics* (Basingstoke: Macmillan and New York: St. Martin's Press, 1997).

Ueberschaer, G.R. and Bezymensky, L.A. (eds) *Der deutsche Angriff auf die Sowjetunion 1941: die Kontroverse um die Präventivkriegsthese* (Darmstadt: Wissenschaftliche Buchgesellschaft, 1998).

Van Dyke, C. *The Soviet Invasion of Finland, 1939–1940* (London and Portland, OR: F. Cass, 1997).

Van Ree, E. *The Political Thought of Joseph Stalin: A Study in Twentieth-Century Revolutionary Patriotism* (London and New York: Routledge, 2002).

Veidlinger, J. *The Moscow State Yiddish Theater: Jewish Culture on the Soviet Stage* (Bloomington: Indiana University Press, 2000).

Vilensky, S. (ed.) *Till My Tale Is Told: Women's Memoirs of the Gulag.* Trans. J. Crowfoot (Bloomington and Indianapolis: Indiana University Press, 1999).

Viola, L. *Peasant Rebels under Stalin: Collectivization and the Culture of Peasant Resistance* (New York and Oxford: Oxford University Press, 1996/1999).

Viola, L. (ed.) *Contending with Stalinism: Soviet Power and Popular Resistance in the 1930s* (Ithaca, NY and London: Cornell University Press, 2002).

Voss, S. *Stalins Kriegsvorbereitungen 1941 erforscht, gedeutet und instrumentalisiert: eine Analyse postsowjetischer Geschichtsschreibung* (Hamburg: Kovac, 1998).

Vucinich, A. *Einstein and Soviet Ideology* (Stanford, CA: Stanford University Press, 2001).

Webb, B. *Pilgerfahrt nach Moskau.* Ed. E. Beumelburg and F. Wacherlein (Passau: K. Stutz, 1998).

Weber, H. and Mählert, U. (eds) *Terror: stalinistische Parteisäuberungen 1936–1953* (Paderborn: F. Schöningh, 1998).

Wehner, M. *Bauernpolitik im proletarischen Staat: die Bauernfrage als zentrales Problem der sowjetischen Innenpolitik 1921–1928* (Cologne, Weimar and Vienna: Böhlau, 1998).

Weiner, A. *Making Sense of War: The Second World War and the Fate of the Bolshevik Revolution* (Princeton, NJ and Oxford: Princeton University Press, 2001).

Westad, O.A. (ed.) *Brothers in Arms: The Rise and Fall of the Sino-Soviet Alliance, 1945–1963* (Stanford, CA: Woodrow Wilson International Center, 1998).

Westad, O.A. (ed.) *Reviewing the Cold War: Approaches, Interpretations, Theory* (London and Portland, OR: F. Cass, 2000–01).

Yakovlev, A.N. *A Century of Violence in Soviet Russia.* Trans. [of *Krestosev*] by A. Austin (New Haven, CT: Yale University Press, 2002).

Young, G. *Power and the Sacred in Revolutionary Russia: Religious Activists in the Village* (University Park, PA: Pennsylvania State University Press, 1997).

Zubkova, E.Yu. *Russia After the War: Hopes, Illusions and Disappointments, 1945–1957.* Trans. and ed. H. Ragsdale (Armonk, NY: M.E. Sharpe, 1998).

Index